D1478592

Painted by R.W.Weir.   Eng.d by M.J.Danforth.

Sa-go-ye-wat-ha

THE

LIFE AND TIMES

OF

RED-JACKET,

OR

SA-GO-YE-WAT-HA;

BEING

THE SEQUEL TO THE HISTORY

OF THE

SIX NATIONS.

BY WILLIAM L. STONE.

"HUMANI NIHIL ALIENUM."

NEW-YORK AND LONDON:

WILEY AND PUTNAM.

1841.

Republished, 1970
Scholarly Press, 22929 Industrial Drive East, St. Clair Shores, Michigan 48080

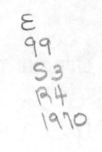

Standard Book Number 403-00227-3

Library of Congress Catalog Card Number: 71-108543

This edition is printed on a high-quality,
acid-free paper that meets specification
requirements for fine book paper referred
to as "300-year" paper

PREFACE.

THE present volume is but one of a series, the composition of which the author has been meditating for several years. The original design contemplated a complete history of the great Iroquois Confederacy, known at first as the Five Nations, and afterward, by the addition of the Tuscaroras from North Carolina, as the Six, from the discovery to the present time. Circumstances, which were explained in the Life of Brant, induced the preparation of that work first. The design of that effort was not merely to embrace the biography of the chief himself, but under the shadow of his name to preserve the history of his people during the half century of his active life, and also to gather up, and reduce to form, the rich materials of the previously unwritten border history of the American revolution. Brant, both as the military leader and civil governor of his people, and also as one of the most active and formidable officers of the border service, was selected as the principal figure around whom to weave the stirring historical details comprised in the two volumes bearing his name.

The present volume, containing the life of the great Seneca orator, Red-Jacket, has been constructed upon the same plan. After the death of Brant, Red-Jacket became the man of greatest distinction among the Six Nations; and in writing his life, the author, as in the preceding work, has used him as the principal figure in illustrating the history of the Six Nations down to the conclusion of the treaty for the sale of the residue of the Seneca lands, in the autumn of 1838. That treaty, when carried into execution, extinguishes the confederacy of the AQUANUSCHIONI, or United People,—a confederacy, the duration of which is lost in the shadowy obscurity of tradition for ages before the sound of the white woodman's axe rang upon the solemn stillness of the forest-continent. The life of Red-Jacket, therefore, may be considered as the sequel, or conclusion, of the History of the Six Nations.

Two divisions of the work meditated by the author, and those the most difficult and laborious,—remain to be executed, viz. : the Life and Times of Sir William Johnson, and the yet earlier history of the Iroquois Confederacy from the discovery down to the year 1735, when Mr. Johnson first planted himself among the Mohawks in the valley of their own beautiful river. The life of the Baronet is the next, which, should health and time allow, the author proposes to take in hand. This work will review an important and most interesting period in the colonial history of New-York, embracing, as it must do, the border history of the colony during the French wars of 1745, and of 1755–63. Nor can that history be properly illustrated without recourse to the archives of the British and French governments. Hitherto the author has been disappointed in the expectation of making a voyage to Europe in connexion with this branch of his historical investigations. But he hopes yet to accomplish this object. At all events, "The Life and Times of Sir William Johnson" is a work the execution of which will not be relinquished except from stern necessity.

The residue of the work, covering the earlier period of the proposed history, will of course be deferred to a yet more distant day.

In regard to the present volume, the author can only say that he has made it as full and as perfect as the materials which he has been able to collect would allow. The subject of the memoir, it must be remembered, could speak but very little English, and could not write at all. He could therefore maintain no written correspondence, and consequently left no letters, or other written memorials, to aid his biographer. Such was not the fact in the case of Brant, whose papers were of vast assistance. It must also be kept in mind that Brant was a man of war, and Red-Jacket a man of peace. Hence in a memoir of the latter a far smaller amount of stirring and bloody incident is to be anticipated, than in one of the former. Indeed in this respect the books are widely dissimilar. And yet it is hoped that it will be found not altogether devoid of interest. The name of Red-Jacket, as the great orator of the Six Nations, is among those most familiar to the American ear; and this volume is the first complete record of his forensic efforts that has ever appeared. Neither diligence nor expense has been spared to make the collection perfect of all the chieftain's speeches, and notes of speeches, that have been preserved. These have been arranged in the text, according to the dates of their delivery, and in connexion with the history of the occasions and events which called them forth. The author is aware that to this feature of his arrangement some may object that the text of the narrative should not be thus interrupted, and that the speeches might better have been thrown back into an appendix. But he thinks differently. Had they been thus disposed of they would not have been read,—such being the usual destiny of speeches, letters and documents, crowded together at the end of almost every book of history. And certainly when they *are* read, they are likely to be better understood and appreciated, if taken in their proper historical connexion,—illustrating the occasions or events by which they were elicited, and in turn receiving such illustrations from the historian as seem to be required.

The general portraiture of the subject of the memoir is ample, and is believed to be just. Nothing has been extenuated without sufficient cause, nor aught set down in malice. The thanks of both author and publishers are due to Mr. Samuel Ward for the use of Wier's fine picture of Red-Jacket, which has been exquisitely engraved by Mr. M. I. Danforth. To the kindness of this accomplished artist the author is likewise indebted for the beautiful and spirited engraved title-page preceding the letter-press title. He also desires to express his thanks to Mr. Osborn, the printer, for the care with which he has supervised the press, and for the typographical elegance of the volume.

As the celebrated chiefs Farmer's-Brother and Cornplanter were intimately associated in public affairs with Red-Jacket for half a century and more, brief sketches of their lives have been added to the principal memoir.

New-York, June 1, 1841.

CONTENTS.

CHAPTER I.

CHAPTER II.

CHAPTER III.

CHAPTER IV.

CHAPTER V.

CHAPTER VI.

CHAPTER VII.

CHAPTER VIII.

CHAPTER IX.

CHAPTER X.

CHAPTER XI.

B

CHAPTER XII.

CHAPTER XIII.

CHAPTER XIV.

SA-GO-YE-WAT-HA,

OR

RED-JACKET.

LIFE AND TIMES OF RED-JACKET.

CHAPTER I.

" I AM an orator!—I was born an orator!"—were the
prompt exclamations of the subject of the present memoir,
in reply to an inquiry, by an obtrusive white man, respecting his deeds in arms. The evasion was alike spirited, quick-witted, and adroit. No man, either savage
or civilized, probably, was ever more conscious of the
strong and the weak points of his own character than the
celebrated Seneca chief, SA-GO-YE-WAT-HA, or "HE-
KEEPS-THEM-AWAKE,"—better known to the public under the less imposing name of RED-JACKET.* His original Indian name was O-TE-TI-ANI—in English—AL-

---

* The Indian name of Red-Jacket, here given in the text, has been variously
spelt, by different authors. I have adopted the orthography of an old MS. record of the Seneca chiefs, invited by Colonel Timothy Pickering to attend a
council in Philadelphia, in 1792. The usual translation of the name, *Sa-go-ye-
wat-ha*, has been, *The Keeper Awake*. It was so rendered by De Witt Clinton, in
his celebrated Discourse before the New-York Historical Society, in 1811. But
that translation is erroneous, as *The Keeper Awake* does not convey the idea intended. The ancient manuscript referred to gives the true meaning, as adopted
in the text—*He-keeps-them-awake*.

1

WAYS READY. The other name was conferred upon him, in after years, on his election to the dignity of a Sachem.

That he was an orator, in the most exalted sense of the term, of great and commanding power, is the universal testimony of all who enjoyed opportunities of forming a just opinion upon the subject. And no other man was more conscious of the fact than himself. That he was a warrior he did not positively deny to his unwelcome catechist, while he studiously avoided its acknowledgment.

It is well for his veracity that he did not, since nothing is more certain than that the impartial testimony of history would have been invoked in vain to sustain the assertion. Yet, notwithstanding the absence of that physical quality, the lack of which is so rare among a people living in the hunter state, and the possession of which is considered so indispensable among all barbarians, few men have arrived at a greater degree of consideration among his own people, or exerted a more commanding influence, than Red-Jacket. He was upon the war-path during both conflicts between the United States and Great Britain. In the former,—the war of the revolution,— he served, with his nation, the cause of the crown. In the war of 1812–1815,—the Senecas having changed their *quasi* allegiance,—he served under the colors of the United States. But in neither contest did he win for himself the *right* to wear the eagle-plume. In the former he was openly charged by his brother chiefs with cowardice and treachery; while in the latter the impression made upon the mind of the General, under whose immediate eye he served, was by no means favorable in regard to his courage.* His entire character formed a bundle of contradictions. If he lacked firmness of nerves, he nevertheless possessed unbending firmness of purpose, and great moral courage. His intellectual powers were unquestionably of a very high order. He was a statesman of sagacity, and an orator of even surpassing eloquence; yet he was capable of descending to the practice of the lowest cunning of the demagogue. But he was still a patriot. He loved his nation, and his race;—and if, in the eyes of his people, the deficiencies of his character were not lost in the blaze of his genius, they were certainly more than counterbalanced by the admiration with which was contemplated the greatness of his mind.

The Seneca Nation, whence Sa-go-ye-wat-ha sprang, and whose principal chief he was for many years, was, even at the time of the discovery by the Europeans, by far the most powerful of the Aquanuschioni, or "United People," known originally as the Five Nations, and afterward as the Six, by the addition of the Tuscaroras to the confederacy, about the year 1712. The reason of this addition to the number of their communities has been variously given. It is well known that the Five Nations carried their arms as far south as the country of the Cherokees, with whom they waged a bloody war, even within the last century.† The Tuscaroras were

* General Peter B. Porter, late Secretary of War, whose opinion will be quoted hereafter.

† A fierce battle, continuing two days, was fought between the Cherokees, Catawbas, and their associates, and the warriors of the Six Nations, at the

natives of a territory now forming the state of North
Carolina. Bancroft speaks of them as "kindred with
the Five Nations," and refers to several villages in that
region, of the Huron-Iroquois, or Wyandot family. According to some authorities, the Tuscaroras, having
formed a deep and general conspiracy to cut off the
whites, were signally defeated, and driven from their
country, under which circumstances they were adopted
as a Sixth Nation by the Iroquois.* It has been asserted
by others that they were conquered by the Iroquois, and
by them removed to their own country, where they were
planted down, and reckoned as an additional nation, but
only upon the condition that, like the Delawares, they
were to be ranked as women, and inhibited the use of
arms in war. This is a most unlikely tale of their removal,—since they "were the most powerful tribe in
North Carolina," occupying, in 1708, fifteen towns in the
upper country, on the Neuse and the Tar, and numbering
twelve hundred warriors, as brave as the Mohawks.†
Other authors have assigned a kindlier motive for the
transplantation, viz : the discovery, by the Five Nations,
of the marked similarity of the Tuscarora language to
their own—there being no labials in either. Hence they
concluded that the latter either were, or of right ought to

junction of the Cumberland and Red Rivers, in Kentucky, near the present line
between the states of Kentucky and Tennessee, in the year 1731. The leader of
the Six Nations on that occasion was Hiokatoo, a celebrated Seneca chief, who
died in 1811, at the great age of 103. The slaughter was great on both sides,
but Hiokatoo was victorious.

* Smith's History of New-York, sanctioned by the Historical Discourse of De
Witt Clinton.

† Bancroft's United States, vol. iii. p. 245.

have been, members of their own great family. Hence, also, probably, Bancroft speaks of the Mohawks as their " brothers."

The Senecas were the fifth nation of the original confederacy—their duty being to keep the western door of " the long house," as the territory occupied by their principal range of towns was called. The Mohawks guarded the eastern door, at Schagh-nack-ta-da.* Whenever, at either door of " the long house," other nations, or their ambassadors, knocked upon business, the first duty of the nation keeping the door was to ascertain its character and importance. If not of great moment, the council of the separate nation attended to it. But whenever the subject matter presented from without was of interest to the whole confederacy, or of sufficient weight to require the consideration of the united council, the messengers charged with it were sent forward to the Onondaga Valley, where the Grand Council fire was kindled, and it was discussed by the National Congress. The Mohawk nation was the first in rank of the confederacy, and to it appertained the office of principal war-chief. To the Onondagas, in like manner,—the nation whose peculiar province it was to guard the council fire,—appertained the office of principal civil chief, or Chief Sachem. Still, numerically considered, for a long time past, and per-

---

* The present site of Albany. The meaning of the term, literally, is—" Beyond-the-Pine-Plains." These plains are those between Schenectady and Albany—separating the Mohawk valley from that of the Hudson. By some mistake, the name was erroneously bestowed by the whites upon the Indian town of *Con-nugh-harie-gugh-harie*, literally *A-great-multitude-collected-together*. Standing at their castles, and looking toward the east, *Schagh-nack-ta-da*, (now Albany,) was Beyond-the-Pine-Plains to the Mohawks.

haps always, the Senecas were by far the most powerful of the confederacy.

The questions as to the origin of the Seneca Indians,
the entire confederacy to which they belonged, and the
length of time they had been in the occupancy of "the
long house," when first visited by the white man, are all
involved in darkness, too deep, probably, for human
penetration. According to the early French historians
and tourists of America,—among whom Charlevoix is
probably the best authority,—the Iroquois were occupying
the country along the St. Lawrence, in the neighborhood
of Hochelaga, at the time of the discovery of Canada by
Jacques Cartier. "When Cartier went to Hochelaga,
now Montreal, in 1535, he discovered a town of the Iroquois, or Hurons, containing about fifty huts."* Cartier
landed about six miles from the town, to which the way
was well beaten and frequented. "It was situated in
the midst of large fields of Indian corn, and from the
description, it must even then have been a considerable
place, and the metropolis of the neighboring country. It
was encompassed by palisades, or probably a picket
fence in three rows, one within the other, well secured
and put together. A single entrance was secured with
piles and stakes; and every precaution adopted against
sudden attack or siege. The town consisted of about
fifty houses, each fifty feet in length by fourteen in
breadth, built of wood and covered with bark, 'well and
cunningly joined together.' Each house contained
small chambers, built round an open court in the centre,

* Clinton's Historical Discourse.

in which the fire was kindled."* The inhabitants were
devoted to husbandry and fishing, and the lands of the
island were well cultivated to the base of the mountain,
three miles from the present city of Montreal.† In a
word, according to the history of Cartier's voyage, the
Indians of Hochelaga were more than usually civilized,
for barbarians, and greatly in advance of the Iroquois a
century afterward. It has also been held that the war
in which the Iroquois were engaged with the Adirondacks, a powerful division of the Hurons,—now generally known by the name of Wyandots,—at the time
when Champlain ascended the St. Lawrence, in 1603,
was the same in which they conquered the territory or
the Mohawk Valley, and that lying south of Lake Ontario, in the possession of which they were found by the
Dutch and English. Such is, moreover, the received
opinion of various writers, European and American, who
have glanced superficially at this question.

But this supposition, though entertained by Governor
Colden, and afterward by Governor Clinton, is beyond
doubt erroneous. At the time of Cartier's discovery
the five Huron nations occupied the Island of Orleans,
below Quebec, and the country of the St. Lawrence and
the Ottawa. The Adirondacks, the most powerful clan
of that people, then lived chiefly upon the Ottawa; and
it is more than probable that those were the occupants of
Hochelaga. The town at Hochelaga, described by Cartier, had dwindled into insignificance at the time of
Champlain's visit, having probably been destroyed by

* Hawkins's History of Quebec, pp. 50, 51.   † Idem.

the Iroquois—a body of whom were met by Champlain, while voyaging upon the lake since bearing his name, on their way against the Hurons, with hostile intent. Champlain was accompanied during this voyage by a war party of the latter, with whom he fought in alliance against the Iroquois, who were struck with amazement at the reports and the execution of the fire-arms used against them,—engines of death which they had never seen before,—and defeated, of course.

But, in addition to these circumstances, all the principal towns and cantons of the Five Nations gave evidence, at the period of the discovery, of a much longer occupancy of the territory in question than most authors have conceded ; while according to their own traditions, affording yet better authority, they had been in the actual possession of that fair region of country for a length of time whereof the memory of man runneth not to the contrary.* It is true that there is a dim and shadowy tradition among some of the people of the Five Nations, that they originally came from the north ; but they date the period of their migration a long number of centuries back. Cusick, the Tuscarora author,—and the only Indian who has written upon that subject,—dates the event more than twenty-five hundred years before the discovery by Columbus,—as correct, probably, as the Chinese chronology.† The tradition of the Senecas is, that the original people of their nation broke forth from the earth, from the crest of a mountain at the head of

* Charlevoix; Colden's Six Nations; Moulton's New-York.
† This tract of Cusick's is a wretchedly puerile performance.

Canandaigua Lake. The mountain which gave them birth is called " Ge-nun-de-wah-gauh," or the Great Hill. Hence the Senecas are called the Great Hill People, which was their original title. The base of the Genundewah mountain, as it is usually called, they believe to have been encircled, when their nation was in its infancy, by a huge serpent,—so vast in his proportions that he was enabled to coil himself entirely around the mountain. The head and tail of the monster united at the gateway of the path leading to and from the steep; and few who attempted either ingress or egress escaped his voracious jaws. Thus environed, the people remained a long time, as it were, in a state of siege,—the serpent rendering their condition almost insupportable, not only by his war upon their lives, but by reason of his fœtid and poisonous breath. At length, their sufferings becoming severe beyond longer endurance, the Indians determined to make a sally. Arming themselves, therefore, with such weapons as they had at hand, they descended the hill, but in attempting to escape the gate, were all seized and swallowed by the serpent, with the exception of two children, who by some means overleaped this fearful line of circumvallation, and avoided the terrible fate of the body of their infant tribe. Having escaped, these children were reserved for a yet higher destiny. They were informed, by an oracle, of means by which they might rid the world of the great monster so inimical to their race. They were directed to form a bow of a particular kind of willow, and an arrow of the same, the barb of which

2

was to be dipped in poison, and shot in a direction that would allow it to penetrate the skin beneath the scales. The children obeyed the divine injunction, and the result was the serpent's death. No sooner had the arrow penetrated the skin than he was thrown into violent convulsions. Uncoiling himself from around the mountain, and writhing into the most frightful convolutions, in his agony he threw up the heads of the people he had devoured, which rolled down the steep into the lake. With agonizing throes the serpent himself then rolled into the lake, sweeping down the timber in his course. The heads of the Indians, that had been disgorged, were petrified by the transparent waters, and are to be seen at the bottom of the lake, in the shape of large round stones, to this day. From the two orphans, thus preserved, and who thus vanquished their terrible enemy, sprang the new race of Senecas. The tradition is equally absurd and puerile; but not more so than are the legends of the aboriginals of other nations, or even of the so-called civilized nations of India and China. But it is cited to show that the Senecas themselves have no idea of a modern occupancy of their territory. And that they were sincere in entertaining the tradition, may be allowed from the circumstance that the Genundewah has been held sacred, as being the place of their birth. For a long time past, and down to a recent period, it was the place of holding their councils. It was also the hallowed place of their religious services, some of which were instituted in commemoration of the death of the serpent, which had thus threat-

ened the extermination of their race.* This legend is
less poetical, perhaps, but it is not more absurd, than the
classic fable of the Hydra of Lerna, or the monster
which, according to Ælian, was the terror of India in the
time of Alexander. The monster of Genundewah did
not discharge volumes of flame and smoke from his
mouth, like another Typhon; but the effluvium of his
breath was even more destructive. The credulity of the
wild Senecas was no greater than that of the polished
Greeks; and they did not fall into the absurdity of paying divine honors to their monster, as the oriental Indians
did the dragon-cotemporary of Alexander.

Connected with this sacred mount of Genundewah,
and a wild precipice in its vicinity, which hangs beetling
over the silver Canandaigua lake, called the "Lover's
Leap," is an interesting story of love to distraction, and
courage to death, on the part of a young Indian beauty,
which may perhaps warrant a digression for its recital—
more especially as the American aboriginals have generally been accounted, comparatively, strangers to *la belle
passion*. The legend is of a later day than that of the
serpent, but, nevertheless, descends from remote tradition. During the wars of the Senecas and the Algonquins of the north, a chief of the latter was captured and
carried to Genundewah, whereon a fortification, consist-

---

* This tradition was related to the author, in November, 1838, by a Seneca
chief, called *The Blacksmith*, a relative of Red-Jacket, and to whom descended
the medal given to the latter by General Washington. It is also given, in substance, by Mr. Seaver, author of the Life of Mary Jemison. Mr. Seaver received it from the late Captain Horatio Jones, for several years a prisoner among
the Senecas, and long a government agent and interpreter among them.

ing of a square without bastions, and surrounded by palisades, was situated. The captive, though young in years, was famed for his prowess in the forest conflict, and nature had been bountiful to his person in those gifts of strength and symmetry which waken savage admiration. After a short debate, he was condemned to die on the following day, by the slow torture of impalement. While he was lying in the "cabin of death," a lodge devoted to the reception of condemned prisoners, the daughter of the Sachem brought him food,* and, struck with his manly form and heroic bearing, resolved to save him or share his fate. Her bold enterprise was favored by the uncertain light of the gray dawn, while the solitary sentinel, weary with his night-watch, and forgetful of his duty, was slumbering. Stealing with noiseless tread to the side of the young captive, she cut the thongs wherewith his limbs were bound, and besought him in breathing accents to follow her. The fugitives descended the hill by a wooded path conducting to the lake; but ere they reached the water, an alarm-whoop, wild and shrill, was heard issuing from the lips of the waking guard. They tarried not, though thorny vines and fallen timber obstructed their way. At length they reached the smooth beach, and leaping into a canoe, previously provided by the brave and considerate damsel, they plied the paddle vigorously, steering for the opposite shore. Vain were their efforts. On the wind came cries of rage, and the quick tramp of savage warriors, bounding over rock and

* The Indians always supply their prisoners with every comfort until the time for their execution arrives.

glen in fierce pursuit. The Algonquin, with the reckless daring of a young brave, sent back a yell of defiance; and soon after the plash of oars was heard, and a dozen war canoes were cutting the billows in their rear. The unfortunate lovers, on landing, took a trail leading in a western direction over the hills. The Algonquin, weakened by unhealed wounds, followed his active guide up the acclivity with panting heart and flagging pace; while his enemies, with the grim old Sachem at their head, drew nearer and nearer. At length, finding farther attempts at flight useless, she diverged from the trail, and conducted her lover to a table-crested rock that projected over a ravine, or gulf, one hundred and fifty feet in depth, the bottom of which was strewn with huge mis-shapen rocks, scattered in rude confusion. With hearts nerved to a high resolve, the hapless pair awaited the arrival of their yelling pursuers. Conspicuous by his eagle plume, towering form, and scowling brow, the daughter soon descried her inexorable sire leaping from crag to crag below her. He paused abruptly when his fiery eye rested on the objects of his pursuit. Notching an arrow on the string of his tried and unerring bow, he raised his sinewy arms—but ere the missile was sent, Wun-nut-hay, the Beautiful, interposed her form between her father and his victim. In wild appealing tones she entreated her sire to spare the young chieftain, assuring him that they would leap together from the precipice rather than be separated. The stern old man, deaf to her supplication, and disregarding her menace, ordered his followers to seize the fugitive. Warrior after warrior darted up the ròck, but on reaching the platform, at the moment when they were grasping to clutch the young brave, the lovers, locked in fond embrace, flung themselves

" From the steep rock and perished."

The mangled bodies were buried in the bottom of the glen, beneath the shade of everlasting rocks; and two small hollows, resembling sunken graves, are to this day pointed out to the curious traveller, as the burial place of " the lovers." It is a sweet, wild haunt,—the sunbeam falls there with a softened radiance,—and a brook near by gives out a complaining murmur, as if mourning for the dead.*

But to return from the alluring field of romance to the graver details of historical inquiry. There is yet farther, if not stronger evidence to sustain the position, that the Five Nations had for ages been in the possession of their Long House. For example, speaking of the mounds in their country, which, like many others scattered between the lakes and the coast of Florida, have occasioned so much of speculation and curious inquiry, some of the Senecas told Mr. Kirkland, the celebrated missionary to the Indians, " that those in their territory were raised by their ancestors, in their wars with the western Indians,

---

* This interesting legend was derived many years ago from a Seneca chief of some note, named " Chequered Cap," and was communicated to me by W. H. C. Hosmer, Esq., of Avon, of whom more hereafter. On the top of Genundewah the remains of an Indian orchard are visible—a few moss-grown and wind-bowed apple-trees still linger, sad, but fitting emblems of the wasted race by whom they were planted.

three, four, or five hundred years ago."* Indeed it was
the belief of that people " that they sprang and grew
up, in that very place, like the trees of the wilderness."†
Still it is and must ever remain a question of doubt
how long the Aquanuschioni had occupied the " Long
House." Their traditions are confused, and not in harmony with each other. De Witt Clinton inclined to the
opinion that they first inhabited the country on the north
side of the great lakes, whence they had been expelled
by the Adirondacks—they in turn driving from the country
south of the lakes a now lost nation, called the Satanas.
But this hypothesis is inconsistent with the subsequent
claim of the Iroquois to the country west of Lake Ontario,
and north of Lake Erie, as a conquest from those same
Adirondacks, or Hurons. Governor Clinton has im-
plicitly followed Colden upon this point; but more
thorough inquiry has shown that Colden was wrong.
The Hurons, without controversy, were driven from the
country of the St. Lawrence, to the north-west, beyond
Lake Superior—" hiding themselves in the dreary wastes
that divided the Chippewas from their western foes."‡
They were afterward driven back by the Sioux to
Detroit, and the northern shore of Lake Erie. The
Indians called Satanas by the English, the Shaouonons
of the French, resided farther west, upon the Mississippi.
Brant, in a letter to Colonel Timothy Pickering, says the

* Clinton's Discourse.
† Note in Drake's Book of the Indians.
‡ Bancroft. Doctor Colden pronounced the Adirondacks " the most warlike
and polite nation of all the Indians in North America." He adds—" they were
almost entirely destroyed by a people they at first despised."

country south of Buffalo Creek and Lake Erie "was obtained by the joint exertions of the Five Nations, in a war with a powerful nation of Indians called Eries, and another nation then living at Tioga Point ;—so that, by our successes, all the country between that and the Mississippi became the joint property of the Five Nations. All other nations now inhabiting this great tract of country were allowed to settle by the Five Nations."*

There is yet another tradition, that the Five Nations came originally from the remote west. But, so far as is known, there is no language in that vast region assimilating to theirs, while the languages of the Indians east of the Hudson river were evidently from the same root as the different dialects of the great Delaware family, who are allowed to have come from that direction. The tradition, imputed by some writers to the Senecas, that they were once occupants of the territory of the Creeks, at the south, is not worthy of consideration. This incidental discussion, therefore, respecting the origin of the Five Nations, or rather the length of time in which they had been in the occupancy of what they figuratively called their "long house," has necessarily left the question involved in as much obscurity as it was before, save that it is believed to have been pretty clearly shown that they were by no means recent occupants of their territory at the time when the white men came among them, nor had they been driven from the north by the Hurons.

* MS. letter from Joseph Brant—Thayendanegea—to Colonel Pickering, dated 30th December, 1794, in the author's possession.

CHAPTER II.

THE Seneca chief, SA-GO-YE-WAT-HA, or " *He-keeps-them-awake*," has, by some writers upon Indian history, been designated as " The Last of the Senecas," and perhaps with figurative justice. He had several able contemporaries, names not unknown to fame, among whom were FARMER'S-BROTHER and the CORNPLANTER. But these chiefs were older than himself, and distinguished rather as warriors than as orators ; while Sa-go-ye-wat-ha, whose eloquence was the glory of his people, has left no one behind who can fill his place at the council-fire. The orator " owed nothing to the advantages of illustrious descent."* On the contrary, his parentage was humble, even in the estimate of his own people, among whom the democratic principle of positive equality

---

* De Witt Clinton's Historical Discourse.

3

is as nearly approximated, perhaps, as in any other country in the universe. He is believed to have been born about the year 1750, at a place called Old Castle, three miles west of the present beautiful and flourishing town of Geneva, at the foot of Seneca Lake.* Of his early history little is known beyond the fact asserted by tradition, that he was remarkably swift upon the chase, and from his fleetness was often employed as a messenger, first among his own people, and afterward, during the war of the American revolution, as a runner for the British officers engaged in the border service. His name of " RED-JACKET," by which he was so long familiarly known among the white people, is said to have been acquired in the following manner : During the war just mentioned, his activity and intelligence attracted the attention of several officers in the service of the British crown, and acquired for him their friendship. One of them, either as a compliment, or for services rendered, " presented him with a richly embroidered scarlet jacket, which he took great pride in wearing. When this was worn out, he was presented with another ; and he continued to wear this peculiar dress until it became a mark of distinction, and gave him the name by which he was afterward best known."† At the treaty of 1794, held at Canandaigua, Captain Parish, one of the interpreters in the service of the United States, gave him another red jacket, " to perpetuate the name to which he was so much attached."‡

---

* Sketch of Red-Jacket, written by the Rev. John Breckenridge, D. D., for M'Kenney's Indian Biography.   † Idem.   ‡ Idem.

The most authentic information that has been obtained respecting his earlier career presents him, in the outset of his slender military service, in a very unfavorable attitude. It was while he was upon the war-path, during the invasion of the Genesee country by General Sullivan, in 1779.

The author of the spirited sketch of his life just quoted speaks of the "activity and intelligence" by which he distinguished himself in that war, "though he had scarcely reached the age of manhood when he engaged in it." But the writer, soon afterward, observes, with greater justice;—"in that contest he took little or no part as a warrior; and it would appear that like his celebrated predecessors in rhetorical fame, Demosthenes and Cicero, he better understood how to rouse his countrymen to war than to lead them to victory."* It is well known to those who are accurately versed in the Indian history of the last half century, that the celebrated Mohawk leader of the Six Nations, Thayendanegea, more commonly known as Joseph Brant, ever regarded the Seneca orator with mingled feelings of hatred and contempt. The Mohawk chief was wont to charge him with conduct perfectly in keeping with the classical parallel indicated by Dr. Breckenridge. According to the statements of

* Sketch by Rev. Dr. Breckenridge. Cicero, it is true, gave evidence of irresolution, if not timidity, in the struggles between Cæsar and the republic; and Demosthenes was accused of having been corrupted by the presents of Alexander. Thus far, between both the ancient orators and the Seneca, it will appear that there is a seeming parallel. Of the former two, cowardice was predicated of the one, and treachery of the other. The Seneca, as will be seen, has been charged with both.

Brant and others,—made, too, with inconvenient direct-
ness in the presence of Red-Jacket himself—the latter
had been known to exert his eloquence to enkindle a
war-spirit in the bosoms of the braves of his nation, and
provoke them to take up the hatchet, while he ingeniously avoided the war-path, and availed himself of the
absence of the warriors, thus procured, to plunder the
goods, and even live stock, wherever he could—not
caring to discriminate between the property of an enemy
and that of the absentees of his own people. Hence the
name of " *Cow-killer*," bestowed upon him by Joseph
Brant, in a letter to the Duke of Northumberland,
written in 1805.*

But the origin of the Mohawk chieftain's enmity is to
be traced to a more remote and still more aggravated
cause, while, as will hereafter appear, there were transactions on the part of Red-Jacket of deep personal concern to Brant, which added to the bitterness of his
hatred. During the campaign of General Sullivan,
already referred to, in which the Americans, like a
stream of fire, swept through the fine country then inhabited by the Cayugas and Senecas, and now forming

* Life of Brant, vol. ii. p. 417. "Red-Jacket was, from the following circumstance, nick-named ' The Cow-killer :' During the revolutionary war, he had
on some occasion exhorted his followers to behave with courage in an engagement expected to take place, promising that he would himself be found in the
hottest of the fight. But when the engagement came on, Red-Jacket was missing,
and was found, during the battle, cutting up a cow, belonging to an Indian, which
he had killed. One day, when dining at my house with Captain Brant, Cornplanter told the story as if the act had been committed by some other Indian.
He and Brant laughed exceedingly at the anecdote, and at Red-Jacket's confusion. The latter attempted to join in the laugh, but was evidently very much
embarrassed."—*Letter to the author from Thomas Morris.*

the western portion of the State of New-York, the
Mohawk chief was the leader, and the master-spirit, of
the Indian forces. The battle of Newtown, so disastrous
to the Indians, the tories, and other more regular troops
in the British service, left Captain Brant no choice but
either to abandon the whole country at once, or adopt the
Fabian system, and harass the American army by coun-
ter-marches and ambuscades. But the Mohawk was not
a man to fly while a blow could be struck, and the latter
alternative was adopted; with, at times, no inconsiderable degree of success. Yet, on the whole, the campaign
of Sullivan resulted in the sad discomfiture of the Indians; and it was in after life urged by Brant, that the
conduct of Red-Jacket had not only caused him much
trouble and embarrassment during that invasion, but had
been the principal cause of the disasters of his people.
Sa-go-ye-wat-ha was then twenty-nine years old, and
although it does not appear that he had yet been created
a chief, he nevertheless seems to have been already a
man of influence. He was in the practice of holding
private consultations with the young warriors, and some
of the younger and less resolute chiefs, for the purpose of
fomenting discontents, and persuading them to sue for
what Brant considered ignominious terms of peace. On
one occasion, as Brant has alleged, Red-Jacket had so
far succeeded in his treachery as to induce some of
the disaffected chiefs to send a runner into Sullivan's
camp, to make known the dissensions he himself had
awakened, and invite a flag of truce, with propositions
of peace to the Indians. But the eagle eye of the Mo-

hawk penetrated the conspiracy. Still his own position was too precarious to allow the exercise of force in crushing it. Watching every movement, therefore, he despatched two confidential warriors to intercept the American flag, possess themselves of the bearer's despatches, and put him to death. This bloody but necessary commission was executed with true Indian adroitness, and the purposes of Red-Jacket were for that time frustrated.*

The charge of positive cowardice, during the same campaign, rests upon the testimony of another—the brave and war-like Cornplanter, a chief of the same nation. It had been the intention of this chief to make a stand against a detachment of General Sullivan's forces, on the beach of the Canandaigua lake—the Indian village at that place having been a very considerable town. But "on the approach of the Americans, a small number of the Indians, among whom was Red-Jacket, began to retreat. Cornplanter exerted himself to rally them. He sprang in front of Red-Jacket and endeavored to persuade him to fight—but in vain. Whereupon the indignant chief, turning to the young wife of the recreant warrior, exclaimed—"Leave that man—he is a coward !"†

The name of Red-Jacket occurs not again in history, written or unwritten, until in connexion with the great Indian Treaty held at Fort Stanwix, in the year 1784. It redounds little to the credit of the British ministry of 1782–83, that in the treaty of peace with the United

* Life of Brant, vol. ii. p. 35.   † Rev. Dr. John Breckenridge.

States, by which the independence of the latter was conceded to the fullest extent, no stipulation was inserted in behalf of the red allies of the crown. Four of the Six Nations, viz., the Mohawks, Onondagas, Cayugas, and Senecas, had adhered to the royal cause with the utmost constancy and with perfect fidelity. They had all poured out their blood like water; their country had been ravaged by fire and sword, and the Mohawks had been entirely driven from their own peculiar and beautiful region; and yet not the slightest provision was interposed in their behalf by those whom they had served so bravely and so long.

But although the hatchet was not formally buried, its use was suspended by the treaty of 1783, and no farther acts of hostility were perpetrated by the Six Nations. Still, smarting as were the borderers of New-York from the cruelties of the Indians, the legislature of that State began to agitate the question of an entire expulsion of the race from beyond its remotest western confines, and the confiscation of their lands. The humane feelings of General Washington revolted against so harsh a measure, as also did those of General Schuyler. The best relations had ever subsisted between the Dutch and the Six Nations, and likewise, for the most part, between the latter and the English colonists; and it was held by Washington and Schuyler, and others whose opinions were entitled to consideration, that the Indians who had been deluded into the service of the crown during the late struggle should be conciliated, if not won back to the interests of the United States, by humane and liberal treatment. In the opinion of Washington, their expulsion by force would inevitably involve the young republic in another general Indian war ;—whereas, were they treated with that degree of kindness and benevolence which the United States could then so well afford to extend to them, and which would be so creditable to the character of the confederation, their country might from time to time be obtained by negotiation as fast as it would be wanted for settlement by the whites, and at much less cost than it could be acquired for by conquest. Happily these principles prevailed, and a grand council was held by the chiefs of the Six Nations at Fort Stanwix, in the autumn of 1784, which was attended by Oliver Wolcott, Richard Butler, and Arthur Lee, on the part of the United States, and at which a treaty of peace was negotiated. The journals of this council have been lost, and nothing remains but the naked treaty, by the provisions of which the Six Nations were received under the protection of the United States, and secured in the possession of all the tracts of country within the boundaries of New-York, of which they were then the occupants.

This treaty was not signed by the chiefs in attendance upon the council, as is the usual practice, but by the names and arms of the nations represented, comprising the whole six of the Iroquois confederacy. There is, therefore, no catalogue extant of the sachems and chiefs present at the council ; but from other and subsequent passages of Indian history, it has been rendered certain that among the more prominent of the Indian leaders on that occasion,—the most influential and the most eloquent—were the Cornplanter and Red-Jacket. At what time the latter had been elevated to the dignity of chieftainship is not known. The means employed to obtain the rank are less uncertain. His conduct upon the war-path could not, by possibility, have purchased for him the favor of his people, for that conduct had been most emphatically stamped both with treachery and cowardice—the latter imperfection being ever an unpardonable offence among warriors of all nations, with whatever leniency the former may perhaps be looked upon by Indians. But the Six Nations, above all others of the American aboriginals, were lovers of eloquence, and cultivators of the art.* Red-Jacket's intellectual powers were of a high order, and he was an orator by nature.† He was, moreover, as artful and ambitious as he was eloquent. Aspiring to the rank of a chief, he not only wrought upon the minds of his people by the exertion of that faculty which was ever with them a high standard of merit, but he succeeded in availing himself of the superstitious constitution of his race, to effect his purpose. "His first essay was to dream that he was, or should be, a chief, and that the Great Spirit was angry that his

* "The most remarkable difference existed between the Confederates [Six Nations,] and the other Indians, with respect to eloquence. You may search in vain in the records and writings of the past, or in the events of the present times, for a single model of eloquence among the Algonquins, the Delawares, the Shawanese, or any other nation of Indians, except the Iroquois. The few scintillations of intellectual light, the faint glimmerings of genius which are sometimes to be found in their speeches, are evidently derivative, and borrowed from the Confederates."—*De Witt Clinton.*

† General Erastus Root once remarked to the author, that he considered John Randolph and Red-Jacket the two most perfect orators whom he had ever heard.

4

natiọn had not advanced him to that dignity. This dream, with the necessary variations, was repeated, until, fortunately for him, the small-pox broke out among the Senecas. He then proclaimed the loathsome infliction a judgment sent by the Great Spirit, to punish them for their ingratitude to him. The consequence, ultimately, was, that by administering flattery to some, working upon the superstitious fears of others, and by awakening the admiration of all by his eloquence, he reached the goal of his ambition."* Hence his appearance in the council at Fort Stanwix, in company with the same brave chief by whom he had been so bitterly reproached for his cowardice, on the margin of Canandaigua Lake, five years before.

Nor is it the least singular circumstance in this portion of his history, that he was the sturdy opponent of Cornplanter in the debates of the council, and although so utterly unfitted, by the absence of physical courage, for war himself, he was nevertheless opposed to peace—at least on the basis upon which it was granted. It appears from the proceedings of a great Indian council held at the mouth of the Detroit river, in 1786, two years after the treaty of Fort Stanwix, that the council at the latter place,—the chiefs especially, who, with their nations, had been engaged on the side of Great Britain, in the struggle then recent—were, for the most part, opposed to the conclusion of any treaty which did not include the Hurons, Ottawas, Shawanese, Chippewas, Delawares, Pottawattamies, and the Wabash confederates, as well as the Six Nations, and cover the

* Life of Brant.

entire question of boundaries for the whole.* They desired that these several nations might be invited to join
the council, that the pacification might include all who
had borne a part hostile to the United States in the war.
Red-Jacket was strenuous upon this point; contending,
with great vehemence, that, unless it were conceded,—
no matter for the withdrawal of Great Britain from the
contest,—the Indians ought to make common cause,
and prosecute the war on their own account. His speech
was characterized, by those who heard it, as a master-
piece of oratory, and it has been declared that every
warrior present was carried away by his eloquence.†
But the commissioners would listen to no such proposition; and the Cornplanter, who was an old and wise
man, though less eloquent than his junior associate, ultimately succeeded in giving a favorable turn to the nego-
ciation. Cornplanter was a warrior of unquestionable
bravery. His trail had been bloody; and he therefore,
at that time, stood high in the confidence of his people,
and of course exerted a corresponding influence. He
saw how utterly hopeless must be a contest between the
Indians, single-handed, and the United States, and he
ultimately succeeded in effecting a pacification—sur-
rendering, by necessity, a large portion of the Indian
territory within the State of New-York, but yet retaining
ample ranges of the forest for his own people. But

---

* Life of Brant.

† General Lafayette, who was present at the treaty of Fort Stanwix. Vide
Levasseur's account of the General's interview with Red-Jacket, at Buffalo, in
1825.

although the result of the negotiation was more favorable to the Six Nations than they had any just right to expect, it nevertheless gave great dissatisfaction to the Indians generally; and several years elapsed before the Senecas became reconciled to it.

After the conclusion of the treaty, the commissioners engaged Cornplanter to make special endeavors to pacify his people, the Senecas and others; as a compensation for which exertions a special grant of land was made to him on the Alleghany river, within the State of Pennsylvania, on which he resided until his death. But his people were not easily reconciled; and they were yet more exasperated at the conduct of Cornplanter, when, five years afterward, at the treaty of Fort Harmar, he gave up a still larger portion of their territory. He was bitterly reproached for this transaction; but, as in the treaty of Fort Stanwix, his motives were beyond impeachment. His life was even threatened,*—a circumstance to which he referred in the pathetic speech delivered by him to "the Great Counsellor of the Thirteen Fires,"† at Philadelphia, in 1790 :—

"Father, we will not conceal from you that the Great God, and not man, has preserved the Cornplanter from the hands of his own people."

The speech here cited is a long and moving appeal to the Thirteen Fires, to reconsider their treaties and other proceedings with the Indians, and especially for a redress

---

* Drake's Book of the Indians.   † Washington.

of alleged grievances, connected with the purchase of a large portion of their lands in Western New-York, by Oliver Phelps and Nathaniel Gorham. In regard to the treaty of Fort Stanwix, the history of which is eloquently reviewed in the speech, the Cornplanter declares that its concessions were yielded only to force.

" You then told us that we were in your hand, and that by closing it you could crush us to nothing, and you demanded from us a great country as the price of that peace you had offered us—as if our want of strength had destroyed our rights. Our chiefs had felt your power, and were unable to contend against you, and they therefore gave up that country." " There were but few chiefs present, and they were compelled to give it up ; and it is not the Six Nations only that reproach us for having given up that country. The Chippewas, and all the nations which lived on those lands westward, call to us, and ask us—' Brothers of our fathers ! Where is the place which you have reserved for us to lie down upon ?' What they agreed to has bound our nation; but your anger against us must, by this time, be cooled, and though our strength has not increased, nor your power become less, we ask you to consider calmly, were the terms dictated to us by your commissioners reasonable and just ?"*

It is evident from the whole strain of this remarkable speech, that Cornplanter was harassed by the murmurs of his own people, and himself grieved at their condition. And it will be seen in the sequel, that the crafty Sa-go-ye-wat-ha afterward availed himself of the position he had himself occupied at Fort Stanwix, to advance his

* Public Documents—Indian Affairs, vol. i. pp. 206, 207.

own ambitious views at the expense of his more ingenuous superior.* Still, it must in justice be conceded to the orator, that the treaty of peace having been concluded, he ever after maintained it with the most unwavering fidelity.

The names of Oliver Phelps and Nathaniel Gorham have been incidentally mentioned a few sentences back, in connection with the griefs which Cornplanter was pouring into the ears of his " Great Father," the " Counsellor of the Thirteen Fires ;" and the name of Red-Jacket appearing in the same connexion, a few words of explanation seem to be required. It is well known that in consequence of the loose and indefinite manner in which patents had been granted by the crown, in the earlier history of the colonies, to vast tracts and regions of lands unknown, several difficult questions of land titles and jurisdiction arose between New-York, Connecticut, Massachusetts, and Pennsylvania. In the adjustment of these difficulties, Connecticut became dispossessed of a tract in the Susquehanna country, called " The Gore," and, on the other hand, received that portion of the State of Ohio, commonly known as " New-Connecticut," or " The Western Reserve." Pennsylvania obtained a tract of land lying immediately beyond the western boundary of New-York, and northeast of her own, embracing the harbor of Presque Isle, upon Lake Erie, familiarly known as " The Triangle." This was an important acquisition to Pennsylvania, affording the

---

* Life of Brant, vol. ii. p. 245.

only passage, upon her own territory, to Lake Erie. The difficulties between New-York and Massachusetts were more serious, and of more difficult adjustment, by reason of the claim of the latter to a very large portion of Western New-York. But an amicable arrangement was effected toward the close of 1786, by mutual concessions. Massachusetts relinquished the *jurisdiction* which she had attempted to claim, and New-York relinquished to Massachusetts the *pre-emptive right*, (or the right of purchasing the soil from the Indians,) to a tract of land embracing six millions of acres, comprehending what is generally known as "the Genesee country," and the territory beyond to Lake Erie and the Pennsylvania border. New-York thus retained her sovereignty, but lost the fee of one of the finest regions of country in the New World.

Pending the adjustment of these difficulties, and emboldened, probably, by the success which crowned the efforts of the Green Mountaineers in robbing New-York of the territory composing the state of Vermont, a daring company of speculators, residing upon the banks of the Hudson, had attempted to grasp the entire country remaining to the Six Nations after the treaty of 1784, with a view, as it was believed, of ultimately dismembering New-York, and creating a separate state from its western territory.* The laws of New-York, even at that early day, prohibited the purchase of any Indian lands what-

---

* The gentlemen concerned in this vast project were, John Livingston, Caleb Benton, Peter Ryckman, John Stephenson, Ezekiel Gilbert, and their associates, of the county of Columbia, and state of New-York.

ever, by individuals, or by companies, within the state. But Colonel Livingston and his associates attempted to escape the legal difficulties by an evasion. Instead of making a *purchase*, they negotiated with the chiefs of the Six Nations, in the autumn of 1787, for a *lease* of their entire territory within the state of New-York, exclusive of certain reservations, for and during the period of *nine hundred and ninety-nine years*, at the nominal yearly rent of two thousand Spanish milled dollars, to be paid annually on the 4th day of July. A lease of such extended duration was equivalent to a purchase of the fee of the land, and was so considered by the lessees, whose object, as it was understood, was to throw a large population as rapidly as possible into that territory, to form the nucleus of another independent state. But the government of the state, and the people, took the alarm. Remonstrances were poured in upon the legislature from Hudson, Poughkeepsie, and other towns, expressing the surprise and anxiety with which the remonstrants had observed the movements of the association, and protesting against the application making by the latter to obtain the sanction of their claim by the government. George Clinton, then governor of the state, was strongly opposed to the transaction, and called the attention of the legislature specially to the subject. Finally the hopes of the company were extinguished by the law of March, 1788, proposed by Egbert Benson, then in the Senate, declaring the pre-emptive right to the lands to be vested in the state, and authorizing the strongest measures of force to be used by the Executive, in the removal of all intruders from the lands.*

Before proceeding farther with these explanations, not as foreign to the purposes of this biography as they may seem at the present stage of the narrative, it must be noted, and the fact should be remembered, that Red-Jacket was a party to the transaction with Colonel Livingston and his associates, as also was the Cornplanter. The importance of keeping the name of Red-Jacket in close connexion with this subject will presently appear.

Meantime, another feature in the great land operations now under consideration must be unfolded. It has just been seen that, in the year 1786, Massachusetts acquired from the state of New-York the pre-emptive right to a large tract of the Indian lands, comprehended in the Seneca country proper. This pre-emptive title to all the lands claimed by, or accorded to, Massachusetts, lying east of the Genesee river, was sold by the legislature of that state, in the following year, to Oliver Phelps and Nathaniel Gorham, for the sum of one million of dollars, payable in three annual instalments. In the next subsequent year,—that is, in the summer of 1788,—Mr. Phelps led an expedition of colonists into the newly purchased territory, and causing a council of the Six

* In order that not even the color of injustice toward the lessees might remain, the legislature, five years afterward, made a grant to them of a district of country, ten miles square, in the northern part of the state, and subsequently they received grants of several large tracts in the Genesee country, from Phelps and Gorham.

Nations to be convened at Buffalo Creek, in the month
of July, succeeded in purchasing the fee of the soil, for
the small sum of five thousand dollars in hand paid,—
one half in cash, and the other in goods,—subject to
an annual rent of five hundred dollars forever. The
deed to Phelps and Gorham was dated on the 8th of
July, 1788, and bears the signature of Sha-go-yagh-
wat-ha,* or Red-Jacket. Joseph Brant was also a party
to the deed.

As the lease of their whole territory, executed the
preceding year by the Indians to Colonel Livingston
and his associates, had not yet been declared invalid by
the government of the state, the sale to Phelps and
Gorham rendered a farther arrangement with the former
parties necessary. Accordingly, in the course of the
same season, a second instrument was executed to
Colonel Livingston and his company, setting forth the
sale to Phelps and Gorham, and for that reason relinquishing to the former one half of the annual rent of
two thousand dollars per annum, for the period of nine
hundred and ninety-nine years. And here, again, it is
necessary to note the fact that Red-Jacket was a party
to this third document, connected with other papers and
transactions, equivalent to an entire sale of the territory
of his people within the state of New-York.

* Thus spelt by the person who wrote the name to which Red-Jacket placed
his mark.

CHAPTER III.

IN the year 1790 the Indian relations of the United States were in a most unhappy, if not unfavorable, condition. A savage war, fierce and bloody, was raging upon the frontier settlements of Pennsylvania and Virginia ; and the strong confederated Indian nations inhabiting the country of the great lakes, even to the regions beyond the Mississippi, acting under the advice of the officers of the British Indian Department, and encouraged in various ways by the government of Canada, were gathering to the contest with a determination that the Ohio river should form the ultimate boundary between the United States and the Indian country. All the sympathies of the Senecas, who had

never been quite satisfied with the provisions of the
treaty of Fort Stanwix, were with their brethren of the
west, as also were not a few of their warriors; although
Cornplanter, their principal chief, remained•unshaken
in his friendship for the United States.   Still, the popular
feeling among his nation was rather hostile; threatening,
in fact, open and general hostilities.   Unluckily, just
at this inauspicious conjuncture, the Senecas found fresh
cause of exasperation in the murder of two of their
people by some of the white border-men of Pennsylvania.   The effect of this outrage had well nigh pro-
voked an immediate outbreak, but the government of
the United States lost not a moment in disavowing the
act, and in the adoption of measures to bring the mur-
derers to punishment, by the offer of a large reward for
their apprehension.   A conference with the Six Nations
was also invited at Tioga Point, at which Colonel Timothy Pickering, who then resided at Wyoming, was commissioned to attend on the part of the United States.
The council-fire was kindled on the 16th of November,
and was kept burning until the 23d.   Among the nations
present, either collectively or by representation, were
the Senecas, Oneidas, Onondagas, Cayugas, a small
party of Chippewas, and also several of the Stockbridge
Indians, among whom was their veteran captain, and the
faithful friend of the United States, Hendrick Apamaut.
The Indians were in a high state of excitement on their
arrival, in regard to the outrage for the consideration of
which they had been convoked, and which was deeply
felt.   The chiefs who took the most active part in the

proceedings of this council were Red-Jacket, Farmer's-Brother, Little Billy, Hendrick, and Fish-Carrier, a very old and distinguished warrior of the Cayugas. Old Hendrick made a very eloquent and pathetic address to the commissioner, in the shape of an appeal in behalf of his people, reminding him of their strong and uniform attachment to the United States during the war of the revolution, of the hardships they underwent, and the losses they had sustained during that war, and complaining bitterly of the neglect with which they had been treated since the peace, in consequence, as he supposed, of the small number to which they had been reduced. In referring to their services in the field, he used these expressions :—

" We fought by your side,—our blood was mingled with yours,—and the bones of our warriors still remain on the field of battle, as so many monuments of our attachment to the United States."*

Cornplanter was not present at this council, and the principal speaker was Red-Jacket, whose efforts produced a deep effect upon his people. Still, by a wise and well-adapted speech, Colonel Pickering succeeded in allaying the excitement of the Indians,—dried their tears, and wiped out the blood that had been shed.

But no sooner had that important business been disposed of than Red-Jacket introduced the subject of their lands, and the purchase of Phelps and Gorham.

* The Stockbridge Indians suffered very severely in the battle of White Plains.

In a set speech to Colonel Pickering he inveighed against the procedure, (although, as has been seen, he had himself been a party to it,) and declared that the Indians had been defrauded. It was not, he said, a sale which they had contemplated, or which they had stipulated to make to those gentlemen, but only a lease; and the consideration, he declared, was to have been ten thousand dollars, together with an annual rent of one thousand dollars, instead of five thousand dollars and a rent of five hundred, which only had been paid to them. He declared that after the bargain was concluded in council at Buffalo Creek, the Rev. Mr. Kirkland,* Colonel John Butler,† and Captain Brant, were designated by the Indians to draw up the papers. The Indians supposed all to have been done correctly until the year following, when they went to Canandaigua to receive their pay. Expecting to receive ten thousand dollars, they were told that five thousand only was their due.

" When we took the money and shared it, we had but about a dollar a piece." " Mr. Street!"‡ said the chief, " you very well know that all that our lands came to was but the price of a few hogsheads of tobacco." " Gentlemen who stand by," (addressing the gentlemen in attendance with Colonel Pickering,) " do not think hard of what has been said. At the time of the treaty, twenty brooches would not buy half a loaf of

* The celebrated missionary to the Indians.

† Of the British Indian Department—the invader of Wyoming, then residing at Niagara.

‡ A gentleman then connected with the Indian Department, who was present at the treaty with Phelps and Gorham, and who was now with Col. Pickering.

bread, so that, when we returned home, there was not a single spot of silver about us. Mr. Phelps did not purchase, but he leased the land. We opened our ears, and understood that the land was leased. This happened to us from our not knowing papers."

The speech under immediate consideration, is the earliest of Sa-go-ye-wat-ha's forensic efforts of which there is any written memorial, nor does it promise much either for the eloquence, genius, or talent of the orator. On the contrary, it is remarkable for its tameness, rather than for spirit or mental power,—sinking indeed below the dead level of mediocrity. But aside from the fact that his theme, for the most part, was not inspiring,—it being chiefly a dry recapitulation of business transactions,— there is reason to believe that great injustice was done him by the interpreter. A gentleman, now venerable in years, who was present at the treaty,* asserts that both in matter and manner, Red-Jacket, during the sittings of the council, spoke with extraordinary eloquence and power. Much depends upon the interpreter in the preservation of Indian eloquence. If he be a dull and prosaic man, without genius himself, and incapable of appreciating the glowing thoughts, the burning words, and the brilliant metaphors of his principal, the most eloquent and stirring passages,—evidently such from the impassioned manner of their delivery, and their kindling effect upon those understanding the language to

* Thomas Morris, Esq., who has favored the author with his written recollections of that council.

whom they are addressed,—will fall from the interpreter's lips as insipid as it is possible to render language by the process of dilution.*   Hence, from the acknowledged genius of Red-Jacket, and the known powers of his eloquence upon his auditors, this speech to Colonel Pickering is to be received rather as a poor paraphrase by a bad interpreter, than as the speech of the orator himself.   The following is the best passage it contains. After recapitulating his own statement of the negotiation with Phelps and Gorham, and asserting the anxiety of his people to appeal to Congress for a redress of their grievances in this transaction, the orator proceeded :—

"Now, BROTHERS, the THIRTEEN STATES, you must open your ears.   You know what has happened respecting our lands. You told us, from this time the chain of friendship should be brightened.   Now, brothers, we have begun to brighten the chain, and we will follow the footsteps of our forefathers.   We will take those steps, that we may sit easy and choose where and how large our seats should be.   The reason we send this message is, that the President, who is over all the Thirteen States, may make our seats easy.   We do it that the chain of friendship may be brightened with the Thirteen States, as well as with the British ; that we may pass from one to the other

* " I have heard an old Indian Sachem speak with much vivacity and elocution, so that the speaker pleased and moved his audience with the manner of delivering his discourse, which, however, as it afterwards came from the interpreter, disappointed us in our expectations.   After the speaker had employed a considerable time in haranguing with much elocution, the interpreter often explained the whole by one single sentence.   I believe the speaker, in that time, embellished and advanced his figures, that they might have their full force on their imagination, while the interpreter contented himself with the sense, in as few words as it could be expressed."—*Colden's Six Nations.*

unmolested. We wish to be under the protection of the Thirteen States as well as of the British."

During the progress of the negotiations with Colonel Pickering at this council, an episode was enacted, of which some account may be excused in this place, as an illustration of Indian character and manners. It was in this year, (1790,) that Robert Morris, of Philadelphia,—the great financier of the revolution,—purchased from the state of Massachusetts the pre-emptive right to that portion of her territory in Western New-York, that had not been sold to Phelps and Gorham, viz: the entire tract bounded on the north by Lake Ontario, on the south by the Pennsylvania line, on the east by the Genesee river, and on the west by the Niagara. Preparatory to the negotiations which Mr. Morris well knew he should be obliged to hold with the Indians, and for the general management of his concerns in that country, his son Thomas had taken up his residence at Canandaigua, and was diligently cultivating an acquaintance with the Indians. In this he was successful, and he soon became popular among them. He was in attendance with Colonel Pickering at Tioga Point, where the Indians determined to adopt him into the Seneca nation, and Red-Jacket bestowed upon him the name he himself had borne previous to his elevation to the dignity of a Sachem,—Otetiani—"Always Ready." The occasion of which they availed themselves to perform the ceremony of conferring upon young Morris his new name, was a religious observance, when the whole sixteen

6

hundred Indians present at the treaty, united in an
offering to the moon, then being at her full. The
ceremonies were performed in the evening. It was a
clear night, and the moon shone with uncommon brilliancy. The host of Indians, and their neophyte, were
all seated upon the ground in an extended circle, on one
side of which a large fire was kept burning. The aged
Cayuga chieftain, Fish-Carrier, who was held in exalted
veneration for his wisdom, and who had been greatly
distinguished for his bravery from his youth up, officia-
ted as the high priest of the occasion,—making a long
speech to the luminary, occasionally throwing tobacco
into the fire as incense. On the conclusion of the address, the whole assembly prostrated themselves upon
the bosom of their parent earth, and a grunting sound of
approbation was uttered from mouth to mouth around
the entire circle. At a short distance from the fire a
post had been planted in the earth ; intended to represent the stake of torture to which captives are bound for
execution. After the ceremonies in favor of Madame
Luna had been ended, they commenced a war-dance
around the post, and the spectacle must have been as picturesque as it was animating and wild. The young braves
engaged in the dance were naked excepting the breech-
clout about their loins. They were painted frightfully,
their backs being chalked white, with irregular streaks of
red, denoting the streaming of blood. Frequently would
they cease from dancing while one of their number ran
to the fire, snatching thence a blazing stick, placed there
for that purpose, which he would thrust at the post, as

though inflicting torture upon a prisoner. In the course
of the dance they sang their songs, and made the forests
ring with their wild screams and shouts, as they boasted
of their deeds of war and told the number of scalps
they had respectively taken, or which had been taken by
their nation. During the dance those engaged in it, as
did others also, partook freely of unmixed rum, and by
consequence of the natural excitement of the occasion,
and the artificial excitement of the liquor, the festival
had well nigh turned out a tragedy. It happened that
among the dancers was an Oneida warrior, who, in
striking the post, boasted of the number of scalps taken
by his nation during the war of the revolution. Now
the Oneidas, it will be recollected, had sustained the
cause of the colonies in that contest, while the rest of
the Iroquois confederacy had espoused that of the
crown. The boasting of the Oneida warrior, therefore,
was like striking a spark into a keg of gunpowder.
The ire of the Senecas was kindled in an instant, and
they in turn boasted of the number of scalps taken by
them from the Oneidas in that contest. They moreover
taunted the Oneidas as cowards. Quick as lightning
the hands of the latter were upon their weapons, and in
turn the knives and tomahawks of the Senecas began to
glitter in the moon-beams, as they were hastily drawn
forth. For an instant it was a scene of anxious and
almost breathless suspense, a death struggle seeming
inevitable, when the storm was hushed by the interposition of old Fish-Carrier, who rushed forward, and striking the post with violence, exclaimed :—

" You are all of you a parcel of boys : When you have attained my age, and performed the warlike deeds that I have performed, you may boast what you have done : not till then !"

Saying which he threw down the post, put an end to the dance, and caused the assembly to retire.* This scene, in its reality, must have been one of absorbing and peculiar interest. An assembly of nearly two thousand inhabitants of the forest, grotesquely clad in skins and strouds, with shining ornaments of silver, and their coarse raven hair falling over their shoulders, and playing wildly in the wind as it swept past, sighing mournfully among the giant branches of the trees above,—such a group, gathered in a broad circle in an " opening" of the wilderness, the starry canopy of heaven glittering above them, the moon casting her silver mantle around their dusky forms,—and a large fire blazing in the midst of them,—before which they were working their spells, and performing their savage rites,—must have presented a spectacle of long and vivid remembrance.

In December of the same year, a deputation of the Senecas, consisting of the Cornplanter, Half-Town and Great Tree, visited Philadelphia, then the seat of the federal government, for the purpose of again remonstrating against the hardship of the treaty of Fort Stanwix, and of reclaiming, if possible, a portion of the terri-

* MS. recollections of Thomas Morris. Mr. M. was known among the Indians by the name conferred upon him on this occasion, for many years. After his marriage, his wife was called by them Otetiani squaw, and his children, Otetiani pappooses.

tory ceded away by that treaty. It was on the occasion of that visit that Cornplanter delivered the speech to General Washington, then President of the United States, cited in the preceding chapter.* They wished, in particular, to obtain a restoration of the territory, bordering upon Pennsylvania, then occupied by Half-Town and his people, who were, and had been from the first, dissatisfied with the treaty.

In the course of his appeal, speaking in reference to Half-Town's clan, Cornplanter exclaimed with moving earnestness :—

" They grew out of that land, and their fathers grew out of it, and they cannot be persuaded to part with it. *It is a very little piece.* We therefore entreat you to restore to us this little piece of land."

The appeal is as simple and touching as that of Lot to be allowed to flee into Zoar. "*Is it not a little city?*" But such has not been the course of events. Vain are the appeals of Indians to the pale faces, for a restoration of territory,—no matter how it may have been acquired. Yet, in the case under consideration, the Indians had less cause of complaint than usual, since the treaty of Fort Stanwix could not justly have been deemed oppressive.

But the provisions of the Fort Stanwix treaty did not constitute the entire burden of Cornplanter's remonstrances. He, too, complained of the conduct of Phelps

* See the entire speech in the sketch of Cornplanter's life, toward the close of the volume.

and Gorham, imputing the same frauds that had been charged by Red-Jacket,—and adding that Street was to receive from Phelps a grant of land ten miles square, for his agency in the deception practised upon the Indians. This feature in the conduct of Cornplanter, considering the general fairness and integrity of his character, as exhibited in his intercourse with the whites subsequent to the revolutionary war, is not of easy explication. He, like Red-Jacket, had been a party to the sale of territory to Phelps and Gorham; and when the subject was afterward brought before Congress, the report of Mr. Butler, from the Committee of Indian Affairs, supplied the most ample testimony, from gentlemen of irreproachable veracity, that the said purchase had been made in the most fair and honorable manner, and that the papers had been thoroughly and truly explained to the Indians, by whom the terms were perfectly understood. The charges of fraud, therefore, first publicly made by Red-Jacket in his speech to Colonel Pickering, and afterward repeated, as has been seen, by Cornplanter, fell to the ground. But how came these chiefs,—the Cornplanter being the head of his nation,— to prefer the charges? May it not have been that Red-Jacket was even then plotting to supplant his principal in the affections of his people, by inducing them to believe that he was more their friend, and a better patriot, than his rival? And may not the latter have taken up the false charge, and repeated it to General Washington, for the purpose only of sustaining himself, and circumventing the crafty demagogue, whose machinations were ultimately but too successful?

The bearing of Washington toward these sons of the forest was such as to allay the unpleasant feelings under which they arrived in Philadelphia, and to send them away in good humor. Nay, the Cornplanter was engaged to accompany Colonel Proctor on a friendly mission to the country of the Miamis, for the purpose of bringing the hostile Indians to reasonable terms of peace. This mission was not undertaken until the following spring, when Colonel Proctor proceeded into the Seneca country, to join Cornplanter. Meeting with him at his own town, situated upon Oil Creek, one of the upper tributaries of the Alleghany river, it was found necessary to convoke a grand council of the Six Nations at Buffalo Creek, before they could safely proceed to the country of the hostile nations. The fact was, that the repulse of General Harmar's expedition in the preceding autumn had greatly emboldened the hostile Indians, with whose cause those four of the Six Nations which had been engaged in the war of the revolution on the side of the crown, especially the Senecas, strongly sympathized. Numbers of their young warriors, disregarding the restraints, feeble at best, of their own principal chiefs, were in the ranks of the enemy, and it was only with the greatest difficulty, during the whole of that border conflict, that the greater part of the Six Nations were kept from joining their brethren. Just about this time, also, the Senecas had again been exasperated by the murder of several of their people, who had given no

offence, by some of the Pennsylvania borderers living at
Big Beaver Creek, in the neighborhood of Pittsburgh.
Hence Cornplanter and Colonel Proctor were obliged to
proceed with the utmost circumspection; and a grand
council at Buffalo being demanded before the nations
would allow Cornplanter to proceed to the west, the
measure was acquiesced in, though attended by great in-
convenience, and necessarily causing a long delay.

It has been necessary to glance at this mission of
Colonel Proctor and the Cornplanter, for the reason that
the leading personage of the present memoir, Red-
Jacket, figured conspicuously in the council at Buffalo
Creek, at which place Cornplanter and Colonel Proctor
arrived on the 27th of April, 1791. The council-fire
had been burning several days, in anticipation of their
presence, and many of the principal chiefs were already
there,—among whom were Farmer's-Brother, Young-
King and Red-Jacket,—the former two being dressed
in the uniforms of British colonels. Red-Jacket was a
much younger chief than the others, but had now, it was
evident, become a man of consideration. Colonel Proctor, in his diary,* mentions him as "the great speaker
and prince of the Turtle tribe."† The Colonel was
received with unusual ceremony. The Indians had
mounted a two-pounder upon logs at the porch of the
council-house, heavily loaded, which they discharged on
the approach of their guests, but to the no small peril of
all who were near, since the explosion up-threw the gun

* Vide Proctor's Journal, Indian State Papers, vol. i. p. 155.
† An Error. Red-Jacket was of the Wolf tribe.

from its position, and sadly deranged its fixtures. Red-Jacket, or, as his people were then accustomed to call him, "the Young Prince of the Wolf Tribe," had been designated by the council to receive the Colonel and Cornplanter, and as they entered the council-house, the orator rose and welcomed the former in the following speech :—

"BROTHER : Listen! It is usual for us to speak; and to you we do it as to a brother that has been absent a long time. Now we all speak to you, and to our Head Warrior that left us last fall :—and we thank the Great Spirit for his and your safe arrival here, as you are together, hand in hand, from Honandaganius,* upon great business.

"You have travelled long, with tears in your eyes, upon account of the bad roads, and bad season of the year. Besides the disturbances between the bad Indians and our brothers the white people, every thing has been trying to prevent your coming, and to stop your. business, and make you lose your way.

"Thus the big waters might have stopped your coming; and the wars might have stopped you; and sickness might have stopped you ; for we cannot know what is to happen until it comes upon us. So, therefore, we thank the Great Spirit who has preserved you from such dangers that might have hindered us from hearing of the good news which you and our head warrior have opened to us. But how could it be that any thing bad could have happened to you, while you have such important business to transact, as we understand you have come on ?

"You must now wipe away those tears occasioned by all the great dangers you have come through. And now we set you upon a seat where you can sit up straight,—and a seat where you are secure from the fears of your enemies ;—where you

* General Washington.

7

can look round and see all your friends and brothers in peace. Besides, you have come along with your heart and your throat stopped up, to secure all that you had to say in your body. But now we open your heart with your brothers' hands, and we run our fingers through to open your mouth, that you may speak clear, and not be molested. Your ears also have been stopped by Honandaganius until you should see your brothers at this place, being spared by the Great Spirit to arrive safe.

" Now, open your ears to hear what your brothers may say after you have made your speech. This is, therefore, the compliment of the chiefs and head men of Buffalo Creek, to you and our great warrior, the Cornplanter, and you may each of you go on safely with your business."

Cornplanter replied in behalf of Colonel Proctor and himself, and at the close of his speech, intended merely as an interchange of compliments, Red-Jacket advanced and presented the colonel with the belt which he held while delivering his salutatory address.

But notwithstanding the apparent frankness and cordiality of this speech of welcome, the conduct of Red-Jacket, even during the first evening's conference, was marked by extreme wariness, giving evidence of disingenuousness, if not of dissimulation. When Colonel Proctor stated " that he had been commissioned by Ge- " neral Washington, the great chief of the Thirteen " Fires," Red-Jacket remarked " that many persons " had occasionally come into their country, who said " they had also come from the authority of the Thirteen " Fires, but of the truth of this they were not always " convinced." But the colonel afterward ascertained that Red-Jacket was only playing *a part* in the ex-

pression of his doubts. The orator and the chiefs at
the council had been fully advised of the colonel's official character, by the chiefs who had met him in the in-
termediate councils, called in some of the Indian towns
through which he had passed on his way thither. It
was also ascertained by Proctor, on the first evening of
his arrival, that Red-Jacket was acting under the advice
of Brant and Colonel John Butler, in order to thwart the
views of the government of the United States, and if possible frustrate the intended visit of Proctor and Cornplanter
to the Miamis. Brant and Butler had been at Buffalo
Creek some days before Proctor's arrival, and after a
conference, the former had departed suddenly for the
country of the belligerent Indians, leaving Red-Jacket
to receive the messengers as already stated, and enact
a part cast expressly for the occasion of their arrival. According to certain intimations given by Captain Powell, an officer in the British Indian service who
had been despatched by the commandant of Fort Erie to
meet Colonel Proctor at the Buffalo Council-house, this
sudden mission of Brant had been "directed from head-
quarters;" but whether reference was had to Quebec,
or the fort at Niagara, does not appear.

The council was numerously attended on the two
succeeding days, during which Colonel Proctor read his
entire instructions to the chiefs, as also the address with
which he was charged to the hostile Indians of the west.
Having concluded the interpretations of these papers,
and informed the Indians of the kindness exercised by
the Great Father of the Thirteen Fires, as manifested

by the liberal concessions made to Cornplanter during his recent visit to Philadelphia, Colonel Proctor was surprised by a speech from Red-Jacket, declaring that the council-fire must be removed to the British fortress of Niagara, to which place he said the colonel must accompany them. As a reason for this proposition, Red-Jacket spoke of the absence of several chiefs of the Six Nations; adding, that in the discussion of matters of such grave importance he wished the presence of the British officers. " Captain Powell," he said, " is always true to " us, and is with us at every treaty."

Conceiving it to be an unwarrantable request, sanctioned neither by his principals nor his instructions, the colonel peremptorily refused to comply with it—declaring, that if the relations of the chiefs with the officers of the British garrison were such that they could not act but upon their counsel and advice, they must send for those officers to join them at Buffalo Creek. A marked silence pervaded the council for some time upon the utterance of Colonel Proctor's refusal; after which Red-Jacket and Farmer's-Brother successively addressed the Indians, and in the end a messenger was despatched to Niagara, with a request that Colonel Butler would join their council without delay.

During the three days intervening before the return of the messenger, Colonel Proctor was urging upon the chiefs the importance of a more rapid despatch of business, that he might resume his journey without farther let or hindrance.

The object of his visit to the Six Nations was two-fold,—first, to allay, if possible, the rising feeling of hostility among the Senecas, and secure the neutrality of the entire confederacy ; and, secondly, to induce a deputation of their chiefs to accompany him and the Cornplanter into the hostile country, to add their persuasions in favor of peace. But Red-Jacket and the leading chiefs were exceedingly adverse, if not to the entire object of the Colonel's mission, at least to the sending of a deputation to accompany him. At first they objected to the distance, pretending that it was the design to take them away to the shores of the distant ocean,—a journey so long that it would require twelve months to reach the point of destination. This excuse having been removed, the next objection interposed by Red-Jacket was fear,—a fear that they would all be murdered by the Miamis and their confederates. Accordingly, on the 3d of May, in reply to the colonel, who continued to press his business with urgency, Red-Jacket dictated the following address :—

" Tell him," (said he to the interpreter,) " Tell Colonel Proctor that some of his language is soft, but that other parts of it are too strong. The danger before us is great. Our enemies are drunk, and they will not hear what we say like a man that is sober ; and we consider that, whatever number of the Six Nations accompany him, (Col. Proctor,) will be in the same danger with himself, and it is likely that we shall not live long when the bad Indians shall see us. Therefore, as it is a business of such great weight to us, we must take counsel, in order to save ourselves, and him, from falling by their hands. Moreover, the Indians are not like white men, for they must think a great while. He (Colonel Proctor) must therefore attend our

councils, and look and hear what we shall speak on his business. To-morrow our head men will meet together, and try
what can be done."

The plea of fear was one that Red-Jacket might very
possibly have interposed in all sincerity; but on the part
of the brave old Farmer's-Brother, Young King, and the
celebrated Cayuga chief, Fish-Carrier, with whom Red-
Jacket was acting in close consultation, it must have
been an artifice of dissimulation. Whatever might have
been the fact with the orator, the emotion of fear was a
stranger to the bosoms of the other three. Indeed the
pretext was transparent. Colonel Proctor had already
seen that their opinions and conduct were to be regulated
by the British agent and the British officers only. At
least if he had not actually seen as much, he was not
long left in doubt as to the fact; since Red-Jacket had
scarcely finished the brief speech recited above, before
a messenger came from Colonel Butler, inviting the
chiefs to meet him on the lake shore, at a distance from
the council-fire, and not to allow Colonel Proctor to accompany them. From that hour forward, the prospect
of a favorable issue to the colonel's mission became
more and more dubious. It is true that Colonel Butler
subsequently met Colonel Proctor, and even entertained
him with courtesy; but the Indians were entirely dis-
suaded from lending him any assistance, or co-operating
in furtherance of his views; while in their conversations
with Colonel Proctor, the British officers assumed the
position that no peace would, or probably could, be negotiated with the hostile Indians, excepting through their

mediation. In a word, it was insisted by His Britannic
Majesty's officers that the adjustment of the entire controversy, and the details of any treaty, with the north-
western Indians, must be left to Captain Brant, the
chiefs at Buffalo, and certain officers of the British Indian department at Detroit. And during the whole of
these conversations and proceedings, the course of Red-
Jacket was manifestly directed by the officers of His
Britannic Majesty. Under these untoward circumstances,—ascertaining, moreover, that Brant had taken
a considerable body of the Mohawk Indians with him
to the Miamis; that the hostile Indians were receiving
large military supplies from the British garrison at Detroit; that Colonel Gordon was strengthening his defences at Niagara; and that preparations were making
for the construction of another fortification on the northern shore, near the foot of Lake Erie; and having also
been explicitly told by Young King, on the evening
of the 14th of May, that they would not send a deputation of their chiefs with him to the Miamis,—Colonel
Proctor determined to end farther procrastination, and
his mission, at once. On the same evening, therefore,
he communicated this determination to the Indians, in a
few brief but energetic words, in the course of which he
forgot not to intimate that his report to the war-chief of
the Thirteen Fires* would not be very favorable, and
probably would not tend greatly to their future advantage. The colonel's decisive manner made a deep im-

---

* General Knox was at that time Secretary at War.

pression upon the Indians, especially the women, to whom his words were reported, and through whose interposition the progress of the mission speedily assumed a different aspect, promising, for the time, a favorable result. The story will be related chiefly as illustrative of Indian character, though not disconnected with the life of Red-Jacket.

Having heard the conversation between Colonel Proctor and Young King, as just recited, on the following morning, being the 14th of May, the elders of the Indian women repaired to Colonel Proctor's lodge, where a number of chiefs were present, and addressed him in the following manner :—

"BROTHER: The Great Spirit has spared us until a new day to talk together : for, since you came here from General Washington, you, and our uncles the sachems, have been counselling together. Moreover, your sisters, the women, have taken the same into great consideration, because that you and our sachems have said so much about it. Now, that is the reason why we have come to say something to you, and to tell you that the Great Spirit hath preserved you, and that you ought to hear and listen to what we, women, shall speak, as well as to the sachems ; for *we are the owners of this land,*—and it is our's. It is we that plant it for our and their use. Hear us, therefore, for we speak of things that concern us and our children, and you must not think hard of us while our men shall say more to you ; for we have told them."

This formal speech of the women being ended, Colonel Proctor acceded to a request that he would meet their sachems in council on the same day, and hear what would be said by the speaker whom they had selected to represent them—"the Young Prince of the Turtle Tribe, Sa-go-ye-wat-ha."* At the given signal, the firing of a gun, the council assembled, and on his arrival at the council-fire, an unusual spectacle was presented to Colonel Proctor, who found the elders of the women seated near their chiefs. It appeared that the women, who, as is natural to the sex, were the lovers of peace, had prevailed upon their lords, including all the leading chiefs of the Six Nations, to alter the determination avowed to Colonel Proctor on the preceding evening by Young King. After a short silence, Red-Jacket took up the speech of his clients as follows :—

"BROTHER FROM PENNSYLVANIA : You that are sent from General Washington, and by the Thirteen Fires : you have been sitting side by side with us every day, and the Great Spirit has appointed us another pleasant day to meet again.

"Now listen, BROTHER ! You know what we have been doing so long, and what trouble we have been at; and you

---

* The women on this occasion spoke of Red-Jacket as of the Turtle Tribe, and it has been thus written elsewhere. But he himself claimed to be of the Wolf Tribe, and thus I have designated him. My authority is the following anecdote, related to me by the venerable Mr. James Wadsworth, of Geneseo, in the summer of 1840. Many years ago, the Six Nations held a treaty, by themselves, at a place about five miles east of Mr. Wadsworth's residence. They continued in council until their provisions were exhausted, and until, in fact, they became very hungry. On breaking up, Red-Jacket, who was well acquainted with Mr. Wadsworth, led some thirty or forty of the leading chiefs to his house, and requested breakfast. Mr. W. spread a table liberally, but such was the voracity of the Indians that the viands disappeared almost as fast as they could be set before them. Steaks, cold hams, tongues, &c., vanished with prodigious rapidity. Red-Jacket lost not his full portion; and reading Mr. Wadsworth's surprise at their voracity in his countenance, the chief drily remarked that his entertainer must excuse him, inasmuch as he belonged to the *Wolf Tribe*—adding " and wolves, you know, are always fond of meat."

8

know that it has been the request of our head warrior,* that
we are left to answer for our women, who are to conclude
what ought to be done by both sachems and warriors.   So
hear what is their conclusion.

"BROTHER : The business you have come on is very troublesome. and we have been a long time considering on it, ever
since you came here, and now the elders of our women, considering the greatness of your business, have said that our
sachems and warriors must help you over your difficulties, for
the good of them and their children.   Moreover, you tell us,
since the treaty of Tioga with us, the Americans are strong
for peace.

" Now all that has been done for you has been done by our
women : the rest will be a hard task for us ; for the people at
the setting sun are bad people, and you have come on in too
much haste for such great matters of importance.   And now,
Brother, you must look when it is light in the morning until
the setting sun, and you must reach your neck over the land,
and take all the light you can, to show the danger.   And these
are the words of our women to you, and the sachems and warriors who shall go with you.   And now we shall name them
as they have first presented themselves in this full council.†

" Now, Brother from Pennsylvania and from General Washington, I have told you what has been directed.   Let us, therefore throw all care on the mercy of our Great Keeper, in hopes
that he will assist us.   You now know that Colonel Butler of
the British told us that he must take our writings down to
Colonel Gordon, as he is a very wise man, and perhaps he
may have something to say to us that may be for our good.

---

* Cornplanter.

† Here followed the names of the delegates, one of whom was Red-Jacket
himself, and among whom was *not* Cornplanter, for a reason presently stated.
The delegates were six in number, of whom were the four following : Kuyscetta,
Red-Jacket, "the Young Prince of the Turtle Tribe," as he was designated,
Captain John, of the Onondagas, and the Grand Carrier, Awangogathe.   (The
names of the two other deputies were lost by Colonel Proctor.)

And we also want his assistance, as he is the man that keeps all the vessels that are on the lake.

"Therefore, my Brother, make your mind easy, for your request is granted, and when we hear from our brothers the British, then we shall know what time we can start. And you must not be uneasy that our brother O'Beel* does not go with you, for he is very tired, and must rest awhile, and take charge of our young warriors while they are playing,† to keep them in peace for fear of danger. And now, while we are speaking, more of our young warriors have given their names to go with you."‡

If the true reason is here given why the Cornplanter was not allowed to proceed upon the mission,—if indeed he had not been kept from the deputation by a British intrigue through Red-Jacket,—there was probably another reason lying still deeper in the minds of the women. Cornplanter was not only the principal war-chief of the Senecas, but he was a man of great bravery and sagacity, and withal a sincere friend of peace. The times were critical, and the Indians at Buffalo Creek and in the circumjacent country were in frequent alarm. Even while Colonel Proctor was with them, two fresh scalps had been brought in, one of which was that of an Indian, accompanied by a story that the white people were making war upon them. And although Colonel Proctor succeeded in convincing them that the tale was without foundation in truth, yet the Indians were not

---

* O'Beel, or O'Bail, was one of the names of Cornplanter, it being the name of his father, who was a white man.

† That is *hunting*—as explained by Colonel Proctor.

‡ Here follow the names, very long, and very Indian, of nine warriors, who volunteered to go upon the mission. It is needless to record them, as none of them were never otherwise distinguished.

without apprehensions of evil. It is, therefore, probable that the women had determined to retain Cornplanter as the chief who could best restrain the warlike propensities of their young braves, while they could repose
greater confidence both in his bravery and discretion,
in the event of actual danger, during the absence of
the messengers to the Miamies, than in any other leader
of their nation.   But the benevolent designs of the
women were circumvented by "the man that kept the
vessels on the lake."   Proctor had previously applied to
Colonel Gordon for permission to charter a vessel for the
proposed voyage upon Lake Erie, to which no answer
had as yet been returned.   The British commander,
probably, was reluctant to be known openly as the agent
in defeating the pacific mission of Colonel Proctor, and
he had, therefore, been intriguing to that effect through
the Indians.   But finding that through the interposition
of the women, who were exercising a sounder discretion
upon the subject than the men, the object could not be
thus frustrated, he at once threw aside his mask, and
brought the mission abruptly to an end, by refusing to
recognise Proctor in his official character, and by pro-
hibiting the passage of the Indian deputies to Sandusky
in any vessel upon the lake.   Thus circumstanced, as
the journey could not with prudence be undertaken by
land, and as the Indians positively refused to attempt
the passage of the lake in canoes, Proctor was compelled
most reluctantly to abandon the enterprise, and return to
the seat of government.   It was well for his personal
safety that he did so ; since by information received sub-

sequently from a captive who escaped from the Miamies, it was ascertained that the noted Simon Girty, and other desperadoes, tories, who had fled from the border settlements of the United States during the war of the revolution, had determined upon the colonel's assassination, should he come among them, even though attended " by a hundred Senecas."*

This council at Buffalo Creek, in regard to the mission of Colonel Proctor, had not been anticipated by the government of the United States. But knowing the feverish tempetament of the Six Nations, and the recent provocations the Senecas in particular had received at the hands of some of the Pennsylvania border men, the President was at the same time engaged in another effort to divert their attention from the wars of their western brethren, and to cultivate with them the most amicable relations. To this end, before the unfavorable result of Proctor's embassy could have been known at Philadelphia, Colonel Pickering had been commissioned to hold a treaty† with the Six Nations at the Painted Post. This treaty was held in June, and was attended by favorable results. Indeed, although most of their principal chiefs were to a very unhappy extent under the influence of the British military authorities in Canada, yet, the greater proportion of their older men, on the republican side of the boundary, were inclined to peace, —the young men of the Senecas, and a few of the Cayugas only, being resolved upon war. The intervention of

---

* Deposition of Thomas Rhea. Indian State Papers, vol. i., pp. 196, 197.

† Holding a council, in Indian parlance, is called holding " a treaty," if there be two or more parties present.

the women, moreover, prior to the departure of Colonel Proctor, had produced a happy effect, by soothing the irritated feelings of their men, and directing their thoughts to the blessings of peace. Very erroneous opinions are generally entertained among civilized people, in regard to the consideration in which their women are held by the American Indians, and the degree of influence they exercise among them. True, as with all barbarians, the women are in some respects the slaves of the men; but those of the American aboriginals are no farther slaves than they are rendered such by the field-labor which is imposed upon them in addition to the ordinary cares of the household; and in this respect the women of the peasantry of Europe are in no better position than they. On the other hand, although the respect with which they are treated by their lords is not as refined and *spiritualized* as among the cavaliers in the days of chivalry, still it may safely be averred that in the adjustment of weighty and difficult matters, no other people are in the habit of treating the opinions of their women with greater deference than the American Indians. On the occasion now passing in review, that influence, as already remarked, was most happily exerted, and the consequence was, that the council called under the auspices of Colonel Pickering, at the *Painted Post*,* was well attended. In-

* The "Painted Post" was a noted land-mark in the early settlement of western New-York, and in the history of Indian affairs, long before. It was literally a post, of oak timber, planted in the ground upon the Conhocton Creek, within the boundary of New-York, but not far from the Pennsylvania line. It was painted in the Indian manner, and tradition avers that it was a monument,

deed, despite the efforts of the British officers in command of Upper Canada, the chiefs began to draw off in the direction of the Painted Post, even before the departure of Colonel Proctor from Buffalo Creek.

The speeches interchanged between the chiefs and Colonel Pickering at this council have not been preserved; but the result was favorable in yet farther diverting the attention of the Six Nations from the affairs of the western Indians in actual hostility; while by a liberal distribution of presents, the young warriors were checked in their propensity to start away upon the warpath whenever blood was snuffed in the tainted breeze. Yet another fortunate measure was accomplished by the employment of the brave old Stockbridge chief, Hendrick Aupamut, upon a pacific mission to the belligerent country of the Miamies,—an undertaking which Colonel Proctor and the Cornplanter had failed to achieve.

More interesting than all to the philanthropist, it was at this council that, in accordance with the benevolent views of Washington, Colonel Pickering made a successful demonstration toward winning the attention of the chiefs to the policy so important to them, of commencing the work of civilization among their people. This was a point upon which Colonel Pickering had been particularly instructed by the President, and no suitable occasion was neglected, during the three weeks'

of great antiquity, erected to commemorate the death of some celebrated war-chief, whose name has been lost in the lapse of ages. The Indians, it is also related, were in the practice, from generation to generation, of erecting new ones on the decay of the old. The *Painted Post* has given the name to a township, now forming the south-east corner of Steuben county.

deliberations of the council, to fulfil this part of the commission. At the close of the council, the colonel regaled the chiefs with a sumptuous entertainment, provided strictly in accordance with the usages of civilized life. The assemblage at the feast was large, including several gentlemen from New-York, Boston and Philadelphia, in the train of the commissioner, and numerous chiefs.

In the course of the entertainment, the commissioner took occasion to renew his appeal to the chiefs, at least to make an effort to introduce among their tribes the arts and customs of civilization,—closing an eloquent address by pointing them to the taste and elegance of the banquet before them. He told them that if they would comply with the advice of the President, and adopt the principles and practices of civilized life, within five years they might spread such a table themselves—the products of their overteeming soil; while by educating their young men, they might be qualified to meet the whites even in the great council of the Thirteen Fires,—in which council they might also be represented.

Red-Jacket replied,—rather doggedly,—but yet with some humor. There were suspicions afloat, that whatever might be the temper of the head men toward each other, upon both sides, the terms between the young white men of the company and the pretty squaws had been sufficiently amicable, of which circumstance the orator was not unmindful to avail himself in his response, which was substantially thus :—

"BROTHER : You have during this negotiation said a good deal on civilization. No chief present can forget what you have told us. They will bear it in mind if they should not follow your advice.

" BROTHER : We thank you for your good counsel ;—and, as an additional inducement to its adoption, I am happy to perceive,"—(casting his piercing eye around the table with an emphasis, look, and tone, peculiarly but insidiously significant,) " that you have introduced to our notice several young men who will doubtless feel that patriotism which your oratory is calculated to inspire,—proud that they can give a practical illustration of its sincerity by intermarrying with our women."*

The satire was as keen as well deserved. But not withstanding the indefiniteness of Red-Jacket's reply, the suggestions of Colonel Pickering had been listened to with more than ordinary attention ; and an invitation to several of the chiefs to visit Philadelphia at some convenient season, to confer with their Great Father, the President, farther upon the subject, was accepted.†

* MS. Collections of Joseph W. Moulton, Esq.

† Message of President Washington to the Senate of the United States, March 26, 1792.

CHAPTER IV.

EFFORTS of General Washington for improving the moral and social condition of the Indians—Mission of fifty chiefs to Philadelphia—Welcomed by the Governor of Pennsylvania—Speech of Red-Jacket in reply—Address to the chiefs by President Washington—Speech of Red-Jacket in reply—Comments upon the speech—Proposition of the government for the improvement of the Indians—Reply of Red-Jacket—Speech of Colonel Pickering to the chiefs—Troubles with the north-western Indians—Reply of Farmer's-Brother to Colonel Pickering—Reply of Red-Jacket—Parting address of Washington—Red-Jacket and the military clothes—Close of the conferences—Continuance of the war with the Indians of the north-west—The Senecas to send a deputation of their chiefs upon a message of peace—Irritation of the Six Nations—Interference of the British—The Fish-Carrier—The deputation returns—Their mission unsuccessful—Close of the Indian war.

ON the thirteenth day of March, 1792, Red-Jacket arrived in Philadelphia, being one of a deputation of fifty chiefs of his people, respectable for their character and influence, invited thither by Colonel Pickering, as stated in the preceding chapter. The brave and true-hearted Farmer's-Brother was of the number; and they had been brought to what was at that time the federal .city, under the guidance of their faithful missionary, the Rev. Mr. Kirkland. In addition to the design, dear to the heart of Washington, of persuading the Indians to exchange the hunter state for that of civilized life, the visit of this deputation had been strongly desired by the Executive, for the purpose, if possible, of attaching them more closely to the interests of the United States.

In order to effect this object, it was thought important, not only to impart to them some just notions of the strength and power of the United States, but to win their confidence by kindness,—by enlightening their understandings as to their own true interests,—and by convincing them of the equitable and benevolent policy of the United States in regard to them.

Nor was this the only object that rendered the visit of this deputation particularly welcome in Philadelphia at that time. Events had occurred in the prosecution of the contest with the hostile Indians of the north-west, of a disastrous character. The campaign against the Miami country, entrusted to the command of General St. Clair, had been brought to a bloody and disastrous termination on the 4th of November, 1791. It was a bitter reverse to the arms of the young republic. The immediate effect of their victory was to elate the Indians beyond measure; and the government was seriously apprehensive that in the flush of the signal triumph obtained by their brethren at the west, the Senecas, and possibly the Cayugas also, might seize their hatchets and fall upon the frontier settlements of New-York and Pennsylvania, in the vain expectation that they might now be able at least to avert, if not to roll back, the tide of white population which was so rapidly crowding them from their seats. In addition to all which, it was the earnest desire of the government to make one more effort to induce them to send a deputation of their most influential chiefs to the hostile country, in the hope of persuading them to reasonable terms of peace. By the defeat of St. Clair, a measure of this character had become far more important, and more urgent withal, than at the time of Proctor's unsuccessful attempt of the preceding year. Under these circumstances, several of which had not been foreseen when the invitation was first extended to the Six Nations by Colonel Pickering. the visit of Red-Jacket and his associates was timely and fortunate.

It is to be regretted that more ample materials for a history of this Indian embassy to the seat of the federal government have not been preserved. The effort was one of the earliest put forth by the government of the young republic, for advancing the substantial happiness of the red man, by persuading him to adopt the habits of civilization. And inasmuch as the policy of the United States toward the hapless race, whose doom it is to disappear before the white man, will be a subject of grave consideration with the future historian, it is important that the facts should stand forth upon the record. The Anglo-Saxon race will have enough to answer for, in regard to this people, in any event. Let it, then, have credit for what it has done, or attempted to do, in their behalf; and if it shall appear that few and small were the advances made by the Indians in the scale of civilization, during the first fifty years of the independent existence of the United States, it will at the same time appear that the government of the latter was not altogether at fault. Certainly it was not until after the administration of the sixth President had terminated, in March, 1829, that the beneficent policy of Washington toward the children of the forest was changed. Until that period they had enjoyed the protection of the federal government, in their ancient " seats," so long as they chose to remain in them ; and the efforts both of the government and of various voluntary associations of a benevolent character, for the improvement of their moral, religious, and social condition, had been unintermitted ; and it may be added, in sorrow, almost unavailing.

Viewed in the aspect here presented, the proceedings attending the mission of Red-Jacket and his associates to Philadelphia, now under consideration, assume more than an ordinary degree of interest. And as Red-Jacket himself bore a prominent part in those proceedings, the narrative will be given as much in detail as the materials that have escaped the ravages of time will allow. The chiefs were welcomed to Philadelphia by the Governor of Pennsylvania, by whom they were addressed in the council chamber of the city. After referring to the fact that every thing which it was supposed might conduce to the comfort of the chiefs during their visit had been provided for them, the Governor closed his speech as follows :—

"BROTHERS ! I know the kindness with which you treat the strangers that visit your country; and it is my sincere wish that, when you return to your families, you may be able to assure them that the virtues of friendship and hospitality are also practised by the citizens of Pennsylvania."

This interview took place on the 28th of March. Five days afterward,—for in all matters of diplomacy and of state the Indians proceed with unexceeded deliberation,—the Governor met the chiefs in council again, when Red-Jacket pronounced an answer to the speech of his Excellency, in the following terms :—

BROTHER ONAS* GOVERNOR : Open unprejudiced ears to what we have to say ! Some days since you addressed us, and what you said gave us great pleasure. This day the Great Spirit has allowed us to meet you again in this council chamber. We hope that your not receiving our immediate answer to your address will make no improper impression upon your mind. We mention this lest you should suspect that your kind welcome and friendly address has not had a proper effect upon our hearts. We assure you it is far otherwise. In your address to us the other day, in this ancient council chamber, where our forefathers have often conversed together, several things struck our attention very forcibly. When you told us this was the place in which our forefathers often met on peaceable terms, it gave us sensible pleasure, and more joy than we could express. Though we have no writings like you, yet we remember often to have heard of the friendship that existed between our fathers and yours. The picture† to which you drew our attention brought fresh to our minds the friendly conferences that used to be held between the former governors of Pennsylvania and our tribes, and showed the love which your fathers had of peace, and the friendly disposition of our people. It is still our wish, as well as yours, to preserve peace between our tribes and you, and it would be well if the same spirit existed among the Indians at the westward, and through

---

* The name which the Indians conferred upon William Penn, and which they continued to bestow upon every succeeding Governor of Pennsylvania. The word itself signifies *a pen*.

† Picture of Penn's treaty with the Indians. *Drake*, in whose Book of the Indians the account of these interviews between the Indians and the Governor of Pennsylvania is found.

every part of the United. States. You particularly expressed that you were well pleased to find that we differed in disposition from the Indians westward. Your disposition is that for which the Onas Governors were remarkable. As you love peace, so do we also; and we wish it could be extended to the most distant part of this great country. We agreed in council, this morning, that the sentiments I have expressed should be communicated to you before the delegates of the Five Nations; and to tell you that your cordial welcome to this city, and the good sentiments contained in your address, have made a deep impression on our hearts, and given us great joy, and from the heart I tell you so. This is all I have to say."

The inference from this speech of Red-Jacket would certainly be that, without diversity of opinion, the Indians of the Six Nations were at length peaceably disposed. But such was not the fact. After Red-Jacket had concluded, Good Peter, another of the delegation, sometimes called Dominie Peter,* and a very worthy man, likewise addressed a short speech to the Governor, which is represented as having been, for the most part, a repetition of the pacific sentiments expressed by Red-Jacket.† But in the course of it the following passage occurred :—

"What is there more desirable than that we, who live within hearing of each other, should unite for the common good? This is my wish. It is the wish of my nation, although I am sorry I can't say so of every individual in it, for there are differences of opinion among us, as well as among the white people."

* For some account of Good Peter, see Clinton's Historical Discourse.
† Drake's Book of the Indians.

On their presentation to the President, General Washington, they were addressed by the latter in the following terms of friendship and cordiality:—*

"SACHEMS AND WARRIORS OF THE FIVE NATIONS: It affords me great satisfaction to see so many of you, who are the respectable chiefs and representatives of your several tribes, and I cordially bid you welcome to the seat of the Government of the United States.

"You have been invited to this place by Colonel Pickering, at my special request, in order to remove all causes of discontent; to devise and adopt plans to promote your welfare, and firmly to cement the peace between the United States and you, so as that in future we shall consider ourselves brothers indeed.

"I assure you that I am desirous that a firm peace should exist, not only between the United States and the Five Nations, but also between the United States and all the nations of this land,—and that this peace should be founded upon the principles of justice and humanity, as upon an immoveable rock.

"That you may partake of all the comforts of this earth, which can be derived from civilized life, enriched by the possession of industry, virtue and knowledge: and I trust that such judicious measures will now be concerted, to secure to you and your children these invaluable objects, as will afford you cause for rejoicing while you live.

"That these are the strong and sincere desires of my heart, I hope time and circumstances will convince you. But in order that our peace and friendship may for ever be unclouded,

* This speech of President Washington has not been preserved by Sparks, although that delivered by him eighteen months before, to Cornplanter, appears in his correspondence. The author is indebted for it to Joseph W. Moulton, Esq., who obtained a copy at Washington, many years ago.

we must forget the misunderstandings of past times. Let us now look forward, and devise measures to render our friendship perpetual. I am aware that the existing hostilities with some of the western Indians have been ascribed to an unjust possession of their lands by the United States. But be assured that this is not the case. We require no lands but those obtained by treaties, which we consider as fairly made, and particularly confirmed by the treaty of Muskingum, in the year 1789.

" If the western Indians should entertain the opinion that we want to wrest their lands from them, they are laboring under an error. If this error could be corrected it would be for their happiness,—and nothing would give me more pleasure, because it would open to both of us the door of peace.

" I shall not enter into further particulars with you at present, but refer you to General Knox, the Secretary of War, and Colonel Pickering, who will communicate with you upon the objects of your journey, and inform me thereof.

" As an evidence of the sincerity of the desires of the United States for perfect peace and friendship with you, I deliver you this white belt of wampum, which I request you will safely keep.

(Signed)   GEO. WASHINGTON."*

The President having thus deputed Colonel Pickering and General Knox to conduct the subsequent conferences with the chiefs, an interview was had with them in the city council chamber, on the 31st of March, at which time Red-Jacket, holding in his hands the white

---

* The manuscript from which the preceding speech has been transcribed bears the date of March 23d, 1792. Hence, in the order of time, it should stand before the antecedent account of the interview between the chiefs and the Governor of Pennsylvania. But the date is believed to be erroneous; and if not, the transposition has been made for the sake of convenience.

10

belt which had been delivered to him by General Washington, addressed Colonel Pickering as follows :—

"I now request the attention of the President of the United States, by his agent, Colonel Pickering, now present. A few days since, when the American chief had spoken to us, he gave us to understand that General Knox and Colonel Pickering should be the agents to negotiate with us on things which concern our welfare. Let me call for your compassion, as you can put all down upon paper, while we have to labor with our minds, to retain and digest what is spoken, to enable us to make an answer.

"BROTHER—whose attention I have called as the representative of the great chief of this Island :—when, the other day, he welcomed us to the great council-fire of the thirteen United States, he said it was from his very heart. He said it gave him pleasure to look around and see such numerous representatives of the Five Nations of Indians, and that it was at his special request we had been invited to the seat of the general government, to promote the happiness of our nation, in a friendly connection with the United States. He then told us that his love of peace did not terminate with the Five Nations, but extended to all the nations at the setting sun; and that it was his desire that universal peace might prevail in this island.

"BROTHER CON-NEH-SAUTY :* I requested your compassion, on account of our different situations, by reason of which I should notice only a few of the principal things in the President's speech, delivered to us the other day. Three things I have mentioned of the introductory part of his speech. What other reply can we, your brothers of the Five Nations, make to that introductory part of the speech, than to thank him, and say that it has given a spring to every passion of our souls ?

* The Indian name of Col. Pickering.

" Brother : The President again observed to us that he wished our minds might all be disposed to peace,—that a happy peace might be established between you and your brothers of the Five Nations, so firmly that nothing might move it; that it might be founded on a rock. This sentiment of your chief has given joy to our hearts,—to compare that peace to a *rock*, which is *immoveable*.

" The President further observed to us that by our continuing to walk in the path of peace, and hearkening to his counsel, we might share with you in all the blessings of civilized life. This also meets the approbation of our minds, and has the thanks of all your brothers of the Five Nations.

" He again observed to us that if we attended to his counsel in this matter, our children, and children's children, might partake in all the blessings which should rise out of this earth. This has taken hold of our minds, and even we who are grown up look forward, and anticipate its fulfilment.

" The President again observed to us that what he had spoken was in the sincerity of his heart, and that time and opportunities would give further evidence that what he said was true. And we believed it, because we saw the words come from his own lips,—and therefore they were lodged deep in our mind.

" The President of the Thirteen Fires, while continuing his speech, made also this remark, ' that in order to establish all his words for the best good of your nation and our's, we must forget all the evils that were past, and attend to what lies before us, and take such a course as shall cement our peace, that we may be as one.'

" The President again observed that it had come to his ears that the cause of the hostilities now prevailing with the Western Indians, was their persuasion that the United States had unjustly taken away their lands. But he assured us this was not the case. That it was not the mind of any of his chiefs to take any land on the whole island without agreeing for it.

He then mentioned a treaty at Muskingum, and he concluded that what land was given up at that treaty was fairly obtained.

"He also observed to us that it was his opinion that the hostile Indians were in an error; that they had missed the true path; whatever evil spirit, or whatever lies had turned them aside, he wished they could be discovered, that they might be removed. He expressed a strong wish that those obstacles to the extending of peace to the westward might be discovered; and he would use all his exertions to remove them, that peace might be extended to the whole Island.— Toward the close of his speech the President informed us that there were many things which concerned the future happiness of the Five Nations, the concerting of which he should refer to you* here present, and the Chief Warrior of the United States.† And at the close he observed that our professions of friendship and regard were commonly witnessed by some token: therefore, in the name of the United States, he presented us with this white belt, which was to be handed down from one generation to another, as a confirmation of his words, and a witness of the friendly disposition of the United States, towards the peace and happiness of the five confederated Nations."

[Red-Jacket here laid aside the white belt received from the President, and taking up a belt of their own, proceeded as follows :—]

"Now let the President of the United States possess his mind in peace. We have made but a short reply to his address to us the other day, for the belt he gave us is deposited with us; and we have taken fast hold of it. What more can we say than to return our united thanks for his address in welcoming us to the seat of the great council, and for the advice he gave us? And our pleasure is increased that you, Con-neh-

* Pointing to Colonel Pickering.   † General Knox, Secretary at War.

sauty, are appointed to assist us in devising the means to promote and secure the happiness of the Five Nations.

"BROTHER! Now open your ears, as the Representative of the Great Council of the thirteen United States, in our present Council. Hear the words we may speak. And all here present, of the great Council,* and our Brethren of the Five Nations, hear!—We consider ourselves in the presence of the Great Spirit, the proprietor of us all.

" The President, in effect, observed to us that we of the Five Nations were our own proprietors—were freemen, and might speak with freedom. This has gladdened our hearts, and removed a weight that was upon them. And therefore you will hear us patiently while we speak. The President has, in effect, told us that we were freemen; the sole proprietors of the soil on which we live. This is the source of the joy which we feel. How can two brothers speak freely together, unless they feel that they are upon equal ground?

" I observed to you, Brother,† that our considering ourselves, by your own acknowledgment, as freemen, has given this joy to our hearts—that we might speak in character. Therefore, we join with the President in his wish that all the evils which have hitherto disturbed our peace may be buried in oblivion; and this wish proceeds from our hearts. Now we can speak our minds freely, as they are free from pressure.

" Now, Brother, while you continue to hear in behalf of the United States, let all here present also open their ears, while those of the Five Nations here present speak with one

* Some members of Congress were present—of which the Indians had been informed.

† It should be borne in mind that the frequent use of the word *Brother* is the effect of the rules of Indian politeness, which enjoin, in all conversations, a constant remembrance of the relation subsisting between the parties, especially where that relation implies any affection, or respect. It is like the perpetual petition, in civilized life, of *Sir*, or *Madam*—or, in England, *Your Lordship*. In the same manner the Indians, at every sentence, repeat, *My Father, My Uncle, My Cousin, My Brother*, &c.

voice. We wish to see your words verified to our children,
and children's children. You enjoy all the blessings of this
life; to you, therefore, we look to make provision that the
same may be enjoyed by our children. This wish comes from
our heart; but we add that our happiness cannot be great if
in the introduction of your ways we are put under too much
constraint.

"BROTHER! Appointed agent to converse with us upon the
affairs of our peace, continue to hear. We, your brothers of
the Five Nations, believe that the Great Spirit let this island
drop down from above. We also believe in his superinten-
dency over this whole island. It is he who gives peace and
prosperity, and he also sends evil. But prosperity has been
yours. American Brethren—all the good which can spring
out of this island you enjoy. We therefore wish that we and
our children, and our children's children, may partake with
you in that enjoyment.

"BROTHER! I observed that the Great Spirit might smile
upon one people, and turn and frown upon another. - This
you have seen, who are of one color and one blood. The
King of England and you Americans strove to advance your
happiness by extending your possessions upon this island,
which produces so many good things. And while you two
great powers were thus contending for those good things, by
which the whole island was shaken and violently agitated, is it
strange that the peace of us, the Five Nations, was shaken and
overturned?

"But, let me say no more of the trembling of our island.
All is, in a measure, now quieted. Peace is now restored.
The peace of us, the Five Nations, is now budding. But still
there is some shaking among the original Americans, at the
setting sun;—and you, the Thirteen Fires, and the King of
England, know what is our situation, and the causes of this
disturbance. Now, here you have an ambassador,* as we are

---

* Mr. Hammond was then the British Envoy to the United States.

informed, from the King of England. Let him, in behalf of the King, and the Americans, adjust all their matters, according to their agreement, at the making of peace—and then you will soon see all things settled among the Indian Nations. Peace will be spread far and near. Let the President and the ambassador use all their exertions to bring about this settlement, (according to the peace,) and it will make us all glad, and we shall consider both as our real friends.

"BROTHER! Continue to hear! Be assured we have spoken from our very hearts, and not from our lips only. Let us therefore make this observation :—That when you Americans and the King made peace, he did not mention us, and showed us no compassion, notwithstanding all he said to us, and all we had suffered. This has been the occasion of great sorrow and pain, and great loss to us, the Five Nations. When you and he settled the peace between you two great nations, he never asked us for a delegation to attend to our interests. Had he done this, a settlement of peace among all the western nations might have been effected. But the neglecting of this, and passing us by unnoticed, has brought upon us great pain and trouble.

"BROTHER! It is evident that we of the Five Nations have suffered much in consequence of the strife between you and the King of England, who are of one color and one blood. Our chain of peace has been broken. Peace and friendship have been chased from us. But you Americans were determined not to treat us in the same manner as we had been treated by the King of England. You therefore desired us, at the re-establishment of peace, to sit down at our ancient fire-places, and again enjoy our lands. And had the peace between you and the King of England been completely accomplished,* it would long before this time have extended far beyond the Five Nations.

* An allusion, probably, to the retention by Great Britain, of the northwestern posts, belonging to the United States, and to other difficulties under the first treaty.

" Brother Con-neh-sauty : You are specially appointed with General Knox to confer with us on our peace and happiness. We have rejoiced in your appointment, and we hope that the great Warrior will remember that though a *Warrior*, he is to converse with us about *peace;* letting what concerns *war* sleep ;—and the counselling part of his mind, while acting with us, be of *peace*.

" Brother ! Have patience, and continue to listen. The President has assured us that *he* is not the cause of the hostilities now existing at the westward, but laments it. Brother, we wish you to point out to us of the Five Nations *what you think is the real cause.*

" Brother ! Agent of the thirteen United States in the present council : We now publicly return our thanks to the President and all the Counsellors of the thirteen United States, for the words which he has spoken to us. They were good—without any mixture. Shall we observe that he wished that if the errors of the hostile Indians could be discovered, he would use his utmost exertions to remove them ?

" Brother ! You and the King of England are the two governing powers of this Island. What are we ? You both are important and proud ; and you cannot adjust your own affairs agreeably to your declarations of peace. Therefore the Western Indians are bewildered. One says one thing to them, and one says another. Were these things adjusted, it would be easy to diffuse peace every where.

" In confirmation of our words, we give this belt, which we wish the President to hold fast in remembrance of what we have now spoken."

This speech was never before published.* Its importance, in several respects, requires a pause in the narra-

---

* The author is indebted for the manuscript to Joseph W. Moulton, Esq., who began writing a history of the State of New-York some fifteen or twenty years ago, but proceeded no farther than a single volume

tive for its consideration. In the first place, if the orator was really as desirous of peace and amity with the United States as would appear from the language of the speech, the English officers in Canada must have lost their hold upon his partialities since the visit of Colonel Proctor to the frontier the preceding year. In the second place, by bearing the declarations of this speech in mind, the reader will hereafter perceive what an entire revolution was subsequently wrought in the feelings of Red-Jacket, in regard to the civilization of his people. But the most important portion of the harangue refers to a prominent cause of the Indian war then raging, which has thus far been but slightly considered, viz.:—The indifference with which the Indians had been cut off, or passed over, by Great Britain, in the treaty of peace. Notwithstanding the loyalty of these untutored sons of the forest, their constancy, and the prodigality with which they had shed their blood in the cause of the crown, when the ministers of that crown found it expedient to negotiate for peace, no one condition or word was interposed in behalf of allies thus faithful, and they were left to shift for themselves as best they might. In the impressive language of Red-Jacket, "the King showed them no compassion." They had been as dependent upon the crown as children upon a parent; and being left to themselves, in a state of war with the United States, although for a time they desisted from actual hostilities, they knew not what to do. In a word, to borrow another expressive phrase from the Seneca orator, "they were bewildered." The consequence was, that, distrusting the people with whom

11

they had so recently been at war, and neglected by those
in whom they had confided, and who ought to have stipulated for an honorable peace for *them*, as well as for
themselves, the poor Indians,—children of ignorance,
caprice, and passion,—were left to the resources of their
own wild natures, and the chances of fortune. Nor was
this all: When, from a variety of untoward circumstances, very shortly after the conclusion of the treaty
between the United States and England, in 1783, the
question of peace or war again hung long and doubt-
fully in the scales, those who ought to have been the
best counsellors of the Indians became their worst.
They were encouraged again to embark in a war, which,
without the aid of England, even the Indians themselves
knew must be hopeless, and during the continuance of
that war, were "paltered with in a double sense;" until,
but for the humanity of those who, though technically
then their enemies, had from the first been in reality their
best friends, their race would have been annihilated.*
True indeed was the assertion of Red-Jacket, that the
Indians were the chief sufferers from the "shaking of
the island" by Great Britain and the United States; nor
is it strange that in their forlorn situation, these untutored
and dependent tenants of the wood looked anxiously to
the united councils of the two white nations with whom
only they were acquainted, to adjust for them the terms
of peace. Red-Jacket has told the story in the preceding

---

* For an ample history of the matters here referred to, and documentary proofs
of the truth of the positions here assumed, see Life of Brant, vol. ii.

speech, with the simple and touching eloquence of nature, and there it may be left.

On the 9th of April Colonel Pickering communicated to the chiefs the propositions which had been matured by the American government, as the basis of its labors in the work of their civilization and social improvement. The details of that project seem not to have been preserved. The general scope of the plan may nevertheless be inferred from the following stipulation, to which the President asked the assent of the Senate by a special message on the 23d of March:—

" The United States, in order to promote the happiness of the Five Nations of Indians, will cause to be expended, annually, the amount of one thousand five hundred dollars, in purchasing for them clothing, domestic animals, and implements of husbandry, and for encouraging useful artificers to reside in their villages."

Perhaps a more accurate estimate of the propositions submitted to the Indians may be formed by a perusal of the annexed speech from Red-Jacket, in which, while he assents to the general tenor of the overtures, he suggests some modifications and improvements. The Indians had indeed been requested by Colonel Pickering to speak their minds upon the propositions, and to propose for consideration any alterations they should think proper. Accordingly, at the next interview, which was on the 10th of April, Red-Jacket spoke the minds of the Senecas as follows:—

" BROTHER CON-NEH-SAUTY : Yesterday, when you made your proposals, the Oneidas accepted them, and thanked you.

They spoke for those Oneidas, Onondagas, and Tuscaroras who *all lie under one blanket.**   We, the Senecas, have considered them, and are now going to speak.

"Yesterday, when you proposed *four* establishments, and that there should be three men for each, you mentioned the rewards to be given to a certain *number* who should learn quickest—of the *biggest* nations, *six*—while those who could not learn fast must be miserable. If you do right, you will give to all something to work with as fast as they learn, so that all may be supplied; otherwise a strife will arise. But if all are to be supplied, all will be encouraged to learn. Another thing :—a great many of our people are poor women, who have no men in their families : now by supplying others in the manner we have suggested, the fields of the poor may be ploughed. This will rouse the minds of the whole nation to learn what the white people know.

"You told us if we liked what you said we should say so : If it was deficient in any thing, we should tell what was wanting ;—if redundant, we should strike off. You mentioned the places for the establishments,—one was at Geneseo, and one at Oneida. We have considered that at Oneida there are a great many people, Tuscaroras and Oneidas, who can help one another ;—and that at Geneseo there are also Oneidas and Tuscaroras, who, being numerous, will want one establishment for themselves. We wish you to use them as you do the Senecas, that their minds may be easy. Perhaps they will learn quicker, so as to desire two establishments at Geneseo.

"You must not suppose that we slight any thing that you have offered. We accept of all. It is all good. But we hope that you will not think of making establishments at Buffalo Creek, or Obeilstown,† *at present*. For there is some shaking‡ at the extremity of our house.§ There may be some danger to the persons who might be employed.

---

* Live in one neighborhood.   † O'Bail,—the Cornplanter's town.
‡ Trouble.   § The border of their country.

" There is one thing which might be of great advantage to us, which you have not mentioned : that is a saw-mill. This would help us greatly. We know the cause of Mr. Allen's leaving our country.* He told us the reason before he went away. And you and we all know that his mill is over the line agreed upon last summer before you, and he has gone away, he says, because he owns nothing. Allen told us if General Washington would buy the mill, paying him just what it cost, it might be our's, and be allowed to stand on our land. And we should rejoice exceedingly if we could become the proprietors of that mill. If General Washington would buy it and give it to us, the superintendent might see to the appraisement of it.

·" You mentioned that this provision was for those of our nations who live on this side of the Lakes. But perhaps our brothers at Grand River, when they see those things introduced among us, may fall in love with them, and want to come and join us. We therefore wish that the plan may be so formed as to comprehend all. For our peace is in a weak, languid condition, just expiring, and we would avoid giving offence to any of our brothers. There are two roads : perhaps they on the other side of the water† may take our road. Therefore we wish you to extend your invitation to the whole Six Nations, and press them to join us when peace shall take place. We shall desire the proposed establishments may be made at Buffalo and Alleghany.

" It was the custom of our fathers, when they had finished any particular business, to talk over affairs of general concern.

---

* Ebenezer Allen, a tory, who fled from Pennsylvania and joined the Senecas. He was a monster of iniquity, according to Mary Jemison, the white woman, whose life contains a chapter devoted to him. After the war he became a trader. He had several successive Indian wives, and afterward married a white woman. He once drowned a Dutch trader, and committed many other enormities. He built the first mill at the Genesee falls, now Rochester, under the authority of Phelps and Gorham,—they having obtained a special grant of a territory at that place, of the Indians, twelve by twenty-four miles in extent, for " a mill-yard!" Allen ultimately fled from the United States, and died at Grand River.

† Meaning the Indians at Grand River, in Upper Canada.

Now we wish Congress to hasten to make peace with the hostile Indians who are alongside of us.   We both have our eyes to the place where the trouble lies.   This is all we have to say."*

This address has not been preserved because of its eloquence.   It is a mere business recital, and claims no higher character.   But it forms a feature in the history of this first effort to introduce the blessings of civilization among the Six Nations, and it also serves to illustrate the views entertained at that time by a notable chief, who subsequently became one of the most steady and implacable opponents of that beneficent policy.   It is therefore neither a useless document, nor out of place in this connexion.

The speeches, or addresses, recited in the preceding pages of the present chapter, had been interchanged before the speech of Red-Jacket in reply to that of the President had been formally answered by Colonel Pickering, upon whom the duty of making such answer had devolved.   The Colonel discharged this duty at an interview, appointed for the purpose, on the 17th day of April.   Under ordinary circumstances, involving matters of less importance, a document of the length of Colonel Pickering's address, instead of being inserted entire in the text, would have been epitomized, or transferred to the appendix.   But the address is so closely interwoven with that benevolent feature of Washington's early Indian policy which contemplated their moral

* The author is indebted to the researches of Joseph W. Moulton, Esq., for a copy of this speech.

and social elevation, and passes in review so many
facts blended with the Indian relations of the United
States at the period under consideration, that its insertion
at length seems to be required. It serves to elucidate, in
language equally concise and clear, the causes, and the
merits, of the war then raging with the north-western
Indians, while it discloses, in refreshing relief, the just
and humane views of the President, and the policy by
which his administration was marked, in regard, not only
to the Six Nations, but to the various tribes of the aboriginal family within the confines of the republic.

The chiefs having assembled, and the council been
opened in due form on the day above stated, Colonel
Pickering addressed them as follows :—

"BROTHERS OF THE FIVE NATIONS : Some days ago you
delivered your answer to the President's speech. According
to your custom, you repeated the principal parts of it, and
expressed your thanks for the friendly sentiments it contained,
which had made your hearts glad. You rejoiced that the
President considered you as freemen, and desired you to speak
with freedom ; and then you joined with the President in his
wish that all the evils which had hitherto disturbed our peace
might be buried in oblivion. You declared your belief that
this island came from the Great Spirit, that you considered
yourselves as in his presence, and that he is the proprietor
of all.

"BROTHERS ! We, your white brethren, have the same belief; as He *made,* so He *governs* the world. He has so disposed
events that we should meet at this place, to consult on those
things which may prove blessings to you and your posterity.
We, your brethren of the United States, rejoice that your
hearts are thus inclined. Many good men have wished to see
such a day, when the knowledge possessed by the white people

might be introduced among you, the nations of this land. Such good men have long been searching, but with small success, for a path by which this knowledge might be carried amongst you. Now we think we have discovered the true path; and you begin to see it. But you must be very careful lest you lose sight of it. Your nephews, the Stockbridge Indians, know the path so well that they can now walk on boldly; and the Oneidas are following in their steps. By and by the path will be extended through all your countries, and I hope to see it so plainly marked that not one of all your nations shall miss it.

"BROTHERS! You not only see this path, but think it a good one; and therefore you express your wishes to see the President's words verified to your children and children's children. You observed that we enjoyed all the good things of this life, and that you looked to us to make provision that the same might be enjoyed by your children. But you desired that this might be done by degrees. This is right. For you know when a traveller gets upon a new track that he can but just discern, if he hurries along he will be in danger of losing it altogether.

"BROTHERS! Some of you are grown old; others are of my age; and some are much younger. But even the oldest of you may see many of your children walking in this new path. Look forward ten, fifteen, or twenty years; for many of us may live so long; and then we may see our children meet together and speak with one tongue. Or if *your* children are in *your* country, and *our's* are *here*, yet they can then *speak on paper*, with the same ease and certainty as if they stood face to face.

"BROTHERS! Does not this thought give you pleasure?

"BROTHERS! You took notice of what the President said to you relative to the war with the western Indians; that he was not the cause of it, but lamented it; and would be happy in the discovery of the means by which peace could be restored.

You then wished me to point out to you what I thought was the real cause of the war.

"BROTHERS! This perhaps would be a difficult task. We have heard that the minds of the western Indians have been disturbed on account of their lands, which at the treaty of peace with Great Britain, fell within the boundary of the United States. But as it has ever been our strong desire to establish peace, and to remove every cause of jealousy and discontent—I now solemnly declare to you that we claim none of those lands, except such of them as we have purchased at treaties held with the Indians, who, as owners, undertook to sell them. All other lands of the Indians we renounce. The President, with his own mouth, has made the same declaration; and if you look into the great parchment which he gave the Cornplanter, you will see it under his hand. Let this be strongly impressed on your mind. But I am informed that some of the western Indians who joined with the British and took up the hatchet sixteen years ago, have never laid it down to this day. Yet measures were taken by Congress for making peace with *all* the Indian nations,—with those at the westward as well as with you: and runners were sent at the same time to invite them to a treaty. The like invitation has been several times renewed. But the Miami and Wabash Indians never would attend. The only nations at the westward who have entered into treaties with us, are the Shawanese, about six years ago, at a council fire at the mouth of the Miami, which runs into the Ohio, and the Delawares, Wyandots, Ottawas, and Chippewas, who attended the treaty at Fort McIntosh, seven years ago, and ceded part of their lands; and the Pottawattamies and Sacs, who, with the Delawares, Wyandots, Ottawas, and Chippewas, attended the treaty at Muskingum, about three years ago, when the treaty at Fort McIntosh was renewed and confirmed. About two years ago a fresh messenger was sent to the hostile Indians, to invite them to a treaty of peace: but they refused to come, and repeated their outrages with increased violence.

12

" Brothers ! It will surprise you to hear that these hostile Indians, in their various incursions on our frontiers since we made peace with the British, have killed upward of one thousand five hundred of our defenceless men, women and children ! I speak not of warriors ;—but only of quiet, harmless people, who were following their peaceable employments. Such is our information. After all these things could we do otherwise than send armies into their country ? It is true we have been unfortunate. But we are not discouraged, though we desire to put an end to the war. For what good can arise from the continuance of it ? We want nothing which belongs to the hostile Indians. Why then should they continue their depredations ? If any of them have made war on account of the lands purchased of them since the peace made with the British, I can only say that the Great Council of the United States appointed Commissioners to treat with them on that subject, and to give them a large quantity of goods. A number of chiefs signed the deeds ; and from the reports of the Commissioners it was supposed the lands were fairly obtained. And in consequence thereof, large tracts have since been sold. Some to the citizens of the United States, and some to the people of your ancient Father, the King of the French, who have gone and built houses and planted corn in that country. Hence you see how difficult it would be to restore that land to the Indians, even if those chiefs who signed the deeds were not a complete representation of the nations who owned the land. But there is one thing which the United States, who desire nothing but what is just, will cheerfully do. They will attentively hear the complaints of the western Indians ; they will re-examine the treaties, and inquire into the manner in which they were conducted ; and if the complaints of the western Indians appear to be well founded, the United States will make them ample compensation for their lands. They will do more. The United States, so far from desiring to injure the western Indians, would rather do them good ; and cheerfully impart to them that knowledge and those arts which you are now convinced will be so beneficial to your nations, and which you have cordially agreed to accept.

" BROTHERS ! What are the obstacles to so much good ? Are they not the jealousies and prejudices entertained by the western Indians against the United States ? As though we wished for their destruction ;—or if they had been wronged, that we were determined never to do what was right. But these obstacles would vanish, if we could persuade them to come near enough to hear our voice. For they would soon find it to be the voice of justice, kindness, and peace.

" BROTHERS ! You have a regard to the people of your own color, and you are the friends of the United States. Perhaps as friends to both parties, you may have it in your power, and be disposed to speak to the western Indians, to convince them that war is not necessary to enable them to obtain justice ; and that the United States have no desire to revenge the injuries they have received.

" BROTHERS ! Some of *you* were once our enemies : but now you are our friends ; and you have strong proof of the kindness of our hearts toward you. In like manner let peace take place with the western Indians, and they will immediately find us equally kind to them.

" BROTHERS ! Perhaps some of the western Indians have never yet distinctly heard our voice inviting them to peace. Possibly our white runners did not go near enough to make them all hear; or perhaps the noise of the guns prevented their hearing. But it may be in your power to go among them and put your voice directly into their ears.

" BROTHERS ! I mention this matter to you, because it is important to us, your friends, and to the people of your own color. If you please you can consider of it. But you are perfectly free to speak and to act according to your own judgment.

" BROTHERS ! You mentioned some other things in your speech, which I have duly attended to ; but it would be tedious to repeat them all. However, as you referred to the treaty of peace made between us and the British, and gave your opinion, that if all the articles of it were completely fulfilled, the difficulties with the western Indians would cease :* I will just observe, that although every thing in that treaty is not accomplished, yet the peace between us and the British is not thereby disturbed. We constantly trade together, and maintain a friendly intercourse with each other ; and all remaining differences will doubtless be quietly settled. This being the case, those must be bad people who make a handle of those differences to encourage the Indians to war. Such bad men, whatever may be their pretences, are equally enemies to the Indians and to us."

To this wise and conciliatory speech, breathing throughout a spirit of benevolence and justice, the two chiefs, Farmers'-Brother and Red-Jacket, rejoined in succession, and at the same interview,—a circumstance rather remarkable in Indian diplomacy. Farmers'-Brother spoke as follows ; first to his own people :—

" BROTHERS OF THE FIVE NATIONS, attend while I address myself in your presence to my Brother Con-neh-sauty, the Representative on this occasion, of the thirteen United States.

Turning then to Colonel Pickering, he proceeded :—

" BROTHER ! You have this day spoken to us. Your speech has been long. As a part of it referred to what you had before communicated to us at large, we shall not now make any reply. But in the close of your talk to us, you mentioned one subject of great importance, which related to the state of the hostile Indians toward the setting sun. You gave us your opinion of the causes of their being in a hostile state ;—we shall now assign some reasons, as they lie in our minds.

* This was the opinion of Fisher Ames. See his masterly speech upon the question of ratifying Mr. Jay's treaty.

" BROTHER ! You desired us to speak our minds freely upon this subject, as we were a free and independent people. We thank you for the declaration. We shall do it. Your Brothers of the Five Nations have been exceedingly distressed in their minds since your peace with the British, that things at the westward were not settled to your satisfaction. We shall now assign but a few of the principal reasons of the hostilities in that quarter ; for there will be no time to descend to all the particulars.

" BROTHER ! Continue to hear us. It is true there was a treaty held at Fort McIntosh, where were a few deputies from several nations composed of such as were hunting round in the bush ; and not of the real chiefs.* About a year after this, a large delegation of the Five Nations went into the Shawanese country, where a great council was called, from all the nations in that quarter. After some time spent in counselling, and it being difficult to continue longer in so great a body, for want of provisions ; the warriors went out to get something to season their broth, and to cover their feet. At the same time some runners were sent out to call in distant nations. And behold ! at this juncture, the Big-Knife came into their country, to the very town where they were assembled, and took and destroyed the town, killed all the old chiefs, and extinguished the council-fire. This happened but one season after the treaty held at Fort McIntosh. I say that this extinguished the council-fire, which was then

---

* This treaty was negotiated by Gen. St. Clair, in 1785. The Indians ever afterward, as well the nations said to have been represented, as the Six Nations, contended that it was not the result of a fair negotiation,—in other words, as Farmer's-Brother maintained, they held that the nations concerned were not properly represented, and they therefore contended that the treaty was not binding. It had doubtless been the policy of the Indians, both the Six Nations and those of the north-west, to act together in one grand confederacy, but General St. Clair availed himself of a moment of jealousy between them, and dexterously contrived to institute separate negotiations. Still the great body of the Indians were never satisfied with that procedure. See letter of Gen. St. Clair to the President. Indian State Papers, vol. i., p. 10–11.

kindled for the purpose of a general peace. For, shocking to tell! the Big-Knife killed the old chief who had then in his hands the treaty of Fort McIntosh, and the flag of the United States then received. Hence we conceive that the Virginians themselves at that time broke the peace.*

"After this, we of the Five Nations, and Delawares, and others, moved the council fire to the place called the Standing Stone. And we, your brothers of the Five Nations, endeavored to quiet their disturbed minds, speaking to them of the disaster which had befallen them.

"Now at this removed council fire, the Wyandot and Delawares replied to us of the Five Nations, in the following manner :—

"'See, Brothers! While you are kindling these council 'fires in the bushes, evil has come upon us. We expected it 'would be so; and we therefore must blame you, for having 'so much confidence in the Big-Knife. Moreover, we must 'thank you that you have come so far into our country, and are 'now at the place where the ancient council fire was kindled, 'the light of which reached to the clouds, and was seen by all 'the Five Nations. We are glad that you still talk to us upon

---

* It is difficult to ascertain with certainty to what transaction the speaker here refers. But it is most likely he was speaking of a friendly town of Indians, called the Piankeshaws, living upon the Wabash. In a report upon the Indian relations of the country, by General Knox, Secretary of War, to the President, dated June 15, 1789, it is remarked that since the conclusion of the revolutionary war, in 1783, the United States had formed no treaties with the Indians of the Wabash country, and that hostilities had almost constantly existed between the people of Kentucky and the said Indians. "The injuries and murders," said the Secretary, " *have been so reciprocal, that it would be a point of critical investigation to know on which side they have been the greatest.*" The Secretary added,—"Some of the inhabitants of Kentucky, during the past year, (1788,) roused by recent injuries, made an invasion into the Wabash country, and, possessing an equal aversion to all bearing the name of Indians, they destroyed a number of peaceable Piankeshaws, who prided themselves on their attachment to the United States." Is it cause of wonder, then, that the less enlightened savages, who were liable to such treatment, should look upon " all the whites with equal aversion?"

' the subject of a general peace, and that we should still use ' our endeavors to effect it among all the Indian nations in this ' quarter.'

" Our elder brother, the Mohawk, then spoke, and gave them great thanks, that they would still endeavor to establish peace, and promised to write the Congress on the subject.

" BROTHER ! The Five Nations were the cause of the attendance on the treaty at the Falls of Muskingum. Some of us went by Fort Pitt, to take all in that route. These first arrived at Muskingum. Another party went by Detroit, to bring all from that quarter. At length, when we had arrived at the place called the High Hills, it was determined that a runner should be sent to Muskingum to know the business of the treaty. Accordingly, Captain David, of the Mohawk Nation, who is since dead, was chosen for this purpose.

" When the runner went to the place (which was at the mouth of the Muskingum) and was returning, he met the main body at the Falls, (which was about half way,) going on to the council fire. Captain David brought back a large piece of writing. And when it was read, (as it was by Brant,) all that it spoke was in regard to their lands ; and they found that all the Commissioner wanted was to get their lands. This disturbed all their minds,—when they found all that was wanted was to get their lands,—and it shocked the minds of the Five Nations.

" All the Indians then went back, except the Senecas, and one out of each other of the Five Nations, and some of the Delawares and Wyandots. These went on to the council fire of the Commissioner, because it had been burning all the season, waiting for them. Here their minds were made uneasy, because the Commissioner marked out their lands as he saw fit, and just told them what he did, saying, " I am going to have so much." The Five Nations tried to assist those nations, but could not. For the Commissioner said, I have nothing to do with you, the Five Nations, but only with these other nations who own the lands.   Then our minds sank within us, and we said no more.

"Then the Commissioner marked off big pieces, describing them, and said, so much I must have.   The nations meant to have the line run along the heads of the small creeks, running into the Alleghany ; but the Commissioner said that was not enough, but that he wanted the line to run so far back as to go upon the heads of the waters running into Lake Erie ; and he extended it accordingly toward the Mississippi.

"BROTHER !   You said perhaps the voice of the runner of the United States had not gone near enough to the western Indians for them to hear it.   This was the case.

"BROTHER !   You desired us to speak our minds freely upon this subject, to wit : the causes of the uneasiness among the western Indians.   We have now candidly related to you from step to step these facts ; which from small beginnings have increased to an extensive breach of our peace.

"BROTHER ! Possess your mind in peace.   This matter does not immediately concern us—but you desired us to speak.

The Farmers'-Brother having ended, Red-Jacket rose and spoke as follows :—

"BROTHER CON-NEH-SAUTY, who have been appointed by the President to represent the United States in the business on which we were invited, now attend !

"You spoke to us on our first arrival ; and a few days since you opened the whole business which respects our national happiness.   After this, you adverted to the troubled state of the nations at the westward ; and mentioned what you supposed were the causes of those troubles among the various nations in that quarter ; and you desired us to speak our minds freely on this subject.

"BROTHER : You have heard the two principal causes of those troubles.   Those two causes, as we apprehend, were these,—the destroying of the town by Big-Knife, and killing the old man, while the nations were met counselling for peace; and the smallness of the number who attended the treaty at Muskingum, and the affair of the lands. For we, the Five Nations, had to give up our judgments to what the Commissioner dictated, and that was the reason there were so many names to the writing.

"BROTHER: You have now heard the causes of the uneasiness among the western Indians; you said you wished to know the causes of those hostilities, that you might remove them. Here they are, as we consider them. Now it is our wish that the President and Congress would exert themselves to remove them. You have manifested a desire to put the burthen of bringing you and the western Indians together, upon our shoulders; but it is too heavy for us to bear without your assistance.

"BROTHER: Continue to hear! We are not able to go forward with this great business alone. Therefore, if you earnestly wish for the restoration of peace as your words have expressed, let us have some assistance. Let there be one voice between you and the British, who are by our fireside, to effect this object. True, you have drawn a line between them and you; and the line comes near to us. But we think you are too proud to act together upon this business. And unless you go to the western Indians, how will you convince them that you mean to do them justice?

"BROTHER: We of the Five Nations have not settled all the affairs pertaining to our peace,—and it will give great joy to our minds if you can extend peace to the western nations. What we have proposed, we think would be a healing medicine. Therefore, when we have completed our business with you, we shall be glad to communicate this to the people of our color to the westward.

"BROTHER: While you are yet hearing, let us remind you of your own words,—'verily you must love those of your 'own color: and we believe also that you are friends to us.'

"BROTHER: You have spoken truly: we do love both,—we

13

also love our common peace. Therefore have we thus advised to this healing medicine, which, alone, we think, will complete a cure of all the wounds.

"BROTHER: This is all we have now to say. You see that it is a pleasant day; an emblem of the pleasure and joy now diffused through all here present, for indeed it has been a counselling day,—a day of business."

The consultations being about to close, on the 25th of April the President transmitted to the chiefs the annexed farewell address :—

"MY CHILDREN OF THE FIVE NATIONS!

"You were invited here at my request, in order that measures should be concerted with you, to impart such of the blessings of civilization, as may at present suit your condition, and give you further desires to improve your own happiness.

"Colonel Pickering has made the particular arrangements with you to carry into execution these objects,—all of which I hereby approve and confirm.

"And in order that the money necessary to defray the annual expenses of the arrangements which have been made, should be provided permanently, I now ratify an article which will secure the yearly appropriation of the sum of one thousand five hundred dollars, for the use and benefit of the Five Nations,—the Stockbridge Indians included.

"The United States having received and provided for you as for a part of themselves, will, I am persuaded, be strongly and gratefully impressed on your minds, and those of all your tribes.

"Let it be spread abroad among all your villages, and throughout your land, that the United States are desirous not only of a general peace with all the Indian tribes, but of being their friends and protectors.

"It has been my direction, and I hope it has been executed

to your satisfaction, that during your residence here you should be well fed, well lodged, and well clothed, and that presents should be furnished to your wives and families.

"I partake of your sorrow on account that it has pleased the Great Spirit to take from you two of your number by death, since your residence in this city.* I have ordered that your tears should be wiped away according to your custom, and that presents should be sent to the relations of the deceased.

"Our lives are all in the hands of our Maker, and we must part with them whenever he shall demand them,—and the survivors must *submit* to events they cannot prevent.

"Having happily settled all your business, and being about to return to your own country, I wish you a pleasant journey, and that you may safely return to your families, after so long a journey, and find them in good health.

"Given under my hand, at the city of Philadelphia, this twenty-fifth day of April, 1792.

(Signed)   GEO. WASHINGTON."

The conferences were finally closed on the 30th of April, to the mutual satisfaction of both parties. The chiefs had not only agreed to *try*, with their people, to become civilized, but had likewise stipulated to send a

---

* One of the chiefs to whose decease General Washington here referred was Peter Jaquette, a leading sachem of the Oneidas, who died on the 19th of March, soon after the deputation arrived in Philadelphia. Peter had been taken to France by the Marquis de la Fayette, (on that nobleman's return home after the close of the revolutionary war,) where he received an education. The Pennsylvania Gazette of that day thus described the funeral of the chief:—" His funeral was attended from Oeler's hotel to the Presbyterian burying ground in Mulberry-street. The corpse was preceded by a detachment of the light infantry of the city, with arms reversed, drums muffled, and the music playing a solemn dirge. The corpse was followed by six of the chiefs as mourners, succeeded by all the warriors; the reverend clergy of all denominations; Secretary of War, and the gentlemen of the war department; officers of the federal army, and of the militia; and a number of citizens."

strong deputation to their brethren in the Miami country, for the purpose of bringing them, if possible, into a more pacific disposition. Colonel Pickering delivered a parting speech to them, embracing their instructions as to their contemplated mission. The hostile Indians had imbibed the idea,—or rather it had been insinuated into their minds by the officers of the British Indian service in Upper Canada,—that the United States were claiming the *fee* of their whole domain south of the great lakes, and east of the Mississippi. Of this idea Red-Jacket and his associates were charged to disabuse them, and to show them by maps with which they were provided, that the United States claimed no farther nor other portions of the soil than were comprehended in the several purchases actually made by treaty, including, of course, the treaties of Fort McIntosh and Fort Harmar, or Muskingum. But it should here be remembered that the Indians invariably protested against the fairness and validity of the two last mentioned treaties; and were then in arms to compel the United States to regard the Ohio as their actual western boundary. Nevertheless, the chiefs departed in good spirits, and great hopes were entertained that their western mission would be attended by auspicious results.*

* It was during this visit to Philadelphia that General Washington presented Red-Jacket with the large silver medal, bearing his likeness, which the chief wore until his death, and of which he was so proud. Soon after the arrival of the chiefs, General Knox directed a military suit of clothes to be delivered to each of them, including a cocked hat, &c., as worn by the officers of the army. When Red-Jacket's suit was tendered to him, he requested the bearer to inform General Knox that he could not consistently wear the dress, because he was a

The members of this deputation arrived at Buffalo Creek early in June; but although returning with the most amicable feelings themselves, their people were found in a very different condition of temper. Many of the young Seneca warriors were among the hostile Indians; but it appeared that the commander of Fort Jefferson had succeeded in winning some of them to the cause of the United States, and a scout of the hostile Indians had been cut off by their assistance. This affair had caused great uneasiness among the Six Nations, and their resentment against the commander of Fort Jefferson was kindled to exasperation, because, as they alleged, "he had excited some of their thoughtless young men to strike the tomahawk into the heads of their brothers." Old Fish-Carrier, the principal chief of the Cayugas, and a man of great consideration among his nation, was for a time after this occurrence exceedingly disaffected; as indeed were the whole Cayuga and Seneca nations. Being advised of this critical state of things, General Chapin, the efficient and influential agent for the Six Nations, whose residence was at Canan-

---

sachem,—a civil officer,—and not a war-chief. He therefore requested that a different suit might be given to him, more suitable to his station. Still he insisted on keeping the military clothes until the other dress was provided for him. But when the plain dress was brought, and the regimentals asked for in exchange, he declined delivering them up,—coolly remarking that although as a sachem he could not wear a military uniform in time of peace, yet in the time of war the sachems joined the warriors, and he would therefore keep it until a war should break out, when he could assume it with entire propriety. *MSS. of Thomas Morris.* Red-Jacket had two brothers upon this deputation, viz: Sa-o-nish-shon-wa, (A Great Breath,) and Sos-son-do-e-wa, (A Great Darkness.)—*Old MS. of Colonel Pickering.*

daigua, hastened to Buffalo Creek, and by much exertion succeeded in allaying the anger of the Cayuga chief, and tranquillizing the minds of the Indians. Such indeed was the change wrought in the mind of the Fish-Carrier, that he promised to recall those of his warriors who had joined the hostiles.* He also acceded to the measure of sending the proposed deputation of chiefs to the Miami country; but owing to the extreme deliberation of their movements, their frequent counselling, and their dilatory manner of conducting business, the messengers did not depart westward until the middle of September. Yet these delays arose from no farther reluctance on the part of the Indians to enter upon the mission. The deportment of the federal government toward them, and the agreeable manner in which they had passed their time in Philadelphia, had completely won their friendship,—even that of the dissembling Red-Jacket, who never afterward gave any good reason for doubting his constancy upon that point. He was himself one of the deputation which proceeded to the west, as also was the Cornplanter.

Meantime, justly appreciating his great talents, and reckoning much upon his influence among the north-western tribes, the government of the United States, by much exertion, had succeeded, after the departure of the Seneca delegation, in persuading Joseph Brant, the Mohawk chief, and the war-captain of the whole Iroquois confederacy, to visit Philadelphia, for the purpose, if

* Letter from General Israel Chapin to the Secretary at War. Indian State Papers, p. 241.

possible, of despatching him also to the Miami country as a messenger of peace. Brant did not leave Upper Canada, to visit the seat of the American government, without encountering much opposition from Sir John Johnson and other officers in the British service. But he nevertheless performed the journey, was respectfully received by the federal authorities at Philadelphia, and was ultimately induced to undertake the western mission. Taking Grand River in the way on his return, he was prostrated by a fit of sickness, and rendered unable, during that season, to fulfil his engagement.

Nor at that time, probably, would a visit, even from him, have been attended by any particular benefit. The hostile Indians were met in council by Red-Jacket and his associates at the Au Glaize, on the Miami river of Lake Erie, but were found in a most implacable humor. In his anxiety for a pacification, the President had sent other messengers of peace to traverse the Wabash country, among whom were the Rev. Mr. Heckewelder, General Rufus Putnam, Colonel Hardin, Major Trueman, and another officer named Freeman. The last mentioned three of these messengers had been intercepted and murdered. The hostile council was large, and no white man was admitted to its deliberations, save the noted Simon Girty, whom, at the expense of their own character, the Wyandots considered as one of themselves. The Shawanese were the only speakers on the side of the hostile chiefs, and Red-Jacket alone was permitted to open his lips in behalf of the pacifica-

tors.* The following passage from the address of the
Shawanese to the Six Nations sufficiently illustrates the
temper by which they were then governed :—

"ELDEST BROTHERS! You come to us with your opinion,
and the voice of the United States. It is your mind to put an
end to all hostilities. Brothers! now we will relate what took
place last fall in our country. General Washington sent an
army into our country, which fell into our hands. Their
orders were thus : to proceed into our country as far as the
Miami towns, to the Glaize; thence to Detroit, but not to
molest the King's people; and if the army should meet any
people that appeared friendly, to leave them behind their
backs without harm.

" The President of the United States must well know why
the blood is so deep in our paths. We have been informed
that he has sent messengers of peace on these bloody roads,
who fell on the way.† And now, as he knows that road to be
bloody, no communication can take place through that bloody
way, as there is a path through the Six Nations' country,
which is smooth and easy. If he wants to send the voice of
peace, it must come through that road.

"ELDER BROTHERS! We have been informed the President
of the United States thinks himself the greatest man on this
island. We had this country long in peace before we saw
any person of a white skin. We consider the people of the
white skin the younger."

There were no stenographers present at that council,
and it is therefore impossible to report as to the manner
in which Red-Jacket acquitted himself. But as he was

* Letter from the Secretary at War to the President, Dec. 6, 1792. See Indian State Papers, p. 322.

† Alluding to the murders of Hardin, Trueman, and Freeman, as just mentioned in the text.

the only speaker in the cause of peace, he doubtless participated in the debates often. The result was a stipulation for an armistice during the winter, and for the holding of a treaty with the United States at the Miami rapids in the ensuing spring, " at any time after the leaves were out." But as a basis of the negotiation they insisted sturdily upon the *status quo ante bellum*,— contending that they had still a claim upon a portion of the territory east of the Ohio, and that under no circumstances would they consent to any farther western boundary than the line of that river. Such was the determination of which Red-Jacket and his associates were the bearers on their return. A report of the whole procedure, drawn up in the Indian style, was forwarded to the President, accompanied by an address from the Six Nations, praying the government of the United States to commission messengers to treat upon the basis proposed. They besought the President to send agents " who were men of honesty, not proud land-jobbers, but men who loved and desired peace." They also suggested that the agents should be " attended by some friend or Quaker,"—a proposition which, as will presently appear, was adopted.*

The deputation returned to Buffalo Creek about the middle of November, and the results of their mission

* The report of this deputation, as returned in form, and rendered into English by Mr. Parish, the interpreter, is a curious document. See Appendix, [A]. The council at the Glaize was very large, including representations from thirty-seven nations beyond the Canadian territory,—as also, chiefs from " the Gora country," who were occupied the whole season in travelling thither.

were forwarded to Philadelphia, by Mr. Jasper Parish, the interpreter. Red-Jacket was desirous of visiting Philadelphia as the bearer of despatches himself, but considerations of economy induced General Chapin, the Indian Agent, to dissuade him from that purpose,—a circumstance which was regretted by the Secretary at War.*

The armistice for which the Miamis and Shawanese had stipulated was not very rigidly observed. The paths were not only made bloody by frequent murders, but at least one sharp and considerable action was fought, late in the fall, between an army of Indians and a detachment of Kentucky volunteers, commanded by Major Adair, in which the former were rather checked than defeated.

The reply of the President to this proposition of the hostile Indians was by them considered evasive, and created great dissatisfaction. They even charged the delegates from the Six Nations with not having advised the American government, in good faith, of their exact determination. The consequence was the convocation of another council of the belligerent confederates, in which they reiterated the conditions upon which only they would agree to treat, in more positive language than before; and they admonished the President to send forward no commissioners, unless prepared to negotiate upon the prescribed basis. Commissioners were, nevertheless, appointed, who proceeded by the way of Alba-

---

* Letter of General Knox to the President.

ny to Niagara, and thence to Sandusky, to meet the Indians at Au Glaize. Moved by the benevolence of their principles, the Quakers, likewise, of Pennsylvania, spontaneously, and before the desire to that effect, of the Six Nations, was known to them, appointed a deputation from their pacific order, to proceed to Detroit and exert their influence in the cause of peace.* Both commissions were alike ineffective. The Indians gathered at the Au Glaize in great numbers, and in the worst possible humor. And although the greatest chieftain of their race, in modern times, Joseph Brant, was there, and exerted himself to the utmost to accomplish a general pacification, the effort was unavailing. The Indians would not relax one iota from their original determination to make the Ohio the *ultima thule* of white possession and civilization. The commissioners could of course entertain no such proposition, and after nearly the entire year (1793) had been consumed, they returned from their bootless errand. Meantime, after the defeat of St. Clair, the command of the army had been confided to General Wayne, who evinced the utmost energy in its re-organization. He was already in the Indian country, at the time when the negotiation failed, and immediately thereafter preparations were made for opening another campaign, on the return of spring,

---

* The commissioners appointed by the government were General Benjamin Lincoln, Beverly Randolph, and Cólonel Timothy Pickering. The Quaker gentlemen deputed upon the mission were John Parish, William Savary, and John Elliott, of Philadelphia; Jacob Lindley, of Westchester county; and Joseph Moore and William Hartshorne, of New-Jersey.

(1794,) with all the vigor the government could put forth. That campaign was short and brilliant. After several rather severe affairs in the early part of the summer, the fierce battle fought by Wayne, at the rapids of the Miamis, on the 20th of August, crowned by a signal victory, put an end to hostilities. This battle was not fought against the Indians alone. They were assisted by "a mixed multitude" of tories and refugees from the United States; half-breeds, French and English fur-traders, and others, residing at Detroit and in the wild regions beyond. The action was, moreover, fought almost under the guns of a British fort, which the assurance of Governor Sinclair had caused to be erected thus far within the territory of the United States, and between the commander of which and General Wayne a sharp correspondence ensued. The American General was so greatly exasperated at the conduct of the British officers and agents in that quarter, that he could scarcely desist from laying siege to the fort itself. There were several skirmishes between scouting parties, after the battle,—affording Wayne an excuse to lay waste the country of the Miamis, which was well cultivated for the distance of fifty miles. Colonel M'Kee, an influential officer in the British Indian department, had extensive possessions there, which were ravaged and his buildings laid in ashes. Wayne continued to occupy the country for a whole year afterward, at the close of which the definitive treaty of Greenville was concluded with the Indians, which was of a character perfectly agreeable to the United States.

CHAPTER V.

THE termination of the war between the United States
and the north-western Indians was mentioned at the
close of the preceding chapter, in anticipation of the
regular historical progress of these memoirs. But the
name of the Seneca orator, Sa-go-ye-wat-ha, does not
occur in connection with that war, or with any other
public event during the year 1793. In February of the
next year, (1794,) he was present at a council convened
at Buffalo Creek, at the instance of the federal government, for the purpose of yet farther conciliating the good
feelings of the Senecas and Cayugas. The wayward-
ness of the Indian character is such, and the desire of
their young men is always so strong to be upon the war-
path at every opportunity, that the most assiduous and
watchful exertions were constantly necessary to keep

the Senecas and Cayugas from joining the belligerents
en masse ;—and these efforts were only crowned with
partial success at the best.   The appliances of the government, on this occasion, consisted of a liberal distribution of presents,—particularly of clothing.   But the
eagle eyes of the British officers in Canada were upon
every movement of the Six Nations, and such was the
lingering attachment of the Senecas for their ancient
allies, or such their actual and continued attachment to
them, that no council could be held upon that frontier
without the presence of one or more representatives of
the crown.   Indeed, his Britannic Majesty's officers were
determined that no peace should be concluded, unless
they might be the principal agents in effecting it.   At
about the time now under consideration, the celebrated
Colonel John Butler, of Wyoming memory, declared
that the only way to make peace with the Indians was
to apply to Lord Dorchester,* Governor General of the
Canadas, and Commander-in-chief at Quebec, for the
appointment of a commission of British officers to designate the boundary between the United States and the
Indians, and assist in the negotiation of a treaty, to be
guaranteed to the Indians by Great Britain.†   Propositions so arrogant on the one side, and an acquiescence
in which would have been so degrading on the other,
were of course spurned with indignation.   Still, the affairs of the war were discussed at the council; but Joseph

* The Sir Guy Carleton of the revolutionary war.
† Massachusetts Historical Collections, vol. i. p. 287.

Brant was the principal Indian speaker, while Red-Jacket enacted only a subordinate and unimportant part.

He came more prominently before the public in the following autumn, at the great and memorable council held with the Six Nations at Canandaigua. General Wayne had not closed the war in the north-west when the preparations for this council were commenced; but aside from the sympathies of the Six Nations in behalf of their belligerent brethren, another difficulty had arisen, nearer home, causing for a season great anxiety. A movement by Pennsylvania, having in view an immediate extension of her settlements to Presque Isle, on the shore of Lake Erie, was a measure that greatly exasperated the Six Nations, who claimed that territory as exclusively their own, and immediate hostilities had well nigh been the consequence. The governor of Pennsylvania claimed the disputed territory by virtue of an alleged purchase from the Cornplanter; but the Six Nations disavowed the transaction, and prepared to defend their soil with the rifle and tomahawk. The military arrangements were matured under the direction of Brant, or Thayendanegea, who was in readiness once more to lead his braves to the onslaught. But the timely interposition of President Washington deterred Pennsylvania from any farther prosecution of her designs in that quarter, at that time.* Still, it was

---

* Life of Brant, vol. ii. pp. 377–381. A council of the Six Nations was holden at Buffalo Creek, in June of 1794, upon this subject, on which occasion Cornplanter delivered a speech, to be forwarded to General Washington, for which, see Appendix B.

deemed proper, on the part of the President, to endeavor
to tranquillize the Indians who had been thus disturbed,
by pacific measures, and a council was appointed, which,
as already mentioned, sat at Canandaigua, in October
and November, 1794.   Colonel Pickering was again detailed as the commissioner on the part of the United
States, with instructions to hold a free conference with
the Indians of the Six Nations, upon all the causes of
discontent then existing between the two peoples.   The
good " Friends" of Pennsylvania and New-Jersey, under
the conviction that the interposition of their pacific
offices was a religious duty, appointed a deputation of
great respectability to attend the council, and if possible,
by indirection at least, exercise some beneficial influence
in its proceedings.*

This was the last general council held by the United
States with the Iroquois confederacy,—and a vast amount
of important business was transacted thereat.   Several
perplexing questions of contested boundaries were settled,
and the relations between the United States and the
confederacy were adjusted upon a basis that has not
since been disturbed.   The results were of great importance, not only to the federal government, but also
in respect to the influence which the adjustment of those
questions had upon the settlement of western New-York
by the white people.   But a proper history of that council is yet a desideratum, which there are no documents

* The delegates were David Bacon, John Parish, William Savary, and James
Emlen.

even in the archives of the government adequate to supply,—the naked treaty itself, which is not of great length, being all that seems to have been preserved.

The council was opened on the 11th of October, in the camp of the Oneidas, they only having yet arrived. But as there were many minor difficulties presented for arrangement by the arbitrament of the commission,—difficulties arising among several of the tribes themselves, and between the Indians and grasping white men, which were not of national concernment,—it was not important that all the nations should be present at the first moment of business. Colonel Pickering opened the council by a conciliatory speech, in which he stated that he had heard of difficulties among them which he would gladly assist in healing. He was addressed in reply by Captain John, and Good Peter, at great length. The first grievance presented related to a lease of about one third of the Oneida reservation to Peter Smith, embracing a territory four miles in breadth, by twenty-four in length, and containing sixty-one thousand four hundred and forty acres of land. This tract, it was alleged, had been leased to Mr. Smith for twenty-one years, by the sachems, or civil magistrates, in opposition to the voice of the warriors; and the attempts to survey the land had brought the two parties in array against each other, and almost into actual conflict. Great complaints were made against the whites in general, for the artifices practised to deceive them and obtain their lands. Captain John spoke in behalf of the sachems, and Good Peter, the head warrior, for the braves. Colonel Pick-

15

ering replied to them on the following day, and proposed
a course of conciliation and compromise,—promising to
visit the Oneida castle on his return, and assist in the
final adjustment of the difficulty.

The Indians, as usual, gathered around the council
fire slowly. By the 14th the Onondagas and Cayugas
had arrived; and on the same day the approach of
Farmer's-Brother was announced, at the head of a large
party of Senecas. He had halted at the distance of four
miles from the village, to paint and dress, preparatory
to a public entrance into the grand camp. At three
o'clock in the afternoon he arrived with his train, the
Oneidas, Onondagas and Cayugas being drawn up in
order, armed, painted and plumed, to receive them.
Marching up in front of the Oneidas and their neighbors, the Senecas fired a salute of three rounds of musketry, which was returned by the others, making the
woods ring long and loud by the reverberations. The
Indian leaders then directed their dusky legions to form
a circle around Colonel Pickering and General Chapin,
the government agents, with their assistants and attendants,—whereupon the commissioner was addressed by
Farmer's-Brother, who on closing returned the belt by
which he had been summoned to the council. Two
days afterward the Cornplanter arrived at the head of
four hundred, being the Alleghany clan of the Senecas.
The same ceremonies of reception and presentation were
observed as on the former day,—the Indians being
dressed and painted with all the brilliancy and beauty

of their wild and fantastic tastes. The number of Indians then present was sixteen hundred.

On the morning of the 18th Red-Jacket made his appearance, and first visited the deputation from the Friends, in company with Cornplanter, Farmer's-Brother, Little Beard, and several other Seneca chiefs, upon private business.* In the afternoon the commissioner and the Friends were summoned by a son of Cornplanter to attend the formal opening of the grand council. The officers and their interpreters were surrounded by a dark assemblage, the chiefs appearing subdued and thoughtful, and the entire *coup d'œil* presenting a striking aspect. The first business was an address of condolence to the Senecas, Cayugas, Tuscaroras, and Delawares, (a deputation of the latter being present,) by Captain John, of the Oneidas, on account of the loss of many chiefs of the Six Nations since they had last met in general council. The Oneidas, in behalf of themselves and the Onondagas, wished, in their figurative language, to wipe the tears from their brethren's eyes, brighten their countenances and clear their throats, that they might speak freely at the council fire. Red-Jacket returned a brotherly salutation, handing the eastern nations of the con-

---

* It appears that the Senecas had invited a private conference with the Friends, respecting the descendants of some Indians who had formerly resided at or near Hopewell, in Virginia. The Indians claimed that the people of whom the Friends had purchased the lands at Hopewell had not paid for them, and therefore had sold what was not their own. The Friends desired that the heirs of the Indians who had been dispossessed at Hopewell should be sought out, that a just compensation might be made to them. Cornplanter now informed them that two of those heirs had been found, residing at Conestoga.

federacy belts and strings of wampum, to unite each to the other, and thus to open the council as with the heart of one man.   They then informed Colonel Pickering that the Six Nations were duly opened as a council for the transaction of business.   The Colonel made a congratulatory address in reply, and informed them that, as it was then Saturday, on Monday afternoon he would hold a council of condolence, to wipe away the tears from the eyes of the Delawares, who had lost a young brother, murdered by a white man at Venango, a few months before.   He would then take the hatchet out of the head of the deceased, and bury it in the earth, preparatory to the treaty.

Accordingly on the 20th, a very large council was held, at which the Colonel performed the promised ceremony of condolement with the Delawares.   By speech and gesture he went through the process of burying the dead, and covered the grave with leaves, so that they could see it no more in passing.   The hatchet which he had taken out of the head of the victim was buried beneath a pine tree, which, *in words*, was torn up for that purpose.   Having placed the hatchet in a deep hole, and covered it with stones, the tree was replanted upon the top, so that the instrument of death should never more be discovered.   The Colonel then wiped the blood from their heads, and the tears from their eyes, and opened the path of peace, which the Indians were invited to keep clear at one end, and the United States at the other, as long as the sun shone.   These and other ceremonies having been performed, the council was adjourned, and the fire covered up for the night.

On the next day, the celebrated Jemima Wilkinson, who, with her followers, resided upon the western margin of the Seneca lake, being at Canandaigua, with several of her disciples, was invited by Colonel Pickering to dine with him, at the house of Mr. Thomas Morris. The invitation was accepted by Jemima, and she was treated with great attention by the Colonel, glad of the opportunity to gratify his curiosity respecting this remarkable woman, whom he had never seen before. The seat of honor was appropriated to her, and she participated freely in the conversation.

At an early hour of the afternoon the commissioner was summoned to the council, to which place he repaired with his friends,—Jemima and her retinue following in the train, and taking seats with the commissioner and interpreters in the centre of the circle. The address of Colonel Pickering, of the preceding day, was answered by the Fish-Carrier,—who took occasion to glance retrospectively at the relations that had existed between the Six Nations and the white men, since the landing of the latter " on this island." When the white people first came, the Indians saw that they were men, and must have something to subsist upon. They, therefore, pitied them, and gave them some land ; and when they complained that the land had become too small for them, the Indians still pitied them, and from time to time gave them more. At length a great council-fire was kindled at Albany, where a silver chain was made,

which was kept bright for many years, until the United
States and the great King over the water differed. Then
their brothers in Canada talked to the Indians, and they
let the chain fall out of their hands. Yet it was not
their fault, but the white people's. The Fish-Carrier
then recapitulated the history of the negotiations with the
white people after the close of the revolutionary war,
referring to the treaties of Fort Stanwix, and complained of many grievances which they had suffered,—
particularly in the curtailment of their territory. The
Indians felt that at the first treaty at Fort Stanwix, in
1784, the commissioners had been too grasping,—a
position which Colonel Pickering, in his reply, labored
rather to extenuate than to deny. Having just come
out victoriously from a bloody war with them, the Colonel told them that great allowances were to be made,
even if the commissioners had shown themselves proud,
and treated them somewhat harshly. But notwithstanding their many causes of complaint, Fish-Carrier,
now that they had taken hold of the chain with the
fifteen fires, pledged the Six Nations to hold on.

In the course of the sitting Colonel Pickering formally introduced the Quaker deputation, who had been appointed at their request, and with the approbation of the
President. The deputies thereupon presented the address from the Friends to the Indians, which was read,
and interpreted by Jasper Parish, and received with
lively approbation by the Indians. The reading of the
address having been completed, Jemima and her disciples dropped upon their knees, and the mistress of

the order uttered something in the form of a prayer. The lady superior afterward desired liberty to address the assembly, which being granted, she proceeded to utter a rhapsody, consisting of disjointed texts of Scripture, mingled with confused and unmeaning sentences of her own, forming together a medley without coherence, relevancy, or point. The proceedings of the day were closed on the part of the Indians, by the interchange of belts, the design of which was to perpetuate the memories and virtues of their departed chiefs, for whose loss they had been performing the ceremonies of condolence.

The council was re-opened on the 23d. When about to proceed to business, a request was made by three Indian women to be admitted to deliver their sentiments. The request was granted, and the women were introduced by Red-Jacket, who appears ever to have been a favorite with the Indian ladies. Addressing himself to the sachems and warriors, he asked their favor in behalf of the women, and also that of the commissioner, craving that they might be heard, especially as on the preceding day a lady of the pale faces had been allowed the same indulgence. The assent of the council having been given, Red-Jacket was designated as the orator through whom they desired to speak. The substance of his communication in their behalf was, that they felt a deep interest in the affairs of their people ; and having heard the opinions of their sachems, they fully concurred in them, that the white people had been the cause of all the Indians' distresses : The

white people, they said, had pressed and squeezed
them together, until it gave them great pain at their
hearts, and they thought the white people ought to give
back all the lands they had taken from them. One of
the white women, (Jemima, meaning,) had yesterday
told the Indians to repent ; and they in turn now called
on the white people to repent,—they having as much
need of repentance as the Indians. They therefore
hoped the pale faces would repent and wrong the Indians no more.

The commissioner thanked them for their speech, observing that it was far from his nature to think meanly
of women, and he should always be happy to hear from
them when they had any thing to say. But in regard
to the conduct of the white woman, on the preceding
day, which they had cited as a precedent, he remarked
that she had forced herself into the council, and had
spoken without his approbation.*

* Jemima Wilkinson was extensively known, by reputation, as a religious impostor, in the western part of New-York, thirty or forty years ago. She was
born in Rhode Island, in 1753, and was educated a Quaker. She was artful, bold,
and zealous. About 1773, on recovering from a fit of sickness, during which
she had fallen into a syncope, so that she was apparently dead, she announced
that she had been raised from the dead, and had received a divine commission
as a religious teacher. Having made a few proselytes, she removed with
them into the western part of New-York, and settled between the Seneca
and Crooked Lakes, at the distance of about eighteen miles from Geneva,
calling her village New Jerusalem. In consequence of the weakness
and credulity of her followers, she was enabled to live in very elegant style,
having half a dozen beautiful damsels in attendance upon her person. She inculcated poverty, but was careful to be the owner of lands purchased in the name
of her companion, Rachel Miller. When she preached, she stood in the door of
her bed chamber, wearing a waistcoat, a stock, and a white silk cravat. She died
in 1819. Joseph Brant once very adroitly discomfited her.—As she professed

An unpleasant incident occurred on the morning of the 25th, which came near breaking up the council in a tempest. It was the appearance in the assembly of a man named Johnson, who came from Fort Erie as a messenger from Brant. He had indeed arrived two days before, and on the day previous he held secret conference with several of the chiefs, and delivered the message with which he had been charged by the Mohawk. Assuming the character of an interpreter, he was now mingling in the council, and appeared rather too intimate with the Indians to please Colonel Pickering, who objected to his presence, and denounced him as a British spy. The Indians either were, or affected to be, greatly surprised at the attitude assumed by Colonel Pickering, in regard to this intrusion. Cornplanter rose to vindicate Johnson and express his surprise that, notwithstanding the conclusion of peace between the United States and the Great King over the water, such an antipathy existed between them that neither party could bear to sit by the side of the other in treaties held with the Indians. The messenger, Johnson, he said, had merely come on a friendly errand from Captain Brant. The Indians, he said, had the year before resolved upon convening a grand council of all their nations at Sandusky, in the (now) following spring, and Brant had sent them a message to remind them of the

---

to be Christ in his second appearing, Brant tested her by speaking in different Indian languages, none of which she understood. He then disclosed her imposture, simply by declaring that Jesus Christ must of course understand all languages,—one as well as another.

16

appointment. But unluckily for the excuse he was making, Cornplanter disclosed too much. "Captain Brant,"
said he, " sends his compliments to the chiefs at Canandaigua, and says, ' you remember what we agreed upon
last year, and the line we marked out: If this line is
complied with, peace will take place ;' and he desires us
to mention this at Canandaigua." The message also
contained an invitation for the chiefs to meet Brant at
Buffalo Creek, at an early day.

Colonel Pickering replied with great indignation,—to
account for which, two or three points must here be
borne in mind. In the first place, such was the tardi-
ness of communication through the deep wildernesses of
the west, that neither the Colonel nor the Indians had
yet heard of the entire overthrow of the Miamies and
their confederates in August, by General Wayne. In
the second place, the Indians at the present council
were striving to re-open, for fresh negotiation, the entire
question of boundaries between the Six Nations and the
United States, and not only that, but they were now
claiming westwardly, between Lake Erie and the Ohio,
as far as the Muskingum—embracing, of course, a large
tract of territory for which the Miamies and their confederates were fighting. Thirdly, although Brant had
been endeavoring to effect a peace, he had always favored the Indian claim that the Ohio should be recog-
nized as the boundary between the white men and the
red. The Senecas, also, had ever avowed the same
opinion ; and lest they might be induced to swerve from
that position, Brant had now taken occasion, in the

midst of a treaty, to throw them a signal of remembrance. Hence the exasperation of Colonel Pickering at the presence of Johnson. Accordingly, in reply to the excuses of Cornplanter, he used language of great severity. He said he considered the intrusion of Johnson as an act betraying great impudence, and as affording fresh proof of British insolence. Then reviewing the whole system of British interference in the Indian relations of the United States, and the ill treatment, in this respect, which his government had received from England, for several years past, the Colonel concluded a long speech by the declaration that either the messenger must be sent back, or he would himself cover up the council fire and depart. His instructions from General Washington, he said, were explicit, that he should suffer no British agents to be present at the treaty.

The Indians were amazed at the vehemence of the Colonel's manner, remarking, as he resumed his seat— "the council-fire grows warm : the sparks fly about very thick." Johnson himself appeared alarmed, and shrunk stealthily away. The Indians then requested Colonel Pickering and his party to withdraw for a short time, as they wished to have a brief conference among themselves. In about half an hour the doors of the council house were re-opened, and Cornplanter again rose in vindication of Johnson, avowing, distinctly, that he came at their own solicitation, and was consequently not to blame. If there were fault in the case, it belonged to the white people, who had deceived the Indians when they were told at Fort Stanwix that the treaty of peace

between England and the United States had been agreed
upon in the presence of the Great Spirit:—

" We now discover," said he, " that the commissioners there
told us what was a lie, when they said they had made the chain
of friendship bright : but I now find there has been an antipathy to each other ever since.   Now our sachems and warriors say, what shall we do ? We will shove Johnson off.
Yet this is not agreeable to my mind, for if *I* had kindled a
council-fire, I would suffer a very bad man to sit in it, that he
might be made better.   But if the peace you made had been
a good peace, all animosities would have been done away, and
you could have sat side by side in council.   I have one request to make, which is, that you would furnish Johnson provisions to carry him home."

There was altogether too much of refinement in the
diplomatic relations between the two white and civilized
nations, for the understandings of the unsophisticated
barbarians.   A *quasi* war between people professing the
most amicable relations with each other, was a state of
things quite beyond their comprehension.   With them,
their relations must be either one thing or the other,—
peace or war,—and in either attitude there would be
nothing equivocal.

After a sitting of five hours the storm passed away,
and the council adjourned.*   In the evening fifteen of

---

* The proceedings against the supposed spy, Johnson, were harsh. By a
MS. letter of Gen. Chapin's, in the author's possession, it appears that the
General had invited Joseph Brant to attend the council.   But it not being convenient for him to do so, at the request of the Indians, Johnson had been sent to
the council by Brant.   On the 4th of November Gen. Chapin wrote to Brant,
attempting to soften down the apparent harshness of the measure toward John-

the principal chiefs, among whom were Red-Jacket, Cornplanter, Farmer's-Brother, Little-Beard, Big-Sky and the Fish-Carrier, dined with Colonel Pickering. Much good humor prevailed on this occasion. The Indians laid aside their stoicism, indulged in many repartees, and manifested the keenest relish for wit and humor. Red-Jacket, in particular, was conspicuous for the readiness and brilliance of his sallies. But there were clouds lowering in the sky on the following day. At the opening of the council, the first business was the presentation of a letter which they had prepared, to be transmitted to Brant by the hand of Johnson. In this letter the chiefs expressed their sorrow that his messenger had not been permitted to remain with them in the council; and for the reasons of his dismissal, the Mohawk captain was referred to Johnson's own relation. They farther assured Brant that they were determined to adhere to the boundary lines as they had been agreed upon among the Indians the year before. In conclusion they expressed to their old war-chief a feeling sense of their present feeble condition. " They were," they said, " a poor, despised, though still an independent people, brought into suffering between two white nations striving which should be the greatest." Nothing could have been more true than this last remark.

son. In this letter Chapin said:—"After Mr. Johnson arrived, some difficulties existed which made it inconvenient for him to attend the treaty, not for any unfavorable regard to the gentleman, but for certain reasons of which he will inform you." Colonel Pickering also wrote to Brant upon the same subject. Brant replied to Gen. Chapin on the 4th of December, and to Colonel Pickering on the 30th, in both of which letters he avows that Johnson went at his request. [The MSS. of these letters are in the author's possession.]

This communication gave high displeasure to Colonel Pickering, and there were again symptoms of an untoward breaking up of the council. The Senecas were displeased that the treaty had not been holden at their old council fire at Buffalo Creek; words ran high, and their eyes at times flashed with vengeful fire. It must have been at this juncture that Red-Jacket made the celebrated unreported speech, a glowing account of which is contained in several modern Indian works*—that is, if the speech was ever delivered, a fact which there is some reason to doubt,—at least in the manner and form described. According to the writer referred to, the treaty was held on a beautiful acclivity that overlooks Canandaigua Lake :—

" The witnesses of the scene will never forget the powers of native oratory. Two days had passed away in negotiation with the Indians for a cession of their lands. The contract was supposed to be nearly completed when Red-Jacket arose. With the grace and dignity of a Roman senator he drew his blanket around him, and with a piercing eye surveyed the multitude. All was hushed. Nothing was interposed to break

---

* Copied into Drake's Book of the Indians, and also Thatcher's Indian Biography, from a correspondent of the New-York American, who wrote some fifteen or twenty years ago. The writer averred that he was present; but he speaks of " the gentle rustling of the tree tops, under whose shade they were gathered," whereas it was now the closing week of October, and according to Mr. Savary's journal, whence the materials for the present history of the treaty are chiefly drawn, the ground was covered with snow to the depth of several inches. The trees were then affording no shade, and the weather was that of winter. Mr. Thomas Morris, moreover, who was then a resident of Canandaigua, and in attendance upon the council, recollects no such speech as that here imputed to Red-Jacket,—nor does Mr. Savary refer to it. The account, therefore, is either an exaggeration, or apocryphal.

the silence, save the gentle rustling of the tree-tops under whose shade they were gathered. After a long and solemn, but not unmeaning pause, he commenced his speech, in a low voice and sententious style. Rising gradually with his subject, he delineated the primitive simplicity and happiness of his people, and the wrongs they had sustained from the usurpations of white men, with such a bold, but faithful pencil, that every auditor was soon raised to vengeance, or melted into tears. The effect was inexpressible. But ere the emotions of admiration and sympathy had subsided, the white men became alarmed. They were in the heart of the Indian country,—surrounded by more than ten times their number, who were inflamed by the remembrance of their injuries, and excited to indignation by the eloquence of a favorite chief. Apalled and terrified, the white men cast a cheerless gaze upon the horde around them. A nod from the chiefs might be the onset of destruction. At this portentous moment Farmer's-Brother interposed. He replied not to his brother chief, but, with a sagacity truly aboriginal, he caused a cessation of the council, introduced good cheer, commended the eloquence of Red-Jacket, and before the meeting had re-assembled, with the aid of other prudent chiefs, he had moderated the fury of his nation to a more salutary review of the question before them."

If the incident, as thus related, occurred at all, it must have been at this stage of the proceedings, since there was no other moment of excitement, during the sittings of this protracted council, that could have awakened such a temper. But the aspect of the negotiation was changed on the following day, by the arrival of a Tuscarora runner, despatched from Niagara by Colonel Butler, with tidings of the signal defeat of Little Turtle and the Miamies, with their confederates, by General

Wayne, or Su-kach-gook,* as he was called by the savages. The news of this event had an immediate and striking effect upon the deportment of the Indians. The successive defeats of Harmar and St. Clair, by the Indians, in the earlier part of that desultory yet bloody war, had inspired the whole race with the hope that their fortunes were about taking a more favorable turn, and that they might still be able to make a stand against the farther advance of the whites, if indeed, by a grand combination of the whole race of red men, they might not one day succeed in driving them back across the great water. In these hopes and aspirations the Six Nations strongly sympathized; and while the contest at the West was undecided, since the arms of their brethren had been twice crowned with success, the Six Nations carried themselves with a considerable degree of arrogance. They were rude and saucy to the white settlers, would impudently enter their houses, take the prepared food from the tables without leave, and commit other offences.† Their deportment was rather haughty at the council until the advices of Wayne's complete success were received. Indeed there is reason to believe that had "The Black Snake" been defeated, neither persuasions nor treaties would have kept the whole Seneca nation from rushing into the contest. But the complete overthrow of Little Turtle and his forces at the Miamies awoke them from their dream,

* The Black Snake.

† MS. letter to the author from George Hosmer, Esq., of Avon, N. Y.,—a resident of the Genesee valley at the period referred to. The valley was then thickly peopled by the Senecas.

and their demeanor was at once subdued into comparative docility.*

But farther embarrassments arose on the next day, in
consequence of the jealousies that had been infused into
the minds of the Indians, against the Cornplanter. His
frequent interviews with Colonel Pickering had been
marked, and were followed by feelings of distrust. Little
Billy took it upon himself to rebuke the warrior sharply,
telling him that he was taking too much upon himself—
that he seemed to forget that he was but a war-chief,
and was transcending the bounds of his proper department, by partaking so largely in the conduct of civil
affairs. Cornplanter replied that he had exerted himself
many years for the good of the nation, but that if they
were displeased with him, or had no farther need of his
services, he would return home. And such was his intention. He did not appear in council on that day; but
after it was opened, Colonel Pickering interposed in his
behalf, and in regard to the private interviews between
the Cornplanter and himself, assumed all the blame:
Cornplanter had not visited him, except when specially
sent for. This explanation pacified the murmurers for
the moment, but their suspicions were re-awakened
within a few days thereafter;—parties were formed
against the warrior; and in a council of the chiefs privately by themselves, which was continued until near midnight, his position became exceedingly critical. It is
necessary to note the difficulties by which the Corn-

* Letter from George Hosmer, Esq. Also conversations of the author with
Thomas Morris.

17

planter was here environed, because of their connexion with an event occurring at a subsequent period in the life of Red-Jacket.

The council having already been continued many days, while yet the main business of the commissioner had scarcely been touched, Colonel Pickering determined, on the 28th of October, to bring the whole subject-matter with which he was charged, directly before the chiefs, and to an issue. The council numbered more chiefs and warriors, on that day, than had met the commissioner on any former occasion. In the opening of a very long speech, the Colonel reminded them that, notwithstanding they had been there so many days, the chiefs had only called his attention to two rusty spots in the chain of friendship. One of these he had already brightened; but the rust of the other was thought by their chief warrior to be so very deep that it could not be rubbed off. This related to the great and always vexatious question of boundaries. Upon this subject the commissioner took an extended review of all the negotiations that had taken place between the whites and themselves, during the administration of their affairs by Sir William Johnson, and since that period, proving to them by successive treaties, and by maps, the justice of the claims of the United States, and the unreasonableness of their own complaints; insisting upon all the cessions of territory that had been made,—and recapitulating the provisions of the treaty of Fort Stanwix, which had been confirmed by the Six Nations themselves at the treaty of Muskingum. Nevertheless the commissioner now offered to stipulate that the

Indians should still enjoy the privilege of hunting upon all the lands they had ceded, and that their settlements thereon should remain undisturbed. He added also that their annuity from the United States should be increased from fifteen hundred to four thousand five hundred dollars,—to say nothing of ten thousand dollars worth of presents he had with him for distribution, on a favorable issue of the council. In consequence of these liberal propositions, the commissioner hoped the Indians would cheerfully comply, and join him in digging a deep pit wherein to bury all former differences, and take hold of the chain of friendship so fast that nothing should ever again force it out of their hands.

The Indians agreed to consider the proposals, and several successive days were spent by them in private deliberations. Red-Jacket had previously informed the Quaker deputation why the Indians had invited them to attend upon this council. Believing the Quakers to be an honest people, and friends to them, they desired their presence that they might see that the Indians were not deceived or imposed upon. On the 31st of October, while yet deliberating upon the propositions of Colonel Pickering in private, a deputation of the chiefs, consisting of Red-Jacket, Clear-Sky, Sagareesa,* and a chief of the Cayugas, waited upon the Quaker deputies, for the purpose of holding a confidential conversation. The white people, and others having no business there, having been excluded, Red-Jacket spoke nearly as follows :—

* A venerable christian chief of the Tuscaroras, yet living, in 1841.

" BROTHERS :—You see here four of us of the Six Nations, who are assembled at this place, in the will of the Great Spirit, to transact the business of the treaty. You have been waiting here a long time, and often visited by our chiefs, and as yet no marks of respect have been shown to you.

" BROTHERS :—We are deputed by the council of chiefs assembled, to come and see you. We understand that you told Sagareesa that you should not have come but at our request, and that you stood ready to afford us any assistance within your power.

" BROTHERS :—We hope you will make your minds easy. We who are now here are but children; the ancients being deceased. We know that your fathers and ours transacted business together, and that you look up to the Great Spirit for his direction and assistance, and take no part in war. We suppose you were all born on this island, and consider you as brethren. Your ancestors came over the great water, and ours were born here. This ought to be no impediment to our considering each other as brethren.

" BROTHERS:—You all know the proposals that have been made by Con-neh-sauty,* as well as the offers made by us to him. We are all now in the presence of the Great Spirit, and we place more confidence in you than in any other people. As you expressed your desire for peace, we now desire your help and assistance. We hope you will not deceive us, for if you should do so, we shall no more place any confidence in mankind.

" BROTHERS :—We wish if you know the will of Congress, or the extent of the commissioner's powers, that you would candidly inform us.

" BROTHERS :—We desire that what we are now about communicating may be kept secret. We are willing to give up the four mile path from Johnson's landing place to the Cayuga Creek, agreeably to our compact with Sir William Johnson

---

* Colonel Pickering.

long ago. The other part proposed by Con-neh-sauty to be relinquished by us, that is from Cayuga to Buffalo Creek, we
wish to reserve on account of the fisheries, that our women
and children may have the use of them. We desire to know
if you can inform us why the triangle on Lake Erie cannot be
given up.

"BROTHERS:—Cornplanter and Captain Brant, who were
only war chiefs, were the persons who attended the treaty at
Fort Stanwix,* and they were to have sent forward the proposals for our more general consideration. At that time Old
Smoke was alive, who was a man of great understanding.
But they were threatened into a compliance, in consequence of
which Captain Brant went off to Canada, desiring Cornplanter
to do the best he could."

The Quaker deputies replied to the committee of the
chiefs on the next day, but the purport of their answer
was not preserved in William Savary's journal, although
he delivered their opinion. Red-Jacket thanked them
for their advice, which he said " would afford them considerable strength." The chiefs having determined
upon their answer, the commissioner met them in grand
council on Sunday, the 2d of November. The business
was opened by Clear-Sky, who apologized for the delay,
which he said had been required by the importance of
the subject they had been considering, and the necessity
of preserving unanimity among themselves. Red-Jacket,
being the principal speaker, then rose and said, first addressing the chiefs:—

* Red-Jacket must have referred in this passage to the second treaty of Fort
Stanwix, viz.: that of Gov. George Clinton, held in 1789. Brant was not at the
treaty of 1784, held at that place, and Red-Jacket himself was. Brant attended
the treaty of 1789.

"BROTHERS :—We request that all the nations present will attend to what we are about to deliver. We are now convened on one of the days of the Great Spirit."

Then addressing Colonel Pickering, he proceeded :—

"BROTHER :—You now represent the President of the United States, and when you spoke to us, we considered it as the voice of the fifteen fires. You desired that we would take the matter under our deliberate consideration, and consult each other well, that when the chain was rusty it might be brightened. We took General Washington by the hand, and desired this council-fire, that all the lines of dispute might be settled.

"BROTHER :—We told you before of the two rusty places on the chain, which were also pointed out by the sachems. Instead of complying with our request respecting the places where we told you the chain was rusty, you offered to relinquish the land on Lake Erie, eastward of the triangular piece sold by Congress to Pennsylvania, and to retain the four mile path between Cayuga and Buffalo Creek, by which you expect to brighten the chain.

"BROTHER :—We thought you had a sharp file to take off the rust, but we believe it must have been dull, or else you let it slip out of your hands. With respect to the four mile path, we are in want of it on account of the fisheries. Although we are but children, we are sharp-sighted, and we see that you want that strip of land for a road, that when you have vessels on the lakes you may have harbors. But we wish that in respect to that land, the treaty of Fort Stanwix may not be broken. You white people have increased very fast on this island, which was given to us Indians by the Great Spirit. We are now become a small people. You are cutting off our lands piece after piece. You are a kind-hearted people,—seeking your own advantages.

"BROTHER :—We are tender-hearted, and desirous of peace. You told us what you would give for our land, to brighten your end of the chain. If you will relinquish the piece of land we have mentioned, our friendship will be strong. You say you are not proud. Neither are we. Congress expects we are now settling the business with regularity. We wish that both parties may have something to say in settling peace. At the time we requested a conference, we also requested that our friends, the Quakers, should come forward, as they are promoters of peace, and we wanted them to be witnesses of what took place. We wish to do nothing private. We have told you of the rusty part, which the file passed over without brightening, and we wish you to take up the file again, and rub it very hard. You told us that if it would not do without, you would apply oil.

"BROTHER :—We the sachems, warriors and others, all depend upon you. Whatever is done we regard as final and permanent. We wish you to take it into consideration, and give us an answer."

There was more of conciliation and concession manifested in this speech than had been anticipated. Colonel Pickering replied in a like amicable tone, urging the reasons why the United States must persist in obtaining the pathway along the lake shore, and between the lakes. As an equivalent for a concession of this on the part of the Indians, the large increase of their annuity had been proposed; and he cheerfully offered to cede back to them all the lands in their former grants, upon which their villages stood, although he said that when he came from Philadelphia it was not expected he would relinquish a single hand-breadth. In conclusion, Colonel Pickering said he was becoming impatient, and he desired a speedy answer.

The proceedings of the day were closed by another

funeral ceremony.   Red-Jacket stated that it was a custom among the Indians, after the decease of one of their
brethren, to return to the donor any present which he
had received in his life time as a mark of respect.   In
conformity with this usage, he now returned to the commissioner a silver gorget, belonging to one of their chiefs
recently dead, which had been presented to him by the
United States.   Farmer's-Brother made a speech of
condolence on the occasion, and presented the customary
strings of black wampum to the family of the deceased.

On the 4th the council-fire was re-opened, and the
Friends, not being present, were sent for, the Indians re-
fusing to proceed unless they were in the assembly.
Red-Jacket then addressed the commissioner :—

"BROTHER :—We the sachems of the Six Nations will now
tell you our minds.   The business of the treaty is to brighten
the chain of friendship between us and the fifteen fires.   We
told you the other day it was but a very small piece that occasioned the rust on the chain.

"BROTHER :—Now we are conversing together to make the
chain bright.   When we told you what would give us satisfaction, you proposed reserving the piece of land between
Cayuga and Buffalo Creek, for building houses,* &c.; but we
apprehend you would not only build houses but towns.   You
told us these houses would be for the accommodation of travellers in the winter, as they cannot go by water in that season,
and that travellers would want a staff to help them along on
the road.   We have taken these matters into serious consideration.

---

* Colonel Pickering had told them in his speech respecting the land for a road—
four miles wide—that the United States also wanted land to build taverns upon,
where the weary traveller might stop to rest.

" BROTHER :—We conclude that we do not understand this
as the white people do.   If we consent to your proposals, we
know it will injure us.   If these houses should be built, they
will tend to scatter us, and make us fall in the street, by drinking to excess, instead of benefitting us.   You want land to
raise provisions, hay, &c.; but as soon as the white people
settle there, they would think the land their's,—for this is the
way of the white people.   You mentioned that when you got
possession of the garrisons,* you would want landing-places,
and fields to plant on.   But we wish to be the sole owners of
these lands ourselves ; and when you settle with the British,
the Great Spirit has made a road for you.   You can pass and
repass by water.   What you want to reserve is entirely in
your own power.

" BROTHER :—You told us, when you left Philadelphia, it
was not expected by the President that you would relinqish a
foot of land.   We thank him for having left you at liberty to
give up what you please.   You have waited with patience at
this council fire, kindled by General Washington.   It is but a
very small thing that keeps the chain from being brightened.
If you will consent to give us this small piece, and have no
houses on it, the chain will be bright.   As to harbors, the waters are between you and the British.   You must talk to
them.   You are of the same color.   I see there are many of
your people now here, watching with their mouth open, to
take up this land.   If you are a friend to us, then disappoint
them.   Our patience is spent.   Comply with our request.
Dismiss, and we will go home."

Colonel Pickering rejoined, and there was considerable farther discussion between the parties.   The Colonel abated somewhat more of his demands, consenting,
on the subject of roads, to reduce his proposition to the

* The posts of Oswego, Niagara, and Detroit, then yet held by England, contrary to the stipulations of the treaty of peace of 1783.

18

liberty of constructing a road from Fort Schlosser to Buffalo Creek. After a consultation among the sachems, Red-Jacket said :—

" We have a right understanding of your request, and have agreed to grant you a road from Fort Schlosser to Buffalo Creek, but not from Buffalo Creek down this way at all."

The difficulties having thus, as it was supposed, all been surmounted by reason of mutual concessions, in a very liberal spirit of compromise on the part of Colonel Pickering, nothing farther remained but to adjust the points, and prepare duplicates of the treaty for signature. The whole day of the 5th was occupied by Colonel Pickering and a few of the leading chiefs upon this business. It was intended that the documents should be executed on the 6th; but on their presentation to the council, fresh difficulties broke out in regard to Presque Isle. Great dissatisfaction was manifested by several of the leading chiefs at the relinquishment of that point of territory. Having ascertained that the Cornplanter and Little Billy had received two thousand dollars worth of goods at Muskingum, and two thousand more at Philadelphia, as the price of Presque Isle, the council was greatly disturbed, and broke up in confusion. No business was transacted on the 7th, the incensed Indians not yet having had time to cool. On the 8th Colonel Pickering canvassed the several articles of the treaty with some of the leading chiefs, and it was arranged that it should be signed on the following day, for which purpose the council assembled. But here, again, most unexpectedly, a new obstacle was interposed from the hitherto fast friend of the United States, the Cornplanter. The moodiness of many of the Indians had been observed when the parchments were unrolled. They held down their heads and manifested their dissatisfaction by silence for half an hour. At length Cornplanter rose and spoke as follows :—

" Brothers :—I request your attention, whilst I inform you of my own mind as an individual. I consider the conduct of the United States, since the war, to have been very bad. I conceive they do not do justice. I will mention what took place at New-York, at one particular time.* After the treaty of Fort Stanwix I went to New-York under an apprehension that the commissioners had not done right; and I laid before Congress our grievances on account of the loss of our lands at that treaty. But the thirteen fires approved of what the commissioners had done, and in confirmation of it, they held up the paper with a piece of silver hanging to it.† Now, Colonel Pickering, you have told us at this treaty that what was given up by the British was only the land around the forts. I am very much dissatisfied that this was not communicated to us before. There has already been too much blood spilt. If this had been known at the close of the war it would have prevented any blood being shed. I have therefore told our warriors not to sign this treaty. The fifteen fires have deceived us ; but we are under the sachems, and will listen to what they do. Though we will not sign it, yet we will abide by what they do as long as they do right. The United States and the Six Nations are now making a firm peace, and we wish the fifteen fires may never deceive them, as they have deceived us warriors. If they once deceive the sachems it will be bad."

* At the time referred to New-York was the seat of government.
† The treaty with England.

He then took his seat, and after a short pause said:—

"I will put a patch upon what I have spoken. I hope you will have no uneasiness at hearing the voice of the warriors. You know it is very hard to be once deceived; so you must not make your minds uneasy."

The Eel, an Onondaga chief, thereupon rose and made a warm speech in reply to the Cornplanter, exhorting the sachems to abide by the decision to which they had arrived. Colonel Pickering followed in an energetic address, insisting that the treaty would be of little effect in securing future tranquillity if signed only by the sachems. The warriors, he contended, must sign it also, or he would have nothing to do with it. Two or three days were spent in endeavoring to soothe the warriors and bring them to terms. These efforts were ultimately successful, and the treaty was finally executed by both sachems and warriors on the 11th of November, 1794. By the terms of the treaty, the United States acknowledged the reservations to the Oneidas, Onondagas and Cayugas, in their treaties with New-York;—the boundaries of the Senecas were established, and their title to all the lands within the same acknowledged by the United States. The Six Nations engaged never to claim any other lands of the United States; the road was allowed from Schlosser to Buffalo Creek; a passage was granted to the United States through their country, together with the use of all their harbors and rivers. Other minor particulars need not be noted.*

* For a letter from Colonel Pickering to Captain Brant, respecting this treaty, and a sensible letter from Brant in reply, see Appendix C.

It has been judged advisable to give an extended account of this council, for several reasons. As has already been said, it was one of the most important negotiations with the Six Nations ever effected by the United States, both as to the magnitude of the council, and the results ; and yet less has been known of its history than of almost any other. The entire proceedings are moreover deemed to be interesting, as affording farther illustrations of the character of the people once forming that extended and daring confederacy, the terror of almost half the continent, but which has now dissolved into a few scattered fragments, each melting rapidly away. There is one feature in the civil polity of that confederacy, which is believed on no other occasion to have been so fully disclosed, or so thoroughly illustrated, as at this treaty,— *the jealousy of the Indians of the military power, and the subordination in which it was held to the civil.* It has been seen that on several occasions the war-chiefs were reminded, with great emphasis, of the superiority in all civil affairs of the *sachems,* or *civil magistrates.* This single fact shows that the untutored Aquanuschioni had made no inconsiderable advances in the science of free government.

Notwithstanding the untoward incidents which occasionally " disturbed the minds" of the Indians, the council broke up, and the parties separated, with the utmost good feeling. The good men forming the Quaker deputation ingratiated themselves into the very hearts of the Indians. Their mission was one of love, nor did they confine their exertions to labors for the temporal benefit of the sons of the forest alone. As ministers of the christian faith, they lost no fitting opportunity of imparting to them a knowledge of the " Unknown God" whom they " ignorantly worshipped." Religious meetings were held by them on the return of every Sabbath, and the fierce chieftains were sometimes melted into tears by their discourses. Nor were the Indians alone the gratified party. The deputies studied their social relations, and were often pleased with what they saw of their manners, their wild sports, and the unrestrained gambols of their children, as may be seen by reference to the valuable journal of William Savary, already referred to.* The different tribes or nations encamped by themselves, and the Senecas, by far the most numerous, occupied several camps, under separate leaders. The following account of Mr. Savary's visit to one of them is graphic and picturesque:—

" *Fifth Day, Oct.* 30. After dinner, John Parish and myself rode to view the Farmer's-Brother's encampment, which contained about five hundred Indians. They are located by the side of a brook, in the woods ; having built about seventy or eighty huts, by far the most commodious and ingeniously made of any that I have seen. The principal materials are bark, and boughs of trees, so nicely put together as to keep the family dry and warm. The women as well as the men appeared to be mostly employed. In this camp there are a large number of pretty children, who, in all the activity and buoyancy of health, were diverting themselves according to their fancy. The vast number of deer they have killed, since coming here, which they cut up, and hang round their huts

* See Friends' Library, vol. i. pp. 332–370.

inside and out, to dry, together with the rations of beef which
they draw daily, give the appearance of plenty to supply the
few wants to which they are subjected.*   The ease and cheer-
fulness of every countenance, and the delightfulness of the
afternoon, which these inhabitants of the woods seemed to enjoy with a relish far superior to those who are pent up in
crowded and populous cities, all combined to make this the
most pleasant visit I have yet made to the Indians; and induced me to believe that before they became acquainted with
white people, and were infected with their vices, they must
have been as happy a people as any in the world.   In returning to our quarters we passed by the Indian council, where
Red-Jacket was displaying his oratory to his brother chiefs,
on the subject of Colonel Pickering's proposals."   On another
page Mr. Savary says of the orator :—" Red-Jacket visited us
with his wife and five children, whom he had brought to see
us.   They were exceedingly well clad, in their manner, and
the best behaved and prettiest Indian children I have ever met
with."

* On another page of his journal, Mr. Savary says they sometimes killed more
than one hundred deers in a day—at Canandaigua, in 1794 !

CHAPTER VI.

NOTWITHSTANDING the difficulties encountered by the commissioner during the protracted negotiation at Canandaigua, and the apparent reluctance of the Indians to accede to the terms demanded, the arrangements stipulated in the treaty gave, on the whole, pretty general satisfaction to both parties,—not less to the Indians themselves than to the United States. "This settlement," said one of the chiefs to Colonel Pickering, "appears like a great light to us." "And to me," said Colonel Pickering, in a letter to Thayendanegea, " it seems like a new era."* The complaints, for the consideration of which the council was called, were removed ; and so many of the individual chiefs expressed their satisfaction with the treaty, in strong terms, that, farther heart-burnings and reproaches for past transactions were not anticipated. The treaty of Green-

* Appendix C.

ville, concluded by General Wayne in the following year, crowned the work of Indian pacification. Henceforward, therefore, fewer occasions arose requiring the national action of the Iroquois confederacy, of whom Red-Jacket had now become the leading sachem, as he had long been the most popular orator. But although the relations of the Six Nations were thus disentangled from those of the United States, yet their own peculiar government remained to be administered; and what with the direction of their own internal concerns, and the holding of occasional councils or treaties, connected with subsequent sales of portions of their remaining lands, there was still business enough to keep the chiefs from leading lives of unusual idleness. Nevertheless the name of Red-Jacket appears on one occasion only, during the three years immediately succeeding the treaty of Canandaigua.

General Israel Chapin, long the Superintendent of Indian Affairs for the northern department, died early in the spring of 1795. He had acquired the entire confidence of the Six Nations, and shared largely of their affection. In consequence of his decease, a council was held at Canandaigua, in honor of his memory, on the 28th of April of that year. Among the chiefs in attendance were the Farmer's-Brother, Red-Jacket, Clear-Sky, and others, representing the several nations, excepting the Mohawks. The following speech of condolence was delivered by Red-Jacket to the son of the deceased, Israel Chapin, Jr., who had served in the capacity of deputy to his father for several years:—

"BROTHER: I wish you to pay attention to what I have to say. You will recollect you forwarded a manuscript to us, informing us of the loss of our good friend. The loss is great to us as well as to you. Yet you will hear what we have to say, and I wish you to pay attention.

"BROTHER: We consider that we have met with a great loss,—we of the Six Nations, as well as the United States,—a person to whom we looked as a father, and a person appointed to stand between the Six Nations and the United States. It gives our minds a great deal of uneasiness to think we have lost so valuable a friend, who has taken so much pains to brighten the chain of friendship between the Six Nations and the United States. We fear that agreeable friendship will be broken up. Let us prevent its failing if we can.

BROTHER: In conformity to the good old ancient customs of our forefathers, we now level the grave of our friend. We gather leaves and weeds, and strew them over the grave, and endeavor to banish grief from our minds as much as we can. [*Fourteen strings of black and white wampum.*]

"BROTHERS: You of the Fifteen Fires: Listen again to the voice of the Six Nations: The man whom you appointed for us to communicate our minds to has left us, and gone to another world. We are now at a loss whom to open our minds to, should there be any thing to communicate from one to another. We used to reveal it to him.

"BROTHERS: You of the Fifteen Fires: We think that you feel this great loss as well as we. While he had the conducting of business, it appeared as though the United States sat close by our sides. If we had any thing to communicate, he took it with care to the Great Council Fire. Now as we have lost our guide, it troubles our minds to find out how to keep up the friendship that we have had heretofore.

"BROTHERS of the Fifteen Fires: You will allow us to speak our sentiments. When you have before appointed a person to guide us in our business, you have chosen one to give satisfaction to us, as we believe he did to you. Sometimes there was more than he could attend to. He then sent forward his son to act in his behalf. We are well acquainted with this young man, as we have frequently transacted business with him, and we find his mind to be good.

BROTHERS : He being well acquainted with our business, and all the papers and belts of wampum being in his hands, we cannot conceive of any other person so suitable to fill his father's seat. His appointment would give us satisfaction. We ask you to grant us the privilege of this our request.

" BROTHERS : This is the second petition of the kind that we have made. But our petition before was not taken into consideration. We hope now you will notice it. We think the son will walk in the steps of his father."

This speech having been transmitted to the seat of government, General Washington, who was yet President, immediately complied with the request, and Captain Israel Chapin was appointed to the agency made vacant by the death of his father.*

The next transaction which brought Red-Jacket conspicuously before the public, was the treaty of " Big Tree,"† held in the year 1797. The purchase from Massachusetts of the pre-emptive right to the territory of New-York lying beyond the Genesee river, by Robert Morris, of Philadelphia, has been incidentally mentioned in a preceding chapter. Massachusetts had contracted to sell this said right of pre-emption to Samuel Ogden, his heirs and assigns, by an agreement

---

* To John Gregg, Esq., of Canandaigua, who married the daughter of the younger Chapin, I have been indebted for several parcels of letters and manuscripts which have been of important service in the present work.

† The site of the present beautiful town of Geneseo.

bearing date March 12, 1791, and on the 11th of May following, Ogden assigned his interest in that agreement to Morris. The title to Morris was confirmed on the same day by the commonwealth. The tract embraced in the purchase contained about four millions of acres of land, and the consideration paid by Morris was one hundred thousand pounds Massachusetts currency. In the year 1792 Robert Morris sold the greater part of this purchase to a company of gentlemen in Holland, since known as the Holland Land Company.

By the terms of his sale Mr. Morris had stipulated to extinguish the Indian title, and survey the whole tract at his own expense,—the company retaining thirty-seven thousand four hundred pounds sterling until the fulfilment of this part of the contract. It was therefore an object for Mr. Morris to procure an extinguishment of the Indian title without unnecessary delay. But it was not until the summer of 1797 that the Senecas, to whom the territory belonged, could be persuaded to negotiate upon the subject. The council was appointed for the 25th of August, about the middle of which month the Indians began to assemble in great numbers,—not the Senecas exclusively, but numerous groups from the other tribes came in to be fed from the stores of the commissioners.* The agents of Mr. Morris were the late Colonel Williamson, (agent of the estate of Sir William Pultney,) and his son, Thomas Morris. The avocations

---

* So greatly hungered were the Indians when they came in, that they were ravenous for food. Several of the oxen first killed for them were devoured raw, reeking in the blood.

of Colonel Williamson not permitting him to attend the
council, the entire duty devolved upon Mr. Thomas
Morris. This was not a negotiation to which the United
States were directly a party; but the humane policy of
the government has always prompted it to appoint commissioners to attend all councils of the Six Nations held
for the sale of their lands, subsequent to the great treaty
of Canandaigua, of 1794. Massachusetts, likewise, had
reserved the right of sending an agent to such councils,
to watch over the interests of the Indians. Accordingly,
at the treaty of Big Tree, Colonel Jeremiah Wadsworth,
of Connecticut, appeared as the commissioner on the
part of the United States, and General Shepherd in behalf of the Commonwealth of Massachusetts. The agent
on the part of the Holland Company was the late William Bayard, of New-York.

The council having been duly opened, the commissioners from the United States and Massachusetts presented their credentials, and addressed the assembly,
declaring the object of their appointment, and assuring
the Indians of their desire to guard their interests, and
see that no injustice was done them. Mr. Morris then
formally opened the business for the consideration of
which the council had been convened, explaining to
them the desire of his father to purchase their lands, or
such a portion of them as they might be willing to sell.
He endeavored to persuade them that an annual income,
derived from the avails of such portions of their territory
as were not required for their actual occupation, would
be better for them than the retaining of a large tract of

country from which they could derive no benefit, save
from their use as hunting-grounds; and as such he assured them that they would be as open to them after the
sale, should they make it, as before. In conclusion, he
offered them the sum of one hundred thousand dollars
for the entire tract, allowing them to retain such reservations as might be required for their actual occupation.
But should they insist upon reservations of unnecessary
size, some deduction from the amount of purchase-
money offered must be made. The proposition having
been submitted, the open council was adjourned, and the
Indians occupied several days in private deliberation.
When at length they were ready to make answer, the
commissioners were notified and the council re-assembled. To Farmer's-Brother, a chief justly enjoying
their confidence for his integrity, was confided the duty
of replying to the propositions. His speech was not
characteristic of the man, for it was not decided in its
tone. He started various objections to selling their
lands, and yet not absolutely declining to do so. To
these objections Mr. Morris replied at considerable
length; whereupon there was a farther adjournment, that
the Indians might have yet another opportunity for private consultation.

On the re-opening of the council, Red-Jacket rose as
the organ to make known the determination of his people. He said they were not yet convinced that it was
their duty to dispose of their lands at any price. Mr.
Morris had said, when speaking of the little value of
their lands while remaining in a wild and unproductive

state, that the only value they had to them while in that condition, arose from the consciousness they felt that they owned them. The truth of this remark was admitted by Red-Jacket, but, said he,—

"That knowledge is every thing to us. It raises us in our own estimation. It creates in our bosoms a proud feeling which elevates us as a nation. Observe the difference between the estimation in which a Seneca and an Oneida are held. We are courted, while the Oneidas are considered a degraded people, fit only to make brooms and baskets. Why this difforence ? It is because the Senecas are known as the proprietors of a broad domain, while the Oneidas are cooped up in a narrow space."

In his rejoinder Mr. Morris attempted to take the conceit out of the Seneca orator, by assuring him that the consequence of his nation was much less than he supposed;—in proof of which assertion he reminded him of the little consideration awarded to a deputation of their chiefs, during their pacific mission to the hostile Indians at the Miamis a few years before. Notwithstanding the extent of their territory, they were treated with so much neglect and indifference that the chiefs returned from the mission deeply mortified. Red-Jacket replied that the statement of Mr. Morris was true ; but, he continued, the reason why they had been thus treated was to be found in the fact that they were in bad company ! They had made that journey to the west with the commissioners of the United States. Had they gone alone, their chiefs would have been treated as Senecas should be treated throughout the world.*

* The reference here is to the mission of Colonel Pickering, Beverly Randolph

A fortnight having been spent in this way, and little
progress made, the commissioners and Mr. Bayard became impatient,—urging Mr. Morris to assume a more
peremptory manner, and bring the Indians to an immediate decision, one way or the other. It was in vain
that Mr. Morris, who understood the Indian character
far better than they, assured them that the course they
were proposing would of all others be most likely to defeat their object. The commissioners insisted upon decisive steps, and Mr. Morris most reluctantly consented.
In answer, therefore, to a proposition from the Indians
that was totally inadmissible, Mr. Morris told them that
such a proposal required no time for consideration. He
refused it at once,—adding, that unless the Indians were
prepared to make some more reasonable offer, it was of
no use to keep the council-fire burning any longer.
They might better rake it up, and terminate all farther
discussion. Upon this remark Red-Jacket sprang upon
his feet and exclaimed :—

"You have now arrived at the point to which I wished to
bring you. You told us in your first address that even in the
event of our not agreeing to sell our lands, we would part
friends. Here, then, is my hand. I now cover up the council-fire."

This decision of the chiefs was received with great
apparent satisfaction by their people. They indulged in

and General Lincoln, to the hostile Indians at the west, in 1793. These commissioners were accompanied by a deputation of Seneca chiefs, but as Red-Jacket
was not of their number, an account of that mission has not been given in the
text. Its full history may be found in the second volume of the Life of Brant.

violent abuse of the commissioners, and of Mr. Morris in particular, and made the surrounding forests ring with their savage yells. Indeed, a person unaccustomed to their character and manners would have trembled for his scalp. Deep was the mortification of the commissioners, of Mr. Bayard especially, at this unexpected issue of the experiment. He had been the most importunate in urging the trial upon Mr. Morris, and his principals, the Holland Land Company, were the most deeply interested in the result. From the prompt and decided manner in which the negotiation had been broken off, moreover, he had little expectation that any thing more favorable was at that time to be anticipated. Yet he urged Mr. Morris very strenuously to make another effort, and if possible to rekindle the fire. To these solicitations that gentleman assented, upon condition that he should be allowed to take his own course with the Indians, without interference on the part either of the agent or commissioners.

On the succeeding day Farmer's-Brother called upon Mr. Morris, and expressed the hope that the failure of the treaty might not cool his friendship for them. Certainly not, replied Mr. Morris, adding that they had a perfect right to refuse selling their lands. Still, he continued, he was dissatisfied with the manner in which the council had been broken up, and with the treatment he had received at the hands of their warriors immediately after the fire had been raked up. Such treatment he had not deserved at their hands. He had been kind to them ever since their acquaintance had begun. His house

20

had always been open when they came to visit him,
and had been well supplied with food and liquor, of
which they had partaken whenever they came; and at
the present treaty all their wants had been supplied.
All this Farmer's-Brother admitted to be true. He regretted that the feelings of Mr. Morris had been wounded
by the violent and indecorous speeches of a few of their
drunken young men, and lamented that the council-fire
had been so suddenly put out, inasmuch as it prevented
another meeting of the council, in which their difficulties
might have been explained and smoothed over. Mr.
Morris in his reply farther remarked that the declaration
of Red-Jacket, extinguishing the fire, was another act
of injustice toward him, though perhaps not so intended.
By that procedure Red-Jacket had usurped a power which
he did not possess, and had departed from an established
custom of the Indians, by which he who lighted a council-fire alone had a right to put it out. This council-
fire had been lit up by him, and he only could put it out.
As he had not done so, the fire was yet burning. To all
this Farmer's-Brother assented, assuring Mr. Morris that
he was glad it was so, as they could meet yet in council and smooth the difficulties over. It need not be added that Mr. Morris assented to this suggestion.

Several days intervened before this meeting could be
convened. Meantime Mr. Morris caused all the chief
women of the nation to be assembled, whom he addressed upon the subject of his mission. He stated to
them the offer he had made to the sachems, and dis-
coursed eloquently of the advantages which would ac-

crue to themselves and their families by the annuity
which would be coming to them, and the comforts they
would be able to procure during the absence of their
warriors,—who often flocked to the white settlements to
sell their skins, where they were comfortably fed while
their families were starving. He then distributed
among the women a liberal present of beads, silver-
brooches, clothes, and a variety of other fancy articles, for
which their people have a great fondness, and which were
received with delight. These articles, Mr. Morris informed them, were intended for distribution only after
the conclusion of a successful treaty. Still, as the women had had no agency in breaking off the negotiation,
he thought they ought not to suffer for the misconduct of
their sachems, and he had consequently determined that
they should have the presents he had intended for them.

It is one of the peculiar features of Indian polity that
their lands belong to the warriors who defend, and the
women who till them, and who, moreover, are the
mothers of the warriors. And although the sachems, as
civil magistrates, have ordinarily the power of negotia-
ting treaties, yet whenever the question of a sale of land
is the subject of a negotiation, if both the warriors and
women become dissatisfied with the course the sachems
are pursuing, they have the right to interpose and take
the subject out of their hands. The politic course adopted
toward the women by Mr. Morris worked like a charm.
In a few days after his meeting with them, as just stated,
he was informed that as the council-fire was yet burning, the negotiation would be resumed, not by the sa-

chems, out of whose hands the business had been taken, but by the women and warriors, who had thrown themselves upon their "reserved rights," and were prepared to "nullify" what the sachems had done.

On a subsequent day the council was re-opened, and the Cornplanter, being the principal war-chief, opened the proceedings. He said the women and warriors had seen with regret the misconduct of their sachems, and he also censured the conduct of Mr. Morris as having been too hasty. Still, he proposed that the negotiation should be renewed, and he hoped it would be conducted with better temper on both sides. Mr. Morris made a few soothing remarks, taking upon himself a share of the blame, and Farmer's-Brother, on the part of the sachems, stated that these proceedings of the women and warriors were in perfect accordance with their customs. The negotiation was thereupon resumed, and was prosecuted to a successful issue without farther procrastination. The terms were as at first proposed,— one hundred thousand dollars for the tract, with such reservations as the parties might be able to agree upon.

From the moment the women and warriors took the negotiation upon themselves, and Cornplanter became the important speaker, Red-Jacket withdrew,—no longer attending the council, but remaining drunk until the proceedings were ended. Yet although the main question of this treaty had been decided, difficulties fresh and formidable arose in the adjustment of the reservations for the different clans. The consequence of a chief depends much upon the number of warriors under his own

immediate command. Hence the different clans, with
their chiefs, were anxious to procure as large reservations
as they could for themselves, and at the same time were
willing to see the territories of the others reduced to
comparatively narrow limits. The chief having the
broadest domains would naturally have the largest collection of his people around him. His own importance
would be consequently increased, while the heads of the
weaker communities would be proportionately dimin-
ished. These jealousies of aggrandizement were the
source of so much difficulty that the adjustment of the
reservations could not be accomplished in full council,
and in the end was only effected by a sub-council, composed of a small number of chiefs selected from the
several clans. Another difficulty was encountered in
designating the boundaries of the reservations. The
Indians insisted upon natural boundaries, such as the
rivers, hills and the courses of streams. But as boundaries like these, with which they were familiar, gave them
all the advantages, Mr. Morris would not listen to the
proposition,—insisting upon the allotment to each clan
of such number of square miles as might be agreed upon,
designating the same upon a map to the view of the
chiefs. In only one instance did Mr. Morris depart
from this determination, and the result taught him what
might have been his fate had he allowed the principle in
other cases. There was a white woman named Mary
Jemison, who occupied a farm upon the Genesee river,
at a place about twenty miles southwest of Big Tree,
for whom the chiefs were desirous of making special

provision. Mary was herself present at the council, and pleaded her own case. She was truly a remarkable woman. When a child, at the breaking out of the French war in 1754, she had been taken prisoner by the Indians in the neighborhood of Fort Du Quesne, with her parents, two brothers, and other inmates of the family. All were murdered except Mary. Her captors were Senecas, and she was brought into the Genesee country. For a season she was discontented with her new situation, and devised various schemes of effecting her escape. These being frustrated, she resigned herself to her fate, and in progress of time became as thoroughly an Indian in all her habits and feelings as Red-Jacket himself. Although she had been religiously instructed in her childhood, she became a pagan, and in a word was thoroughly a squaw in every thing but her complexion. Her life was one of vicissitude and wild adventure. Her first husband was a Delaware chief, with whom she resided for years in the Shawanese country. She afterward married a Seneca chief, with whom she lived until his death at the Gardow flats,—the place which the chiefs now prayed might be reserved for her. Mr. Morris readily assented that a moderate reservation should be made for her, provided the number of acres were defined. But to this she objected, stating that she had various improved places, one of which was a patch of corn, another of potatoes, another of beans, &c. She then named certain boundaries, to which Mr. Morris, in consequence of the impatience of the commissioners, hastily assented, under the impression that the grant would not exceed one hundred and fifty acres. When afterward the survey came to be made, Mary's farm was found to contain thirty thousand acres of land, of an excellent quality!*

There were yet other difficulties to be removed before the negotiation was actually completed. Among these was the arrival at the council of Young King, a descendant of " OLD SMOKE," a notable chief of the Senecas many years before. Old Smoke was the most powerful, as he was deemed the wisest sachem of his time. He was the principal sachem, or civil chief of the nation, and his word was law. When he thought proper to convene a council, it was only for the purpose of announcing his intentions, and none said nay to his behests. His infallibility was never questioned, and although he had been dead many years, his memory was yet held in great reverence. Young King, though literally a young man, and of talents far inferior to Old Smoke, was nevertheless, by inheritance, the chief sachem of the Seneca nation; and the usual deference secured to him by virtue of his office, was greatly augmented by reverence for his descent. As chief sachem, it was necessary to the validity

---

* During the war of the revolution, "The White Woman's" house,—for thus she was designated, became frequently the quarters of Brant and Colonel John Butler when making their inroads upon the frontiers of the colonies. She attended the treaty of the German Flatts, held by General Schuyler in 1775. She would not throw aside her Indian costume, even after the white population had surrounded her residence, but adhered to her Indian habits and customs to the last. She became rich in herds and flocks, as well as in lands. One of her grandsons was educated as a physician. He obtained a commission as surgeon in the navy of the United States, and died a few years ago on the Mediterranean station. Mary died about the year 1825, at a very advanced age.

of the treaty that it should receive his assent and signature.   He was for a time utterly opposed to the sale of
their lands; and both the Cornplanter and Farmer's-
Brother assured Mr. Morris, that without his approbation
the work was all at an end.   Still, by dint of great persuasion, he was ultimately induced to sign the treaty.*

Another obstacle was presented by the instructions of
the President, General Washington, to Colonel Wadsworth, who was directed to withhold his assent from any
treaty that did not provide for the investment of the purchase-money in the stock of the Bank of the United
States, in the name of the President and his successors
in office, in trust for the Seneca nation.   It was found
exceedingly difficult, and in fact impossible, to make the
Indians understand what a bank was, and how it happened that their annual payments should not always be
the same.   They had no conception of the character of
bank dividends, or how they were accumulated.   Their
idea seemed to be that the bank was an extensive place
in Philadelphia, where their money was planted, and
that in some years the crop would be better than in
others.   Frequently, in after years, would they inquire
of Mr. Morris what kind of a crop they were likely to
have in a season like that.   Connected with this subject
of finance, yet another difficulty was experienced from

* Young King died only some five or six years ago. He was engaged with
his warriors in alliance with the forces of the United States, during the war with
England of 1812—1815, and fought bravely. By an act of Congress of 1816, a
pension of two hundred dollars per annum was given him, " as a compensation
for his brave and meritorious services, and as a provision for the wound and disa-
bility which he received in the performance of those services."

their inability to comprehend the amount of the purchase-money. But few of them could count one hundred, while it was necessary to make them comprehend the amount of one hundred thousand dollars. The process by which only this idea could be imparted, was to take a cask, and show them how many dollars it would require to fill it, and then show them how many casks of the same description it would require to contain the whole amount. They were also taught the number of horses it would require to draw the weight.*

It has been remarked that after the negotiation had been resumed by the women and warriors, and Corn-planter took the forum, Red-Jacket absented himself from the council, and remained in a state of intoxication. His object in thus standing aloof from the council was to have the entire responsibility of the treaty thrown upon Cornplanter. In his conversations with the other chiefs he uniformly spoke against any sale of their lands, and he opposed the treaty with great vehemence, eloquence and talent. Yet his opposition was that of a demagogue, and he spoke, to use an expressive metaphor of his own people, with " a forked tongue." In other words his opposition was insincere ; for the fact is no less true than

* The Indians of every tribe are rigidly equitable in the distribution of the avails of all the lands they sell. Every member of a family, even the smallest child, is entitled to, and receives, as much as the highest chief. When the division is made, the father of the family produces as many sticks as there are persons in his household. Blankets are spread upon the ground, and pieces of coin are laid by the side of each parcel of sticks, corresponding with the number, until the whole amount of the money received is fairly divided. At least such was the practice before the chiefs of the Indians learned the art of being bribed from the pale-faces.

disgraceful, that after the negotiation had been completed, he repaired to the lodge of Mr. Morris by night, and
told him that he had in reality no objection to the sale of
their lands, but yet he must seem to oppose the measure, or
he should lose his popularity. That popularity had been
acquired by opposing every land-sale that had been
made, and he must at least *affect* to continue his opposition to the end. It has been seen that the negotiation
was successful. How could it have well been otherwise, under the circumstances, when, to those circumstances, already described, is superadded the fact that
the very leader of the opposition was a traitor to the
cause he pretended to defend? But, as in other popular
communities, the people were the dupes. The arts of
the demagogue blinded their eyes to the sturdy honesty
of Farmer's-Brother, and the at least comparative integrity of the Cornplanter, while their treacherous flat-
terer became their idol. In order to manifest his apparent opposition to the treaty, he refused in council, after
the decision had been made, to sign it; and yet, before
any signature had been made to the document, he arranged with Mr. Morris to have a blank left for the insertion of his name afterward,—desiring that the space
might be high up, among the first, that when General
Washington saw the treaty he might know that Sa-go-
ye-wat-ha was yet a man of consequence among the
chiefs of his people.* It has been related of this extraordinary dissembler, that at the treaty of Canandaigua,

---

* I have derived the facts of this entire history of the treaty of Big Tree, from
the manuscripts of Thomas Morris, and from conversations with him.

during one of his speeches, he observed Colonel Pickering to be writing, as though taking notes of what he was
saying.   He stopped, and drawing himself up, exclaimed with energetic dignity :—" Look up from the
table, brother, and fix your eyes upon my eyes,—*that
you may see that what Sa-go-ye-wat-ha says is the truth, and
no lie!"** Doubtless he would have enacted the part
over again with Thomas Morris, at the Big Tree, had
there been occasion for such a theatrical display.

It was probably about the time of this year that Red-
Jacket made his visit to Hartford, in the state of Connecticut, at the head of a small deputation of the chiefs
of his nation.   In the several land-compromises between
some of the states, Connecticut had acquired the pre-
emptive title to the section of the present state of Ohio,
called New-Connecticut.   This territory was at that
time in the hands of a large association of capitalists
called the Connecticut Land Company, and various negotiations were held for the extinguishment of the Indian
title,—the Six Nations claiming the territory by right of
conquest.   It was in connection with this matter that
Red-Jacket and his associates visited Hartford, where a
council was holden in the state-house.   The documents
connected with this council seem to have been lost; but
tradition preserves a lively remembrance of the visit of
the Indians, and of a great speech delivered by Red-
Jacket.   An eminent member of the Connecticut bar,
afterward distinguished in the national councils of the
United States,† himself a member of the land company,

* O'Reilly's History of Rochester.
† Gideon Granger, Post Master General during the administrations of Presidents

was wont in after years to speak with great enthusiasm of the appearance of Red-Jacket on that occasion, and of the speech which he delivered. "With a step measured, firm and dignified," as he was used to relate,— "a countenance erect, bold and discursive, he entered the vast assemblage without manifesting surprise, fear or curiosity." Of the speech he then delivered, the following passage was preserved in the memory of Mr. Granger :—

"We stand a small island in the bosom of the great waters. We are encircled,—we are encompassed. The evil spirit rides upon the blast, and the waters are disturbed. They rise, they press upon us, and the waves once settled over us, we disappear forever. Who then lives to mourn us ? None. What marks our extermination ? Nothing. We are mingled with the common elements."*

The history of this mission of the orator is necessarily very imperfect. Brant, who took an active interest in the negotiations respecting the Sandusky country, was highly displeased with the course of Red-Jacket at Hartford, and spoke of it with bitterness in a letter to the Duke of Northumberland. Among other things he states that Red-Jacket vowed fidelity to the United States, and sealed his promise by kissing the likeness of General Washington.

Jefferson and Madison, and afterward in the senate of New-York. He died at Canandaigua in 1822, aged 55 years.

* MS. collections of J. W. Moulton. [The author has inquired diligently at Hartford for the records of this council, but without success.]

CHAPTER VII.

A MORE interesting incident, and of yet higher importance as connected with the life, conduct, and subsequent destiny of Red-Jacket, is now approached in chronological order. The unpopularity of the brave old Cornplanter, for the part he had taken at several treaties for the preservation of peace with the United States, even at the expense of parting with large districts of the Indian territory, has repeatedly been spoken of in the progress of the present memoir. That unpopularity was increased by each successive sale, until the chief discovered the unwelcome truth that he had lost almost the entire confidence of his people. Nor is it unlikely that the crafty orator of the "forked tongue" was actively concerned in fomenting the jealousies which lost him the popular favor. Indeed such is believed to have been the fact, which Cornplanter himself was too sagacious not to understand. At all events, in order, as is supposed, to recover his former influence, the warrior,

knowing the credulity of his people, availed himself of
that characteristic, and concerted a plot by which he designed to compass the destruction of his enemies, Red-
Jacket in particular.   It was by playing upon the popular
credulity that Red-Jacket had arrived at the dignity of
a sachem ; and the war-chief may possibly have reasoned that as a victim of intrigue, injustice and ingratitude, he had a right to avail himself of the same means,
for his own restoration to public favor, if not to compass
the overthrow of his rival.   Having determined upon
his course, "he persuaded his brother to announce himself as a prophet, or messenger from heaven, sent to re-
deem the fallen fortunes of his race.   The superstition
of the savages cherished the impostor ; and he acquired
such an ascendancy as to prevail upon the Onondagas,
formerly the most drunken and profligate of the Six Nations, to abstain entirely from spirituous liquors, and to
observe the laws of morality in other respects.   He obtained the same ascendancy among the confederates,
that another impostor, the brother of the celebrated Tecumseh, subsequently acquired among the Shawanese
and other western Indians ; and, like him, he also employed his influence for evil as well as for good purposes.   The Indians universally believe in witchcraft ;
Cornplanter's brother, in his character of prophet, inculcated this superstition, and proceeded, through the in-
strumentality of conjurors selected by himself, to designate the offending familiars of Satan, who were accordingly sentenced to death.   And the unhappy objects
would have been actually executed, if the magistrates of

Oneida, and the officers of the garrison of Niagara, had not interfered. The prosecutions of Cornplanter had proceeded so far that it began to be considered an artful expedient to render his enemies the objects of general abhorrence, if not the victims of an ignominious death. Emboldened by his success, the prophet proceeded finally to execute the views of his brother, and Red-Jacket was publicly denounced at a great council held at Buffalo Creek, and was put upon his trial. At this crisis he well knew that the future course of his life depended upon the powers of his mind. He spoke in his defence nearly three hours. The iron brow of superstition relented under the magic of his eloquence; he declared the prophet an impostor and a cheat; he prevailed; the Indians divided, and a small majority appeared in his favor." "Perhaps," it is added by the distinguished writer who has furnished the account of this great and singular trial,* "Perhaps the annals of history cannot furnish a more conspicuous instance of the triumph and power of oratory in a barbarous nation devoted to superstition, and looking up to the accuser as a delegated minister of the Almighty." And yet it will appear in the sequel that the same orator who triumphed thus over the believers in witchcraft, was a believer himself, or an affected believer, in the same superstition, and caused the execution of at least one victim, as a sacrifice to the delusion.

Red-Jacket's success in this case inflicted a blow upon the influence of Cornplanter, from the effects of

* Clinton's Discourse before the New-York Historical Society.

which he never entirely recovered, although he lived
for more than a third of a century afterward. These
latter years of his extended life were chiefly passed at
his own village, on the margin of the Alleghany river, a
short distance without the confines of the state of New-
York, and within those of Pennsylvania. He retained
his friendship for the people of the United States with
unswerving fidelity; and espousing the Christian religion,
he labored zealously thenceforward to bring the Alleghany clan of the Senecas, among whom he resided, into
a state of civilization.*   He visited Washington in the
winter of 1801,—1802, for the purpose of conferring with
President Jefferson upon this and other subjects connected with the improvement of his people, and was in correspondence with Mr. Jefferson in relation to it, during
the year following. His efforts were particularly directed against the use of ardent spirits, the thirst for
which has ever been the bane of the Indians, and a
beautiful autograph letter from Mr. Jefferson to the chief
is yet extant.†   Pennsylvania had given him a reservation
of nine hundred acres of choice land, upon which he be-

* The name of Cornplanter's brother, the Prophet, was Ga-nio-di-euh. He
began his labors in the cause of temperance in the Alleghany canton. He removed thence to the Tonnewanda reservation, and thence to Onondaga. After
Red-Jacket became thoroughly pagan in his policy, Ga-nio-di-euh, who was never
a Christian, attached himself to the party of the orator against his brother. Cornplanter, at one time, became a religious zealot, and was in a state of excitement
bordering upon hallucination. During that season he too was favored with
visions and revelations.—*Statement of a chief of the Alleghany clan, to the
Author.*

† In the author's possession, vide sketch of Cornplanter, toward the close of
the volume.

came an agriculturist to a considerable extent, and resided thereon till the day of his death.*

A succession of outrages upon the Indians residing along the Pennsylvania border, resulting at different times in the murder of several of their people, induced the Senecas and Tuscaroras in February, 1801, to send a deputation of chiefs to the seat of the federal government, which since the last Seneca embassage had been transferred from Philadelphia to the city of Washington. Red-Jacket was at the head of this deputation, which was received formally, with an appropriate speech, by the acting Secretary at War, Samuel Dexter, on the 10th of February. On the 11th Red-Jacket replied, setting forth the business of his mission in the following speech:—

"BROTHER:—We yesterday received your speech, which removed all uneasiness from our minds. We then told you that should it please the Great Spirit to permit us to rise in health this day, you should hear what we have come to say.

"BROTHER:—The business on which we are now come, is to restore the friendship that has existed between the United States and the Six Nations, agreeably to the direction of the commissioner from the fifteen fires of the United States. He assured us that whensoever, by any grievances, the chain of friendship should become rusty, we might have it brightened by calling on you. We dispense with the usual formality of having your speech again read, as we fully comprehended it yesterday, and it would therefore be useless to waste time in a repetition of it.

"BROTHER:—Yesterday you wiped the tears from our eyes, that we might see clearly; you unstopped our ears that we

* The Indian name of Cornplanter was *Gy-an-twa-ha*, or "*Handsome Lake.*" He died on the 7th of March, 1836, aged upward of one hundred years.

might hear; and removed the obstructions from our throats
that we might speak distinctly.   You offered to join with us
in tearing up the largest pine tree in our forests, and under it
to bury the tomahawk.   We gladly join with you, brother, in
this work, and let us heap rocks and stones on the root of this
tree, that the tomahawk may never again be found.

"BROTHER :—Your apology for not having wampum is sufficient, and we agree to accept of your speeches on paper, to
evince our sincerity in wishing the tomahawk forever buried.
We accompany a repetition of our assurances with these strings.
[*Strings of wampum.*]

"BROTHER :—We always desire, on similar melancholy
occasions, to go through our customary forms of condolence,
and have been happy to find the officers of the government of
the United States willing in this manner to make our minds
easy.

"BROTHER :—We observe that the men now in office are
new men, and, we fear, not fully informed of all that has befallen us.   In 1791 a treaty was held by the commissioners of
Congress with us at Tioga Point, on a similar occasion.   We
have lost seven of our warriors, murdered in cold blood by
white men, since the conclusion of the war.   We are tired of
this mighty grievance, and wish some general arrangement to
prevent it in future.   The first of these was murdered on the
banks of the Ohio, near Fort Pitt.   Shortly after, two men, belonging to our first families, were murdered at Pine Creek;
then one at Fort Franklin; another at Tioga Point; and now
the two that occasion this visit, on the Big Beaver.   These
last two had families.   The one was a Seneca; the other a
Tuscarora.   Their families are now destitute of support; and
we think that the United States should do something toward
their support, as it is to the United States they owe the loss of
their heads.

"BROTHER :—These offences are always committed in one
place on the frontier of Pennsylvania.   In the Genesee country
we live happy, and no one molests us.   I must therefore beg
that the President will exert all his influence with all officers,

civil and military, in that quarter, to remedy this grievance, and trust that he will thus prevent a repetition of it, and save our blood from being spilled in future. [*A Belt.*]

"BROTHER :—Let me call to mind the treaty between the United States and the Six Nations, concluded at Canandaigua. At that treaty Col. Pickering, who was commissioner on behalf of the United States, agreed that the United States should pay to the Six Nations four thousand five hundred dollars *per annum*, and that this should pass through the hands of the superintendent of the United States, to be appointed for that purpose. This treaty was made in the name of the President of the United States, who was then General Washington; and as he is now no more, perhaps the present President would wish to renew the treaty. But if he should think the old one valid, and is willing to let it remain in force, we are also willing. The sum above mentioned we wish to have part of in money, to expend in more agricultural tools, and in purchasing a team, as we have some horses that will do for the purpose. We also wish to build a saw mill on the Buffalo Creek. If the President, however, thinks proper to have it continue as heretofore, we shall not be very uneasy. Whatever he may do we agree to; we only suggest this for his consideration. [*A Belt.*]

"BROTHER :—I hand you the above mentioned treaty, made by Col. Pickering in the name of Gen. Washington, and the belt that accompanied it; as he is now dead, we know not if it is still valid. If not, we wish it renewed—if it is, we wish it copied on clean parchment. Our money got loose in our trunk and tore it. We also show you the belt which is the path of peace between our Six Nations and the United States. [*Treaty and two Belts.*]

"BROTHER :—A request was forwarded by us from the Onondaga nation to the governor of New-York, that he should appoint a commissioner to hold a treaty with them. They have a reservation surrounded by white men which they wish to sell. The Cayugas, also, have a reservation so surrounded that they have been forced to leave it, and they hope that the President's commissioner, whom they expect he will not hesitate to appoint, will be instructed to attend to this business. We also have some business with New-York, which we would wish him to attend to.

"Brother:—The business that has caused this our long journey was occasioned by some of your bad men: the expense of it has been heavy on us. We beg that as so great a breach has been made on your part, the President will judge it proper that the United States should bear our expenses to and from home, and whilst here.

"Brother:—Three horses belonging to the Tuscarora nation were killed by some men under the command of Major Rivardi, on the plains of Niagara. They have made application to the superintendent and to Major R., but get no redress. You make us pay for our breaches of the peace, why should you not pay also? A white man has told us the horses were killed by Major R.'s orders, who said they should not be permitted to come there, although it was an open common on which they were killed. Mr. Chapin has the papers respecting these horses, which we request you to take into consideration."

Mr. Dexter answered the deputation on the 16th, and in the name of the President, (the elder Adams,) promised a thorough investigation into the circumstances of the murders complained of, a compliance with their wishes touching an exchange of certain lands, and payment for the horses killed at Niagara. The expenses of their mission were also directed to be paid.

In the year following, a white man named John Hewitt was murdered at Buffalo Creek by a drunken Indian, and his surrender demanded by the civil authorities of the state. This demand was resisted by the Indians, and no small degree of excitement among them was the consequence. In their own rude jurisprudence, the fact of drunkenness on the part of the offender, when the deed was perpetrated, could be pleaded in extenuation of the crime; whereas by the laws of the white men, such a plea would be held only as an aggravation of the offence. The Indians, moreover, insisted that they were an independent nation, and as such had a right to the entire jurisdiction of the case. Or if not, as they did not exactly understand the divided and nicely balanced relations existing between the United States and the state governments respectively, they supposed they could appeal to their Great Father the President. Buffalo was at that period within the county of Ontario, Canandaigua being the seat of justice. At length, after several meetings between the Indians and the citizens, in which the latter had vainly attempted to persuade the former to surrender the culprit, a council of the principal chiefs of the Senecas, Cayugas and Onondagas, was convened at Canandaigua, to give the question a more solemn consideration. A conference having been arranged betwen the council and the principal inhabitants, Red-Jacket, arguing against the surrender upon the principles already indicated, delivered the following speech, addressed particularly to the white portion of his audience :—*

"BROTHERS :—Open your ears, and give your attention. This day is appointed by the Great Spirit to meet our friends

* For a copy of this speech the author is indebted to James D. Bemis, Esq., (for thirty years the editor of a newspaper in Canandaigua,) by whom it was first published.

at this place. During the many years that we have lived together in this country, good will and harmony have subsisted among us.

"BROTHERS :—We have now come forward on an unhappy occasion. We cannot find words to express our feelings upon it. One of our people has murdered one of your people. So it has been ordered by the Great Spirit, who controls all events. This has been done : we cannot now help it. At first view it would seem to have the effect of putting an end to our friendship ; but let us reflect, and put our minds together. Can't we point out measures whereby our peace and harmony may still be preserved? We have come forward to this place, where we have always had a superintendent and friend to receive us, and to make known to him such grievances as lay upon our minds ; but now we have none ; and we have no guardian,—no protector,—no one is now authorized to receive us.

"BROTHERS :—We therefore now call upon you to take our speech in writing, and forward our ideas to the President of the United States.

"BROTHERS :—Let us look back to our former situation. While you were under the government of Great Britain, Sir William Johnson was our superintendent, appointed by the king. He had power to settle offences of this kind among all the Indian nations, without adverting to the laws. But under the British government you were uneasy,—you wanted to change it for a better. General Washington went forward as your leader. From his exertions you gained your independence. Immediately afterward a treaty was made between the United States and the Six Nations, whereby a method was pointed out of redressing such an accident as the present. Several such accidents did happen, where we were the sufferers. We now crave the same privilege in making restitution to you, that you adopted toward us in a similar situation.

"BROTHERS :—At the close of our treaty at Philadelphia, General Washington told us that we had formed a chain of friendship which was bright: he hoped it would continue so on our part: that the United States would be equally willing to brighten it, if rusted by any means. A number of murders have been committed on our people—we shall only mention the last of them. About two years ago, a few of our warriors were amusing themselves in the woods, to the westward of Fort Pitt; two white men coolly and deliberately took their rifles, travelled nearly three miles to our encampment, fired upon the Indians, killed two men and wounded two children. We then were the party injured. What did we do? We flew to the treaty, and thereby obtained redress, perfectly satisfactory to us, and we hope agreeable to you. This was done a short time before President Adams went out of office: complete peace and harmony was restored. We now want the same method of redress to be pursued.

"Brothers:—How did the present accident take place? Did our warriors go from home cool and sober, and commit murder on you? No. Our brother was in liquor, and a quarrel ensued, in which the unhappy accident happened. We would not excuse him on account of his being in liquor; but such a thing was far from his intention in his sober moments. We are all extremely grieved 'at it, and are willing to come forward and have it settled, as crimes of the same nature have heretofore been.

"Brothers:—Since this accident has taken place, we have been informed that by the laws of this state, if a murder is committed within it, the murderer must be tried by the laws of the state, and punished with death.

"Brothers:—When were such laws explained to us? Did we ever make a treaty with the state of New-York, and agree to conform to its laws? No. We are independent of the state of New-York. It was the will of the Great Spirit to create us different in color: we have different laws, habits and customs, from the white people. We shall never consent that the government of this state shall try our brother. We appeal to the government of the United States.

"Brothers:—Under the customs and habits of our forefathers we were a happy people; we had laws of our own; they were dear to us. The whites came among us and introduced their customs; they introduced liquor among us, which our forefathers always told us would prove our ruin.

"BROTHERS :—In consequence of the introduction of liquor among us, numbers of our people were killed. A council was held to consider of a remedy, at which it was agreed by us that no private revenge should take place for any such murder—that it was decreed by the Great Spirit, and that a council should be called to consider of redress to the friends of the deceased.

"BROTHERS :—The President of the United States is called a great man, possessing great power. He may do what he pleases,—he may turn men out of office,—men who held their offices long before he held his. If he can do these things, can he not even control the laws of this state? Can he not appoint a commissioner to come forward to our country and settle the present difference, as we, on our part, have heretofore often done to him, upon a similar occasion?

"We now call upon you, BROTHERS, to represent these things to the President, and we trust that he will not refuse our request of sending a commissioner to us, with powers to settle the present difference. The consequence of a refusal may be serious. We are determined that our brother shall not be tried by the laws of the state of New-York. Their laws make no difference between a crime committed in liquor, and one committed coolly and deliberately. Our laws are different, as we have before stated. If tried here, our brother must be hanged. We cannot submit to that;—has a murder been committed upon our people, when was it punished with death?

"BROTHERS :—We have now finished what we had to say on the subject of the murder. We wish to address you upon another, and to have our ideas communicated to the President upon it also.

"BROTHERS :—It was understood at the treaty concluded

by Col. Pickering, that our superintendent should reside in the town of Canandaigua, and for very good reasons : that situation is the most central to the Six Nations; and by subsequent treaties between the state of New-York and the Indians, there are still stronger reasons why he should reside here, principally on account of the annuities being stipulated to be paid to our superintendent at this place. These treaties are sacred. If their superintendent resides elsewhere, the state may object to sending their money to him at a greater distance. We would therefore wish our superintendent to reside here at all events.

" BROTHERS :—With regard to the appointment of our present superintendent, we look upon ourselves as much neglected and injured. When General Chapin and Captain Chapin were appointed, our wishes were consulted upon the occasion, and we most cordially agreed to the appointments. Captain Chapin has been turned out, however, within these few days. We do not understand that any neglect of duty has been alleged against him. We are told it is because he differs from the President in his sentiments on government matters. He has also been perfectly satisfactory to us ; and had we known of the intention, we should most cordially have united in a petition to the President to continue him in office. We feel ourselves injured,—we have nobody to look to,—nobody to listen to our complaints,—none to reconcile any differences among us. We are like a young family without a father.*

" BROTHERS :—We understand that the President has appointed a superintendent who is altogether unknown to us, and who is unacquainted with Indian affairs. We know him not in our country. Had we been consulted upon the subject, we might have named some one residing in this country, who was well known to us. Perhaps we might have agreed upon Mr.

---

* Captain Chapin was removed by President Jefferson, as here stated. Shortly afterward he wrote to his friend Brant, the Mohawk chief, announcing the fact, and received a reply from the latter, which, for the intelligence it evinces, and its philosophy, deserves preservation. See Appendix, D.

23

Oliver Phelps, whose politics, coinciding with those of the President, might have recommended him to the office.

"BROTHERS :—We cannot conclude without again urging you to make known all these our sentiments to the President.

But the eloquent pleadings of the Indians were unavailing. They were compelled to surrender the offender to the inexorable law of the white man, though it was done with great reluctance. His name was *Stiff-armed-George*. He was tried and convicted at the Oyer and Terminer of Ontario county, on the 23d of February, 1803,—Brockholst Livingston, one of the justices of the Supreme Court, presiding; but as the murder was without pre-existing malice, and was moreover attended by various mitigating circumstances, the court, the attorney-general, the grand jury that indicted him, together with many of the people of Canandaigua, united in a petition to the Governor, George Clinton, for his pardon. Judge Livingston, in a letter to the Governor upon the subject, after stating the case, and referring to the interpositions of the people in his behalf, observed :—

"It is not for me to urge considerations of policy in favor of a pardon; if any exist they will occur, and be properly appreciated by those with whom this prerogative resides. It may not, however, be impertinent to mention that the convict is well connected; is much beloved by his countrymen, and that his situation has excited an uncommon interest and solicitude in the sachems and warriors of his nation; several of them attended the trial, and behaved with great decorum. Red-Jacket, one of their sachems, addressed the jury at some length; he dwelt on the hardship of making an unlettered savage amenable to laws, of which, from his habits and want of education, he must ever remain ignorant. He complained of the impunity with which white men had, in various instances, committed murders on the Indians, and particularly of the outrages to which those in the neighborhood of Buffalo Creek were constantly exposed. He also insisted that in this affray our citizens were the aggressors. It is proper to add that Judge Hosmer, Judge Atwater, and the Attorney-General, concur with me in recommending the Indian as a fit object of mercy."*

The subject was presented to the consideration of the legislature by a special message from the Governor, and Stiff-armed-George was not executed.

The next act in the public life of Red-Jacket presents him in the character of a conspirator. Flushed with his victory over Cornplanter, the principal war chief of his own nation, the orator meditated an insidious blow at a higher object, and sought to gratify his hate by crushing the military chieftain of the whole confederacy,—the renowned Thayendanegea himself. Between Brant and Red-Jacket no friendship had existed since the exhibitions of cowardice and treachery by the latter, during Sullivan's invasion of the Indian country, in 1779, as heretofore related. They had frequently met in councils, for the transaction of the business appertaining to their government, and the internal relations of their own people, as also in their negotiations with the United States. But the lion-hearted Mohawk despised him in his heart, and could never meet him with cordiality, taking no pains to conceal his feelings.†

* See Journals of the New-York Legislature for 1803.

† The application to Red-Jacket, by Brant, of the insulting *soubriquet* "THE

Brant, it must be borne in mind, was a resident in Canada, whither he had led his Mohawks after the disastrous termination of the war of the revolution. But the fact of his residence, and that of his own particular nation, within the jurisdiction of another government, did not dissolve the confederacy, or change its unwritten constitution. Brant had indeed offered to receive the whole Six Nations in his newly acquired territory upon Grand River, and many from each of the nations joined him there. Still, a large majority of all the Nations, excepting the Mohawks, preferred remaining in their "old seats," in their own beautiful country of western New-York. But the league was not affected, and Thayendanegea remained the war captain of the whole.

At the time now under consideration, Brant was involved in harassing perplexities with the officers of the British Colonial Government. The Grand River territory had been granted to him as a place of retreat for the Mohawks, by Sir Frederick Haldemand, in the name and under the authority of the crown, in fee simple. But as years elapsed, and the lands in that region were continually rising in value, by reason of the tide of emigration that now began to roll against and around them, the colonial authorities chose not so to understand the

---

Cow-KILLER," has been noted in the second chapter of the present work, together with the reason therefor. The name, moreover, must have obtained some currency. Among the manuscripts of General Chapin are the proceedings of one of the Seneca councils, in which *The Cow-Killer* is three times reported as having spoken at as many different stages of the proceedings. But in each of these places the words *Cow-Killer* were crossed by a stroke of the pen, and " *Red-Jacket*" inserted.

grant. They held that Sir Frederick had only conveyed to the Indians the right of occupancy, and that the right of pre-emption was still vested in the crown. Brant resisted this construction to the utmost of his power, and appeals were carried up to the parent government for justice. The ministers uniformly favored the construction claimed by the Indians, but the colonial authorities as uniformly contrived to circumvent their intentions; so that to this day the Mohawks have been excluded from the full enjoyment of their undoubted right to the soil in question. These disputes, and the exertions of Brant in behalf of his people, involved him in a series of troubles that continued until his death. Having attempted to lease portions of the lands to white settlers, the colonial authorities, and the officers of the British Indian Department, interposed, and caused him much difficulty. Disaffection was also stirred up against him, even among the Mohawks, by designing white men; and a plot for his deposition and degradation from office was matured, and attempted to be carried into execution. In order to this, the Senecas, and others of the Six Nations, were induced to claim a right to interfere in the disposition of the Grand River lands, and also in the domestic relations of the Mohawks,—a right with which the laws and usages of the confederacy did not invest them. Brant was likewise charged with peculation, in the management of the revenues of his people,—a charge which he triumphantly repelled. But no matter: It served the purpose of Brant's white opponents in Canada, who were eager to destroy him, and the arch-demagogue Red-Jacket became a ready instrument in their hands. In furtherance of this design, a council was privately convened at Buffalo Creek, early in the year 1805, under the direction of Red-Jacket himself, and a few other Seneca chiefs in his immediate interest, or subject to his influence. Neither chiefs nor sachems of the Mohawks had knowledge of this council, although a pretended representation of that nation was present, selected merely for the sake of form, from the discontents, and the personal enemies of Brant, who were the lowest of the people. The result of this council, clandestinely called and illegally constituted, was the formal deposition of Brant from office, and also the removal from office of all the Mohawk chiefs and sachems who were his friends. There was yet another motive for the instigation of this measure of proscriptive violence by the Canadians, who, with Red-Jacket, were at the bottom of the conspiracy. The celebrated Norton, a Mohawk chief, and the confidential friend of Brant, was then in England, charged by the latter with a mission to the parent government, connected with the long pending controversy respecting the title to their lands. Information had been received that the application was likely to be crowned with success; and those who were hostile to the claim of the Indians sought to defeat the measure of justice by prostrating their noblest champion and most distinguished friend. With this view, having effected his removal, a paper was drawn up for transmission to the parent government, disavowing the mission of Norton, and all the claims and proceedings of

Brant. And to complete the plot, the proceedings were signed by the common Indians who had been convened for the occasion, in the character of chiefs,—each of them being promised a commission from the English government, for their participation in the fraud.*

But the triumph of the orator over the proud Mohawk was of short duration. Although all the charges that had been brought against the latter at this illegal council had been fully investigated and refuted but a few months before, yet the veteran chief was not disposed to sit in silence under the renewal of them, or to acquiesce in his own ostracism. Convening a full council of the Mohawks, including his enemies who had taken a seat in the Buffalo council against him, he made a defence which overwhelmed his enemies. Shortly afterward a full council of the confederacy was summoned, at which, after mature deliberation, the proceedings of the spurious council were revoked, and the chief was restored to his rank by acclamation.

* Letter of Brant to the Duke of Northumberland. Life of Brant, vol. ii. p. 419.

CHAPTER VIII.

THE life and conduct of Red-Jacket are now to be contemplated in a different aspect. It has been seen that at an earlier period of his career by twelve or thir- teen years, he was at Philadelphia, listening with appa- rent approbation to the counsels of Washington for the civilization of his people, and concerting measures with Colonel Pickering to that end. It may indeed be doubted whether he was altogether sincere at that time ; for such was the habitual deceitfulness of his character, that his professions were at all times but an uncertain index to the resolves of his mind. But it is of little im- portance whether he was sincere at the time referred to, or not,—nothing is more certain than that if he was not a dissembler then, an entire revolution must have been wrought in his views previous to the year 1805, at which time, even if it had ever been otherwise, he had become thoroughly pagan. From that year forward, had it been in his power, he would have entirely cut off from his people all knowledge of the Christian religion, and all communication with the Anglo-Saxon race. His language now was, that the Great Spirit had formed the red and white men distinct,—that there was no more reason why the two races should profess the same religious creed, than that they should be of the same color. The Indians, he held, could not be civilized; and he had now become anxious not only to resist all farther innovations upon their manners, but that their ancient customs should be restored.*

It is not unlikely that the ill success attending the experiments made under the auspices of Washington and Pickering, aided by the persevering efforts of the Quakers, might have induced the orator to abandon the project of civilization in despair.† And not without show of reason, since the fact is equally indisputable and lamentable, that from the day on which the Pilgrims landed upon Plymouth Rock to the present, the intercourse between

* MS. Collections of Joseph W. Moulton, Esq.

† The care with which the Friends watched over the interests of the Six Nations on various occasions, particularly at the treaty of Canandaigua, has been repeatedly mentioned in the foregoing pages. But their efforts did not end here. In 1796 several families of Friends were located upon the Oneida reservation, to teach the Indians the art of husbandry, and some of the indispensable mechanic arts. Their women, also, it was sought to teach the skill of household duties, spinning, sewing, knitting, &c. In 1798, the Senecas, who had observed the improvement of the Oneidas, requested the Friends to aid them in the same way, and three families accordingly planted themselves down in the canton of the Alleghany. Their presence, their instruction, and their example, were of great benefit to that canton, although the progress of Indian improvement has been slow. The late Thomas Eddy, of New-York, devoted himself actively to this cause for several years.

the Indians and the white people has resulted in little
more than the acquisition by the former of the vices of
the latter. Red-Jacket had seen this result, and he
doubtless mourned over it. He had seen his people
melting away before the pale-faces, with a rapidity
foreboding their early extinction. He had learned the
failure of every antecedent effort to convert them, as a
people, to Christianity; and he had seen that every attempt thus far made to introduce even the primary arts
and customs of civilization among them, had been equally
abortive. He had therefore become utterly averse to
any farther intercourse or association with the whites,—
having arrived at the conclusion that the only means of
preserving his race, even for a few brief lustres, would
be the erection of a wall of separation, strong and high,
between them. Thenceforward he ever acted rigidly
upon that principle. He was opposed to any farther
sales of their lands. He was opposed to blending the
races by intermarriage,—not unfrequently murmuring,
that whereas before the approach of the white men the
eyes of their children were all black, now they were becoming blue. He was opposed to the introduction of
the arts of civilized life. He was opposed to the acquisition by his people of the English language. Above
all, he was opposed to the introduction among them of
Christianity. Nor indeed, speaking after the manner of
men, was he greatly blameable for his hostility to this
new religion, judging, as both he and his people in their
simplicity naturally would do, of the character of that
religion from such of its fruits as were most perceptible

to them. The irregular and reckless border-men, pressing them closely upon all sides, and setting every bad example possible before them, called themselves Christians. Those who were continually persuading the Indians to drunkenness, in order to cheat or plunder them before they were sober, were called Christians. And the rapacious land-jobbers, who were seeking every opportunity of stripping them of their territory, and who were held in special abhorrence by Red-Jacket and the more considerate of the chiefs, were likewise known to the Indians as Christians. The orator had pondered all these things; and being unable to discriminate between the nominal and the real Christian,—or rather not understanding enough of the nature of Christianity to know that it was a religion of the heart, and that, no matter by what names they were called, those only were Christians who endeavored to live up to its principles,—he could perceive nothing good in the system. So far as he could judge from such lights, and such examples, he saw nothing better in Christianity than in his own paganism. Hence the tone of the speech now to be introduced, which has been regarded as the ablest and most ingenious of his rude forensic efforts.

The occasion was this: In the summer of 1805, a young missionary named CRAM was sent into the country of the Six Nations by the Evangelical Missionary Society of Massachusetts. His design was to plant a missionary station among the Senecas, and a council of their chiefs was convoked at Buffalo Creek to hear his propositions. The agent of the United States for Indian affairs attended the council, and the government interpreter was also present. The proceedings were opened by the agent, who thus introduced the missionary :—

"BROTHERS OF THE SIX NATIONS: I rejoice to meet you at this time, and thank the Great Spirit that he has preserved you in health, and given me another opportunity of taking you by the hand.

"BROTHERS : The person who sits by me is a friend who has come a great distance to hold a talk with you. He will inform you what his business is, and it is my request that you would listen with attention to his words."

The missionary thereupon opened his business in the following terms :—

"MY FRIENDS : I am thankful for the opportunity afforded us of uniting together at this time. I had a great desire to see you, and inquire into your state and welfare. For this purpose I have travelled a great distance, being sent by your old friends, the Boston Missionary Society. You will recollect they formerly sent missionaries among you, to instruct you in religion, and labor for your good. Although they have not heard from you for a long time, yet they have not forgotten their brothers, the Six Nations, and are still anxious to do you good.

"BROTHERS : I have not come to get your lands or your money, but to enlighten your minds, and to instruct you how to worship the Great Spirit agreeably to his mind and will, and to preach to you the gospel of his son Jesus Christ. There is but one religion, and but one way to serve God, and if you do not embrace the right way you cannot be happy hereafter. You have never worshipped the Great Spirit in a manner acceptable to him; but have all your lives been in great errors and darkness. To endeavor to remove these errors, and open your eyes, so that you might see clearly, is my business with you.

" BROTHERS : I wish to talk with you as one friend talks with another ; and if you have any objections to receive the religion which I preach, I wish you to state them ; and I will endeavor to satisfy your minds and remove the objections.

" BROTHERS : I want you to speak your minds freely : for I wish to reason with you on the subject, and, if possible, remove all doubts, if there be any on your minds.   The subject is an important one, and it is of consequence that you give it an early attention while the offer is made you.   Your friends the Boston Missionary Society will continue to send you good and faithful ministers, to instruct and strengthen you in religion, if, on your part, you are willing to receive them.

" BROTHERS : Since I have been in this part of the country, I have visited some of your small villages, and talked with your people.   They appear willing to receive instruction, but as they look up to you as their older brothers in council, they want first to know your opinion on the subject.   You have now heard what I have to propose at present.   I hope you will take it into consideration, and give me an answer before we part."

After about two hours consultation among themselves, Red-Jacket rose and spoke as follows :—

" FRIEND AND BROTHER : It was the will of the Great Spirit that we should meet together this day.   HE orders all things, and has given us a fine day for our Council.   HE has taken his garment from before the sun, and caused it to shine with brightness upon us.   Our eyes are opened, that we see clearly ; our ears are unstopped, that we have been able to hear distinctly the words you have spoken.   For all these favors we thank the Great Spirit ; and HIM *only*.

" BROTHER : This council fire was kindled by you.   It

was at your request that we came together at this time.
We have listened with attention to what you have said. You
requested us to speak our minds freely. This gives us great
joy; for we now consider that we stand upright before you,
and can speak what we think. All have heard your voice,
and all speak to you now as one man. Our minds are
agreed.

" BROTHER: You say you want an answer to your talk before you leave this place. It is right you should have one,
as you are a great distance from home, and we do not wish
to detain you. But we will first look back a little, and tell
you what our fathers have told us, and what we have heard
from the white people.

" BROTHER: Listen to what we say. There was a time
when our forefathers owned this great island. Their seats extended from the rising to the setting sun. The Great Spirit
had made it for the use of Indians. HE had created the buffalo, the deer, and other animals for food. HE had made the
bear and the beaver. Their skins served us for clothing.
HE had scattered them over the country, and taught us how
to take them. HE had caused the earth to produce corn for
bread. All this HE had done for his red children, because
HE loved them. If we had some disputes about our hunting
ground, they were generally settled without the shedding of
much blood. But an evil day came upon us. Your forefathers crossed the great water and landed on this island.
Their numbers were small. They found friends and not
enemies. They told us they had fled from their own country
for fear of wicked men, and had come here to enjoy their religion. They asked for a small seat. We took pity on them,
granted their request; and they sat down amongst us. We
gave them corn and meat; they gave us poison* in return.

" The white people, BROTHER, had now found our country.
Tidings were carried back, and more came amongst us. Yet

* Rum.

we did not fear them. We took them to be friends. They called us brothers. We believed them and gave them a larger seat. At length their numbers had greatly increased. They wanted more land; they wanted our country. Our eyes were opened, and our minds became uneasy. Wars took place. Indians were hired to fight against Indians, and many of our people were destroyed. They also brought strong liquor amongst us. It was strong and powerful, and has slain thousands.

" BROTHER : Our seats were once large and yours were small. You have now become a great people, and we have scarcely a place left to spread our blankets. You have got our country, but are not satisfied ; you want to force your religion upon us.

" BROTHER : Continue to listen. You say that you are sent to instruct us how to worship the Great Spirit agreeably to his mind, and, if we do not take hold of the religion which you white people teach, we shall be unhappy hereafter. You say that you are right and we are lost. How do we know this to be true ? We understand that your religion is written in a book. If it was intended for us as well as you, why has not the Great Spirit given to us, and not only to us, but why did he not give to our forefathers, the knowledge of that book, with the means of understanding it rightly ? We only know what you tell us about it. How shall we know when to believe, being so often deceived by the white people ?

" BROTHER : You say there is but one way to worship and serve the Great Spirit. If there is but one religion, why do you white people differ so much about it ? Why not all agreed, as you can all read the book ?

" BROTHER : We do not understand these things. We are told that your religion was given to your forefathers, and has been handed down from father to son. We also have a religion, which was given to our forefathers, and has been handed down to us their children. We worship in that way. It teaches us to be thankful for all the favors we receive; to love each other, and to be united. We never quarrel about religion.

" BROTHER : The Great Spirit has made us all, but HE has made a great difference between his white and red children. HE has given us different complexions and different customs. To you HE has given the arts. To these HE has not opened our eyes. We know these things to be true. Since HE has made so great a difference between us in other things, why may we not conclude that he has given us a different religion according to our understanding ? The Great Spirit does right. HE knows what is best for his children ; we are satisfied.

" BROTHER : We do not wish to destroy your religion, or take it from you. We only want to enjoy our own.

" BROTHER : You say you have not come to get our land or our money, but to enlighten our minds. I will now tell you that I have been at your meetings, and saw you collect money from the meeting. I cannot tell what this money was intended for, but suppose that it was for your minister, and if we should conform to your way of thinking, perhaps you may want some from us.*

" BROTHER : We are told that you have been preaching to the white people in this place. These people are our neighbors. We are acquainted with them. We will wait a little while, and see what effect your preaching has upon them. If we find it does them good, makes them honest and less disposed to cheat Indians, we will then consider again of what you have said.

" BROTHER : You have now heard our answer to your talk, and this is all we have to say at present. As we are going to part, we will come and take you by the hand, and hope the

---

* This paragraph is not contained in the first edition of the speech, as published by James D. Bemis, in 1811; but I find it in the speech as given by Drake, in his Book of the Indians, and also in Thatcher's Indian Biography. Still, it appears to me to be an interpolation.

Great Spirit will protect you on your journey, and return you safe to your friends."

It has been asserted that, when preparing for this interview, Red-Jacket supposed that possibly he might be drawn into a regular argumentative discussion with the missionary. Like a wary gladiator, therefore, on entering upon the arena he felt disposed to measure the force of his antagonist, and by a searching scrutiny of his countenance, ascertain his intellectual calibre. For this purpose, he approached very near the person of the missionary, and by a rapid but penetrating scrutiny, soon satisfied himself whether it was a great man, like Con-neh-sau-ty,* with whom he was to draw the bow of Achilles, or wield the shield of Ajax. His mind was quickly at ease, and his apprehensions, if he had entertained any, were dissipated at a glance. With a mingled and indescribable expression of countenance, smiling in scornful composure, he turned away, and joined the dusky circle of his own people.† Be this as it may, his reply is ingenious and able. Some of its figures are beautiful,—some of its passages eloquent. It was received by the missionary, probably, with disappointment, and with manifest displeasure,—a displeasure which a wiser man, even if he had felt it, would have concealed. Agreeably to the suggestion at the close of Red-Jacket's speech, as the council was breaking up the Indians moved toward the missionary for the purpose of extending the parting

* Colonel Pickering.
† MS. Collections of Joseph W. Moulton.

hand of friendship; but Mr. Cram rose hastily from his seat, and replied that he could not take them by the hand, "there being," he added, "no fellowship between the religion of God and the devil." These words were interpreted to the Indians, but they nevertheless smiled, and retired in a peaceable manner. Subsequently, on being advised of the indiscretion of his remark, Mr. Cram observed in explanation, that he supposed the ceremony of shaking hands would have been received by the Indians as a token that he assented to what had been said. Being more correctly informed, he expressed his regret at what had so unadvisedly fallen from his lips. Still it cannot be denied that the Indians exhibited better breeding, and more knowledge of human nature, than the missionary. Indeed it is quite probable that Mr. Cram's ill success arose in part from his own repulsiveness of manner, and the want of tact, or, in other words, the power of adaptation, so essential in the composition of a successful missionary. It must be stated in fairness to the Indians, to borrow the langugage of another,* "that the missionaries are not always men fitted for their work. Many of them have been destitute of the talents and information requisite in so arduous an enterprize; some have been bigotted and over-zealous, and others have wanted temper and patience. Ignorant of the aboriginal languages, and obliged to rely upon interpreters to whom religion was an occult science, they doubtless often conveyed very different impressions from those which they intended;" and the worthy and well mean-

* Rev. John Breckenridge, D. D.

ing man who called forth the preceding pagan speech of
Red-Jacket, probably deserved to be classed in this
category. The reader will have observed, from an intimation in the speech itself, that the orator had been at
several of the missionary's meetings, and it has been asserted of Mr. Cram that his first, or at least an early
sermon to the Indians, was exactly such as a wise
man would never have preached to such a congrega-
tion. Instead of being a simple discourse, brought
down to the level of their ignorant, and, upon such a subject, child-like minds, presenting to them the elementary
principles of Christianity in their simplest and most
winning forms, the missionary, according to tradition,
gave them a long argumentative sermon upon the doctrine
of divine decrees, and the deep mysteries of fore-know-
ledge and predestination.* A more repulsive theme,
even for many enlightened congregations reared in the
bosom of the church, could hardly have been selected;
but that it was chosen as the ground-work of an introductory discourse to these simple children of the forest,
argues a want of common sense almost too great for human credulity. Possibly there may be error in the relation. But another circumstance was added, which
favors its truth. Red-Jacket is reported to have been
indignant at the attempt to force doctrines upon him
which were entirely beyond his comprehension; and in
the expression of that indignation, according to unwritten
history, he perpetrated the only pun that is recorded of

* The author's informant is a distinguished gentleman, of high character and
intelligence, then a resident of the Seneca country.

h'm. "Not content," he said, "with the wrongs the white men had done to his people, they were now seeking to *Cram* their doctrines down their throats," &c. And yet the remark will bear repetition, that much of the difficulty in this, and other similar cases, may very naturally have arisen from the ignorance of the parties respectively of the language and modes of thinking of each other. In regard to the American Indians, in particular, the greatest difficulty has always existed in conveying any new ideas to their minds, from the barrenness of their language; and in many instances it has been found impossible to convey to them the sentiments attempted.* "What have you said to them?" inquired a missionary once, of the interpreter who had been expounding his sermon. "I told them you have a message to them from the Great Spirit," was the reply. "I said no such thing," cried the missionary. "Tell them I have come to speak to them of the only living and true God, and of the life that is to be hereafter :—Well, what have you said?" "That you will tell them about Manito, and the land of spirits." "Worse and worse," exclaimed the embarrassed preacher; and such is doubtless the history of many sermons that have been delivered to the bewildered heathen.† The fact is, Red-

---

* General Lincoln's Observations on the North American Indians, in a letter to Dr. Ramsay.

† M'Kenney's Lives and Portraits of the Indians. "The Iroquois have few radical words, but they compound them without end. Sometimes one word among them includes an entire definition of the thing; for example, they call Wine, *Oneharadesehoengtseragherie,* as much as to say, *a liquor made of the juice of the grape.*"[Colden's Six Nations.—] "The Indian language requires many more words to express the meaning of the speaker than ours, as they are

Jacket did not understand the system of the Christian religion, nor did he wish to understand it. It was his belief, and it is that of the Indians generally, that they form a race entirely distinct from the pale faces. They repudiated the idea of a common origin of the human family; and as to the mission of Christ, and his crucifixion, they cannot perceive that they are interested in the one, or have any participation in the guilt of the other. In a conversation with a distinguished clergyman, who was endeavoring to instruct him upon the subject of the Christian religion, not many years before his death, Red-Jacket said :—

"BROTHER : If you white men murdered the Son of the Great Spirit, we Indians had nothing to do with it, and it is none of our affair. If he had come among us, we would not have killed him ; we would have treated him well ; and the white people who killed him ought to be damned for doing it. You must make amends for that crime yourselves.*

obliged to describe objects which a single English word suffices to explain. This will be the more readily understood by the following statement:—When Red-Jacket, Farmer's-Brother, and several hundred Indians arrived at Tioga Point to attend the treaty of 1790, Farmer's-Brother, after thanking the Great Spirit for having permitted them to travel there in safety, narrated all the particulars attending their journey. Wishing among other circumstances to describe their having made a halt at a log hut, where a kind of tavern was kept, the tavern was described *as a house put together with parts of trees piled on each other, and to which a pole was attached to which a board was tied, on which was written,* "*Rum is sold Here.*" This difficulty of expressing in a few words matters which in their own language required a round-about description, demanded a considerable time for them, in their public discussions, to say that which the interpreter would render into a few words of English."—*Letter to the author from Thomas Morris.*

* Conversations between Dr. Breckenridge and the author. See, also, Drake, on the authority of W. J. Snelling.

After the adjustment of the great controversy between the Indians and the United States, at Canandaigua, in 1794, the councils of the Six Nations became of less public importance. With the exception of a few reservations, of a comparatively limited extent, their broad and beautiful domains in the State of New-York had fallen within the greedy and remorseless grasp of the white men, even before the dawn of the present century. From that day to the present, the efforts of those who have become possessed of the pre-emptive title to those reservations have been directed to the acquisition of the fee from the Indians; and so strong and persevering have been the appliances to that end, that slice after slice has been taken away, until but a comparatively few thousand acres now remain to the Indians,—the scattered and disheartened fragments of the once proud lords of the continent.* But after the last great sale to Robert Morris, in 1797, and after the deliberate resolution of Red-Jacket, as already stated, to repel the advances of the whites, and, as the only means of averting the progressive ruin of his people, to re-envelope them in the darkness of paganism, and restore their wildest barbarity, he continued inflexible in his purposes.

* These reservations are as follows:—

Tonnewanda Reservation, near Niagara River, containing about	.	13,000	acres.
Buffalo Reservation, near the city of Buffalo,	" "	. 53,000	"
Cattaraugus Reservation, near Cattaraugus Creek, "	"	. 22,000	"
Alleghany Reservation, near the Alleghany River, "	"	. 31,000	"
		119,000	"

Much of this land is among the most fertile and valuable in the State of New-York.

From the hour of arriving at that determination he never in the slightest degree swerved from his resolution, to drive away, and keep away, every innovation upon the character, and every intrusion upon the territory then remaining to his nation. In the Spring of 1811 an attempt was made by the New-York Company holding the pre-emptive title to the reservations within the Morris, or Holland Purchase, to divest the Indians of their rights by negotiation and purchase. The agent employed by the Company was a Mr. Richardson. He met the chiefs in council at Buffalo Creek, in May, and after opening his business, awaited their reply, which was made by Red-Jacket, a few days afterward, in the following speech :—

"Brother: We opened our ears to the talk you lately delivered to us, at our Council fire. In doing important business it is best not to tell long stories, but to come to it in a few words. We therefore shall not repeat your talk, which is fresh in our minds. We have well considered it, and the advantages and disadvantages of your offers. We request your attention to our answer, which is not from the speaker alone, but from all the Sachems and Chiefs now around our Council fire.

"Brother: We know that great men as well as great nations, having different interests have different minds, and do not see the same subject in the same light,—but we hope our answer will be agreeable to you and to your employers.

"Brother: Your application for the purchase of our lands is to our minds very extraordinary. It has been made in a crooked manner,—you have not walked in the straight path pointed out by the great Council of your nation. You have no writings from our great father the President.

" BROTHER : In making up our minds we have looked back, and remembered how the Yorkers purchased our lands in former times. They bought them piece after piece for a little money paid to a few men in our nation, and not to all our brethren ; our planting and hunting grounds have become very small, and if we sell these we know not where to spread our blankets.

" BROTHER : You tell us your employers have purchased of the Council of Yorkers a right to buy our lands,—we do not understand how this can be,—the lands do not belong to the Yorkers ; they are ours, and were given to us by the Great Spirit.

" BROTHER : We think it strange that you should jump over the lands of our brethren in the East, to come to our Council fire so far off, to get our lands. When we sold our lands in the East to the white people, we determined never to sell those we kept, which are as small as we can live comfortably on.

" BROTHER : You want us to travel with you, and look for other lands. If we should sell our lands and move off into a distant country, towards the setting sun, we should be looked upon in the country to which we go as foreigners, and strangers, and be despised by the red as well as the white men, and we should soon be surrounded by the white men, who will there also kill our game, come upon our lands, and try to get them from us.

" BROTHER : We are determined not to sell our lands, but to continue on them,—we like them,—they are fruitful and produce us corn in abundance, for the support of our women and children, and grass and herbs for our cattle.

" BROTHER : At the treaties held for the purchase of our lands, the white men with sweet voices and smiling faces told us they loved us, and that they would not cheat us, but that the king's children on the other side the lake would cheat us. When we go on the other side the lake the king's children tell us your people will cheat us, but with sweet voices and smiling faces assure us of their love and that they will not cheat us. These things puzzle our heads, and we believe that the Indians must take care of themselves, and not trust either in your people or in the king's children.

" BROTHER : At a late Council we requested our agents to tell you that we would not sell our lands, and we think you have not spoken to our agents, or they would have informed you so, and we should not have met you at our Council fire at this time.

" BROTHER : The white people buy and sell false rights to our lands ; your employers have, you say, paid a great price for their right ; they must have plenty of money, to spend it in buying false rights to lands belonging to Indians ; the loss of it will not hurt them, but our lands are of great value to us, and we wish you to go back with your talk to your employers, and to tell them and the Yorkers that they have no right to buy and sell false rights to our lands.

" BROTHER : We hope you clearly understand the words we have spoken. This is all we have to say."

Thus, as in the great majority of their speeches, the Indians were still endeavoring to brace themselves against what they considered to be the inordinate rapacity of the whites, in the acquisition of their lands. This disposition of the white man to grasp at all their property, with a view, as it appeared, of driving them from the face of the earth, was then, as it is now, and probably ever will be until the race becomes extinct, the source of their jealousy, and the burden of their complaint. Notwithstanding the rapid diminution of their numbers, and their increasingly depressed condition, they still felt that they were independent nations, and they were tenacious of that character. They be-

26

lieved that they had been placed on "this island" by the Great Spirit, and that he had created it for their sole benefit, and they held that nobody could have a right to dispossess them. Hence nothing could have been more inopportune than an effort made at this very council, by a missionary society in the city of New-York, to establish a Christian mission among them.* The former attempts had left no favorable impression upon the mind of Red-Jacket, now their principal civil chief. On the contrary, he had imbibed a fixed and deep-rooted hatred to the system, countenancing, as he supposed, a course of policy on the part of its professors that would eventually sap the foundations of the happiness, and work the ruin of his people.† Least of all was it an auspicious moment to strive farther to persuade them to change their religion, at the very time when those who called themselves Christains were renewing their efforts to dispossess them of their few remaining roods of ground. Hence the following reply, by Red-Jacket, to the advances of the Rev. Mr. Alexander, the agent of the Missionary Society on that occasion :—

"BROTHER: We listened to the talk you delivered to us from the Council of Black Coats‡ in New-York. We have

---

* " In discourse they spoke about preaching, and said, 'they wished many times to hear the word of God; but they were always afraid that the English would take that opportunity to bring them into bondage.' "—*Journal of Christian Frederick Post, to the Delawares of the Ohio.* Proud's Pennsylvania, vol. ii.

† General Lincoln.

‡ So Red-Jacket was wont to call the clergy.

fully considered your talk, and the offers you have made us: we perfectly understand them, and we return an answer which we wish you also to understand. In making up our minds we have looked back and remembered what has been done in our days, and what our fathers have told us was done in old times.

"BROTHER: Great numbers of black coats have been amongst the Indians, and with sweet voices, and smiling faces, have offered to teach them the religion of the white people. Our brethren in the East listened to the black coats,—turned from the religion of their fathers, and took up the religion of the white people. What good has it done them? Are they more happy and more friendly one to another than we are? No, brother, they are a divided people,—we are united; they quarrel about religion,—we live in love and friendship; they drink strong water,—have learnt how to cheat,—and to practice all the vices of the white men, which disgrace Indians, without imitating the virtues of the white men. Brother, if you are our well wisher, keep away and do not disturb us.

"BROTHER: We do not worship the Great Spirit as the white men do, but we believe that forms of worship are indifferent to the Great Spirit,—it is the offering of a sincere heart that pleases him, and we worship him in this manner. According to your religion we must believe in a Father and a Son, or we shall not be happy hereafter. We have always believed in a Father, and we worship him, as we were taught by our fathers. Your book says the Son was sent on earth by the Father,—did all the people who saw the Son believe in him? No, they did not, and the consequences must be known to you, if you have read the book.

"BROTHER: You wish us to change our religion for yours, —we like our religion and do not want another. Our friends*

* Pointing to Mr. Granger, the Agent of the United States for Indian affairs, who was present—Mr. Parish, the Indian interpreter, and Mr. Taylor, the

do us great good,—they counsel us in our troubles, and instruct us how to make ourselves comfortable. Our friends
the Quakers do more than this,—they give us ploughs, and
show us how to use them. They tell us we are accountable
beings, but do not say we must change our religion. We are
satisfied with what they do.

"BROTHER: For these reasons we cannot receive your
offers—we have other things to do, and beg you to make
your mind easy, and not trouble us, lest our heads should be
too much loaded, and by and by burst."

It is a fact that cannot be sufficiently deplored, that
men boasting of their civilization, and calling themselves
Christians, not only in this but in other lands, have by
their own vicious examples interposed the greatest obstacles to the efforts of those who are earnestly laboring
for the moral, social and religious improvement of the
heathen. The missionaries have found such to be the
fact in the Sandwich Islands. And so upon the coasts
of Africa, and at the missionary stations in the China
seas, and in India, the counteracting and contaminating
influences of the seamen and others, belonging to Christian nations, cause the severest trials which the missionaries are obliged to encounter. The natives know them
all alike as Christians,—not understanding the difference
between those who are really and truly governed by
Christian principle,—who, in a word, are Christians at
heart,—and those who are called Christians because they
belong to nations known as such, albeit as individuals
knowing nothing of, and caring nothing about, religion of

agent of the Society of Friends for Improving the Condition of the Indians, residing near the Alleghany settlement, but also present at the Council.

any sort. Most emphatically has such been the fact in respect to the American aboriginals. To borrow a brief passage, without essential variation, from the sainted Milne, the faithful co-laborer of Morrison in China, the meagre specimens of Christianity which they but too often see among the so-called civilized men who first settled around them, have not tended to produce reverence for the system. The total neglect of all religion prevailing too generally in frontier settlements, even among many who have at some time professed to be the followers of Christ,—the public and bare-faced profanation of the Sabbath,—the avarice, lying and cozening which characterize their dealings, sometimes with each other, and most shamefully often in their commerce with the Indians,—the drunkenness, loose morals, and hardness of heart, in daily illustration all around them, have in but too many instances steeled the Indian's soul against Christianity. However earnestly the missionaries may be preaching to him the excellencies of Christianity and civilization, he doubts if they have any of the former, and scoffs at the latter. He cannot think well of a system, the professed adherents of which pay so little regard to God, to truth, and to duty.* Hence the tone of Red-Jacket's speeches to Mr. Cram and Mr. Alexander; hence also the kindred character of the following outline of another of the Seneca orator's philippics against Christianity, delivered on a similar occasion, at about

* Life of Dr. Milne, by Robert Philip, page 146.

the same period of his life with his last mentioned address :—*

" BROTHER :—I rise to return you the thanks of this nation, and to return them back to our ancient friends,—if any such we have,—for their good wishes toward us in attempting to teach us your religion. Inform them we will look well into this matter. We have well weighed your exertions, and find your success not to answer our expectations. But instead of producing that happy effect which you so long promised us, its introduction so far has rendered us uncomfortable and miserable. You have taken a number of our young men to your schools. You have educated them and taught them your religion. They have returned to their kindred and color, neither white men nor Indians. The arts they have learned are incompatible with the chase, and ill adapted to our customs. They have been taught that which is useless to us. They have been made to feel artificial wants, which never entered the minds of their brothers. They have imbibed, in your great towns, the seeds of vices which were unknown in the forest. They become discouraged and dissipated,—despised by the Indians, neglected by the whites, and without value to either,— less honest than the former, and *perhaps* more knavish than the latter.

" BROTHER :—We were told that the failure of these first attempts was attributable to miscalculation, and we were invited to try again, by sending others of our young men to different schools, to be taught by different instructors. Brother, the result has been invariably the same. We believe it wrong for you to attempt further to promote your religion among us, or to introduce your arts, manners, habits, and feelings. We

* The precise time when this speech was delivered, or the particular occasion that called it forth, is not known. The manuscript, from the interpretation of the old Indian linguist, Captain Parish, was obtained by Judge Moulton, from the late Dr. Cyrenus Chapin, of Buffalo.

believe that it is wrong for us to encourage you in so doing.
We believe that the Great Spirit made the whites and the Indians, but for different purposes.*

"BROTHER :—In attempting to pattern your example, the
Great Spirit is angry,—for you see he does not bless or crown
your exertions."

Here, according to the manuscript, Red-Jacket painted
in the most glowing and descriptive colors the curse that
seemed to have descended upon all those Indians who
had been made the objects of pious but mistaken missions,—how imbecile, poor, effeminate, contemptible,
drunken, lying, thieving, cheating, malicious, meddle-
some, backbiting, quarrelsome, degraded and despised,
the poor victims of civilized instruction had become,—
having lost all the noble qualities of the savage, and
acquired all the ignoble vices of the whites,—without one
solitary exception where the Indian had been bettered.
He then proceeded :—

" But, BROTHER, on the other hand we know that the Great
Spirit is pleased that we follow the traditions and customs of
our forefathers,—for in so doing we receive his blessing,—we
have received strength and vigor for the chase. The Great
Spirit has provided abundance,—when we are hungry we find
the forest filled with game,—when thirsty, we slake our thirst
at the pure streams and springs that spread around us.
When weary, the leaves of the trees are our bed,—we retire
with contentment to rest,—we rise with gratitude to the Great
Preserver. Renovated strength in our limbs, and bounding
joy in our hearts, we feel blessed and happy. No luxuries, no
vices, no disputed titles, no avaricious desires, shake the foun-

---

* According to a parenthetical note in the manuscript, Red-Jacket here went
into a train of reasoning-from analogy.

dations of our society, or disturb our peace and happiness. We know the Great Spirit is better pleased with his red children, than with his white, when he bestows upon us a hundred fold more blessings than upon you.

"Perhaps, BROTHER, you are right in your religion:—it may be peculiarly adapted to your condition. You say that you destroyed the Son of the Great Spirit. Perhaps this is the merited cause of all your troubles and misfortunes. But, Brothers, bear in mind that we had no participation in this murder. We disclaim it,—we love the Great Spirit,—and as we never had any agency in so unjust, so merciless an outrage, he therefore continues to smile upon us, and to give us peace, joy and plenty.

"BROTHER:—We pity you,—we wish you to bear to our good friends our best wishes. Inform them that in compassion toward them, we are willing to send them missionaries to teach them our religion, habits and customs. We would be willing they should be as happy as we are, and assure them that if they should follow our example, they would be more, far more happy than they are now. We cannot embrace your religion. It renders us divided and unhappy,—but by your embracing ours, we believe that you would be more happy and more acceptable to the Great Spirit. Here, (pointing his finger to several whites present who had been captured when children, and been brought up among them,) here, Brother, (with an animation and exulting triumph which cannot be described,) here is the living evidence before you. Those young men have been brought up with us. They are contented and happy. Nothing would be an inducement with them to abandon their enjoyments and adopt yours,—for they are too well aware of the blessings of our society, and the evils of yours. But as you have our good will, we would gladly know that you have relinquished your religion, productive of so much disagreement and inquietude among yourselves, and instead thereof that you should follow ours.

"Accept of this advice, BROTHER, and take it back to your

friends, as the best pledge of our wishes for your welfare.
Perhaps you think we are ignorant and uninformed. Go, then,
and teach the whites. Select, for example, the people of Buffalo. We will be spectators, and remain silent. Improve
their morals and refine their habits,—make them less disposed
to cheat Indians. Make the whites generally less inclined to
make Indians drunk, and to take from them their lands. Let
us know the tree by the blossoms, and the blossoms by the
fruit. When this shall be made clear to our minds we may
be more willing to listen to you. But until then we must be
allowed to follow the religion of our ancestors.

" BROTHER :—Farewell !"

A bitter satire ! Humanity weeps that the conduct
of civilized men puts arguments like these into the
mouths of the heathen, against their own best good.
It is a striking coincidence that the Iroquois Indians
were first unhappily made acquainted with their two
greatest enemies, RUM and GUNPOWDER, by the rival
discoverers, Hudson and Champlain, during the same
week of the same year, 1609. While Henry Hudson
was cautiously feeling his way, as he supposed, into
the northern ocean, through the channel of the river
which bears his name, Champlain was accompanying a
war-party of the Hurons against the Iroquois, upon the
lake receiving its name from him. Hudson discovered a
company of the Iroquois upon the bank of the river, whom
he regaled with rum. Champlain discovered a body of
Iroquois warriors upon the coast of the lake, near the spot
afterward selected for the site of Ticonderoga, and
there first taught them the fatal power of gunpowder.
The tradition of the savages, as to their first knowledge

of the former, is substantially this: Many years ago,
before a white skin had ever been seen, some of their
people who were fishing where the sea widens, descried
a huge object, with white wings, moving up the water.
They hurried ashore, and called their friends to view
the phenomenon. None of them could divine what it
was. Some of them supposed it must be a huge fish,
and others a monster of another sort. Onward it
came, growing larger as it approached. The natives
were terrified, and despatched runners in all directions
to collect their warriors. By and by living objects
were seen moving upon the back of the monster. As it
came nearer, they saw that it was a floating house or
castle, and that the living objects on board had the
figures of men, but clothed in a very different manner
from themselves. One of them was in red. They
now concluded that it was the Manitto, or Great Spirit,
coming to make them a visit. Their sensations were,
therefore, changed from fear to adoration. Instantly
they set themselves at the work of preparation to receive their celestial visiter with divine honors. The
men prepared a sacrifice, and the women a feast.
They had no apprehension that the Manitto was coming
to them in anger, for they worshipped him in sincerity.
They descried from the distance various animals in
their Manitto's water-pavilion, and thought that perhaps
he was coming to bring them some new species of
game. While the preparations for the festival were in
progress, the house upon the water stopped. The medi-
cine-men were busy with their charms, to divine the

import of the extraordinary visitation, and the women
and children looked on with awe. At length a voice
sounded from the vessel, speaking words in a language
they could not understand. They replied by a shout
peculiarly their own. A small canoe then left the large
vessel with several persons therein, one of whom was
the being in red. It was certainly the Manitto! The
sachems and warriors formed a circle to receive him
with solemn respect. As the canoe touched the land,
the figure in red, with two attendants, stepped on shore,
and approached them with a friendly countenance.
The figure in red saluted them with a smile, and they
returned his salute. A passage was opened for him
into the circle, and his gorgeous red dress, and ornaments glittering in the bright sun, were viewed
with delight. Surely it must be the Manitto. But
why should he have a white skin? The thought
was perplexing; but he was, nevertheless, regarded
with mingled feelings of amazement and adoration.
After friendly salutations had been interchanged, the
Manitto beckoned to one of his attendants at the canoe,
who brought him a *bockhack*,* clear as the new ice upon
the surface of a lake. He also had a little cup which
was also transparent. The Manitto then poured a
liquid from the *bockhack* into the cup, which he drank.
Then filling the cup again, he handed it to the chief
standing near him. The chief smelled it, and passed it
to the next, who did the same, and in this manner it

---

* A gourd. The reference is to a glass decanter.

went round the circle, without the liquid having been tasted by either.   As the last man of the circle was about returning the cup to the Manitto, the first chief interposed and arrested the movement.   The cup, he said, had been given to them to drink, as the giver had done himself, and it would be offending their Great Benefactor to return it to him untasted.   To drink it would please him,—to refuse might provoke his wrath.   Be the consequences, therefore, what they might, he would drink the cup.   It would be better for him to encounter even a poisoned draught, than for the Great Spirit to become angry with their whole nation.   Saying which, the patriotic chief bade his people adieu, and quaffed the cup to its bottom.   All eyes were now directed to the chief in watching the effects.   There was no sudden change ; but no long time had elapsed before his joints became relaxed,—his movements grew flexible, and ere long his limbs refused to perform their office.   His eyes closed lustreless, and he rolled heavy and helpless upon the ground.   The dusky group stood around him in solemn thought, and the wailings of the women rose upon the gale.   He became motionless, and they supposed him dead.   But perceiving afterward, from the heaving of his chest, that he yet breathed, their grief was abated, and they watched anxiously the result,— not daring, of course, to breathe a murmur against the Great Spirit, whatever that result might be.   After a long time, their chief began to revive.   He rose upon his seat, rubbed his eyes, and at length sprang joyously upon his feet.   He declared that he had experienced the most delightful sensations while in the trance. He had seen visions, and had never been more happy. He requested another draught; and encouraged by his example, the liquor was poured out for them all. They all partook of the ravishing cup,—and all became intoxicated.*

Fatal indeed was that cup ! From the hour when they first tasted the maddening poison to the present, their thirst for it has not abated. In vain have their best advisers and teachers admonished them against it. In vain have humane legislatures endeavored to prohibit its introduction among them. In vain have their own Councils, when sober, passed decrees against it. And equally vain have been the most eloquent and pathetic appeals of their women against it;—whenever and wherever they can lay their hands upon the fire-water, they are sure to drink it. Two hundred years ago, the clergy, and all good men, deplored the evil as deeply as their successors do at this day. With equal vehemence did they then, as now, inveigh against the conduct of the white men, who, knowing their infirmity, supply them with the poison. " Those," says Charlevoix, writing in 1721, " who perhaps have greatest reason to reproach themselves with the horrors of Indian intoxication, are the first to ask whether they are Christians. One might answer them, yes, they are Christians, and new converts, knowing not what they do; but those who, in cold blood, and with a perfect knowledge of what they are

---

* MS. in the New-York Historical Society. Heckewelder, vol. i. Philadelphia Philosophical Transactions.

about, reduce, from sordid motives of avarice, these simple people to this condition, can they be imagined to have any religion at all ? We certainly know that an Indian will give all he is worth for one glass of brandy. This is strong temptation to dealers, against which neither the exclamations of their pastors, nor the zeal and authority of the magistrate, nor respect for the laws, nor the severity of divine justice, nor the dread of the judgments of the Almighty, nor the thoughts of a hell hereafter, of which these barbarians exhibit a very striking picture, have been able to avail."*

* Charlevoix—Voyage to North America.   Letter viii.

CHAPTER IX.

MOVEMENTS of Tecumseh and the Prophet, Elskawatwa, among the western nations—The young Senecas eager to join them—The government of the United States admonished by Red-Jacket—His speech to the Secretary of War—Battle of Tippecanoe—Conduct of the Prophet—War of 1812 with England—Council of the Six Nations at Buffalo—Speech of Granger, the agent—Red-Jacket's reply—Senecas declare themselves neutral—Active hostilities—The Senecas declare war—General Alexander Smyth—General Lewis invites the Senecas to join him—Their arrival at Fort Niagara—Murder of Lieutenant Eldridge—Invasion of Black Rock by the enemy under Colonel Bishop—Repulsed by General Porter's volunteers and Indians—Death of Colonel Bishop—Smart affair of the Indians and volunteers near Fort George.

THE reader will probably be surprised to discover the name of Red-Jacket in connexion with the Indian war between the United States and the Shawanese, and other powerful tribes of the West, under the celebrated Tecumseh, in the year 1811. Like the great Pomatecom, the Wampanoag,* of the eastern Indians, and Pontiac the Ottawa, and Brant the Mohawk, Tecumseh, with the aid of his brother, Elskawatwa,† had for years been laboring to form a vast league of the western and south-

---

* Philip of Pokanoket, commonly called King Philip.

† This name, according to Schoolcraft, signifies " *A-fire-that-moves-from-place-to-place.*" The orthography of Elskawatwa's name has been variously changed by recent writers. Cushing, in his Life of Harrison, writes it Ol-li-wa-chi-ca, upon what authority I know not. In the absence of a reason for the change, the primitive name is preferred.

western Indians, in the vain expectation that they might
be able to arrest the farther advances of the white population. Those Indians were then, as they ever had
been since the conquest of Canada from the French,
more under the influence of the British officers in the
north-west, and of the British Fur Companies and traders, than under that of the Americans. Notwithstanding
all the friendly advances of the Americans toward them,
prior and subsequent to the war of 1789—1795, ended
by General Wayne at the battle of the Miamis and the
treaty of Greenville,—their attachment to England was
much stronger than to the United States, and the movements of Tecumseh were evidently not looked upon with
an unfavorable eye by the British provincial authorities
in the remote interior, inasmuch as the relations between
the United States and Great Britain were at that time
critical, and evidently verging toward a war. The
Prophet had begun to collect his warriors as early as
1808, and in 1810 Tecumseh assumed a semi-hostile
attitude toward General Harrison, in a council held at
Vincennes. The elements of the succeeding storm
thenceforward gathered rapidly; and although the United States had vastly increased in numbers and strength
since the Indians were overwhelmed at the Miamis, yet
the white settlements immediately upon the borders
were in as great peril as were the borderers twenty
years before. For many months, therefore, during these
movements of Tecumseh and his brother, the homes of
the frontier settlers were those of peril. They were in
daily apprehension that their paths would be ambushed.

At every rustling leaf the mother pressed her infant more closely to her bosom. The yells of savage vengeance and the shrieks of torture seemed again in fancy to sigh upon the west winds, and mingle with every echo from the mountains. Families retired to rest, not knowing but that the war-whoop should wake the sleep of the cradle, or that the darkness of midnight might not glitter with the blaze of their own dwellings.*

It has been seen in the glances heretofore given of the former Indian wars, ended by General Wayne, that notwithstanding the friendship of most of the Seneca chiefs for the United States, many of their warriors, especially their young men, would steal away and join themselves to the forces of the Little Turtle and his allies; and although sixteen years of peace had intervened since the treaty of Greenville, and the Senecas had been living in close proximity, and upon cordial terms, with the white settlers of New-York, by whom they were now completely surrounded, yet no sooner did they scent blood upon the western gales than numbers of their warriors again stole away and joined themselves to the forces of Tecumseh and the Prophet.† The fact of this intercommunication between the Senecas and the warriors of Tecumseh could not of course be kept from the knowledge of the chiefs of the former, and it is due to Red-Jacket to place the fact upon record, that he was

---

* Speech of Fisher Ames on the British Treaty.

† MS. Letter of George Hosmer to Henry O'Reilly, Esq., author of History of Rochester.

true to the United States in regard to those transactions, and that as early as 1809 he gave information to the Indian Agent of the gatherings of the western tribes, and the organization of another extensive league, for the avowed purpose, in their own councils, of war. Very early in the year 1810, Red-Jacket visited the city of Washington at the head of a delegation of his people, attended by Erastus Granger the Agent, and Captain Parish the interpreter. During this visit, viz., on the 13th of February, Red-Jacket delivered a speech to the Secretary at War, of which the following passage has been preserved in the archives of the Department:—

" BROTHER :—At the time we were making bright the chain of friendship at Canandaigua, the commissioner on your part told us that the time might come when your enemies would endeavor to disturb our minds, and do away the friendship we had there formed with you. That time, Brother, has already arrived. Since you have had some disputes with the British government, their agents in Canada have not only endeavored to make the Indians at the westward your enemies, but they have sent a war-belt among our warriors, to poison their minds, and make them break their faith with you. This belt we exhibited to your agents in council, and then sent it to the place whence it came, never more to be seen among us. At the same time we had information that the British had circulated war-belts among the western Indians, and within your territory. We rested not, but called a general council of the Six Nations, and resolved to let our voice be heard among our western brethren, and destroy the effects of the poison scattered among them. We have twice sent large deputations to their council fire, for the purpose of making their minds strong in their friendship with your nation; and, in the event of a war between the white people, to sit still on their seats, and take no part on either side. So far as our voice has been heard, they have agreed to hearken unto our counsel, and remain at peace with your nation.

"BROTHER :—If a war should take place, we hope you will inform us of it through your agents, and we will continue to exert our influence with all the Indians with whom we are acquainted, that they will sit still upon their seats, and cultivate friendship with your people."

Of these two councils to which Red-Jacket referred in this speech, they having been probably composed exclusively of Indians, no written memorials have been preserved. Yet it is stated that at about that period there was held at Detroit, or in its vicinity, perhaps the largest Indian Council that had been known in many years, at which were assembled deputations from all the tribes and nations of the upper lakes, and to which the Senecas sent a strong representation with Red-Jacket at its head. The first day of the council there arose a question of the right of precedence in debate,—a point of honor most tenaciously regarded. It was claimed by the Wyandots, and supported by their ablest chiefs, to whom Red-Jacket replied, displaying a knowledge of the history of the several tribes, and powers of oratory, particularly of invective, which according to an eye-witness, who understood the language perfectly, were truly wonderful. At least his speech was so overpowering that no one attempted a reply, and the rank of the Senecas was yielded to them without farther contention.*

* Letter to the author from Hon. Albert H. Tracy.

This may very likely have been one of the Councils to which Red-Jacket referred in his speech to the Secretary of War, in which the Seneca chiefs endeavored to dissuade Tecumseh from a farther prosecution of his designs. But those pacific counsels were of no avail. The storm of war broke out in 1811, but was summarily ended, for that year at least, by General William Henry Harrison, then Governor of Indiana, at the head of a division of United States troops, and several corps of western volunteers, on the bloody field of Tippecanoe. The action was fierce, and many of the noblest spirits of the west fell. But the victory was decisive.* Tecumseh was not himself in this battle, having been

---

* The battle of Tippecanoe was fought on the Wabash, near the Prophet's-Town, on the 7th of November, 1811. The forces of Governor Harrison consisted of a body of Kentucky and Indiana militia, and the 4th U. S. Regiment, under Colonel Boyd. The straggling Indians whom they saw on the march toward the town had behaved in a very threatening manner,—so much so that it was the strong desire of Colonel Daviess and the officers generally, that Harrison should proceed and attack the town, on the afternoon of the 6th; but the Governor's orders were peremptory not to fight, if hostilities could possibly be avoided, and as he was met near the town by several chiefs, disclaiming all hostile designs, and making offers of peace and submission, the Governor, after carefully reconnoitering the country, selected an advantageous position, and encamped for the night. At four in the morning, just after the Governor had risen and dressed, while engaged in conversation with his military family, the attack was commenced,—the Indians, to the number of from six to eight hundred, having crept stealthily up to his very outposts. The camp was furiously assailed on all sides, and a bloody and doubtful contest ensued. It was not until after sunrise that the Indians were finally repulsed, with the loss, on the part of the Americans, of sixty-two killed and one hundred and thirty-six wounded, and a still greater loss on the side of the Indians. Colonel Daviess, a distinguished lawyer, a volunteer from Kentucky, Colonel White, and several other valuable officers, fell on this occasion. Governor Harrison, having destroyed the Prophet's-town, and thrown up some fortifications, returned to Vincennes.

absent on a visit to the Creeks, whom he was endeavoring to persuade to take up the hatchet. The Indians were commanded by White-Loon, Stone-Eater, and Winemac, a Potawatamie chief who had been with General Harrison on his march, and at Fort Harrison, making great professions of friendship. Their master-spirit was the Prophet himself, Elskawatwa. Not that he was actually in the battle, since " he kept himself secure on an adjacent eminence, singing a war-song. He had told his followers that the Great Spirit would render the army of the Americans unavailing, and that their bullets would not hurt the Indians, who would have light while their enemies would be involved in thick darkness. Soon after the battle commenced he was informed that his braves were falling. He told them to fight on, assuring them that it would be as he had predicted, and then began to sing in louder tones."* Numbers of the young Seneca warriors were engaged in this battle.

---

* Dawson's Life of General William Henry Harrison. The Prophet was frequently engaged in practicing incantations and infernal rites and conjurations. There is no better method of working upon the feelings of the Indians than an appeal to their superstition. Tecumseh and the Prophet had conceived the idea of combining all the Indians in a league, and making war upon the United States, as early as 1806. The first account of the pretended divine mission of the Prophet is contained in a *talk* which was circulated widely among the Indian nations, in 1807. This *talk* was delivered at he entrance of Lake Michigan, by the Indian chief *Le Maiquois*, or *The Trout*, on the 4th of May, of that year, as coming from " the first man whom God created," and was addressed to all the Indian tribes. The following is an extract from the *talk* referred to, and is a curiosity :—

" I am the father of the English, of the French, of the Spaniards, and of the Indians. I created the first man, who was the common father of all these people, as well as yourselves ; and it is through him, whom I have awakened from his long sleep, that I now address you. *But the Americans I did not make.*

From the evidence collected by the government of the United States at the time, no doubt can exist that Tecumseh and his followers had been moved to their hostile course by the officers of the British Indian Department in the upper lake country, and by the British fur traders. The relations between the United States and Great Britain had again assumed an unfriendly character, threatening war; and as in former years, the agents of the latter were active in their exertions again to secure the Indians as their allies, in anticipation of a rupture.*

The act of the Congress of the United States, declaring war against England, was approved by President Madison on the 18th of June, 1812, and the proclamation of the President, announcing the fact to the world, was issued on the 19th. The news had no sooner reached the province of Upper Canada, than measures were adopted by the officers of the crown to induce the Mohawks and all other Indians, who could be controlled by their influence, to take up the hatchet. The Shawa-

---

They are not my children, but the children of the evil spirit. They grew from the scum of the great water, when it was troubled by the evil spirit, and the froth was driven into the woods by a strong east wind. They are numerous, but I hate them. My children, you must not speak of this *talk* to the whites. *It must be hidden from them.* I am now on the earth, sent by the Great Spirit to instruct you. Each village must send me two or more principal chiefs to represent you, that you may be taught. The bearer of this talk will point out to you the path to my wigwam. I could not come myself to Abre Croché, because the world is changed from what it was. It is broken, and leans down, and as it declines, the Chippewas and all beyond will fall off and die. Therefore, you must come to see me, and be instructed. Those villages which do not listen to this talk, and send me two deputies, will be cut off from the face of the earth."

This great Manitou, or Indian second Adam, was Elskawatwa.

* Vide American State Papers,—Indian Affairs, pp. 795—804.

nese, and Miamis, and their confederates, who had been
so recently and severely chastised by General Harrison,
were of course eager for the onslaught. The Mohawks,
moreover, residing upon the Grand River, about sixty
miles from Niagara, were no less ready to take part in
the war, and their emissaries were early among the Senecas, for the purpose of influencing them to embark in the
contest, upon the same side. In this effort they were
not successful, as the Senecas, and all others of the Six
Nations remaining within the state of New-York, were
disposed to peace, save some hundreds of the younger
warriors, who seemed impatient to bear a part, though,
for once, not against the United States. But the older
chiefs preferred repose, and they more than once despatched messengers of peace among their brethren the
Mohawks, to dissuade them from their bloody purposes.
Farthermore the American government, in conformity
with the humane policy which had prompted a similar
course at the beginning of the revolutionary war, lost
not a moment in its endeavors to prevent the Senecas
and others of the Six Nations residing in the state of
New-York, from engaging at all in the contest. To this
end a council of those nations was convened at Buffalo,
on the 6th and 8th days of July, by Mr. Erastus Granger,
the Indian Agent, with the view of spreading the whole
matter before them, and consulting with their chiefs as
to the course it would be most wise to adopt. The proceedings of the council were opened by Red-Jacket, who
addressed himself to Mr. Granger thus :—

" BROTHER :—We are glad of having an opportunity once
more of meeting you in council. We thank the Great Spirit
that has again brought us together. This is a full meeting.
All our head men are present. Every village is represented
in this council. We are pleased to find our interpreter, Mr.
Parish, is present. He has attended all our councils since the
last war, and is well acquainted with all the treaties we have
made with the United States. The voice of war has reached
our ears, and made our minds gloomy. We now wish you to
communicate to us every thing which your government has
charged you to tell us concerning this war. We shall listen
with attention to what you have to say."

Mr. Granger thereupon addressed the council at
length, in the following words :—

" BROTHERS OF THE SIX NATIONS :—I am happy to behold
so many of you assembled together at this time. I observe
that the chiefs of the Seneca, Onondaga, Cayuga and Tuscarora
nations, and some of the Delawares, are present. The Mohawks, who live in Canada, are not represented, and the Oneidas, living at a distance, could not attend.

" BROTHERS :—You will now listen to what I say :—

" At the close of the revolutionary war the United States
held a treaty with the Six Nations at Fort Stanwix. They
restored to you the country of land which they had conquered
from you and the British, and set you down once more on your
old seats. Several treaties have since been made with you;
but that which particularly binds us together, was made at
Canandaigua about eighteen years since.

" The chain of friendship then formed has been kept bright
until this time. In this great length of time nothing material
has happened to disturb the peace and harmony subsisting between us. Any momentary interruptions of peace which have
taken place, have been happily settled without injury to either
party. Our friendship has remained unbroken.

" BROTHERS :—The prosperity and happiness of the Six Nations have always been objects which the United States have had in view.

" You have enjoyed with us all the blessings which the country afforded, consistent with your mode and habits of living. We have grown up together on this island. The United States are strong and powerful; you are few in numbers and weak; but as our friends, we consider you, and your women and children, under our protection.

" BROTHERS :—You have heretofore been told that the conduct of Great Britain toward us, might eventually lead to war. That event has at length taken place. War now exists between the United States and the British nation. The injuries we have received from the British, have at length forced us into a war.

" I will now proceed to state to you the reasons why we have been compelled to take up arms.

" For a number of years past the British and French, who live on the other side of the great waters, have been at war with each other, shedding each other's blood. These nations wished us to take a part in their war. France wanted us to fight against Great Britain. Great Britain wanted us to join against France. But the United States did not wish to take any part in their quarrels. Our object was to live in peace, and trade with both nations. Notwithstanding our endeavors to maintain friendship with them, both France and Great Britain have broken their treaties with us. They have taken our vessels and property, and refused to restore them or make compensation for the losses we sustained.

" But the British have done us the greatest injury. They have taken out of our vessels at least six thousand of our own people, put them on board their ships of war, and compelled them to fight their battles. In this situation our friends and connexions are confined, obliged to fight for the British.

" BROTHERS :—If you consider the situation in which we are placed, you cannot blame us for going to war. I will ask

29

you a question. Suppose that the Mohawk Nation, who live in Canada, were at war with a nation of Indians at the westward. Both these nations being your friends, you were determined to take no part in their disputes, but to be at peace with both,—to visit them, and trade with them as usual. In consequence of this determination, you should send messengers with speeches to inform them of the system you had adopted. But the Mohawks not satisfied in seeing you in prosperity, enjoying the blessings of peace, visiting and trading with their enemy,—determine to make you feel the evils of war, unless you agree to give up all intercourse with those they are at war with. This you cannot consent to: you want the privilege of selling your furs and skins where you can find the best market. The Mohawks still continue to flatter you,—say they are your friends,—put on smiling faces and speak good words. But in the mean time, while professing friendship toward you, they fall upon your hunting and trading parties, as they travel back and forth,—strip them of their property,—leave them naked in the world, and refuse to make satisfaction. Not only this, but they come near your villages, and there murder your people,—others they take, when found from home, bind them fast and compel them to go and fight their battles.

"BROTHERS :—Could you for a moment submit to such treatment? Would you not all as one rise from your seats, and let the enemy feel your vengeance? If you are warriors, if you are brave men, you certainly would. What I have stated is exactly our case. The British have done us all these injuries, and still continue to do us wrong without a cause. The United States have risen from their seats,—they have raised their strong arm, and will cause it to be felt.

"BROTHERS :—I feel it my duty at this present time, to point out to you the straight path in which you ought to walk. You well recollect the advice given you by the people of the United States, at the commencement of the revolutionary war against Great Britain. You were then requested to stay at home,—to sit upon your seats at your own council fires, and to take no part in the war.

"It would have been happy for you had you followed this good advice. But the presents and fair speeches of the British poisoned your minds. You took up the hatchet against us, and became our enemies. At the close of the war with Britain, (the event you well know,) the United States had it in their power to cut you off as a people, but they took pity on you, and let you return to your former seats.

"Your great father, the President of the seventeen fires, now gives his red children the same advice that was given you at the beginning of the last war: that is—*That you take no part in the quarrels of the white people.* He stands in no need of your assistance. His warriors are numerous, like the sand on the shores of the great lakes, which cannot be counted. He is able to fight his own battles, and requests you to stay at home, cultivate your fields and take care of your property. If you have any regard for your women and children,—if you have any respect for the country in whose soil repose the bones of your fathers,—you will listen to his advice, and keep bright the chain of friendship between us.

"You have been invited to join the British in this war. Reflect for a moment on the consequence of complying with their request. You will lose your property in the United States. We shall soon take possession of Canada. They will have no land to sit you down upon. You will have nothing to expect from our mercy. You will deservedly, as a people, be cut off from the face of the earth.

"The late delegation which you sent to Canada, was told that they ought not to put any confidence in the United States,—that if you did we should deceive you,—that the United States kept no promises made to Indians.

"BROTHERS :—I now ask, in what have the United States deceived you? Have they not punctually paid your annuities as they became due? Have not the Senecas received annually the interest of their money in the public funds? Has not the

state of New-York honestly fulfilled her engagements with the
Oneidas, Onondagas and Cayugas? Have not the Tuscaroras
been assisted in the sale of their property in North Carolina,
and in obtaining a pleasant seat, purchased of the Holland
Land Company? I again ask, have not the United States observed good faith toward you? Have they deceived you in
any one thing? I answer, they have not.

"Knowing, as you do, that we are your friends, will you
act like children, and suffer yourselves to be imposed upon at
this time by our enemies?

"BROTHERS:—It was our wish that the Six Nations should
all be agreed as one man, but the Mohawks and some few
others living on the British side, have been so foolish as to
declare in favor of war. The good advice you lately gave
them, has not been attended to. They are now at Newark in
arms against the United States. I am sorry they have not listened to good counsel. You, however, have done your duty,
and you are not to blame for their folly. They will soon find
they have done wrong, and must suffer the consequence.

"BROTHERS:—Continue to listen.

"You have been frequently told, that in case we went to
war we did not want your assistance. The same thing has
this day been repeated. But I find some of your young men
are restless and uneasy. They wish to be with our warriors,
and I am sensible the chiefs have not power to control them.
As I observed before, we want not their aid, but we believe it
better for them to be our friends than our enemies.

"If they will not be contented to stay at home, but must
see something of a war, perhaps 150 or 200 will be permitted
to stand by the side of our warriors, and receive the same pay
and provisions which our soldiers receive.

"If they should be permitted to join our troops, they must
conform to our regulations. Your mode of carrying on a war
is different from ours. We never attack and make war upon
women and children, nor on those who are peaceably inclined
and have nothing to defend themselves with. Such conduct
we consider as cowardly, and not becoming a warrior.

" Brothers :—If you have not sufficient time this evening
to deliberate on what I have said, I will meet you to-morrow,
or next day, and receive your answer."

The Agent of the United States having concluded his
speech, the council was adjourned until the 28th, when
Red-Jacket delivered the following reply :—

" Brother :—We are now prepared to give an answer to
the speech you delivered to us in council the other day. We
are happy to find so many of the *white* people present. We
are not accustomed to transact important business in the DARK !
We are willing that the *light* should shine upon whatever we
do. When we speak, we do it with sincerity, and in a manner that cannot be misunderstood.

" You have been appointed by the United States an Agent
for the Six Nations. We have been requested to make you
acquainted with the sentiments of those nations we represent.
None of the Mohawks or Oneidas, it is well known, are present. The number of treaties that have passed between the
Six Nations and the United States, appears to be fresh in
your memory. We shall only mention to you some things
that were agreed upon in the treaty made at Canandaigua.

" We were a long time in forming that treaty, but we at
length made up our minds and spoke freely. Mr. Pickering,
who was then agent for the United States, declared to us that
no breach should ever be made in that treaty. We replied
to him, if it should ever be broken, you will be the first to do
it. We are weak. You are strong. You are a great people.
You can, if you are so disposed, place yourselves under it and
overturn it,—or, by getting upon it, you can crush it with your
weight! Mr. Pickering again declared, that this treaty would
ever remain firm and unshaken, that it would be as durable as
the largest rock to be found in our country.

" This treaty was afterward shown to General Washington.
He said that he was satisfied and pleased with what the agent

had done. He told us that no treaty could be formed that would be more binding. He then presented us with a chain, which he assured us would never rust, but always remain bright. Upon this belt of wampum,* he placed a silver seal.† This belt we always have and always wish to look upon as sacred.

"In the treaty, it was agreed that the Six Nations should receive a small annuity, to show the intention of the United States to continue friendly with them. This has been complied with. It was also agreed that if any injury or damage should be done on either side, satisfaction should be made to the party injured. We were a long time in conference before we could make up our minds upon one article of the treaty,—what punishment should be inflicted for the crime of murder? Mr. Pickering said it should be *hanging*. We told him that would never do: that if a white man killed an Indian, the Indians would not be permitted to hang the white man,— the sacrifice would be considered too great for killing an Indian! We at length agreed that conciliatory measures should be resorted to, such as would give satisfaction to all parties.

"In cases of theft, as in stealing horses, cattle, &c., it was agreed that restitution should be made. In this article, the whites have transgressed twice, where the Indians have once. As often as you will mention one instance in which we have wronged you, we will tell you of two in which you have defrauded us!

"I have related these articles of the treaty to show you that it still remains clear in our recollection, and we now declare to you, in presence of all here assembled, that we will continue to hold fast the chain which connects us together. Some who first took hold of it are gone! but others will supply their place.

"We regret, extremely, that any disturbance should have taken place among the white people. Mischief has com-

---

* Holding up a belt of wampum curiously wrought.

† Upon which an eagle was engraved, representing the United States.

menced. We are now told that war has been declared against Great Britain. The reasons for it are unknown to us. The Six Nations are placed in an unpleasant situation. A part of them are in Canada, and the remainder in the United States.

"Whilst we were endeavoring to persuade those who live in Canada to remain peaceable and quiet, the noise of war suddenly sounded in our ears. We were told that all communication between us and them would be prevented. We have since heard that they have taken up arms. We are very sorry to hear of this. They are our brothers and relations, and we do not wish that their blood should be spilt, when there is so little occasion for it. We hope that the passage is not so closely stopped but that a small door may still be open by which we may again have an opportunity of seeing our brothers, and of persuading them to take no part in a war in which they have nothing to gain.

"We know the feelings of the greater portion of them. We therefore believe, that if we have another opportunity, we can persuade them to have nothing to do with this war. Our minds are fully made up on this subject, and we repeat, that it is our wish to see them once more, and to give them our advice about the path they ought to travel.

"You (Mr. Parish,) are going to the eastward; you will visit the Oneidas. Relate to them faithfully what has taken place in this council; tell them all we have said, and request that a deputation of their chiefs may be sent to attend our council here. We wish that you would return with them."

[The orator then brought forward the belt which he had before held up in his hand, and requested Mr. Granger and the others present to look at it and observe whether it was not the one that had been presented to the Six Nations by General Washington. He likewise held up another belt, much larger, of different colors, which appeared to be very ancient, and then continued :—]

" BROTHER :—I will now state to you the meaning of this belt. A long time ago the Six Nations had formed an union. They had no means of writing their treaties on paper, and of preserving them in the manner the white people do. We therefore made this belt, which shows that the Six Nations have bound themselves firmly together; that it is their determination to remain united ; that they will never do any thing contrary to the interests of the whole; but that they will always act toward each other like brothers.

" Whenever, for the future, you see a small number of our people meeting together to consult about any matter of trifling account, we desire that you would pay no attention to it. It may give you uneasiness, when we have no intention to injure you. This happened but a few days ago : It seems that a white man and two or three Indians, living on the same creek, had a small conversation, which the mischievous talked about until the whole country was in an uproar, and many families left their country and homes in consequence.

" The council held some time since at Batavia, was unauthorized by us, and we now declare to you that none have a right to hold council any where except at this place, around the great council fire of the Six Nations.*

" We hope that you will not accept of any of our warriors, unless they are permitted by our great council to offer themselves to you. And we should be sorry indeed if any of the whites should entice our young warriors to take up arms. We mention these things to show you that we wish to guard against every thing that may interrupt our good understanding.

" BROTHER :—We hope that what has been said will be

* There are no records, that I am aware of, connected with the council here referred to.

generally known to the white people. Let every one recollect and give a faithful account of it. We wish them to know that we are peaceably disposed towards the United States, and that we are determined to keep bright the chain of friendship that we formed with them at Canandaigua.

" BROTHER :—We have one thing more to which we would wish to call your attention. We present you the papers* which secure to us our annuities from the United States. We would be glad to know if this war would affect our interests in that quarter. We also desire that you would inform us whether the monies we have deposited in the [late] Bank of the United States will be less secure, than if this war had not taken place."

To which Mr. Granger, after thanking them for their general and punctual attendance, thus rejoined :—

" BROTHERS :—You have this day brought forward the large white belt, given you at Canandaigua. Your speaker has explained the leading particulars of the treaty made at that time. I am much pleased to find your minds so deeply impressed with them. I now repeat to you that the United States will, on their part, hold fast of the treaty ; they wish you to do the same. Should it be broken on your part, the United States will no longer consider themselves bound by it.

" BROTHERS :—It appears that you are still desirous of sending to Grand River, to endeavor to prevail on your brethren in that quarter to remain at peace. An undertaking of this kind will be of little use. They will only fill your heads with idle talk, and poison your minds against the United States. Perhaps after crossing Niagara river, you will not be permitted to go any farther. Still, should you insist upon it, permission will be granted to four or five of your chiefs to go over, with such instructions as you shall think proper to give them."

* Handing the agent a small bundle of papers.

" But should your young men cross over and join our enemies, they must never expect to be allowed to set their feet
on our shores again as friends. Rest assured they will be
severely punished for it.

" With respect to the property you have placed in the hands
of the United States you have nothing to fear, it will be fully
as secure as if this war had not happened. Your annuities
will be paid you as formerly, and your bank stock be as productive as usual.

" I now return you my thanks for the good attendance you
have given at this council.   I feel pleased that you have again
come forward and renewed the covenant of friendship, that
you have once more declared your steady attachment to the
United States.

" Your friend, Mr. Parish, will soon go to the eastward,
where he will see such of your brethren as were not present
at this council. In a short time he will return, and remain
here, if he should be wanted, through the summer."

The earnestness with which the council, through the
mouth of their speaker, had urged their request for
leave to send yet another peaceable message to their
brothers, the Mohawks, induced the agent to grant the
desired permission; although he had not the least confidence in the measure. He was right in his conjec-
tures. A deputation of five chiefs proceeded to Lewiston, and application was made to General Brock, then
in command of the British forces on the opposite shore
of the Niagara, that they might be allowed to land in
his Majesty's dominions. After deliberating two days
upon the request, the deputation was permitted to cross
over and hold a consultation with some of the Mohawk
chiefs. They did so; but the conference was brief,

and the object was not accomplished. The Mohawks had taken up the hatchet, and were resolved not to bury it; and the friendly messengers of the Senecas were ordered to return.

But the Senecas did not long succeed in maintaining their neutrality. The young men, as already intimated, were restless from the moment of the declaration of war; and the soul-stirring music, the glittering panoply and pomp of war, speedily wrought so powerfully upon the feelings, and indeed the natural propensities, of the older chiefs, that they rather sought occasion to declare hostilities on their own behalf,—considering themselves still an independent nation. That occasion was fast approaching. Not long after the commencement of hostilities, it was rumored at Buffalo, and among the Senecas, that the enemy had taken possession of Grand Island, appertaining to the United States, and then owned by the Senecas. Red-Jacket immediately convoked a council of his people, and invited Mr. Granger to attend there for consultation. After stating the case to the latter, the orator avowed the purpose of the Senecas in the following brief but energetic speech :—

"Brother: You have told us that we have nothing to do with the war that has taken place between you and the British. But we find that the war has come to our doors. Our property is taken possession of by the British and their Indian friends. It is necessary now for us to take up the business, defend our property, and drive the enemy from it. If we sit still upon our seats, and take no means of redress, the British, according to the customs of you white people, will hold it by conquest.

And should you conquer the Canadas, you will claim it upon the same principles, as though you had conquered it from the British. We therefore request permission to go with our warriors, and drive off those bad people, and take possession of our lands."

The request was granted, and at a subsequent meeting of the council, strengthened by a larger attendance, a formal declaration of war was issued in the following terms :—

" We, the chiefs and councillors of the Six Nations of Indians, residing in the State of New-York, do hereby proclaim to all the war-chiefs and warriors of the Six Nations, that war is declared on our part against the provinces of Upper and Lower Canada. Therefore, we hereby command and advise all the war-chiefs and warriors of the Six Nations to call forth immediately the warriors under them, and put them in motion to protect their rights and liberties, which our brethren, the Americans, are now defending."*

No speech of Red-Jacket delivered at this council has been preserved, but from the address of one of the oldest warriors present, it would appear that it was their expectation to put as many as three thousand braves upon the war-path.† But there surely must have been some mistake in this computation, since the whole Iroquois confederacy was never able to call forth so large a number of warriors, even in the palmy days of Sir William Johnson; and at the time under consideration, the number of warriors within the confines of the State of New-York,—Senecas, Oneidas, Onondagas,

* Drake and Thatcher.   † Drake and Thatcher.

Cayugas and Tuscaroras, all included,—could not have exceeded two thousand fighting men. Not more than a fourth of that number ever took the field at any one time during the war of 1812. Still, the friendship of the nation was unwavering, and considerable bodies of their warriors were occasionally in the service of the United States upon that frontier, until near the close of the contest. The Mohawks, and the other red allies of England, it is true, endeavored to poison their minds with disaffection, for which purpose emissaries were occasionally discovered amongst them, but without effect.

Yet, notwithstanding their preparations, and their formal declaration of hostilities,—the first Indian declaration of the kind, it is believed, ever issued in writing,—they seem not actually to have entered the field as the allies of the Americans during that year,—at least such is the presumption from the following circumstances: After the brilliant, though in the end, disastrous affair of Queenston, and after the relinquishment of the command of that frontier by General Van Rensselaer, General Alexander Smyth succeeded to the station. He made preparations to retrieve the fortunes lost at Queenston, but his demonstrations were failures, and the results proved him to be a man of words rather than of deeds. His name is only here introduced because of the declaration contained in one of his inflated proclamations, illustrating the fact just asserted, that the Senecas were not in actual service in that year. In the proclamation referred to, General

Smyth, in order to stimulate the militia into the field, told them that "even the Indians of the friendly Six Nations had offered their services, but that, through regard to the cause of humanity, he had refused to follow a disgraceful example by letting loose these barbarous warriors upon the inhabitants of Canada."*

No corresponding feelings had deterred the enemy from employing Indians, and using them at every opportunity. It was, therefore, at length thought advisable by the government of the United States to bring the same description of warriors into the field, though not into battle, if that alternative could be avoided. The Spring of 1813 found Major-General Lewis in command of the American fortress of Niagara; and it occurred to that officer, that inasmuch as the relationship between the Mohawks, and others of the Six Nations who had joined their settlement upon the Grand River, and the Senecas, Cayugas and Onondagas upon the American side, was near and intimate, they might feel reluctant to come into conflict, brother against brother. The idea was accordingly suggested, that the actual employment of the Senecas might possibly induce the Mohawks to retire,—in which case the Senecas were forthwith to have been dismissed. With this object the Seneca warriors were invited to meet General Lewis at Niagara, and they responded to the invitation, to the number of from three to four hundred, armed, painted, and with distended nostrils breathing eagerly for the

* H. M. Breckenridge's History of the War.

contest. They were led by Farmer's-Brother, the most noble Indian in form and mould, in carriage and in soul, of that generation of his race.* The forest warriors were received by General Lewis, and addressed in accordance with the views already indicated. But very great was the disappointment of the Indians. They had supposed themselves invited to a feast of blood in earnest, and their dissatisfaction at the suggestions of the General, who intended to use them rather to prevent than to participate in fighting, was but ill concealed, if indeed concealment was intended. Their countenances fell; their murmurs were deep and strong; and they left the fort with a degree of displeasure bordering upon indignation. Red-Jacket was among them on this occasion, and was as usual their orator; but he appeared not in the character of a war-chief, being now the head sachem or civil magistrate of his nation.†

But fastidiousness in regard to the employment of this description of force by the Americans soon ceased to be a virtue. The campaign of that year against Upper Canada was auspiciously commenced by the capture of York, on the 27th of April. The plan of this brilliant exploit was conceived by General Pike, whose blood was a dear purchase of the triumph.

---

* The opinion and nearly the same language of Colonel William J. Worth, of the army, who at the time was in the staff of General Lewis, and from whose conversations the facts concerning the Indian service upon the Niagara frontier in the campaigns of 1813—1814, have in part been drawn.

† In the account of the great treaty at Canandaigua, it has been seen how jealous the Indians were of the power of their war-chiefs. But that was a time of peace. In peace the voice of the chief sachem is potential. In war he is but a counsellor, while the war-chief becomes the dictator.

This achievement was followed, a month afterward, by the conquest of forts George and Erie. Still, these successes not being followed up with corresponding vigor, a war of outposts succeeded in that quarter, continuing through the season, unattended by any important results. "On the 8th of July a severe skirmish was brought on, in which nearly the whole force on each side was engaged, without any thing of moment resulting from it. An incident, nevertheless, occurred which exasperated the Americans to a greater degree than any thing that had previously transpired in that quarter during the war. Lieutenant Eldridge, a gallant and accomplished youth, with about forty men, was drawn by his impetuosity too far, and was surrounded by British troops and Indians. The greater part resisted until they were killed; but Lieutenant Eldridge and ten others were taken prisoners, and never afterward heard of. The bodies of the slain were treated in the most shocking manner by the Indians. Their heads were split open, and their hearts torn from their bodies. General Boyd, considering the forbearance hitherto practised in declining the aid of Indian allies as no longer justifiable, and by way of preventing a recurrence of such barbarities, accepted the services of four hundred Senecas, under Henry O'Bail, the Young Cornplanter.* But it was positively stipulated that the unresisting and defenceless should not be hurt, and that no scalps should be taken."†

* This young chief had been partially educated in Philadelphia; but not liking the restraints of civilization, he had again resumed the blanket.

† Breckenridge's History of the War.

The first affair in which these auxiliaries took an active part in the contest, was the defence of Black Rock and Buffalo against an attack by the British troops, in July, 1813; and, although in proportion to the numbers engaged, it was, both in its style of execution and its issue, one of the most brilliant and useful achievements of the war, it was but little noticed either in the army despatches, or in the public journals, by reason of its having occurred at a time when there was a sort of *interregnum*, or shifting of commands, between Generals Dearborn, Lewis and Boyd; and the public attention, as well as that of the army, was engrossed with the scenes, far from creditable to the American arms, which were enacting at the Beaver Dams, Cross Roads, and other places in the immediate vicinity of head quarters.*

After the capture of Fort George, in May, General Dearborn withdrew nearly the whole of his forces from the upper parts of the Niagara River, to the support of his position at Fort Niagara; leaving the provisions, naval stores and equipments, collected for the squadron with which Commodore Perry, soon after, did such signal execution, in the ware-houses at Black Rock; and also a large supply of provisions and quarter-master's stores for the army, at Buffalo,—wholly unprotected.

On being strongly urged by those who were more conversant with the affairs of the frontier, and the pro-

---

* The affairs here referred to were the discomfiture and captivity of Generals Winder and Chandler, on the morning of June 4th, 1813, and the sad and humiliating defeat of Colonel Boerstler, at the Beaver Dams, on the 23d of June, by a small party of British troops and a few hundred Mohawks.

bable views of the enemy, than himself, General Dearborn ordered a guard of eight or ten artillerists to take charge of the block-house at Black Rock, and made a call for five hundred of the neighboring militia,—about one hundred and fifty or two hundred of whom arrived early in July, and were stationed near the ware-houses at Black Rock, under command of Major P. Adams, who was furnished with two or three pieces of artillery. For Buffalo he ordered about ninety or one hundred regular troops, being a body of infantry and dragoon recruits on their march from the south to head quarters, under Captain (now Colonel) Cummings. Besides which, Mr. Granger, the Indian Agent, was directed to engage as many Seneca warriors as would consent to remain in camp. At the same time requesting General Peter B. Porter, who was then residing at his house in Black Rock, to take command of the whole, in case of an emergency.

Notwithstanding this show of force, an expedition was fitted out against these places, at the British head-quarters on Lundy's Lane, and placed under the command of Lieutenant-Colonel Bishop, of the forty-first regiment, comprising three hundred regulars of his own regiment, and a body of Provincials and volunteers, under Colonel T. Clark ; and making in the whole a force estimated at four hundred.

This detachment embarked in boats at Chippewa, early in the evening of the 10th of July; and, passing up the Niagara, landed in the course of the night on the American shore, two or three miles below Black Rock ;

and soon after daylight on the 11th, surprised the encampment of Major Adams, who fled to Buffalo with his militia, leaving his artillery with its ammunition on the ground, without taking the precaution to disable it.

The enemy, after setting fire to the marine and military barracks and block-house, and ordering breakfast at General Porter's house for their principal officers, (little anticipating that a less palatable one was preparing for them in the field,) proceeded to the plunder of the inhabitants as well as of the public stores, assisted by constant reinforcements of men and boats from the British shore.

General Porter, after a narrow escape from his own house, and an unsuccessful attempt to reach Major Adams's camp, retired on foot toward Buffalo ; but before reaching there was met by Captain Cummings, who, having heard the alarm, was promptly advancing with his command to the support of Black Rock. After directing the captain to proceed to an open ground between the two villages, and there to halt until a sufficient force could be collected to justify an attack on the enemy ; and after supplying himself with a horse and equipments taken from one of the captain's dragoons, the general left him for Buffalo ; and, in the course of an hour and a half, rejoined him with about ninety or a hundred of Major Adams's militia, who had retreated by the lake route, and been kept together by their officers, and about fifty volunteer citizens of Buffalo, who were found in the streets making preparations to abandon the town with their effects.

Captain Cummings having, in the meantime, ascertained by his videttes that the enemy,—that is to say, their three hundred regular troops, their volunteers being engaged in plundering,—were in possession of the commanding position left by Major Adams, and prepared for defence, General Porter determined to divide his force into three parts, and by a simultaneous attack from three different points, throw the enemy into confusion, and prevent the effective use of their artillery. The smallest of these divisions consisted of but twenty resolute volunteers, who were directed to associate themselves with a body of Indian warriors, understood to be gathering in the woods a short distance in advance,—provided the Indians would consent to join them,—and take a position, unobserved, in a deep ravine close upon the enemy's left, remain concealed until the action commenced, and then raise the war-whoop and rush forward. These Indians, numbering between thirty and forty, did join, behaving throughout in the most admirable manner.

By a bold and united attack with these forces, the enemy at 8 o'clock in the morning, after a spirited resistance of a few minutes, were beaten, routed and driven in great confusion to the neighborhood of their boats. Here they again rallied with their entire force, and with the apparent intention of renewing the fight. But being again attacked by the united and organized force of the assailants, fled with precipitation into their boats, taking with them most of their wounded, and leaving eight or ten dead on the field, and sixteen or eighteen prisoners, among whom was Captain Saunders of the forty-first, badly wounded.

But their principal loss was after they had entered their boats, particularly the last, which, besides some sixty men, contained most of their officers. The pursuit was so close that some of the American warriors actually plunged into the water, seized upon the gunwales of the boat, and would have brought it to shore but for the fire from the rear, which obliged them to desist. The occupants of the boat made great efforts at first to gain an offing in the river, but the firing from the shore became so intense that they dropped their oars and hoisted signals for surrender; in consequence of which, the firing in a few minutes ceased. Taking advantage of this interval, they dropped down the river with the current, followed *pari passu* by the troops on shore, making in the meantime some slight movements with their oars, as if to return to shore, and proclaiming their inability to do more by reason of their disabled state, until they reached the upper point of Squaw Island, when, by a sudden and vigorous effort, they sheered their boat to the outside of the island, and soon escaped under its protection; but not without again suffering from a renewal of the fire. The apology afterward given for this act of bad faith was, that the soldiers in the boat declared that they had seen Captain Saunders tomahawked and scalped by the Indians, after he had surrendered; and that they could have expected no better fate if they had done the same.

Colonel Bishop and several of his officers were slain

in their boats, the former having received a severe but
not mortal wound while on horseback in the field, and
four or five others after he had embarked, of which he
died in the course of the day.

The Indians throughout this affair displayed the most
admirable tact and gallantry, and evinced no disposition
to commit acts of barbarity on the prisoners or the
slain,—other than to take the scalps of the latter,
had they been permitted, according to their usages in
war.   When passing Captain Saunders, they divested
him, in the gentlest manner, of his cap, epaulettes, sword
and belt, but offered him no personal insult. He was
wounded by a rifle ball passing through his chest and
lungs, which it was not supposed he could survive, and
a musket shot shattering his wrist; but he had no cut
or mark of the knife or the tomahawk.

He was carried, after the action, by the Indians, in
blankets to General Porter's house, where he was suffered to remain, under the kindest treatment,—accompanied by his wife, who was written for at his anxious request,—for two or three weeks, when he was sent to the
depot at Williamsville, and is now a British pensioner.

The whole loss of the British,—whose numerical force
exceeded that of the Americans, in that expedition,—
was estimated at one hundred, inclusive of killed,
wounded and prisoners; while the American loss was
only one sergeant and three or four privates of the militia, killed, and as many more wounded; and Young-
King, the leader of the Indians, and one of his warriors
badly wounded. The disproportionate loss of the mili-

tia, compared with the regulars and Buffalo volunteers, was the consequence of their having been permitted to retrieve the reputation they had lost by the retreat, by taking the advance in the charge on the British line, which they executed most gallantly. Major Adams being in too bad health to permit him to take an active part, his battalion was led by his adjutant, now General Phinehas Staunton, of Genesee county, who had kept them together on their retreat, and who distinguished himself in that as well as many subsequent occasions on the Niagara. Captain Cummings was joined by Colonel King of the army, on their march from Buffalo to the Rock, and both of them took efficient parts in the operations of the morning.*

* For this account of the invasion of Black Rock by Colonel Bishop, and his defeat, I am indebted to General Peter B. Porter. I had written an account myself, from such materials as could be obtained; but finding that the publications of the day, and the books subsequently written, gave but a very unsatisfactory idea of the gallant affair, I gave my manuscript to General Porter, who not only corrected, but re-wrote the narrative. This, therefore, is the first correct account that has appeared of that brilliant exploit. General Porter adds, in a note, that in writing this account more details have been indulged than was otherwise necessary, for the purpose of correcting the misrepresentations contained in General Armstrong's book lately published, and intended as a repository of historical truth for posterity, entitled "Notices of the War of 1812." In this book, (vol. 1st, pages 147–8 and 9,) the General attempts to depreciate and ridicule the militia of the state, by representing them as having run away on the first sight of the enemy, but giving them no credit for their prompt return and subsequent good conduct; and ascribing the gallant attack and defeat of the British, on that occasion, to about one hundred and fifty United States infantry and a few Indians, whom he represents as having casually assembled at Buffalo.

It is true as asserted by General Armstrong, and admitted in the preceding account, that the militia stationed at Black Rock did flee most ignominiously on the first appearance of the British troops, and without firing a gun; but it is equally true, that these same militia a short time afterward nobly returned to their duty, and fought and achieved the only severe battle of that morning, un-

The next affair in which the Indians were engaged,
occurred in the neighborhood of Fort George, on the

aided by the regular troops from Buffalo,—who, by-the-bye, amounted,—not to
one hundred and fifty men, as represented by General Armstrong,—but to only
about one half that number, and they too, with the exception of the officers, raw
recruits, nine tenths of whom had never seen a battle or a camp.

The attacking force was on that morning divided by the commanding officer
into three columns, which were to advance by different routes, and make a simultaneous assault on the British position, which was on high, open and commanding
ground.   The militia and Indians arrived in season and commenced the attack;
but the column composed of the regular infantry and the volunteer citizens attached to it, being commanded at the time the order for the attack was given by
Captain Cummings of the army, but who was superseded at the critical moment
when the troops were advancing, by another officer of the army of higher rank,
who happened to arrive and to insist on his right to command the column, lost
the favorable moment for rendering efficient service.   Misapprehending the precise orders under which they were acting, the officer who thus assumed the
command over Captain Cummings, made an awkward, although but momentary
diversion, which prevented him from reaching the ground until the battle had
been fought, and the enemy had fled in the direction of their boats.

Subsequently, when the enemy had rallied and again presented a line of battle
in the vicinity of their boats, the regular infantry from Buffalo, being now incor-
porated with the other troops, advanced to the charge with all the zeal and spirit
that distinguished their associates: but the British, abashed by the vigor and
resolution manifested by their assailants, made and received but one or two fires,
when they took to their boats and hurried to the opposite shore of the Niagara.

This explanation is made in no feeling of unkindness toward the regular
troops; but is richly due to the gallant little band of militia, who, it is believed,
set the first example during the late war,—but afterward so often and so glori-
ously repeated on the Niagara frontier,—of a body of raw militia advancing and
meeting, in open field and regular order, an equal, or as in this case, even a superior number of disciplined British troops, and dispersing them at the point of the
bayonet.   For the conflict on this occasion was closer and more desperate than
happens in nine out of ten battles said to be fought by British troops at the bayonet's point.

There are other misrepresentations in General Armstrong's account of this
affair,—such as materially underrating the number of combatants, and the numbers
slain and made prisoners; and in his assertion that the British had accomplished,
before they were driven back, most of the important objects of the expedition, in
burning barracks and block houses, and carrying away the *whole* of the plunder
that invited it,—when in fact they did not carry away or destroy more than one
third of the valuable naval stores prepared at Black Rock for Commodore Perry,

17th of July. A body of volunteers and Indians, under Major Cyrenius Chapin, having crossed over to the fort, and being somewhat impatient to see the enemy, a plan was concerted to cut off his pickets. The forces of Major Chapin, Indians and militia, consisted of about three hundred. To these was added a detachment of two hundred regulars, under Major Cummings, and the command of the whole entrusted to General Porter. The British and Indian encampment was surprised at daylight, seventy-five of their number killed, and sixteen taken prisoners. It has been stated that the success of the expedition was almost entirely owing to a stratagem of the Indians, who, when they had formed their plan of attack, succeeded in decoying the opposing Indians into an ambuscade, so artfully disposed that when they raised the war-whoop their dusky opponents mistook it for a signal of a party of their own friends.* An official account of this affair was given by General Boyd, then commanding the post of Fort George, in which he says :—

" Those who participated in this contest, particularly the Indians, conducted with great bravery and activity. General Porter volunteered in the affair, and Major Chapin evinced his accustomed zeal and courage. The principal chiefs who led the warriors this day were Farmer's-Brother, Red-Jacket, Little-Billy, Pollard, Black-Smoke, Johnson, Silver-Heels, Captain Half-Town, Major Henry O'Bail, and Captain Cold,

---

nor touch a particle of the military stores in *depot* at Buffalo for the use of the army. But these are errors of minor consideration, and would not have been noticed but for the cruel attack upon the militia of the Niagara frontier.

* Drake's Book of the Indians.

who was wounded.   In a council which was held with them yesterday, they covenanted not to scalp or murder ; and I am happy to say that they treated the prisoners with humanity, and committed no wanton cruelties on the dead."

The chiefs named in this despatch were all Senecas excepting Captain Cold.   In a subsequent bulletin General Boyd spoke a second time of the good conduct of the Indians in this brisk affair, thus :—" The bravery and humanity of the Indians were equally conspicuous ;" and another authority* says :—" They behaved with great gallantry, and betrayed no disposition to violate the restrictions imposed upon them by General Boyd."   The despatch of General Boyd, just quoted, contains the first official information extant, of Red-Jacket's personal service in the field during that contest.

* Article in Niles's Weekly Register.

CHAPTER X.

NOTWITHSTANDING the brilliant successes with which it had been opened, the Niagara campaign of 1813 closed disastrously to the American arms. Forts Erie and George were successively evacuated by the forces of the United States,—the latter withdrawing to the republican side of the river, while their pathway was lighted by the conflagration of the beautiful town of Newark, wantonly laid in ashes by General M'Clure, under a misapprehension of his instructions from the Secretary of War. This event, the remembrance of which is painful to every American of just feelings, occurred on the 10th of December. But the Vandal act was not allowed to pass unavenged. On the night of the 18th, the enemy crossed the river in force, and the fortress of Niagara was carried by surprise. Pursuing his success, the enemy swept rapidly along the frontier from Ontario to Erie, carrying the works at Lewiston, Manchester, Black Rock and Buffalo, laying those fair villages in ruins, and ravaging the adjacent country with fire and sword. It is true that this frontier had been left comparatively defenceless, by the withdrawal of the regular troops for the memorable descent of the St. Lawrence, with a view to the capture of Montreal,—an enterprise which signally failed. Still, the fall of Niagara was inglorious, while but few laurels were won in defence of either of the posts, successively and immediately thereafter falling into the hands of the invaders. Among the villages destroyed in this retaliatory invasion was that of the Tuscaroras; but the Indians themselves appear to have borne no part even in the feeble defence interposed by the militia, and the handful of regulars stationed among them.

But the contest was renewed in that quarter in the following year, more vigorously than ever, and the Senecas, with their confederates upon the American side, roused by the stirring eloquence of Red-Jacket, were upon the war path as early at least as the American troops were prepared to resume offensive operations.

On the 1st of July, 1814, General Brown found himself in Buffalo, at the head of a military force so strong as in his judgment to authorize the invasion of Canada, for which movement the country at large as well as his own troops appeared to be impatient. His army consisted of two brigades of infantry, commanded respectively by Generals Scott and Ripley, to each of which was attached an efficient train of field artillery, under

Colonel Towson and Major Hindman, and a small squadron of cavalry under Captain Harris,—the whole in the highest state of discipline and equipment. To these was added a brigade of miscellaneous troops, comprising a regiment of Pennsylvania volunteers about five hundred strong, a corps of six hundred New-York volunteers, one hundred of them mounted,—then on their march from Batavia,—and five hundred and fifty to six hundred Indian warriors, embracing nearly the whole military force of the Six Nations,—all under the immediate command of General Peter B. Porter, as the Quarter-master General of the militia of New-York; who, without intending to adopt permanently the military profession, was induced to accept this heterogeneous command, under a belief that his local knowledge of the country, at least, might enable him to be useful in the prosecution of a war which, in another situation, he had been instrumental in recommending, but which thus far had been attended with so little success.*

General Brown proposed to open the campaign by the capture of Fort Erie; and thence, proceeding rapidly down the Niagara river, reduce in succession the British posts of Chippewa, Queenston Heights, Forts Mississaugua and Niagara; anticipating the co-operation of Commodore Chauncey's squadron on Lake Ontario, in the achievement of the two last objects.

Fort Erie, situated at the foot of Lake Erie, was garrisoned by one hundred and seventy men, and comman-

---

* General Porter, as a member of Congress, had been a strong and eloquent advocate for the Declaration of War.

ded by Major Burke of the British army. Chippewa, eighteen miles below, and then the head quarters of the British forces, was occupied by General Real, with an army,—inclusive of troops at available distances in his rear,—of about the same numerical force, and of the same composition with that of General Brown, save that the number of his Indian allies was somewhat less.

In order to form any just estimate of the merits of the battle of Chippewa,—no just or adequate account of which has yet appeared in history,—a correct and minute knowledge of the positions of the two armies and their surrounding localities, at the time of the engagement, is indispensably necessary. The Chippewa or Welland River, the north or left bank of which, near its mouth, was occupied by the British army and their defences, consisting of two block-houses connected and flanked by a parapet, is a considerable stream, about one hundred yards wide and from twelve to twenty feet deep, coming from the west and entering the Niagara at a right angle. Street's Creek, the mouth of which was selected by the American commanders as a suitable position before the battle, is a small sluggish stream parallel to the Chippewa, and entering the Niagara two miles above, or to the south of it. The Chippewa is bordered on the south by a flat, open plain, about three-fourths of a mile wide and terminating in the rear in a dense forest of primitive growth ; so wet, and so much obstructed by fallen timber, as to be impracticable for carriages or horses. The west bank of the Niagara is precisely similar to the south bank of the

Chippewa,—with this difference only, that about mid-
way between the Chippewa and Street's Creek there is,
or was at that time, a strip or tongue of woodland which
had never been cleared, about one-fourth of a mile in
width, extending from, or being a continuation of, the
forest in the rear to a narrow clearing of one hundred
yards width, on the bank of the river, used as the public highway,—thus forming a mask between the two
positions of Chippewa and Street's Creek, by which the
occupants of each were excluded from all knowledge or
observation of what was passing at the other.

On the 2d of July General Brown, with Generals
Scott and Porter, made a reconnoissance of Fort Erie
and the upper parts of the Niagara, and concerted a
plan for the attack of the fort on the following morning.
By this plan General Ripley, with part of his brigade,
was to embark in boats at Buffalo in the course of the
night, and passing up and across the lake, land at daylight on the British shore, a mile above Fort Erie; and
General Scott with his brigade to cross the Niagara
River, through a difficult pass in the Black Rock
Rapids, and make a simultaneous landing, a mile below
the fort; when the two brigades, closing and surrounding the fort, would prevent the escape of the garrison
until artillery could be brought from Buffalo to reduce
it. General Ripley, although punctual in his departure,
did not reach the point of debarkation until some hours
after the appointed time, in consequence of a heavy fog
by which his pilots were misled. But General Scott,
with his accustomed promptitude, made good his land-

ing at the hour indicated, and was able, with the assistance of a few Indians and volunteers who accompanied him, to invest the fort in such a manner as to secure its garrison.

The rising sun disclosed to the British commandant and his officers, who were deliberately viewing the scene with their glasses from the top of their works, not only their fort already surrounded, but the hurried transit of boats at the ferry below freighted with Indians, artillery and other means for their destruction. Whether influenced most by the formidable appearance of the artillery or of the Indians, who are held even in greater terror by European than by American soldiers, the commanding officer, soon after mid-day, and too soon perhaps to satisfy the claims of military etiquette, surrendered the fort and garrison to the demand of General Brown, without firing a gun.

On the same evening General Scott, with his brigade and Towson's artillery, proceeded down the Niagara, and on the morning of the 4th, having driven in on his march some advanced posts of the enemy, established his camp in the open field on the south side of Street's Creek, near its mouth and two miles from Chippewa. On the evening of the same day (4th) he was joined by General Brown, with General Ripley's brigade, which took post in the same field in rear of General Scott. In the course of the night of the 4th, General Porter crossed the Niagara at Black Rock, with the Pennsylvania volunteers and Indians; and at sunrise on the morning of the 5th, marched for the camp, where they arrived at twelve o'clock. On their way down they were met about five miles above Chippewa by General Brown, who on joining and returning with them gave General Porter to understand that the position of the American army, although probably the best that could have been selected, was a most uncomfortable one on account of its contracted limits,—there being but about three-fourths of a mile distance between the river and an almost impenetrable forest, infested by a band of Indians and militia, conversant with its haunts and sent out from the British camp to annoy and assail his pickets; that he had that morning been under the necessity of making an example of a valuable officer for suffering his guard to be driven in, and the army thus exposed to the direct fire of these troublesome visitants,— that it was absolutely necessary for the quiet and safety of the camp that these intruders should be dispersed; and, as regular troops were ill qualified for such service, proposed to General Porter that he should with his corps of Indian warriors, aided if necessary by the volunteers, scour the adjoining woods and drive the enemy across the Chippewa, handling them in such a manner as would prevent a renewal of this kind of warfare,—*assuring him in the most confident terms* that there was not and would not be in the course of that day a single British regular soldier on the south side of the Chippewa. But still, to be prepared for such improbable contingency, that he would direct General Scott's brigade to cross Street's Creek and occupy the plain on the north side of it, (which afterward became the principal battle

33

ground,) and be in readiness to sustain him. The proposition was of course acceded to by General Porter, and when afterward communicated to his brigade, received by them with enthusiasm.

By three o'clock in the afternoon, the men having been refreshed from the fatigues of the preceding twenty-four hours,—the plan of march and attack settled, and the warriors duly arrayed in their battle dress,*—General Porter's command,—with the exception of two hundred Pennsylvanians who were left on parade, subject to future orders,—was formed about half a mile in rear of the main camp, into a single or Indian file, with Indians on the left; and thence marching into the woods in the same order, in a line at right angles to the river, until the whole Indian force was immerged in the forest, leaving the white troops in the open field,—they had only to halt and face to the right, when the whole were formed in line of battle, three-fourths of a mile long and *one man deep*, looking in the direction of Chippewa. Red-Jacket was placed at the extreme left of the line, and General Porter took his station on the margin of the woods between the white and red troops, accompanied by Captain Pollard,—a Seneca chief, who was considered as the first in command among the In-

---

* It was the uniform practice of our Indian warriors, when going into action, to divest their persons of all covering excepting moccasins, perhaps leggings, a breech-cloth, a large tuft of white feathers fastened to the hair on the crown of the head, and a small strong plaited line or belt, three or four yards long, (called a matunip line,) girt about their waist, to secure the tomahawk, knife, powderhorn, &c., and used if necessary to bind their prisoners. Their naked bodies and faces were then painted with bold and gaudy colors, without uniformity, and generally, though not always, without much taste or design.

dians,*—Colonel Flemming, the Quarter-master of the Indian corps, Lieutenant (now Major) Donald Fraser, his aid, Henry Johnson, his interpreter.† He was also accompanied by Major (now Adjutant-General) Jones, and Major Wood of the Engineers, who afterward fell in the sortie from Fort Erie, as volunteers ; and supported by a company of regular infantry, marching in column in the rear as a reserve. The Indians were commanded by their war-chiefs who were indulged in their own mode of conducting the attack, marching about twenty yards in advance of the warriors of their respective tribes.   General Porter having sent out scouts to re-

* The selection of their leader for this battle, or perhaps for the campaign, was made in council but a short time before the action took place.   The chief who expected the distinction was an Onondaga, named *Ka-was-kwant*, or the *Spring-Trap*, commonly known as Captain John.   He was an aged warrior, who had shown his bravery at Wyoming, Cherry Valley, and Newtown, and in short at almost every place where fighting was to be done during the war of the revolution.   He was now seventy-five years old ; but hearing that his people were about to go again upon the war-path, the fire of heroism rekindled in his bosom, and he hastened to the frontier, confident, that from his well-known character of old, he should be chosen the leader on the present occasion.   But he was not even named in council, the choice falling with great unanimity upon Pollard.   Captain John was greatly affected by this neglect, and the tears rolled down his cheeks as he related the circumstance to Mr. Tyler, the author's informant.   " They think me too old, and that I am good for nothing," said the veteran chief, in the bitterness of his heart; and with a countenance saddened with disappointment he left the warriors, and retraced his steps to Onondaga. As they did not want his services, he would not trouble them with his presence.

† Henry Johnson, (called Cattaraugas Hank,) was a white man by birth ; but having been made a prisoner in infancy, was in all his associations, habits and dispositions, a thorough Indian.   He was honest and possessed a handsome property, was endowed with great physical power and enterprise, and being withal an admirable hunter, there was, probably, not an Indian or a white man on the Niagara, who could boast of having slain the number of foes that fell by his unerring rifle.

connoitre the enemy, the march was commenced by signal, and proceeded at first with great stillness and caution. The chiefs have signals, by which, on the discovery of any circumstance requiring consultation or a change of route or action, they convey notice through their ranks with great celerity, on which the whole line of warriors drop instantly to the ground, and remain there until farther orders. Two manœuvres of this kind occurred on the march,—the first of little moment, but the second communicating, through the scouts, the exact position of the enemy, who, apprised of their assailants' approach, lay concealed in a thicket of bushes along the margin of Street's Creek. A consultation was thereupon held and new orders given, the purport of which was to change the line of march so as to meet the enemy to more advantage, to increase the speed as much as was consistent with the preservation of order, to receive their first fire, but not to return it except singly and when it could be done with certain effect, and then to raise the war-whoop, pursue, capture and slay as many as practicable, until they should reach the open ground in front of Chippewa, and thence return to camp.

The march was accordingly resumed, the fire of the enemy received, and a rush accompanied with savage yells made upon them and continued for more than a mile, through scenes of frightful havoc and slaughter, few only of the fugitives offering to surrender as prisoners, while others, believing that no quarters would be given, suffered themselves to be cut down by the tomahawk, or turning back upon their pursuers, fought hand to hand to the last.

On reaching the open field in front of Chippewa, the assailants were met by a tremendous discharge of musketry, by which the warriors, who were principally in front, were thrown back upon the volunteers and reserve, who for want of equal speed were a short distance in the rear. Presuming that the fire had come from the enemy he had been pursuing, and who had rallied on reaching the open ground, General Porter made an effort, not without success, to reform his line with the volunteers, reserve, and a portion of the warriors; but on again advancing to the margin of the woods found himself within a few yards of the whole British regular army formed in line of battle, and presenting within a given space at least three men fresh from their camp, to a single one in his own attenuated and exhausted line. After receiving and returning two or three fires, the enemy rushed forward with charged bayonets, when, hearing nothing from General Scott, he gave the order to retreat, *sauve qui peut*, and form again on the left of General Scott's brigade, wherever it should be found.

It appears that the British commander had resolved on making a general attack that day on the American camp; and in execution of this purpose had marched his whole force across the Chippewa a short time before General Porter entered the woods with the Indians; and having sent forward his Indians and militia,—which was the British force met in the woods,—to commence his attack on the left flank of the Americans, formed in the meantime his battalions of regulars on the plain, under cover of the strip of wood land which divided the two camps, with his artillery on his left, near the gorge occupied by the road along the bank of the river ; ready to act the moment the effect of the flank attack should be developed.

The repulse of General Porter's command was thus effected by the main body of the British army, while General Scott's brigade was more than a mile in the rear, and had not yet crossed the bridge over Street's Creek. The error therefore of General Porter,—if he committed one,—consisted in remaining as long as he did under so unequal a fire ; or perhaps in attempting to rally at all against so superior a force ; and if the Indians were more censured for cowardice than the volunteers, in consequence of being foremost in the flight, they owe· their degradation to their greater speed and bottom, for every fugitive, whether white or red man, exerted his utmost power of locomotion to escape, restrained by no other consideration than a passing regard to the safety of his immediate companions in flight.* In a retreat of

* Colonel Worth, of the U. S. army, has given me in conversations some amusing reminiscences of this retreat of the Indians. The Colonel was a young officer at that time, attached to the military family of General Scott. Some of the Indians, it seems, had taken their sons, lads of twelve to fourteen, into the battle, to teach them early in the trade of war. As the Indians came rushing along in a diagonal direction, some of them ran up in front of Scott's brigade, which opened a passage through for their retreat. Among them Colonel Worth observed one stalwart Indian, with his son upon his shoulder, bounding forward with the utmost expedition. Just as he was passing near the position of the General and staff, a shell of the enemy's exploded apparently over his head. With the usual exclamation of "Ugh!" the Indian bounded nearly ten feet high, and as he came down, his son, who was about fourteen years old, tumbled sprawling upon the ground,—the father continuing his speed, and the young "brave" picking him-

a mile in a diagonal direction to the right, so as to un-
cover the enemy to the fire of the American line, then
just beginning to form, they gained but little distance on
the British columns who were in hot pursuit. When
General Porter and his staff arrived at Street's Creek,
they were met by Major (now General,) Jesup's battalion, then in the act of taking its position, which was
on the left, and a short distance from the remainder of
General Scott's brigade ; and the volunteers, fatigued as
they were, aided Major Jesup's evolutions, which were
executed with great order and celerity, by breaking
down the fences to enable him to pass from the road
bordering on Street's Creek, to his position in the field.
Nothing could exceed the coolness and order with which
General Scott's brigade crossed the bridge and formed
its line, under the galling fire of the enemy's artillery,
and the headlong approach of his infantry, who, when
only fifty yards distant, were received by a tremendous
discharge of musketry from the American line, which
forced them to fall back for a considerable distance.
But they speedily rallied and advanced again, when
they were met in the same gallant manner, which proved
decisive of the battle ; and they thereupon fled the field
with as much precipitation as they had entered it,—not
halting until they had recrossed the Chippewa and destroyed their bridge. General Scott pursued them
around the point of woods, beyond which he could only

---

self up and scampering after him as fast as possible. The scene was so ludicrous
as to create merriment among the young officers, even on so grave an occasion,—
calling forth a rebuke from General Scott. W. L. S.

advance in face of their batteries, and these he could
not reach by reason of the intervening river. He therefore deployed to the left, and forming a line in the open
field in front of Chippewa, directed his men to lie down
with their heads toward the batteries, the better to avoid
the effect of their fire.

The battle between the regular troops was but of a
few minutes duration, with the exception of the artillery,
which, on both sides, was earliest and longest engaged,
and served with the most destructive effect,—Colonel
Towson occupying the right of the American line, on
Street's Creek, and the British artillery the left of theirs,
at the point of woods, and both commencing with the
first movements of the regular troops.

Immediately after the two lines had encountered on
Street's Creek, a magnificent charger completely capari-
soned, but without a rider, was seen prancing and cur-
veting in the centre of the battle field, and endeavoring
to make his escape through the American line to the
rear. Presuming that he had belonged to some officer
who had fallen, he was forthwith secured by the servant
of General Porter, and immediately mounted by the
general, to whom he was a most acceptable acquisition
after the labors of the day which he had performed on
foot.*

* This powerful steed was the property of Major M'Neal, who commanded
one of General Scott's battalions, and never having before been in action, was so
much alarmed by the sudden and tremendous discharge of musketry and artillery in every direction, as to be, for a few moments, wholly unmanagable ; and
the major was obliged to dismount and abandon him. He, nevertheless, soon
became familiarized, as his owner had been long before, to the dangers of his
new profession, and was the next morning restored to the major.

Riding up to General Brown, who was also in the midst of the action, General Porter received his orders to march with the two hundred Pennsylvanians who had been left in camp, to the support of General Scott; which orders were promptly executed by following General Scott's brigade around the point of woods, receiving the fire of the British batteries, and taking post on his left with the men in the same recumbent position. Here they awaited the arrival of General Ripley's brigade, which, on the first discovery that the whole British army was in the field, had been ordered to make a detour through the woods, and attack the enemy's right. They soon came up, in the same muddy plight with the volunteers and Indians who had previously traversed the same ground; when the whole army at about sundown quietly retired to their camp on the south side of Street's Creek. And thus ended the battle of Chippewa, which probably produced more important results in favor of the American arms than any other engagement by land in the course of that war; although there were several battles fought on the Niagara, if not elsewhere, during the same campaign, exhibiting a greater number of combatants engaged, a larger number slain, and a result equally creditable to the gallantry and good conduct of the American soldiers.

The first advantage gained was in driving from the British army those troublesome enemies, their Indian allies, who had been the terror of our troops in the west, during all the preceding stages of the war, and had kept the camps of General Dearborn, General Lewis and

34

General Boyd, in a perpetual panic during the campaign of 1813. Terrified and disheartened by the reception they met with at Chippewa, they fled from the battle field to the head of Lake Ontario, a distance of thirty miles, without halting, and never again during the remainder of the war appeared in the British camp,—thus giving a practical and decisive proof that they held the prowess of their red American foes in much higher estimation than some of the allies of the latter were disposed to accord to them.

Another immediate effect of this battle was to give the American people confidence in the courage and efficiency of their army, and to the latter, confidence in themselves. A great blunder had been committed at the commencement of the war, in the appointment of incompetent and unworthy men, taken perhaps from the gambling table or the race course, as officers of the army, owing their places to the importunities of influential friends, who sought this mode of providing for those who were useless in civil life.

It is a well known fact, and it is fortunate for the purposes of war that it is so, that the tone, temper and spirit of the common soldier will, in most instances, and especially on occasions of great peril, conform to, and identify themselves with those of his commanding officer; so that if an officer prove recreant in battle, his example will poison and make cowards of the whole corps to which he belongs; and it was to this circumstance that the Americans were indebted for most of their early discomfitures.

But in 1814 this difficulty had in a great measure
been overcome by the resignation or dismissal of unde-
serving incumbents, and the army of Niagara entered
the field under a complement of as gallant officers as
could be found in any army or country.

The victory of Chippewa and those which followed
it were achieved by men three fourths of whom,—including the regular troops as well as the volunteers and
Indians,—had never before been in action,—thus establishing the important fact, which should not be lost
sight of in the future organization of our army and militia, that the efficiency of a military force depends more
on the judicious selection and arrangement of the original
material of which it is composed, than on prolonged discipline ; and that a farmer fresh from the plough may,
by a drill of six weeks, *under proper officers*, be rendered
as efficient in all the duties of the field, as a soldier of
ten years standing, although he may not within this short
space become enured to the habits of the camp.

The *eclat* of these victories created such an enthusiasm throughout the country, that not only the youth,
but men of every age and condition in life, were pressing
for opportunities to enter the service ; and had the war
continued, the campaign of 1815 would have opened
with an army of any desired extent, selected from the
choicest materials of the country. But these same events,
so brilliant on our part, had a corresponding influence in
depressing the hopes and expectations of our enemy, and
led to the peace of December, 1814, so honorable to both
parties, and which, it is to be hoped, will not soon be
again disturbed.

On reviewing the several incidents connected with the battle of Chippewa, it is evident that, had General Scott's brigade been at hand to support the volunteers and Indians when first met by the regular columns of the British army, the contest as a whole would have presented quite a different aspect from the one it actually assumed ; but that the result would have been equally auspicious to the American arms is not to be doubted. Why they were not there has never been satisfactorily explained to those who were most interested in the movement. There can be no question that General Scott was as full a believer as General Brown, in the proposition and prophecy so confidently advanced by the latter in the morning, "that there was not and would not be, in the course of that day, a single regular British soldier on the south side of the Chippewa," and that General Porter's force was amply sufficient to dispose of the Indians and militia. But whether the tardy execution, or rather non-execution, of the promised order for his support, proceeded from delay in the issuing, or in the performance of it, is a question which seems not to have been settled.

Still, the successive mistakes committed by the two armies on that day, by reason of their mutual ignorance of each other's positions, plans and movements, were probably quite as injurious in their consequences to the British as to the Americans. The first error, in throwing the volunteers and Indians, in their exhausted condition, into the power of the British battalions, without support, was immediately followed by an equal one on the part of the latter, who, on seeing the sudden check and rapid retreat they had given to their assailants, and elated too, as they evidently were, with the idea that victory was already achieved, pursued them for a mile with a precipitation which at once exhausted their strength, and threw them into a degree of confusion, which was so much increased by the astounding reception they met with from General Scott's line, that they could never afterward restore that order which was necessary to enable them to cope with the cool and compact ranks of the Americans. And these mutual blunders probably hastened the termination of the battle, and rendered it less sanguinary than it would have been had the parties met more deliberately, and with a better knowledge of each other's views and comparative strength.*

The rumor which was industriously spread, that the whole of the American Indians, immediately on their repulse at Chippewa, fled to Buffalo, and were never seen again in the American camp, was destitute of foundation. The Indians never coerce their warriors into battle or compel them to remain there, and it is true that a considerable number of them fled from sheer cowardice and fright, on the first fire ; but the number of fugitives was much exaggerated for want of a knowledge of Indian customs. When they take a prisoner, the captor, with surprising dexterity and despatch, binds his hands behind his back with his maturnip line and leads him off to the rear,

* General Riall had seventeen hundred men engaged in this battle, while the American troops actually brought into the battle did not exceed thirteen hundred.

like a horse by a halter, on a trot; and the frequent appearance of these parties gliding along the skirts of the woods at the commencement of the action,—the guard generally outnumbering the prisoners,—led the other troops by whom they were observed to believe that they were all fugitives. But that the great body of warriors as well as volunteers, engaged in the opening attack, fought with a boldness, not to say desperation, unsurpassed by any other troops until they were placed,— and that not by their own fault,—in a situation where it would have been madness not to retreat, was fully attested by their officers; and was, moreover, proved by the fact that the loss of the British Indians and militia in the woods, inclusive of killed, wounded and prisoners, was not less than that of their regular troops in the subsequent engagement in the field.

Most of the warriors remained in camp for some fifteen days longer, and until the eve of the battle of Bridgewater, when, for reasons which were plausible, if not satisfactory, they retired from the army to their respective villages.

On the morning of the 6th of July, General Porter was waited on at his tent by about twenty chiefs, each accompanied by a warrior bearing the scalps which his tribe had taken during the preceding day. They had, it seems, been informed that they were to receive a bounty for every scalp taken in battle. But on being apprised of their mistake, these unseemly trophies were immediately buried or thrown into the river. Still they were allowed a premium for the prisoners they had

taken, amounting to sixteen or eighteen,—among whom
were two or three chiefs,—proportioned to the rank they
held.

At their request General Porter gave them permission to visit the battle ground, for the purpose of bringing off the bodies of their friends who had fallen,
which in the hurry of the preceding day they had not
been able to do,—it being understood that Colonel
Flemming should accompany them.

After an absence of a few hours they returned, bringing in the bodies of fifteen warriors, among whom were
three chiefs, all of which were buried in the course of
the evening with the honors of war.* They reported
also that among the numerous bodies of their enemies
strewed along the woods, they had discovered three
who, although mortally wounded, were still living.
Two of these they despatched by cutting their throats,
but recognizing in the third a late member of one of
their own villages, who was burning with fever and
thirst, Johnson had filled his own canteen with water
at a neighboring creek and given it to him, to die by
himself. On being reproached with the savage proceeding of taking the life of an unresisting foe, the only
answer given by Johnson, with marks of evident con-
trition, was,—"That it did seem hard to take the lives

* Among the slain chiefs was Captain Le Fort, an Onondaga, of courage and
reputation. His son, Abraham Le Fort, yet resides at Onondaga. He has procured a good education, adopted the costume of the whites, and his children are
inmates of the English common school in his neighborhood. He was a lad of
fourteen at the time of the battle of Chippewa, and accompanied his father
in that campaign. W. L. S.

" of these men, but that we ought to recollect that these
" were very hard times."

Two days after the battle a passage was forced
across the Chippewa at a point three miles above its
mouth, by Major Hindman's corps of artillery, supported
by General Ripley's brigade and the New-York volunteers, just arrived. After a short and gallant resistance
by the enemy at the cannon's mouth, they fled in great
haste and confusion,—destroying their works at Chippewa and Queenston heights,—to Fort Mississagua, at
the mouth of the Niagara River.

On the march of the army to Queenston, the Indians,
whose roving habits it was impossible to restrain, committed some depredations upon the neighboring farmers,
besides capturing some fifty to one hundred barrels of
wine, brandy, and other stores belonging to the British
army, which they found concealed in the woods. This
property was taken from them by the United States
Quarter-master, in virtue of an order issued by General Brown on entering the province, and as regarded
the public stores, much to their dissatisfaction.

About this time, on the suggestion of Red-Jacket, approved by General Brown, two young chiefs distinguished for their bravery, prudence and address, were
despatched to the camp of the British Indians at the
head of the lake, with secret propositions for the mutual
withdrawal of the whole Indian forces from both armies.
After three days absence they returned, and reported
that they were kindly received by the few chiefs with
whom they dared to communicate or to be made

known to ; and that measures would be immediately taken by them to carry the proposition into effect. This embassy,—which Red-Jacket was disposed to turn to the best advantage,—resulted in the retirement of all the American warriors to their respective villages, with a positive engagement, nevertheless, that they would immediately return if the British Indians should again appear in the field. But they did not appear; still, some forty or fifty American Indians, among whom was Johnson, lured by the love of war and by the exciting scenes through which they had already passed, returned to the army and were useful auxiliaries during the remainder of the campaign,—having been in Fort Erie at the time of its investment, and performed a conspicuous part in the sortie of the 17th September, on which occasion they were among the first to scale the enemy's works.

The writer of the preceding account has relied almost wholly on his memory,—having had recourse to scarcely a single written document, except to ascertain dates,—for the facts it contains.* His principal object has been to vindicate the men of the Six Nations, who have no historian to chronicle their good or bad deeds, against the charges both of bad faith and cowardice

* General Porter is himself the author of this account of the crossing of the Niagara by the American army; the capture of Fort Erie; and the battle of Chippewa. I had written as good an account of these events as all the materials I could obtain enabled me to collate. But not being satisfied with it myself, I placed the manuscript in the hands of General Porter, who kindly favored me with a far more correct, extended, and impartial account of that portion of the campaign of 1814, than I could obtain the means of composing. See letter from General Porter to the author, Appendix E.

35

preferred against them during their brief connexion with the army. He will close it with a few remarks on their character, and more especially that of Red-Jacket, as warriors.

Although these people are unable, for want of the necessary science, materials, and machinery, to wage a systematic and independent war, they are nevertheless most valuable auxiliaries to an army in this country. Indeed, a corps of Indian warriors, bearing a due proportion to the size of the army with which they act, may be considered as worth at least double their numbers in any other description of troops. Equal, at least, to white men in physical strength, intelligence, and military ambition, the athletic habits in which they are educated, their familiarity with the woods and fields, and their abstemious modes of living, confer on them an activity and fleetness and a power of endurance far beyond what white men possess; while the lightness of their arms and dress and the scanty means required for their subsistence and sleeping, relieve an army from a vast amount of the lumber and material of war. The prevailing impression that they are more cowardly than white men,—which is an inference from their well known repugnance and refusal to fight hand to hand in the open field,—is known to be unjust by those intimately acquainted with their character and customs. It should be recollected that the sentiment of true valor, which is as much respected and cherished by the Indians as by white men, is not less the offspring of education than of instinct. Among the qualifications of a great war-chief, prudence, sagacity, and skill in circumventing and prostrating an enemy with the least possible loss to his own people, are not less regarded and venerated than his prowess in the field. They are taught from their infancy to hold in detestation that sort of blind chivalry which induces two men, or two equal bodies of men, to march into a field and deliberately hack each other down. Yet many of our Indians were repeatedly seen, not only charging with the other troops in the field, but performing,—when acting by themselves,—feats of open, bold, and daring bravery, from the execution of which few even of our best troops would not have recoiled. But when they do indulge in such feats it must be when the chances of success are strongly in their favor, and in prospect of a boon commensurate with the hazard they run.

As to Red-Jacket, he was considered by his own friends as well as by his enemies, constitutionally a coward,—that is to say, as formed with nerves more sensitive to danger than those of most other men; and yet so powerfully was he influenced by the feelings of pride, and the necessity of sustaining in every situation the reputation of a great chief, that he was said by those who were near him to have behaved exceedingly well in the battle of Chippewa. But he took care to keep himself out of all minor engagements and skirmishes, where, if the hazard would have been less, so also was the object to be achieved. During the whole period of the war, the powers of his great eloquence were constantly exerted both on the government and on the chiefs and warriors; first, to keep them from joining in the war, and after they had become engaged to withdraw them from it; and in this his counsels were those of a wise man and a provident father of his people. His principal arguments were,—that the Indians had no interest in the quarrel between the two parties, and nothing to gain or lose in the result,—that they had no voice in the declaration of war, nor could they have in its conduct and termination,—and above all, that the Six Nations had but few young men, who, if permitted to be drawn into the contest and employed in such enterprises as the white officers by whom they would be commanded should direct, and their own ambition court, would be very soon exterminated, and leave the remainder of their nation poor and powerless.

Four days after the battle of Chippewa, the army resumed its march down the Niagara, for the investment of Fort George, the passage of the Chippewa being but feebly opposed, and General Riall falling back upon Twelve Mile Creek, and throwing a portion of his troops into the last mentioned fortress.

In the hard fought battle of Lundy's Lane, on the 25th of July, among the wounded were the Commander-in-chief Major-General Brown, General Scott, and his favorite aid-de-camp Captain Worth. The latter officer was carried back to Buffalo to be healed of his wounds. While lying there, an incident occurred connected with the Indian department of history, which is worthy of record. Captain Worth had become quite a favorite with the Indians in that and the preceding campaign, and during the several weeks of his confinement, they were wont to hang around his quarters in considerable numbers, watching him with great solicitude. Farmer's-Brother, in particular, was in the habit of attending his bed-side several hours almost every day. On one occasion, a Chippewa Indian crossed over from the Canada shore, and joined a large party of Indians near Captain Worth's quarters, in the character of a deserter. According to his story, he had left the British camp below the falls, swum the Chippewa, and finding means of crossing the Niagara, he had now come over to join the Americans. Desertion is not an Indian vice, being peculiar to the more elevated race of the whites. His statement was therefore received with distrust. Nevertheless, for a short time he mingled among the Senecas undetected. But his true character could not be long concealed. The Indians having indulged rather more freely than common in drink one afternoon, and consequently waxing valiant, began vauntingly to recount their exploits,—each one relating how many of the British red-coats and Indians he had killed. The spirit of the Chippewa kindled at the recital; and forgetting for the moment his assumed character, he held up his fingers and boasted of the number of Yankees and Senecas whom he had slain. Words ran high, and ere many minutes had elapsed the Chippewa stood in the midst of a circle of some twenty warriors, self-convicted, not only as an enemy, but a spy. The veteran Farmer's-Brother happened at the time to be sitting with Captain Worth, and the noise of the excitement called him into the street. The weather was extremely hot, and the windows of the Captain's apartments were open, so that he was enabled to see from his couch all that was passing without. After a few words to the old chief, apparently of explanation, but which Captain Worth could not understand, Farmer's-Brother stepped up to the Chippewa, who drew his blanket over his head, and fell from a blow inflicted by the veteran's war-club. He was stunned, and for a few seconds lay motionless,—when, springing suddenly upon his feet, he leaped through the circle, and ran swiftly away to the distance of several rods. Recovering from the momentary surprise into which they had been thrown by this unlooked for action, the Senecas called after the fleeing Chippewa, and taunted him for his cowardice in refusing to die like a brave man. The retreating spy, stung by the reproach, stopped short in his flight, wheeled about, and deliberately retraced his steps to the fatal circle. Having resumed his place, he once more drew his blanket over his head, and laying himself quietly down, received the contents of Farmer's-Brother's rifle in his breast, and expired,—atoning for his crime with as much calmness and resignation as Socrates displayed in drinking the deadly hemlock.*

From the preceding narrative it must be apparent that Red-Jacket bore no very prominent part among his people while upon the war-path. Yet, in other respects, while with the army, his influence upon his people was great. Their councils were frequent

---

* Notes of the Author's conversations with Colonel Worth.

during the campaign, and Red-Jacket was uniformly their principal orator. His manner was graceful and imposing in the eye of every beholder, and his voice music,—especially to the ears of his own people. He had the power of wielding them at will, and the soul-stirring trumpet could not produce a more kindling effect in the bosoms of a disciplined army, than would his appeals upon the warriors of his race. Still, they were all aware of his infirmity, and sometimes when he was speaking of the war-path, those who were waggishly inclined would exchange significant glances at his expense.* And yet they were strongly attached to him, from their admiration of his talents, their love of his eloquence, and their confidence in his patriotism. He had years before this period become addicted to that almost universal vice of his race, intemperance, and was now indeed almost a confirmed drunkard. But he always abstained from the fire-water for a season before a council, and made due preparation for any intellectual effort he might be expecting to put forth. " Often have " I known him to make a great speech, rich in elo- " quence,—and in an hour afterward seen him drunk " upon the ground."†

In the course of the campaign sketched in the pre-

---

* An anecdote in point has been related to the author by a western gentleman who knew Red-Jacket well. He says that the Indians were often in the habit of jeering him for his cowardice, notwithstanding their strong affection for him. On one occasion this gentleman heard a conversation between the orator and two Indians, who were walking with him. They were reminding him of the circumstance of their having once in compassion given him a scalp that he might take it home as a trophy, but they said that he was afraid to carry it!

† Remark of Colonel Worth to the author.

sent chapter, Red-Jacket is said to have formed a strong friendship for Colonel Snelling, of the army, who had shown him some particular attentions. The colonel having been ordered to the command of Governor's Island, in the harbor of New-York, the orator waited upon him to bid him farewell. His parting speech was thus reported :—

"Brother :—I hear you are going to a place called Governor's Island. I hope you will be a governor yourself. I understand that you white people think children a blessing. I hope you may have a thousand. And above all, I hope, wherever you go, you may never find whiskey above two shillings a quart."*

* Published in the New-England Galaxy, by William J. Snelling.

CHAPTER XI.

IN process of time, subsequent to the negotiations of Thomas Morris with the Indians in behalf of the Holland Land Company, this association disposed of its preemptive right to the several reservations yet held by the Senecas, to Colonel Aaron Ogden and others, since known in connexion with this subject as " The Ogden Company." Thenceforward it of course became the interest of this last mentioned association to induce the Indians to relinquish those reservations, and seek a new home in a more distant territory. Negotiations to this end have often been instituted since, attended, from time to time, by partial success. It appears, moreover, that the Senecas themselves began to think of " removing their seats," at an early day after the peace of 1815. There is some reason also to suppose that connected with this projected removal was the revival, by Red-Jacket and his fellow chiefs, of the scheme so

36

ardently prosecuted by Brant twenty-five or thirty years before, of forming a great confederacy of the northwestern nations, at the head of which the Senecas would have claimed their position. Such, at all events, is the inference, irresistible, to be drawn from the proceedings of a grand Indian council held at the upper rapids of the Sandusky, in the autumn of 1816. Among the northwestern nations represented in this council were the Wyandots, Shawanese, Delawares, Ottawas, Monseys, Piankishaws, and several others. A deputation of the chiefs of the Six Nations was likewise in attendance, at the head of which was Red-Jacket, accompanied by Jasper Parish, the interpreter, and likewise by George Hosmer, Esq., a resident of the Genesee Valley, who had been a warm friend of the Seneca chiefs from his youth up, and who made this journey with them at their express solicitation.*

Among Mr. Hosmer's memoranda of his journey to Sandusky on this occasion, he has recorded an agreeable incident, illustrating the fact that notwithstanding the scorn with which he looked upon the laws and usages of civilization, Red-Jacket was not an entire stranger to the rules of propriety and delicacy in the social circle. In travelling up the shore of Lake Erie, when in the neighborhood of Cleveland, they were overtaken by a heavy storm of rain, which thoroughly drenched the party and their baggage. Stopping for

---

* I am indebted exclusively to Mr. Hosmer for the accompanying account of this council, and the sketches of the speeches delivered, which were reported by him.

the night at a comfortable log-tavern, after having partaken of some refreshments, the whole party were seated
in a large circle around a cheerful fire, drying their baggage and clothes. The chiefs, with the exception of
Red-Jacket, were earnestly and with much animation
and glee engaged in a jocular conversation with Captain Parish, and by the keenness of their wit, and the
readiness and briskness of their sallies, greatly annoyed
him, as was evident from his exertions to sustain himself. During all this time Red-Jacket sat opposite to
Mr. Hosmer, calmly smoking his pipe, and apparently
taking little interest in the conversation farther than occasionally to cast toward Mr. H. a gratified expression of
his sparkling eye. Mr. Hosmer was ignorant of the
Seneca language,—a circumstance which Red-Jacket
very well knew,—and the idea crossed his mind that his
friend might possibly suppose that their sport was at his
expense, which, situated as he was, would have been
inexcusable rudeness. After their mirth had been indulged for some time, Red-Jacket interposed a word to
Mr. Parish, and instantly all were silent. He then addressed a few sentences to Mr. Parish, which he desired him to interpret to Mr. Hosmer. It was done in
the following words :—

"We have been made uncomfortable by the storm; we are
now warm and comfortable; it has caused us to feel cheerful
and merry. But I hope our friend who is travelling with us
will not be hurt at this merriment, or suppose that we are
taking advantage of his ignorance of our language, to make
him in any manner the subject of our mirth."

To which Mr. Hosmer replied, that knowing himself to be in company with brave and honorable men, he could not allow himself to entertain any such impression. After which they resumed their merriment, and Red-Jacket his gravity.

Arriving at the council-fire, and the council having been organized for business, on the 7th of November Red-Jacket delivered the following speech :—

" BROTHERS OF THE COUNCIL,—LISTEN ! You must recollect that a few years since some delegates from your elder brethren, the Six Nations, came to you. That council fire was kindled at Brownstown, by the mutual consent of the Six Nations; but we then requested that all important business should thereafter be transacted at this place. A few years after this, another delegation came to this council fire from your elder brethren, the Six Nations. We then thought appearances looked squally. We thought the United States and Great Britain were looking with jealous eyes at each other. It appeared to us a tremendous and destructive storm was approaching, bearing blood and carnage upon its wings. We then told you that if we were not on our guard we should feel that storm. We also told you that it was the policy of the red-coats* to request at such times the aid of the Indians. We admonished you to take warning from the past, and told you to recollect the calamities which have befallen our nations in the wars of the pale faces. We then therefore solemnly requested you would be neutral in that contest. We advised you not to listen to their requests, but to sit still on your seats.

" At length the tremendous storm burst, and first in this quarter you were disturbed by the Virginians. Others of our brothers who listened to the voice from the other side of the water, and some of your warriors, united with the Virginians.

* The English.

Those warriors you took without consulting your elder brethren, the Six Nations. The consequence was, your whole land, and the place of your council fire, was smeared with blood. Our ancient records were dispersed, and many were wholly lost. Thus are we situated. There is now a delegation present from the Indians at large. A great council fire is kindled, whose smoke shall ascend to the heavens ; and we now appoint this the place for kindling a great council fire, where all important business shall be transacted. In token we give you a large belt of wampum, brown and white, intermixed with strings.

" BROTHERS :—When we received your message to attend at this time and place, you requested a full representation should arise from their seats, for the purpose of making some general arrangement for the benefit of the Indians. We have attended agreeably to your request,—and shall now make some communications to remind you of former transactions. Whenever the two white nations are about falling into difficulties, we discover different languages are held out by the British that we must adhere to them, and when the storm is near by, they will present you with a sharp iron. This has always been the course of the red-coats.

" BROTHERS :—You must be sensible that this continent was the gift of the Great Spirit. But in consequence of the wars that have taken place, we have been the perpetual sufferers. In all wars within my memory, we have lost territory by taking up the hatchet. The British have sold our country to buy peace. By the experience of the past let us learn wisdom, and close our ears to British counsel. War may again happen ; and when it does you will be invited to mate with the British. If we continue to listen to their counsel, we shall soon be exterminated. Let us guard against this by forming a permanent union which shall protect us in future. To decoy you into their measures, the British allure you with many fanciful trinkets. But these are trifles when compared with our general and individual happiness. We now earnestly request you will exert yourselves to extend the sound of our voices to our brethren who are absent from this council.

"WARRIORS, LISTEN!—You recollect that we have now established at this place a council fire, to be under the care of the Wyandots. I request you to submit to the direction of the sachems, and not through pride to attempt to control them. It is planted in the centre of your country. Do not be flattered away by any white people who may wish to purchase your land. To command respect you must possess extensive territory. Keep your seats sufficiently large that you may not be crowded on any side by the whites. And do not ever attempt to transact any business except at this place, and then in the presence of the sachems. I hope that you will aid and assist the sachems in bringing back from the other side of the water* those of our brothers who have gone astray to the British. Take them by the hand in friendship, and forget their errors. They will add to your strength.

"MY YOUNGER BRETHREN OF THE SHAWANESE:—I now address myself to you. When we were created by the Great Spirit, we were all of one color. But it was his pleasure that we should speak different languages, and be placed in different countries. You must be sensible that you are foreigners. A number of years since you came to this country, and were taken under the protection of our brethren the Wyandots, who gave you a pleasant seat, where you enjoyed a delightful country, and shared in common with them the game of the forest. These proceedings came to the knowledge of the Six Nations. You had not resided here long before you became uneasy, and you have been first to produce disturbances, and been forward to effect the sale of lands which did not belong to your nation. You have been the authors of other difficulties between the red and white people. You have been forward in the late difficulties, by listening to the voice from across the waters. Where is now your head sachem? Where a part of your people?

---

* Not the ocean, but the great lakes meaning. The same phrase, in the same sense, occurs frequently in the course of this speech.

They lent an ear to the red-coats, and are now in exile beyond the waters. We admonish you to recall them,—unite them with their brethren,—form a band of union with the Wyandots. Settled on the seats of the Wyandots, your friends, listen to their counsel. It will be good. Listen also to the counsels of the Six Nations, your elder brethren. Do not attempt to transact important business, involving the rights of others, unless at the great council fire, and with the approbation of the Wyandots.

"SACHEMS OF THE MUNSEE AND DELAWARE INDIANS :—You are sensible that you are not the original proprietors of the country you now enjoy. You came from the east. We know the country you came from. You wasted away your inheritance and became wanderers. We gave you a seat on White River, where is plenty of game and pure water. And notwithstanding this, your nation is dispersed. Some of your people have taken up the hatchet, united with the red-coats, and are now across the water. We request you will collect yourselves in one body, and settle yourselves on your lands at White River. Do this, and we will then unite ourselves together under one confederacy. We shall then have strength and be respected as well by the whites as by the more western nations."

[The speaker next proceeded to address the dispersed members of the Six Nations, residing on the lands of the Wyandots, admonishing them as he had admonished others, and counselling them to act in union and harmony, and to follow the advice of the Wyandots. He then addressed himself to Mr. Parish, and another officer in the Indian department, named Johnston :—]

"BROTHERS :—We are happy to meet you both at our council. We of the Six Nations transact all our business openly, and not under the curtain. I have observed with what attention you have listened to me. I hope you will be

willing to unite with us in bringing back our friends from beyond the water, and making us one band.   Then we shall become one great family of children, under our great Father, the
President.   We ask your assistance.   Let the communication
with the other side of the water be opened, and then we shall
be able to bring back our friends from across the water.   Our
great Father we hope will not forget his red children ; and as
he now possesses much of our finest land, we hope he will be
more liberal of presents than he has been.   You must now be
sensible that we are well pleased with presents.   You may
know this by the influence of British presents.   They have won
to the British cause many brave warriors.   I hope that you
will take much pains, now that we are at peace, in uniting all.
Treat us well.   We in common with you possess this soil.
We have frequently heard your voice, when it was for our interest and happiness to listen to it.   It would conduce much
to our happiness to listen to the voice of the United States,
and not be poisoned by the language of the red-coats.   To
make us happy do not crowd our seats.   When you purchase
lands still leave us some to move upon.   This you will make
known to our Father the President, and solicit his aid in opening our passage across the water to our friends.

"Brothers of the Delawares :—We received a message
fom you a number of years since, offering us a seat of land in
your country.   You said you had not forgot the favors heretofore received from the Six Nations, who took you under their
care, until at length you travelled west to the country of White
River.   As you say you have not forgot past favors, are you
now willing to offer the Six Nations, or any part of them, a
seat in your country ?   This invitation has been often repeated.
We now come forward to accept the offer.   We request you
will designate its extent, situation and boundary.   We have
applied to our Father the President for leave to move into
that country, and to be assured that he will confirm your grant.
We find it is necessary by his answer, that when you shall
make such a grant, it must be done on paper, so that such

conveyance may be confirmed. We should be unwilling to leave our present seats without a secure and permanent grant, securing a seat for us, our children, and children's children to the remotest generation. We request that if you are not authorized of yourselves to make such location, you will communicate our wishes to the neighboring nations, proprietors of the land, that they may make such location. This seat we shall expect to receive not as our exclusive property, but to be held in common for the benefit, as well of such of the Six Nations who may wish to settle upon it, as of any other Indians who may choose to take their seats there with us."

Such is the only report preserved of Red-Jacket's speech at this great council, the apparent design of which was entirely of a pacific character, intended by the Indians to heal the wounds among each other inflicted during the then recent war between the United States and England, in which they had indiscreetly taken a part, and likewise to improve their social condition, by means of a more extensive and perfect union among themselves. The speech has lost much of its Indian character in the process of translation, or else Red-Jacket's language and course of thinking had become somewhat assimilated to those of the white man. Still, the character of the speech was well adapted to the occasion, and its counsels were those of wisdom. It is, moreover, worthy of preservation, not only as appertaining to the life of Red-Jacket, but as forming a fragment of Indian history. Mr. Hosmer, who took down the speech from the lips of the interpreter, notes that the orator concluded by a general address to the council, recommending the cultivation of friendly intercourse among themselves,—and at the close gave them a string of wampum which he called "the path of peace." He again admonished them to avoid the British and their shores, and to hold their communications on the south side of the lakes.

On the day following the speakers of the several nations addressed by Red-Jacket made their replies. The Wyandots spoke first, by Teãr-unk-to-yor-on, or "Between-the-Logs," as follows :—

"BROTHERS OF THE SIX NATIONS :—You say that at Brownstown was a great council fire, whose smoke ascended to the heavens. I must remind you of an omission. At that fire was a large tree. A strong root ran to the east. At its foot lay a staff and a broom. The root moving eastward was to represent the Six Nations. The staff was for the support of the aged, who sought shelter there. The broom to brush away any destructive worm, or other thing that might endanger the tree."

[The orator next proceeded to rehearse the speech of Red-Jacket, as the Indian manner is, in order to show that all had been understood. He then said :—]

BROTHER :—This has been your conversation as I have rehearsed it. You have appointed this place for the council fire of the Six Nations. As it is your choice we accept it as a friendly act toward us. Brothers, we return you many thanks, warriors and women all. You may expect due attention paid to it.

"BROTHER :—We are happy to hear that you have not forgot the customs of our forefathers. By these strings,—do not think them too small,—you will return to your respective nations, and say their wishes are accepted of. As to your request

that we use our influence in getting back our brothers beyond
the water, we will do so. We will use our best endeavors to
win them back by gentle means. You may expect that our
younger brethren, the Shawanese, and our nephews, the Delawares, will unite with us in recalling the dispersed of our tribes.
And now, BROTHERS, I enjoin that you do the same thing on
your part. You are similarly situated. This winter will pass
and the next summer will come, before we shall hear from you
again on this subject. I am not certain whether we shall come
to you, or you to us. We will take care to suppress our pride,
and lest I should be thought to possess it, I will say but little.
It is easy to say all that is necessary.

" BROTHERS :—As to your speech yesterday, relative to our
assisting our sachems, depend upon it we will take due care;
if we see any thing go amiss, we will put it right. Do you the
same. It has often been an injury that the counsels of the
war chiefs have not been heard. We have now closed our reply to your speech. You will now open your ears to the reply of the Shawanese."

The Shawanese chief, Cutte-we-ga-saw, commonly
called Black-foot, then spoke to the following effect:—

" BROTHERS OF THE SIX NATIONS :—We heard you yesterday. You shall soon hear our reply. We are pleased that
the council fire is established at this place by our friends the
Wyandots, and that our Brothers, the Six Nations, have agreed
to unite with us.

" BROTHER :—I remember what you said relative to our
people being dispersed. Some of them are scattered, it is
true, and I shall do all in my power to collect them. What
you say relative to our making difficulties I admit is truth.
The way it happened was this: A man came among us who
pretended he had communication with the Great Spirit,* and

* Elskawatwa, the brother of Tecumseh.

that if we followed him we could regain our lands. The whites were crowding upon us. He said they would eat land, and that they would soon eat all our land up. I was deceived and led away by him, and many of my nation. We took him for the Great Spirit. But we soon found him to be a devil, and forsook him. This great man, who pretended to be the Great Spirit, has not only intermeddled with us, but he has been among you,* and has misled many of all nations. I am not surprised that you should bring this charge against us. This prophet exerted such influence over us that we were no longer governed by our ancient customs, but were entirely led by him. You, my elder brother, are of the same people who flocked to him, and listened to him, expecting he would carry his point. I disbelieved it. You, when you went there, were shown a great map, and on it the prophet traced out a great tract of land for you on the Wabash, which was promised you. There was a battle there, and some of your men were in it; and there were others on the way who did not arrive in season. The next place where we found the prophet was at Malden, with some of the Senecas as his followers. And this man was the cause of the destruction of our council fire at Brownstown. This prophet was driven back into Canada. He again attempted to strengthen himself. He promised to your people the land on the Wabash. We heard it. Of all our people who followed the prophet, only eight families remain with him. His power is broken. He is nothing."

The council was next addressed by a chief called Colonel Lewis, but his nation is not designated in Mr. Hosmer's manuscript. He expressed his concurrence in the views presented by Red-Jacket, and exhorted the Indians to be of one mind, and as Americans all, to be

---

* Alluding to the fact that some of the warriors of the Six Nations were in the battle of Tippecanoe.

faithful and true. He was succeeded by Black-Hoof,
(of what nation is not stated,) who said :—

"BROTHERS OF THE WYANDOTS :—You have invited me to
this council, and you see me standing before you. I address
myself to all present. I have heard all that has been said, and
am well pleased with it. I agree with my brothers the Wyandots, in all they have said.

"BROTHERS OF THE SIX NATIONS :—You were the first to
make away with your lands, on which you ought to have reared
your women and children. You advise us to take good care
of our lands. We thank you for that counsel, and are very
sorry you did not take better care of yours. We now give the
same advice to you. Take care of your land. We shall take
good care of ours. We have not much left. But what we
have we mean to keep, and we recommend the same counsel
to our brothers the Wyandots. We have made peace with
the United States, and I shall keep it. To my brothers the
Wyandots I recommend that great care should be taken of
their lands. Let the rights of all be established and carefully
guarded.

"MY BROTHERS OF THE DELAWARES :—I understand you
have promised a seat to the Senecas. I invite your attention
to this subject. I have frequently talked with the President.
He has sent Mr. Johnson as our agent, through whom we may
communicate with him. If you have any thing to do in trans-
ferring your land, consult him.

"BROTHER SENECAS : I wish to remind you of one thing,
I understand our brothers, the Delawares, have invited you to
settle at White River. They own no land, and were only
permitted to settle there and hunt. But they have been there
so long that they pretend a claim, and have in two instances
made sales of land."

The Delawares, their chief being absent, declined
saying any thing in reply to the imputation of having

sold what was not their own; neither did Red-Jacket respond to the sharp rebuke directed to the Six Nations, for having been among the first after the war of the revolution to dispose of their domains. No farther information in regard to this council has been obtained from the manuscripts of Mr. Hosmer, or from any other source. As it was a meeting in which the United States had no concern, the archives of the Indian bureau contain nothing respecting it; and the council seems to have broken up without the adoption of definitive measures of any description, for the benefit of any of the parties concerned therein.

But in the summer of 1819, the Ogden Company determined to open negotiations directly with the Seneca chiefs, for the purpose either of securing their removal from all the reservations yet held by them, or of inducing them to concentrate the several fragments of their nation upon a single one of these reservations. Arrangements having been made for holding a treaty with them at Buffalo, the Hon. Morris S. Miller was appointed a commissioner to conduct the proceedings by the United States.* The Hon. Nathaniel Gorham, of Canandaigua, was designated by Massachusetts, as agent to attend the negotiation.† The council was opened on the 5th of July,—Colonel Ogden and his associates being present, with Captain Parish, the interpreter. Major

---

* Mr. Miller is since deceased. He was a resident of Oneida County, and was for several years an able member of Congress from Oneida.

† From her former interest in the Indian country of western New-York, Massachusetts has ever appointed an agent to attend these land negotiations with the Senecas, for the purpose of guarding them from wrong.

Joseph Delafield, at that time an agent of the United States for the adjustment of boundaries under the sixth article of the treaty of Ghent, happening to be in the village of Buffalo, and having a few days of leisure on his hands, complied with a request from Judge Miller to act as secretary.

It was well known that Red-Jacket was to appear in the character of principal speaker in opposition to the objects of the land company, and the deep and general interest felt in the result of the negotiation drew together a large concourse of people,—pale faces and red. No subsequent assemblage of Indians within the State of New-York has presented so numerous and imposing an array, nor is it likely that so many of them will ever again meet upon the soil of their fathers.

The council having been opened for business, Captain Pollard, the brave Seneca chief who had signalized himself upon the war-path in the Niagara campaign of 1814, rose to welcome the commissioner and the other officers, agents, and parties in attendance upon the council,—a duty which he performed with much courtesy. The credentials of the commissioner on the part of the United States having been read and interpreted, Judge Miller proceeded to explain the objects of his mission.

" He stated that their great Father (the President) had deputed him to meet them at their council fire : that he came to give them his good advice, and the assurance of their great Father, who protected both the red and the white men, that it was his wish to extend to them security and the useful arts. That, situated as they now were, his wishes would not be so well effected as if the Indians were more closely concentrated. He explained to them the tenures by which they held their reservations ; the rights of the pre-emptioners, and the guardianship of the United States. He then submitted to them these several propositions :—*First*, that they should all concentrate on the Alleghany reservation, the title to which should be ceded to them in fee, as white men hold their lands. *Second*, if they preferred to join their red brothers at Sandusky, or to settle in the Territories of the United States, upon other lands to be given to them, they were at liberty to do so. In case they chose the latter proposition, the offer made by their great Father was not to impair the price they were to receive from the pre-emptioners, nor in any manner to influence the bargains to be made. It was meant as a free gift, and for the mutual benefit of the red and white men. Judge Miller proceeded with much eloquence to describe the present situation of the Six Nations, more particularly that of the Senecas, and predicted the time when they must be overwhelmed by the force of the white population, if they continued in their little villages so closely surrounded. He cautioned them against the antipathies of bad men, and against the hasty adoption of the advice of good white men, and concluded by admonishing them that they must reflect more for themselves, and take time to deliberate in council."

An adjournment was then proposed by Governor Ogden, to give time to consider these propositions, whereupon Captain Pollard spoke as follows :—

" BROTHERS : We have listened attentively to what the commissioner has said to us : as well to the authority by which he meets us at this council as also to the views our great Father the President entertains, relative to the affairs of his red children here. In doing this, brother, you have addressed yourself principally to the Senecas. The Six Nations are present.

They are our confederates. For myself, I am gratified that they are present, and that they, too, have heard what you have said to us. You have told us, that the propositions which we now hear from our great Father have not been made by him in haste ; that he has deliberated a long time, and taken a full view of the interests of his white and red children. In doing this, he has sometimes addressed the Senecas, sometimes the Six Nations. He has considered fully, you tell us, the situation of his red children, and he knows their wants, their poverty, and their troubles. You have told us, too, of his solicitude for the red men, and also of the solicitude of his great council, as expressed during the last year. You are not now to expect that we will reply to these subjects. We think it proper now to make but a short talk ; to thank you for what we have heard, and to thank the President for what he has said to us through you, to which we have listened attentively. We rejoice that this council has been made so public. We are pleased that so many white men have attended. We rejoice that your squaws have come with you, and we thank you that they are present."

Then turning to Colonel Ogden, he proceeded :—

" The Commissioner has not spoken solely to the red men. You are also interested in what our Great Father has said, and the result of this council will also interest you as well as us. After our brother's talk you told us this, and that you wanted time to reflect upon the propositions, which are serious and important. We too, brother, have had a short consultation upon your proposal to meet the day after to-morrow. We wish to give you time, and to have time ourselves to hold our councils, and to reflect. We will meet you again the day after to-morrow. Knowing that our proceedings are slow and dilatory, and not like yours, we propose to meet you at 10 o'clock on that day."

The Commissioner then explained that he had ad-

38

dressed the Senecas more particularly, because his commission appointed him to treat with that nation; but as
the Six Nations were assembled, he had also addressed
them jointly; and again advising them to a full and calm
deliberation, the council was adjourned.

The council fire was re-kindled by Red-Jacket on the
7th of July, who spoke as follows :—

"BROTHERS :—We have been preserved in health, strength
and spirit, to meet you again at our council fire. The Great
Spirit has protected us, and we are thankful again to meet
you. You will recollect, brothers, that we listened with attention to what the Commissioner said, and to the words of our
Great Father through his mouth. As this council was called
by the voice of our Great Father, you barely told us of his
care for his red children. You further promised us that the
Yorkers, (meaning the pre-emptioners,) had communications
for us. We now welcome you all to this council, and are
ready to hear what you have to say. We see here our brother
from Massachusetts. He, too, is welcome, and we are ready
to hear from him.

"BROTHERS :—We wish you to open your minds to us. Let
us hear frankly all that you have to communicate, that we
may be ready to answer."

Having thus spoken, Red-Jacket resumed his seat,
and Judge Gorham addressed the council, approving
of the propositions in behalf of the company, from the
President. Mr. David A. Ogden succeeded him, and
discussed at greater length the views of the pre-emptioners,—explaining the nature and extent of their rights,
and the relations subsisting respectively between the
Indians and the United States, the state of Massachu-

setts, and the company. In conclusion, he offered in behalf of the company to accede to the propositions that
had been submitted by the commissioner at the first
meeting. Red-Jacket then addressed the council and
said :—

" We have now heard our great Father and Mr. Ogden.
We must take time to deliberate upon these propositions and
agreements. When we are ready we will send you word.
We are slow, and the subjects are important. We have
nothing farther to decide at this council fire."

The council convened again on the 9th of July, when
Red-Jacket, first addressing the commissioner, spoke at
large as follows :—

" BROTHER : We understand that you have been appointed
by our great Father the President to make these communications to us. We thank the Great Spirit for this pleasant day
given us for our reply, and we beg you to listen.

" BROTHER: Previous to your arrival at this council fire, we
were told that our great Father had appointed a commissioner
to meet us. You have produced your commission, and it
has been read and explained to us. You have also explained
the object of your mission, and the wishes of the President in
sending you to the council fire of the Six Nations. We do
not doubt that the sealed document you produced contained
the words of the President, our great Father. When first informed of your appointment, we supposed that you were
coming to meet us on a very different subject. Since the war
of the revolution we have held various councils with our white
brothers, and in this same manner. We have made various
speeches and entered into several treaties, and these things
are well known to our great Father; they are lodged with
him. We, too, perfectly understand them all. The same in-

terpreters were then present as now.   In consequence of what took place during the late war, we made it known to our great Father, through our interpreter, that we wished to have a talk.   Our application was not complied with.   We sent a messenger to brighten the chain of friendship with our great Father, but he would not meet around the council fire, and we were disappointed.   We had supposed that the commissioner he has now sent came forward to brighten the chain of friendship, to renew former engagements.   When we made a treaty at Canandaigua with Colonel Pickering, in 1794, we were told and thought that it was to be permanent, and to be lasting between us and the United States forever.   After several treaties had been entered into under our great Father, General Washington, large delegations from the Six Nations were invited to meet him.   We went and met him in Philadelphia.   We kindled a council fire.   A treaty was then made, and General Washington then declared that it should be permanent between the red and white brothers : that it should be spread out on the largest and strongest rocks that nothing could undermine or break ; that it should be exposed to the view of all.

"BROTHER : We shall now see what has been done by the United States.   After this treaty had been formed, I then said that I did not doubt but that the United States would faithfully perform their engagements.   But I told our white brothers at that time, that I feared eventually they would *wish* to disturb those contracts.   You white brothers have the faculty to burst the stoutest rocks.   On our part we would not have disturbed those treaties.   Shortly after our interview with our great Father, General Washington, at Philadelphia, a treaty was made at Canandaigua, by which we widened our former engagements with our white brothers, and made some new ones.   The commissioner,—Colonel Pickering,—then told us that this treaty should be binding and should last without alteration for two lives.   We wished to make it extend much farther, and the Six Nations then wished to establish a lasting chain of friendship.   On our part, we wished the treaty to last as long as trees grow and waters run. Our brother told us that he would agree to it.

"BROTHER: I have reminded you what had taken place between our confederates, the Six Nations, and our white brothers, down to the treaty of Canandaigua. At the close of that treaty it was agreed,—it being as strong and binding as by my former comparisons I have explained,—that if any difficulty should occur, if any monster should cross the chain of friendship, that we would unite to remove those difficulties, to drive away the monster; that we would go hand in hand and prolong the chain. So it was agreed.

"BROTHER: Many years ago we discovered a cloud rising that darkened the prospect of our peace and happiness. We heard eventful things from different quarters, from different persons, and at different times, and foresaw that the period was not very distant, when this threatening cloud would burst upon us.

"BROTHER: During the late war we intended to take no part. Yet residing within the limits of the United States, and with the advice of General Porter, we agreed around our council fire that it was right, and we took a part. We thought it would help to promote our friendship with our white brothers, to aid the arms of the United States, and to make our present seats still stronger. These were our reasons. What were the results? We lost many of our warriors. We spilt our blood in a cause between you and a people not of our color.

"BROTHER: These things may be new to you, but they are not new to your government. Records of these things are with our great Father the President. You have come, therefore, for a very different purpose from the one we expected. You come to tell us of our situation, of our reservations, of the opinions of the President that we must change our old customs for new ones; that we must concentrate in order to enjoy the fair means you offer of civilization and improvement in the arts of agriculture.

"BROTHER: At the treaty of Canandaigua we were promised that different kinds of mechanics,—blacksmiths and carpenters,—should be sent among us; and farmers with their families, that our women might learn to spin. We agreed to receive them. We even applied for these benefits. We were told that our children were too young to be taught. Neither farmers nor mechanics were sent.

"BROTHER: We had thought that the promises made by one president were handed down to the next. We do not change our chiefs as you do. Since these treaties were made you have had several presidents. We do not understand why the treaty made by one is not binding on the other. On our part, we expect to comply with our engagements.

"BROTHER: You told us when the country was surrounded by whites, and in possession of Indians, that it was unproductive, not being liable to taxes, nor to make roads and improvements, it was time to change. As for the taxing of Indians, this is extraordinary; and was never heard of since the settlement of America. The land is ours by the gift of the Great Spirit. How can you tax it? We can make such roads as we want, and did so when the land was all ours. We *are* improving in our condition. See these large stocks of cattle, and those fences. We are surrounded by the whites, from whom we can procure cattle and whatever is necessary for our improvement. Now that we are confined to narrow limits, we can easily make our roads and improve our lands. Look back to the first settlement by the whites, and then look at our present condition. Formerly, we continued to grow in numbers and in strength. What has become of the Indians who extended to the salt waters? They have been driven back and become few, while you have been growing numerous and powerful. This land is ours from the God of Heaven. It was given to us. We cannot make land. Driven back and reduced as we are, you wish to cramp us more and more. You tell us of a pre-emptive right. Such men, you say, own one reservation, and such another. But they are all ours,—

ours from the top to the bottom. If Mr. Ogden had come from heaven, with flesh on his bones, as we now see him, and said that the Heavenly Father had given him a *title*, we might *then* believe him.

" BROTHER : You say that the President has sent us word that it is for our interest to dispose of our lands. You tell us that there is a good tract of land at Alleghany. This, too, is very extraordinary. Our feet have covered every inch of that reservation. A communication like this has never been made to us at any of our councils. The President must have been disordered in mind, when he offered to lead us off by the arms to the Alleghany reservation. I have told you of the treaty we made with the United States. Here is the belt of wampum that confirmed that treaty. Here, too, is the parchment. You know its contents. I will not open it. Now the tree of friendship is decaying; its limbs are fast falling off. You are at fault.

" Formerly, we called the British brothers. Now we call the President our Father. Probably among you are persons with families of children. We consider ourselves the children of the President. What would be your feelings were you told that your children were to be cast upon a naked rock, there to protect themselves. The different claims you tell us of on our lands, I cannot understand. We are placed here by the Great Spirit for purposes known to him. You have no right to interfere. You told us that we had large and unproductive tracts of land. We do not view it so. Our seats, we consider small; and if we are left here long by the Great Spirit we shall stand in need of them. We shall be in want of timber. Land after many years' use wears out; our fields must be renewed, and new ones improved, so that we have no more land in our reservations than we want. Look at the white people around us and back. You are not cramped for lands. They are large. Look at that man.* If you want

* Mr. Ellicott, the agent of the Holland Land Company.

to buy apply to him. He has lands enough to sell. We have none to part with. You laugh, but do not think I trifle. I am sincere. Do not think we are hasty in making up our minds. We have had many councils, and thought for a long time upon this subject. We will not part with any,—not with one of our reservations.

" We recollect that Mr. Ogden addressed his speech to you, therefore I have spoken to you. Now I will speak to Mr. Ogden.

" BROTHER: You recollect when you first came to this ground that you told us you had bought the pre-emptive right, —a right to purchase, given you by the government. Remember my reply. I told you, you had been unfortunate in buying. You said you would not disturb us. I then told you as long as I lived, you must not come forward to explain that right. You have come. See me before you. You have heard our reply to the commissioner sent by the President. I again repeat that, one and all, chiefs and warriors, we are of the same mind. We will not part with any of our reservations. Do not make your application anew, nor in any other shape. Let us hear no more of it. Let us part as we met,— in friendship. You discover white people on our reservations. It is my wish, and the wish of all of us, to remove every white man. We can educate our children. Our reservation is small. The white people are near. Such as wish can send their children to the white people's schools. The schoolmaster and the preacher must withdraw. The distance is short for those who wish to go after them. We wish to get rid of all the whites. They make disturbances. We wish our reservations clear of them."

Colonel Ogden and Judge Miller both made replies to Red-Jacket, correcting him in several particulars wherein he had misunderstood them, as well as the views of the President, Mr. Monroe. It is but just, moreover, to say, that these replies were made with a degree of feeling and frankness carrying with it the conviction of a sincere desire that the Indians should be dealt with justly and generously. But their breath was expended to no good purpose. The counsels of Red-Jacket prevailed, and the treaty was broken off without even an approach to success.

The speech of Red-Jacket, it will have been observed, in some respects bordered upon rudeness, and in one instance upon irreverence to heaven. Great pains had been taken by his people that he should be well prepared for this council, and that he should appear in his best condition. The consequence was, that whatever excesses might have marked his conduct before or after the council, there was on this occasion no evidence of intemperance. On the contrary, his personal conduct was marked throughout by the utmost propriety, and his manner was calm, deliberate and decided. Still, there had been intemperate expressions in his speech, which gave pain to some of the most considerate and respectable of the chiefs, and which they feared would be sources of unpleasant reflection, if not of irritation, to the commissioner and the other white gentlemen of his company. It must be here remarked that the Senecas had, some time before the holding of this treaty, become divided into two bodies,—the Pagan and Christian parties. At the head of the former was Red-Jacket, of the latter, that fine old chief Captain Pollard.* It was this latter party,

* Captain Pollard, or Ka-o-un-do-wand, is yet living, (1841,) a venerable looking old man,—with a finely developed head which would form a noble subject of

of course, that felt chagrined at some of Red-Jacket's remarks, and they determined that an apology or explanation ought to be tendered to the commissioner. On the day after the adjournment of the council, therefore, the commissioner received a message from Captain Pollard, informing him that thirteen of their chiefs were then in council deliberating upon the occurrences of yesterday, and that they wished to make a communication to him. In the afternoon a deputation of chiefs presented themselves, consisting of Young King, Pollard, Destroy-Town, Jim Nickerson, White Seneca and Captain Johnson, when Pollard, addressing the commissioner, said :—

"BROTHER : You recollect what took place in council yesterday. The speaker first made a reply to you, and then to the proprietors. You must have discovered some things in that reply that were not correct, and some that were improper. You must also have observed from our different meetings that there was a division among ourselves. This is true. It has been so for a long time. We, although a minority, have been reflecting, for a long time, how we could adopt the advice of good white men, and how it could be possible that you would have told us any thing that did not come from the President our great Father, when you said it came from him. An intimation of this kind, you might have perceived, was given. The speaker yesterday acknowledged your authority, and that your commission contained the President's words ; but he did not admit that your subsequent words came from

study for Dr. Combe. The author visited him in the autumn of 1838, to make certain historical inquiries connected with the invasion of Wyoming. Pollard was a young chief in that bloody expedition. He declares that neither Brant nor the Mohawks were there.

our great Father. One expression grieved us. He said that the President, our great Father, must have been disordered in mind to offer to lead us off to the Alleghany. This remark made us very unhappy. Another expression of his was very extraordinary,—one that we are not accustomed to. He said that if Mr. Ogden should come from heaven with life and with flesh on his bones, and tell us he had a title to these lands, then we might believe him. This we, as Christians, think very wrong; and it gave us much pain. After the council dispersed, the followers of the speaker collected around him, and took him to task for these things. They proposed that an apology should be made for him. But he said no; it has gone forth, let it stand. This gives us an opportunity to come forward. He told you also of many treaties down to Pickering's. Speaking of that, he exhibited the wampum in confirmation, with the parchment. He would not open the parchment, saying that you had a copy at Washington, and had misrepresented it. This we consider improper, rude and indecorous. He spoke, too, of our great Father the President,—calling him President. We call him and consider him as father, friend and protector. The speaker has attempted to explain what he meant by the disordered mind of the President, but as we think, he has made the matter worse,—because he casts aspersions upon the Quakers, and others who have been long praying for our good. We view the commissioner as coming from a father to his children. Your advice to concentrate and improve in our mode of agriculture we approve of. We see that the time has come when we should change our condition and improve our husbandry. But we all agree in what he said about parting with our lands; and we all agree that his harsh and rude language was improper.

" Another motive for asking this interview is, to make you acquainted with our peculiar views and feelings. We, the Senecas, are divided. The Tuscaroras are all united and wish to receive instruction and civilization. The Alleghanies are divided, but are principally with our party,—wishing to receive instruction from the whites.

"When I look back among our forefathers, I see nothing to admire, nothing I should follow, nothing to induce me to live as they did. On the contrary, to enjoy life I find we must change our condition. We who are present have families and children; we wish them to be instructed and enlightened,—if we have not been,—that their eyes may be opened to see the light, if our's have not been. We are getting old and cannot receive the instruction we wish our children to have. We wish them to know how to manage their affairs. After we are dead and gone,—are covered with the dust,—they will bless us for giving them instruction that our fathers had not given us. The Tuscaroras have for a long time received instruction, and they continue to improve. They see and know the advantage of it, and their children will enjoy it. We wish our great Father the President to know of this interview and our explanations. Hereafter when he makes communications to the Senecas, we wish to have them made to us, the Christian party. This we think would do good, and be a lesson to our children. We wish to adopt his advice in improving our condition, because we see that by following Indian habits we must decay and sink to nothing. We are sensible that we cannot remain independent, and would therefore wish to undergo a gradual change. In cases of crimes committed we are not independent now. We are punished, and this is right.

"One cause of division among us is, that one party will school their children,—the other will not. Another cause is, the placing of white men on our lands as tenants. I did so, because advised by a white friend, and because I wished to show our people how the white men farmed the land."*

* The author is indebted entirely to the kindness of Major Joseph Delafield for the speeches at this council, by whom they were taken down from the lips of the interpreter. Major Delafield remarks in a note at the close of his report, which has never before met the public eye, that the speeches were taken down as nearly in the language of the interpreter as was possible,—such corrections as were obviously necessary having been made at the time. The only liberty

The hopes of the pre-emptioners were thus again deferred ; but they ceased not in their efforts to accomplish their purposes by proposing treaties, and using such appliances as were within their power. Indeed such were their perseverance and pertinacity in pushing their designs, that the Indians, in their ignorance, were at times apprehensive that means would be found to dispossess them of their lands without their own free consent. A strong and eloquent address from the Senecas to the President of the United States, upon this subject, was transmitted to Washington in January, previous to the council held by Judge Miller, and two years afterward another appeal was made to the executive of the state of New-York,—Governor De Witt Clinton. In his reply to their memorial, dated February 9, 1820, Governor Clinton said :—

" All the right that Ogden and his company have, [to your reservations,] is the right of purchasing them when you think it expedient to sell them,—that is, they can buy your lands, but no other person can. You may retain them as long as you please, and you may sell them to Ogden as soon you please. You are the owners of these lands in the same way that your brethren, the Oneidas, are of their reservations. They ar all that is left of what the Great Spirit gave to your ancestors. No man shall deprive you of them without your

taken in transcribing them, has been to omit the repetitions for which both Red-Jacket's and Pollard's speeches were remar ble. The interpreter stated that he could not translate some of Red-Jacket's figurative l ts,—they were too wild and difficult to appear in English,—and he did not attempt it. Should his speech be improved by omitting its tautology, it has no doubt lost much of its most characteristic beauty and interest from the acknowledged omissions of the interpreter.

consent.   The State will protect you in the full enjoyment of
your property.   We are strong, and willing to shield you from
oppression.   The Great Spirit looks down on the conduct of
mankind, and will punish us if we permit the remnant of the
Indian nations which is with us to be injured.   We feel for
you, brethren : we shall watch over your interests.   We know
that in a future world we shall be called upon to answer for
our conduct to our fellow creatures."*

But the Anglo-Saxon race is seldom diverted from its
purpose, especially if that purpose be the acquisition of
territory.   Treaty after treaty succeeded the abortive
council held by Judge Miller; and although at all these
treaties, so long as he lived, Red-Jacket exerted himself
to the utmost to prevent the sale of another rood of
ground, yet the arts and appliances of the Ogden Company and its agents, by degrees prevailed over the patriotism of the Indians, and the chief, already stricken
in years, lived yet long enough to mourn the loss, by
piece-meal, of almost the entire of that beautiful region
which he loved so well, and over which he had been
wont to roam, free as the air he breathed, with so much
delight.

A distinguished gentleman, long a resident of Buffalo,
has supplied a few notes of one of the treaties just referred to, between the Senecas and the Ogden Company, and of the part borne thereat by Red-Jacket,
which is both spirited and interesting.   According to the

---

* Manuscript answer of Governor Clinton, to a speech from the Senecas.
Would that the elevated morality of that great philanthropist had governed
every American negotiation with the children of the forest.

memoranda of that gentleman,* this treaty, or council, was holden at the Seneca village near Buffalo, in 1822 or 1823. The council having been addressed by the commissioner, and also by Governor Ogden, Red-Jacket, in a single speech, replied to both. After a concise and appropriate exordium, addressing himself to the commissioner, and repeating in form the speech in which the desire of the United States had been communicated, that the Senecas should sell their lands, he gave a succinct but connected history of the transactions between the Indians and the whites, from the first settlement of the country, down to that day. Some of his figurative illustrations were very happy.

" We first knew you," said he, " a feeble plant which wanted a little earth whereon to grow. We gave it you,— and afterward, when we could have trod you under our feet, we watered and protected you;—and now you have grown to be a mighty tree, whose top reaches the clouds, and whose branches overspread the whole land ; whilst we, who were then the tall pine of the forest, have become the feeble plant, and need your protection."

Again, enforcing the same idea, he said :—

"When you first came here, you clung around our knee, and called us *father*. We took you by the hand and called you BROTHERS. You have grown greater than we, so that we no longer can reach up to your hand. But we wish to cling round your knee and be called YOUR CHILDREN."

* The Hon. Albert H. Tracy.

Referring to their services in the then recent war with England, he said :—

"Not long ago you raised the war-club against him who was once our grea. Father over the waters. You asked us to go with you to the war. It was not our quarrel. We knew not that you were right. We asked not: we cared not: it was enough for us that you were our brothers. We went with you to the battle. We fought and bled for you :—and now," said he with great feeling, pointing to some Indians who had been wounded in the contest, "dare you pretend to us that our Father the President, while he sees our blood running yet fresh from the wounds received while fighting his battles, has sent you with a message to persuade us to relinquish the poor remains of our once boundless possessions,—to sell the birth-place of our children, and the graves of our fathers. No! Sooner than believe that he gave you this message, we will believe that you have stolen your commission, and are a cheat and a liar."

In reply to an explanation as to the nature of the preemptive claim of the company to their lands, and an assurance that the object was not to wrong them in the purchase, but to pay the full value, he referred to the different treaties,—the great cessions the Indians had made,—the small equivalents they had received,—and the repeated solemn assurances given by the government that they should not be importuned to relinquish the reservations remaining to them.

"You tell us," said he, "of your claim to our land, and that you have purchased it from your State. We know nothing of your claim, and we care nothing for it. Even the whites have a law, by which they cannot sell what they do not own. How, then, has your state, which never owned our land, sold it to you? We have a title to it, and we know that our title is good; for it came direct from the Great Spirit, who gave it to us, his red children. When you can ascend to where He is,"—pointing toward the skies,—" and will get His deed, and show it to us, then, and never till then, will we acknowledge your title. You say that you came not to cheat us of our lands, but to buy them. Who told you that we have lands to sell? You never heard it from us."

Then drawing up, and giving Mr. Ogden a look of earnestness, if not of indignation, he said :—

" Did I not tell you, the last time we met, that whilst Red-Jacket lived you would get no more lands of the Indians? How, then, while you see him alive and strong," (striking his hand violently on his breast,) " do you think to make him a liar ?"*

Red-Jacket was doubtless sincere, at this time, and during the latter years of his life, in his opposition to any farther disposition of their already contracted territory,

---

* Speaking in reference to the real eloquence of Red-Jacket, the gentleman referred to in the last note remarks :—" It is evident that the best translations of Indian speeches must fail to express the beauty and sublimity of the originals,— especially of such an original as Red-Jacket. It has been my good fortune to hear him a few times, but only of late years, and when his powers were enfeebled by age, and still more by intemperance. But I shall never forget the impression made on me the first time that I saw him in council :—

> Deep on his front engraven,
> Deliberation sate, and public care,
> And princely counsel in his face yet shone,
> Majestic, though in ruin.

I can give no adequate idea of the strong impression it made upon my mind, though conveyed to it through the medium of an illiterate interpreter. Even in this mangled form, I saw the *disjecta membra* of a regular and splendid oration.

40

although, as has been seen at an earlier stage of his life, he could speak with a "forked tongue" upon the subject,—declaring eloquently in open council against the selling of an acre, and meeting the agent of the purchase by night to facilitate his operations. But however sincere at the last mentioned and at subsequent councils, in his opposition to the views of the pre-emption company, their persuasives were stronger than his,—less eloquent, but far more effective. It is believed that no sales of land were made at either of the two councils last mentioned; but shortly afterward, viz., in the summer of 1826, another negotiation was opened, which was attended by better success for the company. The commissioner on the part of the United States was the Hon. Oliver Forward, of Buffalo. The agent for the commonwealth of Massachusetts was the Hon. Nathaniel Gorham. The agent of the company was John Greig, Esq., of Canandaigua, who succeeded in extinguishing the Indian title to about eighty thousand acres of their smaller reservations along the course of the Genesee River, of which there were several. Red-Jacket participated largely in the proceedings of the council, and opposed every cession step by step. Yet his eloquence, though earnest as ever, was exerted to but little purpose;—the Indians acceded to the terms proposed to them. After the treaty was concluded, and its terms were reduced to writing, Mr. Greig remarked to Red-Jacket that as he had opposed the sales he need not sign the paper. But the chief would listen to no such proposition. He was proud of having his name appear upon

every document connected with the fortunes of his people, whether he approved of them or not, and insisted
on signing the instrument, which he accordingly did.*
Still, although this negotiation was conducted with the
utmost fairness in respect to the Indians, loud complaints
were made against it by Red-Jacket and the non-con-
tents, and a commission was subsequently instituted by
President Adams, to inquire into the true character of
the transaction. This duty was confided to Richard
Montgomery Livingston, of Saratoga. A powerful effort
was made by Red-Jacket to cause the treaty to be set
aside as fraudulent, but without success, and it was allowed to be carried into effect.†

Another negotiation was instituted in the year 1828,
and others still have followed, until, yielding to the pertinacity of the company, in the autumn of 1839 the Indians so far relinquished the contest that a treaty was
concluded, by virtue of which all the remaining territory
of the Senecas in the state of New-York was conveyed

---

* Conversations of the Author with Mr. Greig.

† The treaty here referred to was concluded on the 31st of August, 1826. By
it the Seneca nation of Indians sold to the proprietors of the pre-emptive right
87,526 acres of their reservations, being 33,637 from the Buffalo, 33,409 from
the Tonnewanta, 5,120 from the Cattaraugus, all of the Caneadea, (10,240,) and
all of the Gardow, Squacky Hill, Big Tree and Canawagus reservations, containing
1,280 acres each. The last four were situated in the county of Livingston, and contain each a portion of the Genesee river flats. The papers connected with this
treaty were once partially examined by the author, at the house of the late Mr. Livingston, but they were subsequently burnt with his office-building. Red-Jacket
was again active and eloquent in opposition to the views of the company; but he
was out-voted in council, and compelled to yield to the overpowering numbers of
" democracy,—savage and wild," literally—as Governeur Morris once pronounced
it in another place.

to the company that had so long and intently been striving to grasp the prize.*   This treaty was ratified by the Senate of the United States in March, 1840; but although yet unexecuted, and doomed, perhaps, to encounter opposition in regard to the appropriations necessary for its fulfilment, still it requires no special gift of prophecy to foretell that the remains of the once proud and powerful Senecas, comprising now but a few scattered and dissolving bands, must soon turn their backs upon the fair region which they have possessed for centuries, to seek out a new home toward the setting sun. Lost amid the boundless regions beyond the Mississippi, and mingled with nations of their own race more numerous than themselves, not many years will elapse before the Senecas will be numbered as among the nations that were.

* There remained to the Senecas after the treaty of 1826, at Buffalo 49,920 acres, at Tonnewanta 12,800, at Allegany 30,469, at Cattaraugus 21,760, and at Tuscarora 1,920,—in all 116,869 acres, all of excellent quality. With the exception of the Tuscarora reservation, which is small, all have now been sold by the Indians. For an account of the provisions of the last mentioned treaty, and a history of the arts and management by which it was obtained, see Appendix F.

CHAPTER XII.

NEITHER civilized nor savage wars occurring again in
the neighborhood of the Seneca country during the residue of Red-Jacket's life, few public events with which
his name is associated remain to be discussed. The
most considerable exception to this remark is to be found
in the celebrated case of Tommy-Jemmy, a chief of the
Senecas, who, in the year 1821, was tried for murder at
Buffalo. The case was substantially this :—In the spring
of the year just mentioned, a Seneca Indian fell into a
state of languishment, and died. The character and
course of the disease were such that the Indian medi-
cine-men did not understand it; and from a variety of
strange circumstances attending the sick man's decline
and death, it was sagely concluded that he had been

destroyed by sorcery. Nay more, the woman who had nursed him, and anxiously watched him at his bed-side, was fixed upon as the beldam who, by the aid of an evil spirit, had compassed his death. The woman fled the territory and crossed into Canada, but was followed thither by the sachems and others, arrested, and tried by a council, in due form, according to the immemorial usages of her people in such cases made and provided. She was proved guilty, and sentenced to death. But the Indians were too well informed, and too wary, to carry the execution into effect beyond the confines of their own territory, either in Canada or the United States. The poor culprit was therefore artfully inveigled back to the American side of the Niagara, and thence within the bounds of their own jurisdiction, where it was determined she should meet her doom. Still the Indian who had been designated as the executioner faltered in his duty. Either his heart or his hand failed, or his conscience smote him, and he declined the fulfilment of his bloody commission. In this emergency, a chief named So-on-on-gise, but who was usually called Tommy-Jemmy, seized a knife, and despatched the sorceress by cutting her throat. The white inhabitants of the neighborhood were shocked at the deed ; and forgetting that, to a certain extent at least, the Indians constituted an independent community, Tommy-Jemmy was arrested by the civil authorities of Buffalo, and thrown into prison. In due time he was indicted for the capital crime of murder, and arraigned at the bar of the oyer and terminer to take his trial. This trial, interesting in itself, became in its progress both curious and instruc-

tive; and before the close of all the proceedings had in
connexion therewith, attracted very general attention
throughout the state, especially with the legal profession.
The death of the woman, by the hand of the accused, of
course was not denied. But the prisoner, by his counsel, pleaded to the jurisdiction of the court, that the
Seneca Indians were a sovereign and independent nation, exercising exclusive jurisdiction of all offences committed by any of its members within their own territory,
and that the prisoner, as well as the person killed, was
a member of the Seneca nation, and the offence, if any,
was committed within their own territory. The woman,
it was held, had been judicially executed, according to
their own laws and usages, and it was therefore insisted
that it was a matter of which the tribunals of the state of
New-York could take no cognizance. To this plea a
replication was filed by the public prosecutor,* denying
the allegations, and an issue to the country tendered.
In this issue the prisoner joined, and a jury was sworn
to try the same. Among the witnesses introduced to
support the plea of the accused was Red-Jacket, who
was examined at large touching the laws and usages of
his people. The eminent counsel who conducted the
prosecution wished to exclude his testimony, and to that
end inquired whether he believed in the existence of a
God. "More truly than one can who could ask me
such a question," with an indignant look, was the instant
reply.† Afterward, on his cross-examination, the chief

---

* The Hon. John C. Spencer, now, (1841,) Secretary of the state of New-
York.

† Letter to the author from the Hon. Albert H. Tracy.

was asked by one of the counsel, what rank he held in his nation : to which he answered with a contemptuous sneer,—" Look at the papers which the white people keep the most carefully,"—(meaning the treaties ceding their lands,)—" they will tell you what I am !"*

The testimony of the orator, as also did that of the other Indian witnesses, went to show that in the apprehension of the Indians the woman was clearly a witch, and that she had been tried by a properly constituted council, and executed, in pursuance of their laws, which had been established for a time whereof the memory of the white people, at least, ran not to the contrary, inasmuch as these laws were in force long before the English came to this island. In the course of his examination, perceiving that their superstition on the subject of witchcraft was the theme of ridicule, as well with the legal gentlemen as among the bystanders, Red-Jacket found an opportunity to break forth as follows :—

"What! Do you denounce us as fools and bigots, because we still believe that which you yourselves believed two centuries ago ? Your black-coats thundered this doctrine from the pulpit, your judges pronounced it from the bench, and sanctioned it with the formalities of law ; and you would now punish our unfortunate brother for adhering to the faith of *his* fathers and of yours ! Go to Salem ! Look at the records of your own government, and you will find that hundreds have been executed for the very crime which has called forth the sentence of condemnation against this woman, and drawn down upon her the arm of vengeance. What have our brothers done more than the rulers of your people have done ? And

* Drake's Book of the Indians.

what crime has this man committed, by executing, in a summary way, the laws of his country, and the command of the Great Spirit ?"*

The appearance of Red-Jacket, when delivering this sarcastic philippic, was noted as remarkable, even for him. When fired with indignation, or burning for revenge, the expression of his eye was terrible, and when he chose to display his powers of irony, which were rarely excelled, the aspect of his keen sarcastic glance was irresistible.† The result of the trial was a verdict that the *allegations* contained in the prisoner's plea were true. The court suspended giving judgment, and the proceedings were removed by certiorari into the Supreme Court. At the August term of that tribunal, in the same year, a motion was made by the attorney-general for judgment that the prisoner answer farther, notwithstanding the verdict of the jury. The argument was opened, in behalf of the people, by Mr. Spencer, who was followed by Mr. Oakley,‡ in behalf of the prisoner. Mr. Samuel A. Talcott, attorney-general, closed the argument, which was sustained throughout, on both sides, with great ability. The discussion produced a very thorough examination of all the laws, treaties, documents, and public history relating to the Indians, from the time of the discovery; and the court, intima-

* Albany Argus, 1821,—one of the editors of which paper, at that day, was present at the trial.

† William J. Snelling, who was also present at the trial. Vide Drake's Book of the Indians.

‡ Thomas J. Oakley, formerly attorney-general, and now (1841,) one of the judges of the Superior Court of the city of New-York.

ting that there was considerable difficulty in the question, took time for mature consideration. The conclusion of the whole matter was the discharge of the prisoner by consent. The court, not liking to make a decision recognizing the independent jurisdiction of the Indians in such cases, and yet being unable to deny to them the existence of a qualified sovereignty,—perceiving, moreover, very clearly that the case was not one of murder, as the Indians " understood it,"—took the middle course, and allowed the liberation of the prisoner.

After the close of the war between the United States and Great Britain, in 1815, the whole attention of Red-Jacket was devoted to the government of his people, and the advancement of what he doubtless honestly conceived to be their true interests. The leading feature of his policy was to exclude the white people from mingling with his nation, and to prevent Christian missionaries and school-masters from coming amongst them; in furtherance of which design, all his influence, and all that remained of his power, were exerted to the utmost. In a word, he labored with all his energies to shut out every thing like moral and social improvement, and to preserve his people in their primitive Indian character. But his arm was too feeble to check the advances of the Anglo-Saxon race, and the residue of the Six Nations at length found themselves hemmed closely within the comparatively narrow reservations yet remaining to them. Both school-masters and missionaries, also, the objects of the chieftain's peculiar hate, were still insinuating themselves among them; for the New-York Missionary Society, nothing daunted by the repulse of Mr. Alexander, in 1811, had succeeded in establishing several missionary stations. Indeed, the Tuscarora Indians had received the missionaries as early as the year 1805, and the consequence had been a rapid improvement of their moral and social condition. A missionary house had likewise been opened at the Seneca village, about five miles from Buffalo, and another upon the Cattaraugus reservation.* These humble efforts in the cause of Christian civilization were crowned with very considerable success, so that previous to the year 1820 the Senecas had become divided into two distinct parties, Christian and Pagan, —as mentioned incidentally in a preceding chapter. The former was headed by the veteran Captain Pollard, or Ka-oun-doo-wand, Gishkaka, commonly called Little-Billy, and several other chiefs of note, and the latter by Red-Jacket and the Young Cornplanter, who, notwithstanding the conversion of his father to the Christian faith, and his own education in Philadelpha, adhered still to the heathenism of his ancestors. There were likewise other pagan chiefs acting in concert with Red-Jacket, who, with their followers, probably at that period composed considerably more than half the nation. The hostility of this pagan party to these inroads of civilization was uncompromising, and at the close of the year 1819, or early in 1820, an appeal was made to Governor Clinton for protection against the " black-coats." This appeal was embodied in a letter, dictated by Red-Jacket, and addressed to Mr. Parish, their favorite in-

* Reports from the missionary, in the Missionary Herald.

terpreter, then on a visit to the seat of the state government, upon business appertaining to the Indians :—

RED-JACKET TO CAPTAIN PARISH.

"BROTHER PARISH : I address myself to you, and through you to the governor. The chiefs of Onondaga have accompanied you to Albany, to do business with the governor; I, also, was to have been with you, but I am sorry to say that bad health has put it out of my power. For this you must not think hard of me. I am not to blame for it. It is the will of the Great Spirit that it should be so. The object of the Onondagas is to purchase our lands at Tonnewanta. This and another business that they may have to do at Albany, must be transacted in the presence of the governor. He will see that the'bargain is fairly made, so that all parties may have reason to be satisfied with what is done ; and when our sanction shall be wanted to the transaction, it will be freely given. I much regret that, at this time, the state of my health should prevent me from accompanying you to Albany, as it was the wish of the nation that I should state to the governor some circumstances which show that the chain of friendship between us and the white people is wearing out, and wants brightening. But I will proceed now to lay them before you by letter, that you may mention them to the governor, and solicit redress. He is appointed to do justice to all, and the Indians fully confide that he will not suffer them to be wronged with impunity.

" The first subject to which we would call the attention of the governor, is the depredations that are daily committed by the white people upon the most valuable timber on our reservations. This has been a subject of complaint with us for many years ; but now, and particularly at this season of the year, it has become an alarming evil, and calls for the immediate interposition of the governor in our behalf. Our next subject of complaint is, the frequent thefts of our horses and cattle by the white people ; and their habit of taking and using them whenever they please, and without our leave. These are evils which seem to increase upon us with the increase of our white neighbors, and they call loudly for redress.

"Another evil arising from the pressure of the whites upon us, and our unavoidable communication with them, is the frequency with which our chiefs, and warriors, and Indians, are thrown into jail, and that, too, for the most trifling causes. This is very galling to our feelings, and ought not to be permitted to the extent to which,—to gratify their bad passions,— our white neighbors now carry this practice.

"In our hunting and fishing, too, we are greatly interrupted by the whites. Our venison is stolen from the trees where we have hung it to be reclaimed after the chase. Our hunting camps have been fired into, and we have been warned that we shall no longer be permitted to pursue the deer in those forests which were so lately all our own. The fish, which, in the Buffalo and Tonnewanta creeks, used to supply us with food, are now, by the dams and other obstructions of the white people, prevented from multiplying, and we are almost entirely deprived of that accustomed sustenance. Our great Father the President has recommended to our young men to be industrious,—to plough and to sow. This we have done, and we are thankful for the advice, and for the means he has afforded us of carrying it into effect. We are happier in consequence of it.

"But another thing recommended to us has created great confusion among us, and is making us a quarrelsome and divided people ; and that is, the introduction of preachers into our nation. These black-coats contrive to get the consent of *some* of the Indians to preach among us, and wherever this is the case, confusion and disorder are sure to follow : and the encroachments of the whites upon our lands are the invariable consequence. The governor must not think hard of me for speaking thus of the preachers. I have observed their progress, and when I look back to see what has taken place of old, I perceive that whenever they came among the Indians, they were the forerunners of their dispersion; that they always excited enmities and quarrels among them; that they introduced the white people on their lands, by whom they were robbed and plundered of their property; and that the Indians were sure to dwindle and decrease and be driven back, in proportion to the number of preachers that came among them. Each nation has its own customs and its own religion. The Indians have theirs,—given to them by the Great Spirit,—under which they were·happy. It was not intended that they should embrace the religion of the whites, and be destroyed by the attempt to make them think differently on that subject from their fathers.

" It is true, these preachers have got the consent of some of the chiefs to stay and preach among us, but I and my friends know this to be wrong, and that they ought to be removed; besides, we have been threatened by Mr. Hyde,—who came among us as a school-master and a teacher of our children, but has now become a black-coat, and refused to teach them any more,—that unless we listen to his preaching and become Christians, we will be turned off our lands. We wish to know from the governor if this is to be so; and if he has no right to say so, we think he ought to be turned off our lands, and not allowed to plague us any more. We shall never be at peace while he is among us. Let them be removed, and we will be happy and contented among ourselves. We now cry to the governor for help, and hope that he will attend to our complaints, and speedily give us redress.

" SA-GO-YE-WAT-HA, or *Red-Jacket*."*

In consequence of this representation, and others of corresponding import, an act was passed by the legisla-

---

* This letter was dictated by Red-Jacket, and interpreted by Henry O'Bail, in the presence of the following Indians: Red-Jacket's son, Cornplanter, John-Cobb, Peter, Young-King's-Brother, Tom-the-Infant, (Onnonggaiheko,) Blue-sky, (Towyocauna,) John-Sky, Jemmy-Johnson, Marcus, Big-fire, Captain-Jemmy.

ture of New-York, during the session of 1821, for the more effectual prevention of encroachments upon the lands of the Senecas. The enactments of this law were peremptory,—requiring the district-attorney and sheriff of the county, on complaint being made, to remove from the reservation " all persons other than Indians." Resistance to the mandate for such removal was punishable by imprisonment. It is not supposed that in the enactment of this law the legislature intended to molest the missionaries, or to interfere with their schools. The design was to afford more efficient protection to the Indians against intruders in general, who were crowding upon them in considerable numbers, destroying their timber, and endamaging them in other respects. Against such it was occasionally enforced; but in regard to the missionaries its energies were allowed to slumber for two or three years. Meantime the New-York Missionary Society had transferred its stations to the care of the American Board of Foreign Missions, by which latter association the Seneca missions had been re-organized upon a more efficient and commanding basis. In 1821, the Rev. Thompson S. Harris, with an augmented mission family, had been stationed at the Seneca village, with a commission as superintendent of the stations in the several cantons. A church was soon afterward organized, and schools, male and female, were opened. In the year 1822, the Rev. Mr. Thayer, with his family and suitable teachers for schools, was stationed at the Cattaraugus reservation. The labors of both of these families,—missionaries and teachers,—were greatly blessed; and Red-

Jacket and his pagan adherents were doomed to the mortification of beholding a rapid increase of the Christian party at the expense of their own. The children were flocking to the schools, and the adults almost daily renouncing their heathen rites and superstitions, and avowing themselves Christians. Among the notables of the tribe who came out from among the pagans, was the principal chief of the Cattaraugus clan, O-qui-ye-sou, well known in English as Captain Strong. He was a chief of talent and great influence among his people,— a sober, deep-thinking man, who for judgment and penetration surpassed most others of his nation. His family was connected with that of Red-Jacket by ties of consanguinity, and, with all the members of that family, he remained a pagan until 1823. Red-Jacket himself had not been more decided in his opposition to the missionaries than Captain Strong, down to the period just mentioned. But observing the salutary influences which the missionaries and their schools were exerting upon his people, he was brought to reflect seriously upon the subject. His pagan friends became alarmed at the symptoms they discovered of a change in his views, and a council was convened, at which the most strenuous efforts were put in requisition to prevent his defection. But their efforts were vain. To the disappointment and grief of the pagans, after they had exhausted their stock of dissuasives, O-qui-ye-sou rose and in a manly speech abjured his pagan creed, and avowed himself a member of the Christian party,—to which he has stedfastly adhered until this day. Alarmed at the loss of

such a chief as Captain Strong, and at the rapid diminution of his adherents, foreshadowing his own loss of
influence and power, the project of a forcible ejectment
of the missionaries and school-teachers, under the act of
1821, was conceived by Red-Jacket, and by the aid of
several *white pagans* in Buffalo, who were ever on the
qui vive to facilitate his anti-christian purposes, carried
into prompt execution. Complaints having been duly
entered against Mr. Harris and his teachers at the
Seneca village, the district-attorney and sheriff, having
no discretion in the premises, were compelled to proceed against them, and the mission at the Seneca village
was broken up in March, 1824. There were forty-three
children in the school at the time, who, with their teachers and assistants, were removed to the Cattaraugus
station. Mr. Harris and his family retired to Buffalo,
to watch the course of events, and render such offices
to the Indians of his spiritual charge as might yet be in
his power. This was a sad disappointment to the mis-
sion-family, and was deeply lamented by the Christian
Indians, upon whom the happiest influences had been
exerted. A lively concern had been awakened in their
bosoms for the salvation of their souls, and they were in
the habit of resorting to the woods for their private de-
votions. They therefore felt deeply the loss of their
minister, to whom they owed so much, not only for his
instructions in religion, but for his labors in the improvement of their social condition. The American Board
had no sooner heard of these transactions, than an appeal was made to the legislature for such a modification

42

of the law of 1821 as would allow the missionaries to resume their labors. The people of Buffalo, also, with the exception of a small knot of unbelievers in alliance upon this subject with Red-Jacket, sustained the application. Judge Wilkinson, then a senator from Buffalo, made a strong speech in favor of the proposed modification of the law, and bore powerful testimony to the advantages that had resulted to the Indians from the labors of the missionaries. In this posture of affairs, while the question was yet pending, Red-Jacket addressed the following letter to Governor Clinton :—

"TO THE CHIEF OF THE COUNCIL FIRE AT ALBANY.

"BROTHER : About three years ago, our friends of the great council fire at Albany wrote down in their book that the priests of white people should no longer reside on our lands, and told their officers to move them off whenever we complained. This was to us good news, and made our hearts glad. These priests had a long time troubled us, and made us bad friends and bad neighbors. After much difficulty we removed them from our lands; and for a short time we have been quiet, and our minds easy. But we are now told that the priests have asked liberty to return ; and that our friends of the great council fire are about to blot from their book the law which they made, and leave their poor red brethren once more a prey to hungry priests.

"BROTHER : Listen to what we say. These men do us no good. They deceive every body. They deny the Great Spirit, which we, and our fathers before us, have looked upon as our creator. They disturb us in our worship. They tell our children* they must not believe like our fathers and mothers, and tell us many things we do not understand and cannot believe. They tell us we must be like white people,—but they

* Several of Red-Jacket's children had joined the Christian party.

are lazy and won't work, nor do they teach our young men to do so. The habits of our women are worse than they were before these men came amongst us, and our young men drink more whiskey. We are willing to be taught to read, and write, and work, but not by people who have done us so much injury.

" BROTHER : We wish you to lay before the council fire the wishes of your red brethren. We ask our brothers not to blot out the law which has made us peaceable and happy ; and not to force a strange religion upon us. We ask to be let alone, and, like the white people, to worship the Great Spirit as we think best. We shall then be happy in fulfilling the little share in life which is left us, and shall go down to our fathers in peace.

" SA-GO-YE-WAT-HA."*

In one of the parables of the Great Author of Christianity, it is said that on a certain occasion, when a husbandman had been scattering good seed in his field, " an enemy" came afterward and sowed tares. It was even so at the village of the Senecas. There were a few individual white men in the vicinity of the reservation, unbelievers in the Christian religion,—of whose number was a man of some political notoriety in Buffalo,—who labored with a zeal worthy of a better cause, to thwart the efforts of the missionary and teachers at the Seneca village. By these men the prejudices of Red-Jacket and his pagan adherents were fomented, and their hands strengthened. No man labored with

* The original of this document is in the office of the Secretary of State, at Albany. It was subscribed with the mark of Sa-go-ye-wat-ha, or Red-Jacket, first, and then follow those of the Young Cornplanter, Green-Blanket, Big-Kettle, Robert Bob, Twenty Canoes, senior and junior, Two-Guns, Fish-Hook, Hot-Bread, Bare-Foot, and several others of the pagan party.

greater industry in sowing the good seed than Mr. Harris.   None could have labored with greater assiduity in
sowing tares in the same field than the persons referred
to.   And these men were doubtless the counsellors of
Red-Jacket, as they had been on other similar occasions,
in the composition of the foregoing letter to Governor
Clinton.   It was a grievous libel upon the character and
conduct of the missionaries, and probably was not without its influence for temporary evil, inasmuch as the application in their behalf was not at that time sustained
by the legislature.   But at a period not long subsequent,
the rigors of the law were meliorated, and both missionaries and teachers were allowed to resume and continue their labors without farther molestation.

There is indeed, in one passage of the letter under
consideration, an apparent qualification of the old chieftain's hostility to the introduction of the arts of reading
and writing among the Indians; but he was nevertheless
averse to the acquisition of those accomplishments from
Mr. Harris and his assistants.   But toward the Quakers,
who had exercised a watchful guardianship over the
Alleghany clan of the Senecas, by means of boards of
visiters and resident agents, almost from the hour of
their laying down the hatchet in 1783, Red-Jacket was
much better disposed.   He made an earnest appeal to
them, at about the same time, for assistance, or for the
exertion of their influence in keeping the missionaries at
a distance.   In his communications with the Quakers
upon this subject, he was more grievously libellous
against the missionaries even than in the letter to Go-

vernor Clinton, charging them with stealing the horses of
the Indians, driving away their cattle, and with other
grave offences. Charges like these, against men holding
the commissions of the American Board of Foreign Missions, stationed, as it were, under the very eye of the
Board itself, carried their own contradiction upon their
face. Still it may be possible,—barely possible,—that
miscreants may have assumed the missionary garb in
order to accomplish some sinister purpose against this
much-abused race. And when the orator told the Quakers, as it is alleged he did by at least one authority,
that such of the Senecas as were nominally converted
from heathenism to Christianity by those pretended
teachers, only disgraced themselves by paltry attempts
to cover the profligacy of the one with the hypocrisy of
the other,* he must either have adverted to some isolated
instance of imposture and affected conversion, or coined
the libel with malignant intent.

But his hostility to Christianity and its teachers was
implacable, and broke forth on every possible occasion.
About the year 1824, a gentleman who had much official
and personal intercourse with the Senecas, and with
Red-Jacket in particular, while in conversation with him
in company with the late Colonel Chapin, asked the
question why he was so much opposed to the missionaries. The inquiry awakened feelings of real or affected
surprise in the bosom of the chief, and after a brief
pause as though for reflection, he replied with a sarcastic
smile, and an emphasis peculiar to himself:—

* Thatcher's Indian Biography.

" Because they do us no good. If they are not useful to
the white people, why do they send them among the Indians?
If they are useful to the white people, and do them good, why
do they not keep them at home ? They are surely bad enough
to need the labor of every one who can make them better.
These men know we do not understand their religion. We
cannot read their book,—they tell us different stories about
what it contains, and we believe they make the book talk to
suit themselves. If we had no money, no land, and no country to be cheated out of, these black-coats would not trouble
themselves about our good hereafter. The Great Spirit will
not punish us for what we do not know. He will do justice to
his red children. These black-coats talk to the Great Spirit,
and ask for light, that we may see as they do, when they are
blind themselves, and quarrel about the light which guides
them. These things we do not understand, and the light they
give us makes the straight and plain path trod by our fathers
dark and dreary. The black-coats tell us to work and raise
corn : they do nothing themselves, and would starve to death
if somebody did not feed them. All they do is to pray to the
Great Spirit ; but that will not make corn or potatoes grow ;
if it will why do they beg from us and from the white people?
The red men knew nothing of trouble until it came from the
white men; as soon as they crossed the great waters they
wanted our country, and in return have always been ready to
teach us to quarrel about their religion. Red-Jacket can
never be the friend of such men. The Indians can never be
civilized,—they are not like white men. If they were raised
among the white people, and learned to work, and to read, as
they do, it would only make their situations worse. They
would be treated no better than negroes. We are few and
weak, but may for a long time be happy if we hold fast to
our country and the religion of our fathers !"*

* Colonel M'Kenney's Indian Biography.

It need scarcely be added that this outpouring of invective against the missionaries was no more bitter than unjust; and were it not for the close resemblance it bears to the preceding letter to Governor Clinton, it would be charitable to hope that the reporter imparted to the language of the speaker a tone of severity beyond his design. No doubt can exist that his feelings of hatred to Christianity were at that time settled and deep; but, as has been previously intimated, there were white pagans in the Seneca neighborhood, who, with a vigilance that never slumbered, were watching for opportunities to infuse into the bosom of Red-Jacket a portion of the poison rankling in their own. Such may have been the fact in regard both to the last mentioned speech and the letter. Perhaps, therefore, a more just conception of the old chieftain's general views upon this important subject,—his manner of reasoning respecting it,—and the position in which he supposed the Indians stood in regard to it,—may be formed by a perusal of the notes of a protracted colloquy between him and a young candidate for clerical orders,—now an eminent divine,*—which occurred at about the period of his life now under consideration. These notes, or more properly sketches, in addition to their dramatic interest, will serve as vivid illustrations of the manners of the orator in his old age, and the character of his mind;—while the missionaries are at the same time vindicated.

* The Rev. John Breckenridge, D. D.

REV. DR. BRECKENRIDGE TO THE AUTHOR.

" The first opportunity I ever enjoyed of seeing that deservedly celebrated Indian chief Red-Jacket, was in the year 1821, at the residence of General PETER B. PORTER, Black Rock, New-York. Being on a visit to the General and his family, it seemed a peculiarly fit occasion to become acquainted with the great Seneca orator, whose tribe resided within a few miles of Black Rock. General Porter embraced the Indian warriors who fought with us on that line, during the late war with Great Britain, in his command. From this cause; from his high character; his intimate acquaintance with the chiefs; and his known attachment to these interesting people, he had great influence over them;—and his lamented lady, who it is not indelicate for me to say was my sister, had by her kindness won the rugged hearts of all their leading men. So that their united influence, and my near relationship to them, secured to me at once access to the chiefs, and their entire confidence.

" I had not only a great desire to see Red-Jacket, but also to use this important opportunity to correct some of his false impressions in regard to Christianity and the missionaries established in his tribe. To this end it was agreed to invite Red-Jacket and the other chiefs of the Senecas, to visit Co-na-shus-tah,* and meet his brother at his house. The invitation was accordingly given, and very promptly and respectfully accepted.

" On the appointed day they made their appearance

---

* The name given to General Porter by Red-Jacket.

in due form, headed by Red-Jacket, to the number of perhaps eight or ten, besides himself. Red-Jacket was dressed with much taste, in the Indian costume throughout. He wore a blue dress, the upper garment cut after the fashion of a hunting-shirt, with blue leggings, very neat moccasins, a red jacket, and a girdle of red about his waist. I have seldom seen a more dignified or noble looking body of men than the entire group. It seems,—though no such impression was designed to be made by the terms of the invitation,—that some indefinite expectation had been excited in their minds of meeting an official agent on important business. And they have been so unworthily tampered with, and so badly treated by us, as a people, and many of their most important treaties have been so much the result of private and corrupting appeals, that they very naturally look for some evil design in every approach to them,—however open and simple it may be. So it was on this occasion. As soon as the ceremonies of introduction had passed, with the civilities growing out of it, the old orator seated himself in the midst of the circle of chiefs, and after a word with them, followed by a general assent, he proceeded in a very serious and commanding manner,—always speaking in his own nervous tongue, through an interpreter, to address me in substance as follows :—

" ' We have had a call from our good friends,' (pointing to the general and his lady,) ' to come down to Black Rock to meet their brother. We are glad to break bread and to drink the cup of friendship with them. They are great friends to

43

our people, and we love them much. Co-na-shus-tah is a
great man. His woman has none like her. We often come
to their house. We thank them for telling us to come to-day.
But as all the chiefs were asked we expected some important
talk. Now, here we are :—What is your business ?' "

" This, as may be readily supposed, was an embar-
rassing position to a young man just out of college. I
paused. Every countenance was fixed upon me, while
Red-Jacket in particular seemed to search me with his
arrowy eye, and to feel that the private and informal
nature of the meeting, and the extreme youth of the
man, were hardly in keeping with the character and
number of the guests invited ;—and his whole manner
implied, ' that but for the sake of the general and his
good viands, I should have waited for you to come to
us.' With these impressions of his feelings, I proceeded
to say in reply :—

" ' That I should have thought it very presumptuous in me
to send for him alone,—and still more for all the chiefs of his
tribe,—to come so far to see me ;—that my intention had been
to visit him and the other chiefs at his town ;—but the general and his lady could not go with me to introduce me.
Nor were we at all certain that we should find him and the
other chiefs at home ; and at any rate the general's house was
more convenient. He intended, when he asked them, to keep
them as long as they could stay, and to invite them to break
his bread, and drink his cup, and smoke his pipe ;—that
his woman, and he as well as I, desired to see them at their
house ;—that as to myself, I was a young man, and had no
business with them, except that I had heard a great deal of
Red-Jacket, and wished to see him and hear him talk ;—and
also that I had some things to say to him when we were better

acquainted, which, though not *business*, were important to his people ;—and I thought it would be interesting to him, as I knew he loved his people much ;—and finally that I would return his visit, and show him that it was not out of disrespect, but out of great regard for him, and great desire to see him, that we had sent for him,—this being the way that white men honor one another.'

" Mrs. Porter immediately confirmed what I had said, and gave special point to the *hospitality* of the house, and the great desire I had to see Red-Jacket. Her appeal, added to the reply, relaxed the rigor of his manner and that of the other chiefs, while it relieved our interview of all painful feelings.

" After this general letting down of the scene, Red-Jacket turned to me familiarly and asked :—' What are you ? You say you are not a government agent,—are you a gambler ?* or a black-coat ? or what are you ?' I answered : ' I am yet too young a man to engage in any profession; but I hope some of these days to be a black-coat.' He lifted up his hands accompanied by his eyes, in a most expressive way, and though not a word was uttered, every one fully understood that he very distinctly expressed the sentiment,—' What a fool !' I had too often been called to bear from those reputed ' great and wise' among *white* men, the shame of the cross, to be surprised by his manner; and I was too anxious to conciliate his good feelings to attempt

* By the term "gambler," Red-Jacket meant a land speculator, and by the way not a bad definition,—especially of those base men who have so long conspired to cheat the poor Indians out of their little remaining lands.

any retort,—so that I commanded my countenance, and
seeming not to have observed him, I proceeded to tell
him something of our colleges, &c., &c.   That gradually led his mind away from the ideas with which it was
filled and excited when he arrived.

" A good deal of general conversation ensued,—addressed to one and another of the chiefs,—and we were
just arriving at the hour of dinner, when our conference
was suddenly broken up by the arrival of a breathless
messenger, saying that an old chief, whose name I forget, had just died, and the other chiefs were immediately needed, to attend his burial.   One of the chiefs shed
tears at the news;—all seemed serious; but the others
suppressed their feelings and spent a few moments in
a very earnest conversation, the result of which Red-
Jacket announced to us.   They had determined to return at once to their village; but consented to leave
Red-Jacket and his interpreter.   In vain were they
urged to wait until after dinner, or to refresh themselves
with something eaten by the way.   With hurried farewell and quick steps they left the house, and by the
nearest foot-path returned home.

" This occurrence relieved me of one difficulty.   It
enabled me to see Red-Jacket at leisure, and alone.   It
seemed also to soften his feelings, and make him more
affable and kind.

" Soon after the departure of the chiefs, we were
ushered to dinner.   Red-Jacket behaved with great
propriety, in all respects; his interpreter, Major Berry,
though half a white man and perhaps a chief, like a true

savage. After a few awkward attempts at the knife and fork, he found himself falling behind, and repeating the old adage which is often quoted to cover the same style among our white urchins of picking a chicken-bone, '*that fingers were made before knives and forks,*' he proceeded with real gusto, and much good humor, to make up his lost time upon all parts of the dinner. It being over, I invited Red-Jacket into the general's office, where we had for four hours a most interesting conversation on a variety of topics, but chiefly connected with Christianity ; the government of the United States ; the missionaries ; and his loved lands.

"So great a length of time has passed since that interview that there must be supposed to be a failure in the attempt perfectly to report what was said. I am well assured I cannot do justice to his *language*, even as diluted by the ignorant interpreter ; and his *manner* cannot be described. But it was so impressive a conversation, and I have so often been called on to repeat it, that the substance of his remarks has been faithfully retained by my memory. It is only attempted here to recite a small part of what was then said, and that with particular reference to the illustration of his character, mind and opinions.

"It has already been mentioned and is largely known, that Red-Jacket cherished the most violent antipathy toward the American missionaries who had been located among his people. This led to very strenuous resistance of their influence, and to hatred of their religion, but of the true character of which he was totally ignorant. His

deep attachment to his people, and his great principle
that their national glory and even existence depended
upon keeping themselves distinct from white men, lay
at the foundation of his aversion to Christianity. Though
a pagan, yet his opposition was *political,* and he cared
very little for any religion except so far as it seemed to
advance or endanger the glory and safety of the tribe.

"He had unfortunately been led by designing and
corrupt white men, who were *interested* in the result,
falsely to associate the labors of the missionaries with
designs against his nation; and those who wished the
Senecas removed from their lands that *they* might profit
by the purchase,—and who saw in the success of the
mission the chief danger to *their* plans, artfully enlisted
the pagan party, of which Red-Jacket was the leader,
to oppose the missionaries,—and thus effectually led to
the final frustration of Red-Jacket's policy,—in and by
the defeat of the missionary enterprise. But as this
question is discussed in the sequel, I will not anticipate.
Thus much it was necessary to premise, in order to explain the nature and ends of my interview with Red-
Jacket. My object was to explain the true state of the
case to him, and after this to recommend the doctrine of
Christ to his understanding and heart. My first step,
therefore, was to ask him why he so strongly opposed
the settlement and labors of the missionaries? He replied, because they are the enemies of the Indians, and
under the cloak of doing them good are trying to cheat
them out of their lands. I asked him what proof he had
of this. He said he had been told so by some of his

wise and good friends among the white men, and he observed that the missionaries were constantly wanting more land,—and that by little and little, for themselves, or those who hired them to do it, they would take away all their lands, and drive them off.

"I asked him if he knew that there was a body of white men who had already bought the exclusive right to buy their lands from the government of New-York, and that therefore the missionaries could not hold the lands given or sold them by the Indians a moment after the latter left the lands and went away. He seemed to be startled by the statement, but said nothing. I proceeded to tell him that the true effect of the missionary influence on the tribe was to *secure* to them the possession of their lands, by civilizing them and making them quit the chase for the cultivation of the soil, building good houses, educating their children, and making them permanent citizens and good men. This was what the speculators did not wish. Therefore they hated the missionaries. He acknowledged that the Christian party among the Indians did as I said; but that was not the way for an Indian to do. Hunting, war and manly pursuits, were best fitted to them. But, said I, your reservation of land is too little for that purpose. It is surrounded by the white people like a small island by the sea; the deer, the buffalo and bear, have all gone. This wont do. If you intend to live so much longer, you will have to go to the great western wilderness where there is plenty of game, and no white men to trouble you. But he said, we wish to keep our lands, and to be buried by our fathers. I know it,—and therefore I say that the missionaries are your best friends; for if you follow the ways they teach you can still hold your lands,—though you cannot have hunting grounds; and therefore you must either do like white men, or remove from your lands,—very soon. Your plan of keeping the Indians distinct from the white people is begun too late. If you would do it and have large grounds, and would let the missionaries teach you Christianity far from the bad habits and big farms of the white people, it would then be well: it would keep your people from being corrupted and swallowed up by our people who grow so fast around you, and many of whom are very bad. But it is too late to do it here, and you must choose between keeping the missionaries and being like white men, and going to a far country : as it is, I continued, Red-Jacket is doing more than any body else to break up and drive away his people.

"This conversation had much effect on him. He grasped my hand and said if that were the case it was new to him. He also said he would lay it up in his mind, [putting his hand to his noble forehead,] and talk of it to the chiefs and the people.

"It is a very striking fact, that the disgraceful scenes now passing before the public eye over the grave of Red-Jacket, so early and so sadly fulfil these predictions; and I cannot here forbear to add that the thanks of the nation are due to our present chief magistrate,* for the

* This letter was written in January, 1841, and the President alluded to is Mr. Van Buren. W. L. S.

firmness with which he has resisted the recent efforts to force a fraudulent treaty on the remnant of this injured people; and drive them against their will, and against law and treaties sacredly made, away from their lands, to satisfy the rapacity of unprincipled men.

"It may be proper here to say likewise, that I do by no means intend to justify all that may possibly have been done by the missionaries to the Senecas. It is probable the earliest efforts were badly conducted; and men of more ability ought to have been sent to that peculiar and difficult station. But it is not for a moment to be admitted, nor is it credible that the authors of the charges themselves believe it, that the worthy men who at every sacrifice went to the mission among the Senecas, had any other than the purest purposes. I visited the station, and intimately knew the chief missionary. I marked carefully their plan and progress, and do not doubt their usefulness any more than their uprightness; and beyond all doubt it was owing chiefly to malignant influence exerted by white men, that they finally failed in their benevolent designs. But my business is to narrate, not to discuss.

"My next object was to talk with Red-Jacket about Christianity itself. He was prompt in his replies, and exercised and encouraged frankness with a spirit becoming a great man.

"He admitted both its truth and excellence, as adapted to white men. He said some keenly sarcastic things about the treatment that so good a man as Jesus had received from white men. The white men, he said,

44

ought all to be sent to hell for killing him; but as the
Indians had no hand in that transaction, they were in
that matter innocent.   Jesus Christ was not sent to
them; the atonement was not made for them; nor the
Bible given to them; and therefore the Christian religion
was not meant for them.   If the Great Spirit had intended that the Indians should be Christians, he would
have made his revelation to them as well as to the white
men.   Not having done so, it was clearly his will that
they should continue in the faith of their fathers.   He
said that the red man was of a totally different race,—
and needed an entirely different religion,—and that it
was idle as well as unkind, to try to alter their religion
and give them ours.   I asked him to point out the difference of the races, contending that they were one, and
needed but one religion, and that Christianity was that
religion which Christ had intended for, and ordered to
be preached to, all men.   He had no distinct views of
the nature of Christianity as a method of salvation, and
denied the need of it.   As to the *unity* of the races, I
asked if he ever knew two distinct races, even of the
lower animals, to propagate their seed from generation
to generation.   But do not Indians and white men do
so? He allowed it; but denied that it proved the matter
in hand.   I pressed the points of resemblance in every
thing but color,—and that in the case of the Christian
Indians there was a common mind on religion.   He
finally waived this part of the debate by saying " that one
thing was certain whatever else was not,—that white

men had a great love for Indian women, and left their traces behind them wherever they could."*

"On the point of needing pardon, from being wicked, he said the Indians were *good* till the white man corrupted them. "But did not the Indians have *some* wickedness *before* that?" "Not so *much.*" "How was *that* regarded by the Great Spirit? Would He forgive it?" He hoped so,—"did not know." "Jesus," I rejoined, "came to tell us He would, and to get that pardon for us."

"As to suffering and death among the Indians, did not they prove that the Great Spirit was angry with *them,* as well as with white men? Would He thus treat men that were *good?* He said they were not wicked before white men came to their country and taught them to be so. But they *died before* that? And why did they *die,* if the Great Spirit was not angry, and they wicked? He could not say, and in reply to my explanation of the gospel doctrine of the entrance of death by sin, he again turned the subject by saying he was a "great doctor," and could cure any thing but *death.*

"The interpreter had incidentally mentioned that the reason the chiefs had to go home so soon, was that they always *sacrificed a white dog on the death of a great man.* I turned this fact to the account of the argument, and endeavored to connect it with, and explain by it, the doctrine of *atonement,* by the blood of Christ, and

* In another conversation upon this subject, I believe with Dr. Breckenridge, Red-Jacket expressed this idea more pungently, as may be seen by referring back to page 186. W. L. S.

also pressed him on the questions, how can this *please* the Great Spirit, on *your* plan? *Why* do you offer such a *sacrifice*, for so it is considered? And *where* they got such a rite from? He attempted no definite reply.

"Many other topics were talked over. But these specimens suffice to illustrate his views, and mode of thinking.

"At the close of the conversation he proposed to give me a *name*, that henceforth I might be numbered among his friends, and admitted to the intercourse and regards of the nation. Supposing this not amiss, I consented. But before he proceeded he called for some whiskey. He was at this time an intemperate man,—and though perfectly sober on that occasion, evidently displayed toward the close of the interview the need of stimulus, which it is hardly necessary to say we carefully kept from him. But he *insisted* now, and after some time a small portion was sent to him at the bottom of a decanter. He looked at it,—shook it,—and with a sneer said,—" Why, here is not whiskey enough for a name to float in." But no movement being made to get more, he drank it off, and proceeded with a sort of pagan orgies, to give me a name. It seemed a semi-civil, semi-religious ceremony. He walked around me again and again, muttering sounds which the interpreter did not venture to explain; and laying his hand on me pronounced me " Con-go-gu-wah," and instantly, with great apparent delight, took me by the hand as a brother. I felt badly during the scene, but it was beyond recall,— and supposing that it might be useful in a future day, submitted to the initiation.

"Red-Jacket was in appearance nearly sixty years old at this time. He had a weather-beaten look; age had done something to produce this,—probably intemperance more. But still his general appearance was striking, and his face noble. His lofty and capacious forehead, his piercing black eye, his gently curved lips, fine cheek, and slightly aquiline nose, all marked a great man, and as sustained and expressed by his dignified air, made a deep impression on every one that saw him. All these features became doubly expressive when his mind and body were set in motion by the effort of speaking,—if effort that may be called which flowed like a free full stream from his lips. I saw him in the wane of life, and I heard him only in private, and through a stupid and careless interpreter. Yet notwithstanding these disadvantages, he was one of the greatest men and most eloquent orators I ever knew. His cadence was measured and yet very musical. In ordinary utterance it amounted to a sort of musical monotony. But when excited he would spring to his feet, elevate his head, expand his arms, and utter with indescribable effect of manner and tone, some of his noblest thoughts.

"After this interesting conference had closed, the old chief with his interpreter bade us a very civil and kind farewell, and set forth on foot for his own wigwam.

"It was four years after this before I had the pleasure of again seeing my old friend. I was then on a flying visit to Black Rock. At an early day I repaired to his village, but he was not at home. Ten days after, as we were just leaving the shore in the steam-boat to go up the lake, he suddenly presented himself. It was unhappily too late to return. He hailed me by name, and pointed with much animation to such parts of his person as were decorated with some *red* cloth which I had at parting presented to him, and which, though not worn as a *jacket*, was with much taste otherwise distributed over his person. These he exhibited as proofs of his friendly recollection.

" The last time I ever saw him, was at the close of Mr. Adams's administration. He, with a *new* interpreter, (Major Berry having been removed by death,) had been on a visit to his old friend Co-na-shus-tah,—then Secretary of War. After spending some time at the capital, where I often met him, and had the horror to see his ' dignity often laid in the dust,' by excessive drunkenness, he paid me by invitation a final visit at Baltimore, on his way home. He took only time enough to dine. He looked dejected and forlorn. He and his interpreter had each a suit of common infantry uniform, and a sword as common, which he said had been presented to him at the war department. He was evidently ashamed of them. I confess I was too. But I forbear. He was then sober, and serious. He drank hard cider, which was the strongest drink I could conscientiously offer him,—so I told him. He said it was enough. I said but little to him of religion,—urged him to prepare to meet the Great Spirit, and recommended him to go to Jesus for all he needed. He took it kindly,—said he should see me no more,—and was going to his people to die. So it was,—not long after this, he was called to his last account. **JOHN BRECKENRIDGE.**"

On another occasion, at no great distance of time from his first interview with Doctor Breckenridge, the superior benefits of husbandry, education, the enjoyments and refinements of civilized life, and the blessings of Christianity having been urged upon him by a benevolent gentleman with great earnestness, Red-Jacket replied in the following strain :—

" As to civilization, among white people, I believe it is a good thing, and that it was so ordered that they should get their living in that manner. I believe in a God, and that it was ordered by him that we, the red people, should get our living in a different way, viz : from the wild game of the woods and the fishes of the waters. I believe in the Great Spirit who created the heavens and the earth. He peopled the forests, and the air and the waters. He then created man, and placed him as the superior animal of this creation, and designed him as governor over all other created beings on earth. He created man differing from all other animals. He created the red man, the white, the black, and yellow. All these he created for wise, but inscrutable purposes," &c.*

To prove this he reasoned from analogy, from the varieties in the same species, and from the different species under a common genus in all other animals, whether quadruped, fowl, or fish,—pointed out their different modes of living, and showed that they each had a distinct designation assigned to them in the grand

* MS. collection of Joseph W. Moulton.

arrangement of the animal economy by the Great Spirit.
He proceeded :—

" This being so, what proof have we that he did not make
a similar arrangement with the human species, when we find
so vast, so various, and so irreconcileable a variety among
them, causing them to live differently, and to pursue different
occupations. As to religion, we all ought to have it. We
should adore and worship our Creator for his great favors in
placing us over all his works. If we cannot with the same
fluency of speech, and in the same flowing language, worship as you do, we have our mode of adoring, which we do
with a sincere heart,—then can you say that our prayers and
thanksgivings, proceeding from grateful hearts and sincere
minds, are less acceptable to the Great God of the heavens
and the earth, though manifested either by speaking, dancing,
or feasting, than your's, uttered in your own manner and
style ?"*

Doctor Breckenridge laments, in the preceding letter,
his inability to make even an approach to justice as to
the language and figures in which Red-Jacket clothed
his thoughts, and by which he illustrated and enforced
them. The same confession has been uniformly elicited
from every writer who enjoyed opportunities of listening
to the chief or conversing with him. General Porter,

* In their mode of worship, the Six Nations addressed the Great Spirit with
thanks and prayer by particular speakers. They then feasted, or celebrated a
thanksgiving, closing with dancing and other amusements and recreations.
Their great religious festivals, when the convocations were general, were semi-
annual, and continued from three to six days. While prayer is offered, the dust
of tobacco is sprinkled on live coals of fire, that the incense may ascend with
their supplications. Thanks are returned for all their temporal mercies,—their
lives, health, crops, game, and in a word for all the bounties received from the
Great Spirit.

than whom no one knew him better, speaks of him as a man "endowed with great intellectual powers, and who, as an orator, was not only unsurpassed, but unequalled, *longo intervallo*, by any of his cotemporaries. Although those who were ignorant of his language could not fully appreciate the force and beauty of his speeches, when received through the medium of an interpretation, —generally coarse and clumsy,—yet such was the peculiar gracefulness of his person, attitudes and action, and the mellow tones of his Seneca dialect, and such the astonishing effects produced on that part of the auditory who did fully understand him, and whose souls appeared to be engrossed and borne away with the orator, that he was listened to by all with perfect delight."* He drew his arguments from the natural relations and fitness of things. His mind glanced through the visible creation, and from analogy he reasoned in a way that often baffled and defied refutation. His figures were from the same inexhaustible fountain, and were frequently so sublime, so apposite, and so beautiful, that the interpreters often said the English language was not rich enough to allow of doing him justice. Such, at least, have been the representations of those who knew him well, and who have had the best opportunities of arriving at correct conclusions. Nevertheless, the character of nearly all his speeches that have been preserved, *as* they have been preserved, bears evidence rather of the enthusiasm of his admirers, than of their judgment.

* MS. letter to the author from General Porter.

45

CHAPTER XIII.

THE domestic relations of Red-Jacket have thus far scarcely been adverted to. Indeed, the materials for his family history are very slender. The orator had two wives. The first, after having borne him a large family of children, he forsook, for an alleged breach of conjugal fidelity, and never received her to his favor again. In William Savary's journal of the treaty of Canandaigua, in 1794, that excellent Friend gave an account of a visit to Red-Jacket's lodge, and spoke of his children, in regard to their appearance and manners, in terms of gratified commendation. But a large number of his children by the first wife died of consumption while yet "in the dew of their youth." In a conversation with that eminent medical practitioner, Doctor John W. Francis, of New-York, a few years before the chieftain's death, on the subject of the diseases incident to the Indians, Red-Jacket refuted the popular notion that they were not equally obnoxious with others to pulmonary complaints. In support of his position he instanced the case of his own family, of which he said seventeen had died of consumption, ten or eleven of whom were his children. He felt the bereavement deeply, and sometimes evinced strong emotion when conversing upon the subject. On one occasion, when visiting an aged lady of his acquaintance at Avon, who had known him almost from his youth,* and who was aware of his domestic afflictions, she inquired whether any of his children were living. He fixed his eyes upon her with a sorrowful expression of countenance and replied :—

"Red-Jacket was once a great man, and in favor with the Great Spirit. He was a lofty pine among the smaller trees of the forest. But after years of glory he degraded himself by drinking the fire-water of the white man. The Great Spirit has looked upon him in anger, and his lightning has stripped the pine of its branches !"

For his second wife Red-Jacket married the widow of a deceased chief, whose English name was " Two-Guns." She was one of the most amiable and respectable women of her tribe. Her mind was of a superior order, and the dignity of her manners and fine personal

* The late Mrs. Berry, of the Genesee Valley, wife of Gilbert R. Berry, one of the earliest settlers of western New-York, and a trader at the Indian town, once standing near the place where the turnpike crosses the Genesee river at Avon. Mrs. Berry was the mother of Mrs. George Hosmer, from whom I received this touching incident. Mrs. B. was a great friend of the Senecas, and spoke their language, (as does Mrs. Hosmer,) fluently.

appearance rendered her a very suitable counterpart to
the noble form and bearing of her husband. It is an interesting, if not remarkable fact, that notwithstanding
the inveterate hostility of Red-Jacket to the missionaries,
and his confirmed paganism, his wife became a Christian,
and several of his children were believed to have died
in the same faith.

It was in the year 1826 that his wife first became
interested in the subject of religion. She was frequently seen in the Christian assembly, an attentive listener
to the truths of the gospel, as presented from Sabbath
to Sabbath in the plain familiar address of the missionary. She at length abandoned her pagan worship altogether, became a constant attendant at the mission
chapel, and in the following year proposed connecting
herself with the little church then under the pastoral
charge of the Rev. Mr. Harris. This proposal was strongly resisted on the part of Red-Jacket. He represented
to her "that they had hitherto ever lived in peace and
harmony, and had been prosperous and happy; and
now if she was going to leave him and go over and
join herself to the company of his political and personal
opponents, one thing was certain, that he should leave
her for ever; he should never come to see her again."
Soon after this somewhat arbitrary communication, she
went one day to the house of Mr. Harris, apparently in
much distress, to ask counsel as to the course she ought
to pursue. The advice can readily be anticipated. She
was told that God required her to be a Christian under
all possible circumstances;—that it was best to follow

the dictates of her conscience and the commands of
Jesus Christ;—and that if she would humbly look to the
Saviour for grace, He would strengthen and comfort
her under this trial, and cause it "to work for her
good." Still, although holding the course thus indicated
to be the path of duty, the missionary very properly observed to her that she must be governed in her decision
by the voice of conscience, and the dictates of her own
judgment.

Her resolution was soon taken to abjure the dark and
senseless superstitions of her people; and in a short
time thereafter she was received on the profession of
her faith into the fellowship of the Christian church.
True to his threat, Red-Jacket left her; and retiring to
the Tonnewanta reservation, connected himself with a
woman of that nation. No one questioned the sincerity
or the strength of the attachment of the woman thus
abandoned for her husband, yet she followed not after
him, nor made any efforts to induce his return. The
injury was borne with a meek and submissive spirit,—
so much so as to endear her greatly to the members
of the mission family, to whom she became much attached, and with whom she was wont to spend several
hours almost every week, in Christian conversation
and prayer.

Red-Jacket continued absent, in his new alliance, for
six or seven months, by which time he repented of his
folly and returned to his lawful wife, whom he urgently so-
licited to receive him back. She *did* receive him, with the
same meek and forgiving spirit that marked her character

and conduct during her desertion. But it was with the condition that she should be unmolested in regard to her religious opinions, and the discharge of her Christian duties,—a condition to which Red-Jacket willingly acceded. Their conjugal relations having been thus reestablished, the chieftain and his wife continued to live together with their usual harmony, until a divorce was pronounced by a summons from another world.*

When, in the year 1825, General Lafayette, as the guest of the nation, was making his memorable tour of the United States, being at Buffalo, Red-Jacket was among the visitors who in throngs paid their respects to the veteran. Having been presented to the General, the orator inquired whether he remembered being at the treaty of peace with the Six Nations, at Fort Stanwix, in 1784. Lafayette answered that he had not forgotten that great council, and asked his interrogator if he knew what had become of the young chief who, on that occasion, opposed with so much eloquence " the burying of the tomahawk." " *He is before you*," was the instant reply. The General remarked to him that time had wrought great changes upon both since that memorable meeting. "Ah," rejoined Red-Jacket, "time has not been so severe upon you as it has upon me. It has left you a fresh countenance, and hair to cover your head; while to me ...... behold ......!" and taking a handkerchief from his head, with an air of much feeling, he disclosed the fact that he was nearly bald. It is

---

* I have derived the facts of this relation respecting Red-Jacket and his second wife, directly from Mr. Harris, the missionary, himself.

added by M. Lavasseur, the secretary of General Lafayette, and the French historian of his tour, that the
people in attendance could not help laughing at the simplicity of the Indian, who appeared to be ignorant how
to repair the ravages of age in this respect. But his
simplicity was presently enlightened by the disclosure
of the fact that the General was furnished with a wig,—
whereupon the chief, confounding a wig with a scalp,
conceived the idea of regarnishing his own head by an
operation truly Indian, at the expense of some one of
his neighbors. But this was a suggestion of pleasantry.
M. Lavasseur remarked of the appearance of Red-Jacket at that time,—"This extraordinary man, although
much worn down by time and intemperance, preserves
yet, in a surprising degree, the exercise of all his faculties. He obstinately refuses to speak any language but
that of his own people, and affects a great dislike to all
others, although it is easy to discern that he perfectly
understands the English. He refused, nevertheless, to
reply to the General before his interpreter had translated
his questions into the Seneca language."*

Red-Jacket was ever gratified with the attentions of
distinguished men, with whom, no matter for the height
of their elevation, he felt himself upon a footing of perfect
equality. It is related that "about the year 1820, a
young French nobleman, who was making the tour of
the United States, visited the town of Buffalo. Hearing

---

* Lavasseur—Drake—B. B. Thatcher. M. Lavasseur was perfectly correct
in this last suggestion. Red-Jacket understood the English language very well,
as the author had occasion to ascertain. But he could not speak it well.

of the fame of Red-Jacket, and learning that his residence was but seven miles distant, he sent him word that he was desirous to see him, adding a request that the chief would visit him in Buffalo the next day. Red-Jacket received the message with much contempt, and replied:—
" Tell the *young man* that if he wishes to visit the *old chief*, he may find him with his nation, where other strangers pay their respects to him; and Red-Jacket will be glad to see him." The count sent back his messenger, to say that he was fatigued with his journey, and could not go to the Seneca village; that he had come all the way from France to see the great orator of the Senecas, and after having put himself to so much trouble to see so distinguished a man, the latter could not refuse to meet him at Buffalo. " Tell him," said the sarcastic chief, "that it is very strange he should come so far to see me, and then stop short within seven miles of my lodge." The retort was richly merited. The count visited him at his wigwam, and *then* Red-Jacket accepted an invitation to dine with him at his lodgings in Buffalo. The young nobleman was greatly pleased with him, declaring that he considered him a greater wonder than the Falls of Niagara. This remark was the more striking, as it was made within view of the great cataract. " But," adds the relator,* " it was just. He who made the world, and filled it with wonders, has declared man to be the crowning work of the whole creation."

But the chieftain did not always stand so sternly upon his dignity, and in the case just related, it is quite pos-

* Rev. Dr. Breckenridge—vide M'Kenney's Indian Sketches.

sible that he was more particular because of the rank of the stranger, and because he *was* a stranger to the country. On one occasion, not many years before his death, a gentleman from Albany on a visit to Buffalo, being desirous of seeing the chief, sent a message to that effect. The gentleman was affluent in money, and in words, the latter flowing forth with great rapidity, and in an inverse ratio to his ideas. He had also a habit of approaching very near to any person with whom he was conversing, and chattering with almost unapproachable volubility. On receiving the message, Red-Jacket dressed himself with the utmost care, designing, as he ever did when sober, to make the most imposing impression, and came over to the village. Being introduced to the stranger, he soon measured his intellectual capacity, and made no effort to suppress his disappointment, which indeed was sufficiently disclosed in his features. After listening for a few moments to the chatter of the gentleman, Red-Jacket, with a look of mingled chagrin and contempt, approached close to him and exclaimed,—" cha, cha, cha !" as rapidly as utterance would allow. Then drawing himself to his full height, he turned proudly upon his heel, and walked away in the direction of his own domicil, "as straight as an Indian," nor deigned to look behind while in sight of the tavern. The gentleman with more money than brains was for once lost in astonishment, and stood longer motionless and silent than he had ever done before.*

A prominent trait in the Indian character is vanity.

* This incident was related to the author by the Hon. Mr. Moseley, of Buffalo.

46

The Indians are vain of their dress, of their achievements, and of their talents, whenever marked by superiority; and it cannot have escaped the observation of the reader, that this weakness was prominent in the disposition of Red-Jacket. The organ of self-esteem, according to the classification of the phrenologists, was beyond doubt strongly developed upon his head. A few illustrations of this feature in his character may not be amiss.

In the earlier years of his public life, as the reader is well aware, Red-Jacket was frequently engaged in negotiations with Timothy Pickering, of whose vigorous intellectual powers there is no occasion to speak in this connexion. Some time after the diplomatic intercourse between the colonel and himself had ceased, the former was called to the State Department of the federal government.* On meeting Red-Jacket soon afterward, the fact of this appointment was mentioned to him by his friend Thomas Morris. " Yes," observed the chief : " we began our public career about the same time. He knew how to read and write, but I did not, and therefore he has got ahead of me. But had I possessed those advantages I should have been ahead of him."†

At the treaties held by him, Colonel Pickering was in the practice of taking down the speeches of the Indians, from the lips of the interpreter, in writing, and in

---

* The last treaty between the United States and the Six Nations was held at Canandaigua, in 1794. Colonel Pickering was appointed Secretary of State by Washington, in December, 1795.

† Letter of Thomas Morris to the author.

order to expedite business, he would sometimes write
while the orator in chief was himself speaking. On one
occasion, when Red-Jacket occupied the forum, observing that the colonel continued writing, he abruptly
came to a pause. The colonel desired him to proceed.
" No," said the orator,—" not while you hold down your
head." " Why," inquired the commissioner, " can you
not go on while I write ?" " Because," replied the chief,
" if you look me in the eye you will then perceive
whether I tell you the truth or not."*

On another occasion, Colonel Pickering turned to
speak to a third person while Red-Jacket was addressing him. The chief instantly rebuked him for his inat-
tention with great hauteur, observing, with emphasis,
" When a Seneca speaks he ought to be listened to with
attention from one extremity of this great island to the
other."†

On returning from his visits to the seat of the federal
government, where, at different periods, he had several
interviews with General Washington, he would magnify
to the other Indians the importance of his reception by
the great chief. " I remember having seen him on one
of those occasions, when, after having seated the Indians around him in a semi-circle, taking the cocked-hat
that had been presented to him by General Knox, then
Secretary of War, in his hand, he went round bowing
to the Indians, as though they were the company at the
President's house, and himself the President. He
would then repeat to one and another all the compli-

* Letter of Thomas Morris to the author.   † Idem.

ments which he chose to suppose the President had bestowed upon him, and which his auditors and admiring people supposed had been thus bestowed."*

Toward the close of his life he was present by invitation at the launching of a schooner at Black Rock, bearing his name. He made a short address on the occasion, showing the estimation in which he held his own high merit. In the course of this speech, addressing himself directly to the vessel, he said :—

"You have had a great name given to you,—strive to deserve it. Be brave and daring. Go boldly into the great lakes, and fear neither the swift winds nor the strong waves. Be not frightened nor overcome by them, for it is by resisting storms and tempests that I, whose name you bear, obtained my renown. Let my great example inspire you to courage and lead you to glory."†

He was not deficient in tact, and with true Indian circumspection, and his own characteristic cunning, was careful to conceal his ignorance as to the usages of society in the better circles into which he was occasionally thrown. "He once, on his return from Philadelphia, told me that when there he perceived many things the meaning of which he did not understand, but he would not make inquiry concerning them there, because they would be imputed to his ignorance. He therefore had determined on his return to ask me. He said that when he dined at General Washington's, a man stood all the time behind his chair, and would every now and

* Letter from Thomas Morris.
† Letter from the Hon. Albert H. Tracy to the author.

then run off with his plate, and knife and fork, which he
would immediately replace by others. ' Now,' said
Red-Jacket, ' what was this for ?' I replied to him, that
he must have observed on the President's table a variety
of dishes, that each dish was cooked in a different manner, and that plates, and the knives and forks of the
guests, were changed as often as they were helped from
a different dish. ' Ah,' said he, after musing a moment, ' is that it ?' I replied in the affirmative. ' You
must then suppose,' he continued, ' that the plates, and
knives and forks, retain the taste of the cookery ?' Yes,
I replied. ' Have you then,' he added, ' any method
by which you can change your palates every time you
change your plates ; for I should suppose that the taste
would remain on the palate longer than on the plate ?' I
replied that we were in the habit of washing that away
by drinking wine. ' Ah,' said he, 'I now understand it.
I was persuaded that so general a custom among you
must be founded in reason, and I only regret that when
I was in Philadelphia I did not understand it,—when
dining with General Washington and your father. The
moment the man went off with my plate, I would have
drunk wine until he brought me another ; for although I
am fond of eating, I am more so of drinking."*

Red-Jacket could never become reconciled to the
criminal law of the white men, the operation of which,
in many respects, he thought unequal, and consequently
unjust. It has been seen in a former chapter, on the
trial of Stiff-armed George, indicted for murder, that

* MS. letter of Thomas Morris to the author.

the Indians supposed that drunkenness might with propriety be pleaded in mitigation of a crime, whereas the white men hold it to be but one crime superadded to another, and therefore aggravating the offence. In like manner, he could not understand the justice of the law that would punish an offender by as long an imprisonment for stealing a trifling article as for a larger one. An incident in point occurred in the county of Genesee, about twenty years ago, which will at once illustrate his views upon this subject, and his humor. It happened that an Indian was indicted at Batavia, for burglary, in breaking and entering the house of Mr. Ellicott, agent of the Holland Land Company, and stealing some trifling article of small value, the punishment for which was imprisonment in the state prison for life,—the crime of petit larceny merging itself in the greater offence. Red-Jacket, with other chiefs, attended the trial for the purpose of rendering all the aid and obtaining all the favor in their power for their brother in bonds. The proof was clear, and a verdict of guilty followed without hesitation. When the prisoner was arraigned for sentence, and the usual question propounded, why the sentence of the law should not be pronounced, Red-Jacket, who had been watching the proceedings with intense interest, asked permission to speak in his behalf. The request being granted, he rose with his usual dignity, and boldly questioned the jurisdiction of the court, and asserted the independence of his nation. He contended that the Senecas were the allies, not the subjects of the whites,—that his nation had laws for the punishment of theft,—and that the offender in the present case ought to be delivered up to them, to be tried according to the usages, and suffer according to the laws of his own people,—assuring the court that, in the event of his surrender, the culprit should be thus tried and punished. His manner on the occasion was particularly fine, even for him. But his argument was not sufficiently powerful to avert the sentence, which was pronounced in due form. The orator was dissatisfied at the result. Estimating the measure of delinquency by the pecuniary loss, he could not perceive the justice of incarcerating a man for life, who had only stolen a few spoons of small value, when another offender, who had stolen a horse, was sentenced to but a few years imprisonment. After the proceedings were over, in passing from the court-house to the inn, in company with a group of lawyers, Red-Jacket discerned upon the sign of a printing-office the arms of the state, with the emblematical representation of Liberty and Justice, emblazoned in large figures and characters. The chieftain stopped, and pointing to the figure of Liberty, asked in broken English,—"*What—him—call?*" He was answered, " LIBERTY." " Ugh !" was the significant and truly aboriginal response. Then pointing to the other figure, he inquired,—"*What—him—call ?*" He was answered, "JUSTICE,"—to which with a kindling eye he instantly replied, by asking,—"*Where—him—live—now?*"*

Captain Jones, who was so long connected with the

---

* Related to the author by George Hosmer, Esq., of Avon, who was present at the scene in the court-house, and also in the street.

Indians as a resident of their country, and an interpreter, had been adopted by Red-Jacket as a son, according to the customs of that people.   On a certain
occasion, owing to the slanderous imputations of some
mischief-makers of his nation, Red-Jacket entertained a
suspicion that Jones was actuated by motives of self-
interest, and did not regard the welfare of the Indians.
Shortly after his mind was thus poisoned in reference to his
friend, he met the captain at the hotel of Timothy Hosmer, in Avon.   Jones advanced to greet the chief with
his accustomed cordiality of manner, but was received
with haughty distrust and coldness.   After the lapse of
a few minutes, during which time the questions of Jones
were answered in monosyllables, the captain asked an
explanation of Red-Jacket for his conduct.   Fixing his
searching glance upon him as if reading the secrets of
his soul, Red-Jacket told him of the rumor circulated in
reference to his fidelity to the Indians, and concluded by
saying with a saddened expression,—" And have *you* at
last deserted us?"   The look, the tone, the attitude of
the orator, were so touching, so despairing, that Jones,
though made of stern materials, wept like a child, at the
same time refuting the calumny in the most energetic
terms.*   Convinced that Jones was still true, the chief,
forgetful of the stoicism of his race, mingled his tears
with his, and embracing him with the cordiality of old,

---

* This incident, and the touching and almost pathetic inquiry of Red-Jacket,
remind one of the dying words which the dramatists have put into the mouth of
Cæsar, when he discovered Brutus among the conspirators,—" *Et tu Brute ?*
Wilt thou stab Cæsar too?"   Or in the words of another author;—"And Brutus
thou my sonne, whom erst I loved best."

RED JACKET'S HOUSE, RESIDENCE OF JONES,

Seneca Village.   The Interpreter.

the reconciled parties renewed old friendships over a social glass.*

Red-Jacket did not relish being trifled with, even in playfulness. At one of his visits to the house of Captain Jones, on taking his seat at the breakfast table with the family, Mrs. Jones, knowing his extreme fondness for sugar, mischievously prepared his coffee without the addition of that luxury. On discovering the cheat, the chief looked at the Captain with an offended expression, and thus rebuked him:—"My son!"—stirring his cup with energy,—"do you allow your squaw thus to trifle with your father?" Perceiving at the same time by the giggling of the children, that they had entered into the joke, he continued,—"And do you allow your children to make sport of their chief?" Jones and his wife thereupon apologized, and the latter made the *amende honorable* by handing him the sugar-bowl, which he took, and with half-angry sarcasm filled his cup to the brim with sugar. The liquid not holding so large a quantity in solution, he ate the whole with his spoon.†

Red-Jacket was not gratified with scenes of human suffering. Some four or five years before his death, there was an execution of three brothers at Buffalo, named Thayer. They had been convicted of murdering a man several years before, named Lane, the discovery of whose remains caused much excitement, and altogether the extraordinary circumstances with which the case was invested, caused a great sensation in Western New-

* Related to the author by W. H. C. Hosmer, of Avon.
† Related to Mr. Hosmer by Mrs. Jones, in May, 1840.

47

York.   On the day when the unhappy brothers were executed, while the whole civilized population of that region,
of both sexes, was crowding the roads to Buffalo to behold the exit of three of their fellow beings upon the scaffold, Red-Jacket was met by Judge Walden, of Buffalo,
wending his way from the town to his own home.   The
judge inquired where he was going, at the same time
expressing his astonishment that he did not join the multitude who were pressing the other way to see the execution.   The answer of the chief was brief:—"Fools
enough there already.....Battle is the place to see men
die."   This reply was a severe rebuke, as just as sententious, of that strange and discreditable curiosity un-
accountably prevailing among both sexes of all nations,
to witness the awful spectacles of public executions.*

Although fond of the pleasures of the table himself,
yet no man had a more thorough contempt for the mere
sensualist or gourmand than Red-Jacket.   Many years
ago, before the Indian towns were broken up along the
valley of the Genesee, a clan of the Senecas resided at
Connawaugus, in the vicinity of the present town of
Avon.   The chief of this clan was a good easy man
named *Hot-Bread*.   He was a hereditary sachem, not
having risen by merit,—was weak and inefficient, and
of gluttonous habits.   On a certain occasion, when Mr.
Hosmer was accompanying Red-Jacket to an Indian council, in the course of general conversation he inquired
the chief's opinion of Hot-Bread.   "Waugh!" exclaimed

---

* Related to the author by the lady of George Hosmer.

Red-Jacket: "He has a little place at Connawaugus,—big enough for him. Big man here," (laying his left hand upon his abdomen,) "but very small here," bringing the palm of his right hand with significant emphasis upon his forehead.

As to the general manners of Red-Jacket, his intellectual character, his personal appearance, and the power and studied graces of his oratory, a gentleman who knew him intimately for almost half a century has written thus:—"When I first knew Red-Jacket he was in his prime, being probably about thirty-six years of age. He was decidedly the most eloquent man amongst the Six Nations. His stature was rather above than below the middle size. He was well made. His eyes were fine, and expressive of the intellect of which he possessed an uncommon portion. His address, particularly when he spoke in council, was very fine, and almost majestic. He was decidedly the most graceful public speaker I ever heard. He was fluent, without being too rapid. You could always tell when he meant to speak, from the pains he would take before he arose to arrange the silver ornaments on his arms, and the graceful fold that he would give to his blanket. On rising he would first turn toward the Indians, and bespeak their attention to what he meant to say in their behalf to the commissioner of the United States. He would then turn toward the commissioner, and bending toward him with a slight but dignified inclination of the head, proceed. There is much more decorum in the Indian councils than in any of our public bodies. When any chief thinks that the speaker has omitted or forgotten any thing that ought to be dwelt upon, he places himself quite near to the speaker, and in the most delicate and quiet manner, his voice not louder than a whisper, prompts him, while the whole assembly in their peculiar manner encourage by cheering the orator."*

Deprived as were the Indians of the unspeakable advantages of a written language, and depending altogether upon tradition for the preservation of both their official and unofficial history, the cultivation of the memory was an object of the first importance among them.† The provisions of their treaties, it is well known, were preserved with great accuracy, and for generations, by means of belts, with strings of wampum,—each string, being different, was in fact a record of some

---

* Letter to the author from Thomas Morris.

† There is reason to believe that the orators of the Six Nations were as careful in the study of their speeches,—those especially which were to be delivered on great occasions,—as were the orators of Greece and Rome. The author has been informed by that veteran legislator, General Erastus Root, that he was a member of the Senate of New-York when the celebrated letter, or speech, of Farmer's-Brother, containing the passage which has been so much admired,—" *The Great Spirit spake to the whirlwind and it was still,*" was presented to that body. The General says that it struck him so forcibly at the time, that he called for a second reading, which was had. Soon afterward, in a conversation with Mr. Parish, so long the interpreter of the Senecas, the General inquired of him whether it was not the habit of the interpreters to embellish the speeches of the Indian orators. His reply was an exclamation of surprise at the suggestion. So far from it, Mr. Parish averred that it was altogether impossible for him to impart to the translations any thing like the force and beauty of the originals. He also stated that on great occasions, the Indian orators, Red-Jacket and Farmer's-Brother in particular, not only studied their speeches, and conned them well, but would send to him for rehearsals, in order that they might be assured that he understood them fully, and could translate them with accuracy. They were alike vain and ambitious of appearing well in the reports of their speeches.

particular article or provision of a treaty. These belts were deposited in their council lodges with great care, and the signification of each particular string was carefully repeated from father to son, or from chief to chief in the succession, until thoroughly fixed in the memory. By this process, the stipulations of every treaty were so deeply impressed upon the mind, that by the aid of the belt they were at any time, when occasion required, brought to fresh remembrance. This cultivation of the art of mnemonics would necessarily be carried to its greatest perfection by a chief of Red-Jacket's intellectual powers and ambition, and the following incident has been preserved as an illustration of his accuracy. " In a council which was held with the Senecas by Governor Tompkins, of New-York, a contest arose between that gentleman and Red-Jacket, as to a fact connected with a treaty of many years' standing. The American agent stated one thing, and the Indian chief corrected him,—insisting that the reverse of his assertion was true. But it was rejoined :—' You have forgotten. We have it written down on paper.' ' The paper then tells a lie,' was the confident answer; ' I have it written down here,' he added, placing his hand with great dignity upon his brow. ' You Yankees are born with a feather between your fingers, but your paper does not speak the truth. The Indian keeps his knowledge here,—this is the book the Great Spirit gave them ; it does not lie.' A reference was immediately made to the treaty in question, when to the astonishment of all present, and the triumph of the unlettered statesman, the document confirmed every word he had uttered."*

There are no portraits of Red-Jacket extant, taken in early life, or even when in the prime of his manhood, although many efforts were made by the artists of New-York and Philadelphia, and also by other gentlemen, during his visits to those cities, to induce him to sit. His reply to all importunities upon the subject, for many years, was, that when Red-Jacket died, all that appertained to him should die with him. He wished nothing to remain. But this purpose was changed in the autumn of 1820, through the interposition of the blacksmith of the tribe, and he was induced to sit to Mr. Mathies, a self-taught artist, residing at Rochester. Indeed, his reluctance was readily overcome by an appeal to his vanity, —Mr. Mathies having assured him that his only motive was to obtain a likeness to be placed by the side of the portraits of other great men of the United States. He sat three times to Mathies, and the picture is said to be very good. The Rubicon having been passed, there was less difficulty in prevailing upon him to favor other artists, among whom was the distinguished delineator of Indians, Mr. George Catlin, who painted him twice. Henry Inman also made a sketch of him,—a head only, —which is thought very spirited. But the picture by Mr. Robert W. Weir, taken in 1828, at the request of Doctor John W. Francis, of New-York, is of far the highest order of merit, and has become the standard likeness of "the last of the Seneca orators." An ac-

* M'Kenney's Indian Biography.

quaintance of several years, and the reception of some trifling presents from Doctor Francis, had enabled the latter to induce a promise from the old chief to sit, on his next visit to New-York. This happened in the year last mentioned; when, with his interpreter, Jemison, he very promptly repaired to the painting-room of Mr. Weir. " For this purpose he dressed himself in the costume which he deemed most appropriate to his character, decorated with his brilliant overcovering and belt, his tomahawk and Washington medal. For the whole period of nearly two hours, on four or five successive days, he was as punctual to the arrangements of the artist as any individual could be. He chose a large arm-chair for his convenience, while his interpreter, as well as himself, was occupied, for the most part, in surveying the various objects which decorated the artist's room. He had a party of several Senecas with him, who, adopting the horizontal position, in different parts of the room, regaled themselves with the fumes of tobacco to their utmost gratification. Red-Jacket occasionally united in this relaxation; but was so deeply absorbed in attention to the work of the painter as to think, perhaps, of no other subject. At times he manifested extreme pleasure, as the outlines of the picture were filled up. The drawing of his costume, which he seemed to prize, as peculiarly appropriate, and the distant view of the falls of Niagara,—scenery at no great distance from his residence at the reservation,—forced him to an indistinct utterance of his satisfaction. When his medal appeared complete in the picture, he ad-

dressed his interpreter, accompanied by striking gestures ; and when his noble front was finished, he sprang
upon his feet with great alacrity, and seizing the artist
by the hand, exclaimed, with great energy, " Good !
good !" The painting being finished, he parted with
Mr. Weir with a satisfaction apparently equal to that
which he doubtless, on some occasions, had felt, on
effecting an Indian treaty. Red-Jacket must have been
beyond his seventieth year when the painting was
made. He exhibited in his countenance somewhat of
the traces of time and trial on his constitution. Nevertheless he was of a tall and erect form, and walked with
a firm gait. His characteristics are preserved by the
artist to admiration ; and his majestic front exhibits an
attitude surpassing every other that I have ever seen of
the human skull. As a specimen for the craniologist,
Red-Jacket need not yield his pretensions to those of the
most astute philosopher. He will long live by the painting of Weir, the poetry of Halleck, and the fame of his
own deeds."*

Red-Jacket loved his native forests, and no music was
to him so sad as the sounds of approaching civilization,
before which they were destined to fall. Every blow of
the woodman's axe sent a pang to his heart. The crash
of a falling tree sounded more painfully upon his ears

* Letter from Doctor J. W. Francis to William Dunlap, vide Dunlap's History
of the American Arts of Design. Doctor Francis held many conversations with
Red-Jacket, some of which were upon the subject of the diseases to which the
Indians were subject. He was quite descriptive in his statements, and seemed
sufficiently qualified to make a number of very fair distinctions in relation to
the subject.—*Conversations of Dr. Francis with the author.*

than the jar of an earthquake. An anecdote, illustrative of his feelings upon this subject, will complete the present chapter. In the days of his youth he was wont to join the hunters in the beautiful valley of the Genesee with great enthusiasm. Game was then plenty, and those were indeed the finest hunting grounds he could traverse. Toward the close of his life he went thither to indulge once more in the chase, where a forest, apparently of considerable extent, yet remained. He entered it, recognizing some of his ancient friends among the more venerable of the trees, and hoping yet to find abundant game. But he had not proceeded far before he approached an " opening," and his course was presently impeded by a fence, within the enclosure of which one of the pale-faces was engaged in guiding the plough! With a heavy heart he turned in another direction, the forest seeming yet to be deep, and where he hoped to find a deer, as in the days when he was young. But he had not travelled long before another " opening" broke upon his view, another fence impeded his course, and another cultivated field appeared within. He sat down and wept.*

* Related to the author by a Seneca chief.

CHAPTER XIV.

THE last three years of Red-Jacket's life afforded him no season of repose. For a long period after he obtained the ascendancy over the Cornplanter, and especially after the death of Farmer's-Brother, which event occurred shortly after the close of the last war between England and the United States, Red-Jacket had borne almost undisputed sway over his people,—those of them, especially, whom he could so far control as to keep in a measure from what he conceived to be the contaminating influences of Christianity and civilization. But notwithstanding his vigilance, his inflexibility and his energy, those influences were too powerful for him to resist. A dense white population had by this time surrounded each of their several reservations. The missionaries and school-masters were indefatigable in their efforts, and his people, on every hand, were at length in daily and necessary communication and association with the whites. Those who yet adhered to their paganism were nevertheless neglecting to celebrate their feasts by the usual rites, and were in fact abandoning their grosser ceremonies and superstitions.* It may readily be conceived that, to a mind like Red-Jacket's, at once vigorous and clear, these superstitions, or at least the uncouth observances by which they were attended, had no intrinsic value ; but he looked upon them as conservative in their operation,—as potent and effectual barriers against the tide of innovation which he could not but perceive, would in the end prove fatal to his own authority, and from which he apprehended the most disastrous consequences to his people. He was deeply impressed with the conviction that the white and red races could not exist together ; and it was his anxious policy and wish to keep up between them every wall of separation afforded by difference of habits, language, costume and religion. Therefore he deprecated and resisted to his utmost ability every attempt at departure from the ancient nationality of his race. The arts of civilization were gradually advancing among them, though in their

* Yet incredible as the statement may appear, in the year 1830 there was an infidel white man in a neighboring town, who went among the Indians at Cattaraugus, convened a meeting of them, and endeavored to persuade them against Christianity. He even went so far as to endeavor to induce them to renew their Pagan dances, and other cast-off abominations of heathenism. But the Indians scouted his proposals, and one of them denounced him, not inaptly, as " the Devil's Minister."—*Vide Missionary Herald for* 1830.

simplest state ; and the indomitable Indian, who looked with scorn upon these things, and beheld their advance with vexation, was doomed to see the ranks of his Pagan followers almost daily thinned by the desertion both of chiefs and people to the Christian party.*   By this latter party he had for years been looked upon with no eye of friendship, much as they admired his talents.   Those who had truly imbibed the principles of Christianity could not longer repose confidence of any kind in the great champion of Paganism ; and those who had begun to taste the comforts of civilization, having incurred the hostility of the orator, by showing a disposition to throw off the savage state, could not of necessity remain upon terms of cordiality with him.   On the contrary, by his continued opposition to their moral and social improvement, they came to regard him as an enemy—or

---

* The Rev. Mr. Harris, whose own particular station was at the Seneca village—Red-Jacket's town—was likewise the general superintendent of the several missions among the Six Nations, and his labors for the nine years of his residence there were equally unwearied and effective. In the year 1826 the school at the Seneca village had become so forward as to be an object of curiosity for strangers to visit. The children had indeed made a remarkable degree of proficiency. At the same date the Cattaraugus mission had made very encouraging progress. Not only were the children taught in the schools, but under the impulse given by the missionaries, the people were making rapid advances in the arts of husbandry—in the fencing and general cultivation of their farms. They had also, voluntarily, and at their own cost, built a church. In the year 1827 the Sunday school of the Seneca village was attended numerously, and with great interest. In addition to the children, about eighty adults were in attendance upon these schools, receiving instruction from their own children, and in some instances from their grand-children. It was in this year that Red-Jacket's wife began to manifest an interest in Christianity, as stated in the preceding chapter ; visiting Mr. Harris and acknowledging the struggles of her conscience in conforming to heathen rites. In the year 1828 the Indians of the Seneca village built a comfortable church, contributing one thousand dollars in money, and supplying the lumber from their own saw-mill. There were at that time

SENECA MISSION CHURCH.

Seneca Village, Western View.

at least as a foe to their best interests. Meantime his habits had become so extremely dissipated, that by all the better portion of his people he was considered as in every respect morally worthless. Under these circumstances, the Christian party determined upon his deposition,—a measure of exceedingly rare occurrence among the Indians. The council for this purpose was held in September, 1827, and the following act of deposition was drawn up, adopted, and signed by the chiefs. It was written in the Seneca tongue, but translated into English for publication, by Dr. Jemison, himself a half-breed, retaining his connexion with the Indians :—

" We, the chiefs of the Seneca tribe, of the Six Nations, say to you, Sa-go-ye-wat-ha, (or Red-Jacket,) that you have a long time disturbed our councils; that you have procured

twenty-one members of the church. In 1830 the church at Seneca village contained forty-nine members; at Tuscarora, fourteen; at Cattaraugus twenty-three. The Seneca school had then fifty children; the Cattaraugus thirty-five; the Tuscarora twenty. Temperance societies had also been formed, and the use of ardent spirits totally abandoned by the members. A white farmer among them having brought a barrel of whiskey upon the reservation, for his harvest, the Indians took possession thereof, and poured it upon the ground. Mr. Harris had translated the Gospel of Luke into the Seneca language, and also a small collection of prayers, and a spelling-book, all of which had been printed. In cases of church discipline, there were instances in which offending members, their feelings softened, and their savage natures changed by the spirit of the Gospel, instead of showing the implacable and revengeful dispositions characteristic of their race, submitted to the church authorities with the docility and quietness inculcated by the principles of the new religion they had professed. In consequence of the improvement of their moral and social condition their numbers, instead of longer diminishing, began to increase. On the three reservations of Seneca, Cattaraugus, and Alleghany, by a census taken by order of the Secretary of War, in 1830, there had been an increase to the number of 294 in three years. There was also a corresponding increase of flocks and herds, and an augmentation of the means of domestic comfort.—Consult the Missionary Herald, from 1821 to 1831.

some white men to assist you in sending a great number of
false stories to our Father the President of the United States,
and induced our people to sign those falsehoods at Tonna-
wanta as chiefs of our tribe, when you knew they were not
chiefs ; that you have opposed the improvement of our nation,
and made divisions and disturbances among our people ; that
you have abused and insulted our great Father the President ;
that you have not regarded the rules which make the Great
Spirit love us, and which make his red children do good to
each other; that you have a bad heart, because in a time of
great distress, when our people were starving, you took and
hid the body of a deer you had killed, when your starving
brothers should have shared their proportions of it with you ;
that the last time our Father the President was fighting
against the king across the great waters, you divided us,—you
acted against our Father the President, and his officers, and
advised with those who were not friends; that you have prevented, and always discouraged our children from going to
school, where they could learn, and abused and lied about our
people who were willing to learn, and about those who were
offering to instruct them how to worship the Great Spirit in
the manner Christians do ; that you have always placed yourself before them who would be instructed, and have done all
you could to prevent their going to schools ; that you have
taken goods to your own use, which were received as annuities, and which belonged to orphan children, and to old people ; that for the last ten years you have often said the communications of our great Father to his red children were
forgeries made up at New-York by those who wanted to buy
our lands; that you left your wife, because she joined the
Christians, and worshipped the Great Spirit as they do, knowing that she was a good woman; that we have waited for
nearly ten years for you to reform and do better; but are
now discouraged, as you declare you never will receive instructions from those who wish to do us good, as our great
Father advises, and induced others to hold the same language.

" We might say a great many other things, which make you
an enemy to the Great Spirit, and also to your own brothers,
but we have said enough, and now renounce you as a chief,
and from this time you are forbid to act as such ;—all of our
nation will hereafter regard you as a private man, and we say
to them all, that every one, who shall do as you have done,
if a chief, will in like manner be disowned, and set back
where he started from by his brethren."

Declared at the Council-house of the Seneca
nation, Sept. 15, 1827.*

* This remarkable document was signed by the following chiefs, among whom
it will be observed, were Young-King, Captain Pollard, Little Billy, Twenty-
Canoes, Doxtater, Two-Guns, Barefoot, and others who had been partizans of
Red-Jacket in his better days.

Ga-yan-quia-ton, or Young King, ✕ his mark.

Ha-lon-to-wa-nen, or Captain Pollard, ✕ his mark.

Jish-ja-ga, or Little Billy, ✕ his mark.

Ya-on-yau-go, or Seneca White, ✕ his mark.

Is-nish-har-de, or James Stevenson, ✕ his mark.

Go-non-da-gie, or Destroy Town, ✕ his mark.

Ho-no-ja-cya, or Tall Peter, ✕ his mark.

Yut-wau-nou-ha, or Little Johnson, ✕ his mark.

White Chief, ✕ his mark.

Ha-sen-nia-wall, or White Seneca, ✕ his mark.

Yen-nau-qua, or Doxtater, ✕ his mark.

Ha-ja-on-quist, or Henry Two-Guns, ✕ his mark.

Ska-ta-ga-onyes, or Twenty Canoes, ✕ his mark.

Ha-squi-sau-on, or James Stevenson, jun., ✕ his mark.

O-qui-ye-sou, or Captain Strong, ✕ his mark.

Ya-yout-ga-ah, or Captain Thompson, ✕ his mark.

George Silverheels, ✕ his mark.

William Jones, ✕ his mark.

James Robinson, ✕ his mark.

Blue-eyes, ✕ his mark.

John Pierce, ✕ his mark.

Sa-he-o-qui-au-don-qui, or Little Beard, ✕ his mark.

Barefoot, ✕ his mark.

Lewis Rainy, ✕ his mark.

Captain Jones, ✕ his mark.

A melancholy picture of fallen greatness! Nor can it be denied that in many of its lineaments it was drawn with but too much fidelity. Still, the artist may have been moved to darken the portraiture by personal animosity or political hate. The charges may have been multiplied in the heat of party asperity, and magnified by the bitterness of religious dissension; while it may well be questioned whether one of the most heinous items in the declaration was not positively untrue. Certainly there is no evidence, of antecedent date, whereon to found a charge of treachery to the cause of the United States, by Red-Jacket, during the last war with England. On the contrary, although not often personally valiant in fight, yet, almost from the day of the declaration of that war by the United States, until its close, Red-Jacket was active and eloquent in their behalf. He was no more suspected of treachery than he was of courage, by the American officers in the service, and his character should be relieved from *that* imputation. Yet there were charges enough specified in the declaration, that *were* true, to warrant the procedure.

But the orator was not prepared to submit to his official degradation without an effort to regain his position; nor had the energy of his mind been so far impaired by his intemperance as to render him incapable of exertion. Perhaps he yet felt, occasionally, both the consciousness of his power and the sting of his shame.* Be it so or not, he " was greatly affected by this decision, and made a journey to Washington to lay his griefs

* Thatcher's Indian Biography.

before 'his Great Father the President.' His first call, on arriving at the seat of government, was upon Colonel M'Kenney, the commissioner then in charge of the Indian Bureau. That officer had previously been informed of all that had occurred upon the subject among the Senecas, and of the decision of the council, and the cause of it. After the customary shaking of hands, the old Seneca thus opened his message :—'I have a talk for my Father.' 'Tell him,' answered Colonel M'Kenney to the interpreter,—' I have one for him. I will make it first, and will then listen to him.' The chief of the Indian Bureau then proceeded to narrate all that had passed between the two parties, taking care not to omit even the minute incidents that had combined to produce the rupture between the Christian and Pagan parties, and the deposition of the chief of the latter. He sought to convince Red-Jacket that a spirit of forbearance on his part, and the yielding to the Christian party of the right, which he claimed for himself, to believe as he pleased on the subject of the Christian religion, would have prevented the mortifying result of his expulsion from office and power. At the conclusion of this talk, during which Red-Jacket never took his eye from the speaker, the chief turned to the interpreter, saying, with his finger pointing in the direction of his people,—' Our Father has got a long eye !' He then proceeded to vindicate himself and his cause, and to pour out upon the ' black-coats' the vials of his wrath. The result of the conference was an arrangement between the Indian commissioner and the chief, that the latter should return home,

49

and there, in a council to be convened for that purpose, express his willingness to bury the hatchet, and leave it to those who might choose to be Christians, to adopt the ceremonies and creed of that religion; whilst for himself, and those who thought like him, he claimed the privilege to follow the faith of his fathers.*

On his return to the reservation, Red-Jacket entered upon the work of retrieving his character, and wiping off the disgrace, by regaining his position, in earnest, and with an energy becoming the meridian of his manhood. "It shall not be said of me," thought the venerable orator, with the gleam of a fiery soul in his eye, "it shall not be said that Sá-go-ye-wat-ha lived in insignificance and died in dishonor. Am I too feeble to revenge myself of my enemies? Am not I as I have been?"† In a word he aroused himself to a great effort, and pains were taken to procure a full attendance at a Grand Council, to be composed of all that could be gathered from the remaining of the whole Six Nations. The council was holden at the upper council-house of the principal reservation, in the neighborhood of Buffalo. The business for which it was assembled having been stated, and the act of deposition by the Christian party read, Half-Town, a chief from the Cattaraugus reservation, rose and declared that there was but one voice in his section of the nation, and that of general indignation at the contumely cast on so great a man as Red-Jacket.

* The authority for this interview is Colonel M'Kenney himself, whose language has in part been adopted.

† Thatcher's Indian Biography.

Several other chiefs addressed the council to the same effect.* After these declarations, and a farther interchange of views, the condemned orator rose slowly, as if grieved and humiliated, and after a solemn pause, but with somewhat of his ancient dignity and grandeur of manner, spoke as follows :—

" My Brothers ! You have this day been correctly informed of an attempt to make me sit down and throw off the authority of a chief, by twenty-six misguided chiefs of my nation. You have heard the statements of my associates in council and their explanations of the foolish charges brought against me. I have taken the legal and proper way to meet those charges. It is the only way in which I could notice them. They are charges which I despise, and which nothing could induce me to notice, but the concern which many respected chiefs of my nation feel in the character of their aged comrade. Were it otherwise I should not be before you. I would fold my arms, and sit quietly under these ridiculous slanders. The Christian party have not even proceeded legally, according to our usages, to put me down. Ah! It grieves my heart when I look around me and see the situation of my people,—in old times united and powerful,—now divided and feeble. I feel sorry for my nation. When I am gone to the other world,—when the Great Spirit calls me away,—who among my people can take my place ? Many years have I guided the nation."

*   *   *   *   *   *

In the report of these proceedings the connected speech ends thus abruptly. But it is added that the

* Such is the statement of Thatcher, the only authority the author has discovered for the account of this council. But the statement of Half-Town must certainly have been exaggerated, inasmuch as O-qui-ye-sou, or Captain Strong, always a chief of consideration among the Cattaraugus Indians, was one of the signers of the act of deposition.

chief proceeded in an artful manner to rehearse the history of what some have called his "persecution," and to repel the various attacks that had been made against him. Recurring again to the subject with which his heart was always full, viz:—the evils befalling his people by reason of the countenance they were giving to Christianity, and the disgrace which should attach to them for their abandonment of the faith of their fathers, —he proceeded once more to denounce, with his wonted vehemence, the "black-coats." He said that in a conference with Mr. Calhoun, four years before,* he had been told that the Indians might treat these black-coats just as they thought proper, and the government would not interfere. "I will not consent," he concluded,—sagaciously identifying his disgrace with his opposition to Christianity,—"I will not consent silently to be trampled under foot. As long as I can raise my voice I will oppose the 'black-coats.' As long as I can stand in my moccasins I will do all I can for my nation."

The result of the council corresponded with the promises made to him at Washington, and he was restored to his former rank by a unanimous vote. But the excitement of the occasion being over, the orator sank rapidly into a state of comparative imbecility,—a condition, both of body and mind, prematurely superinduced by strong drink. Indeed, the energies he had put forth in these proceedings resembled rather the un-

---

* Mr. Calhoun was, at the time referred to, Vice-President of the United States. He had been Secretary at War, in which capacity he probably became acquainted with Red-Jacket.

natural mental and bodily vigor often exhibited by dying
people, arousing from stupor and exhaustion just before
the hour of dissolution, than the healthful intellectual
action which characterized his better days.

He nevertheless visited the Atlantic cities once or
twice after his restoration. His last journey to the city
of Washington was made in the spring of 1829, soon
after the accession of General Jackson to the office of
President. On his return, he travelled eastward as far
as Boston, having become so lost to the pride of character, as to allow the keepers of the museums in Boston
and Albany to exhibit him for money. At Albany great
pains were taken to collect a political audience to meet
him at the museum, and listen to a speech which he was
advertised to deliver. The legislature was in session,
a large majority of which body was composed of the
political friends of the new President. It was noised
abroad that the orator would speak of his visit to the
President, and the impression somehow obtained currency, that the savage orator, having been struck with
great admiration of the character and bearing of the
hero of New-Orleans, would pronounce a panegyrick
upon his character and services; the loftiest strains of
forest eloquence were anticipated. The audience was
large, and the majority consisted of the most ardent
friends of the President, hurrying with impatience to
hear him extolled from the lips of an orator so renowned
as the great Seneca. But he had not completed half a
dozen sentences of his speech, before their kindling impatience was changed into disappointment, which was

in turn succeeded by chagrin; for instead of eulogizing the man who was at that time the popular idol of the nation, he spoke of his former visit to General Washington, drew an outline of *his* character, and then instituted a comparison between it and that of General Jackson, greatly to the disadvantage of the latter. The applause with which the orator was greeted on his first appearance, was changed into rude manifestations of displeasure, and the audience rapidly grew thin by the departure of those who had been the most eager to come. Justice, moreover, requires the acknowledgment that the speech was feeble and puerile in itself, and delivered without energy or grace. There was not even enough of the orator left to show that he had ever had any valid pretensions to that character.*

But his career was now drawing rapidly to a close, and he lived not to behold the opening flowers of another spring. The circumstances of his decease were striking. "For some months previous to his death, time had made such fearful ravages on his constitution as to render him fully sensible of his approaching dissolution. To that event he often adverted, and always in the language of philosophic calmness. He visited successively all his most intimate friends at their cabins, and conversed with them upon the condition of their nation, in the most impressive and affecting manner. He told them that he

* The author speaks not at random. He was present on the occasion referred to, and well remembers the whole scene,—not forgetting the disappointment which sat on the countenances of those who had been anticipating a rich display of Indian eloquence in behalf of their favorite President.

was passing away, and his counsels would be heard no more. He ran over the history of his people from the most remote period to which his knowledge extended, and pointed out, as few could, the wrongs, the privations, and the loss of character, which almost of themselves constituted that history. " I am about to leave you," he said, " and when I am gone, and my warnings shall be no longer heard or regarded, the craft and avarice of the white man will prevail. Many winters have I breasted the storm, but I am an aged tree, and can stand no longer. My leaves are fallen, my branches are withered, and I am shaken by every breeze. Soon my aged trunk will be prostrate, and the foot of the exulting foe of the Indian may be placed upon it in safety ; for I have none who will be able to avenge such an indignity. Think not I mourn for myself. I go to join the spirits of my fathers, where age cannot come ; but my heart fails when I think of my people, who are so soon to be scattered and forgotten." These several interviews were all concluded with particular instructions respecting his domestic affairs, and his funeral." " Bury me," said he, " by the side of my former wife ; and let my funeral be according to the customs of our nation. Let me be dressed and equipped as my fathers were, that their spirits may rejoice at my coming. Be sure that my grave be not made by a white man ; let them not pursue me there."*

But notwithstanding these brave resolutions in anticipation of the time of his departure, to die as he had lived

* Sketches of Red-Jacket in M'Kenney's Indian Biography.

and to be buried a pagan, there is reason to believe that he relented not a little in the bitterness of his hostility toward the missionary and the religion he taught. The conduct of his wife toward him after her conversion to Christianity, during the troubles of his latter years, notwithstanding his temporary desertion of her, had afforded a beautiful illustration of the spirit of her new religion; and this circumstance may have softened and won upon his feelings.

While the lamp of life was flickering in its socket, he convened a general council of the nation, embracing both the Christian and Pagan parties, for the express purpose of exerting his influence to cause a better understanding between them. Not that he spoke, or made any direct movements, in favor of Christianity, but his desire was to bring both parties to a resolution to quarrel no more respecting their religion, leaving every man to choose for himself, without let or hindrance, and to have his children taught in whatever school he might prefer.* He was taken mortally sick of cholera morbus during the sittings of this council, but he yet lived long enough to see his recommendation adopted by mutual resolution, and he spoke of the act with great satisfaction, a little previous to his departure. Two days before his last sickness, moreover, he sent a friendly message to the chief missionary, the Rev. Mr. Harris, desiring him to come and talk with him. But there was

---

* At this time the pagans were sending their children to a Quaker school, while the Christian party sent their's to the schools under the supervision of Mr. Harris.

an ecclesiastical council sitting at the time, in which Mr. Harris was engaged; and in the multiplicity and confusion of business, the message was not received until after his decease. The object of the request was, therefore, not positively known; but his wife believed his desire was to express more friendly feelings toward the religious character of the missionary than he had previously manifested. He remarked " that the minister knew that he had always been his opposer, and now, as by the resolution of the council there was a prospect of seeing his people more united than they had been for years, he desired to have some talk with him."

When his last attack of illness came upon him, he said he should not survive, and refused all medical assistance. His request of his wife was, that at the moment of his departure she should place in his hand a certain vial of water, possessing, as he supposed, a charm sufficiently potent to keep away the devil, should the latter attempt, as he was not without apprehension might be the fact, to take away his soul. That vial, he believed, would be all-sufficient to secure his spirit an unobstructed flight to the fair hunting-grounds. He died on the 20th of January, 1830, at his residence, near the church and mission-house at the Seneca village.* The management of his funeral was committed

---

* The women among the Indians regulate the household affairs altogether,— prescribing the locations of their cabins, or houses, as the case may be, and dictating removals at their own pleasure. By virtue of this authority, after the wife of Red-Jacket embraced Christianity, she removed the residence of her lord to the vicinity of the church and the house of the missionary, for the convenience of public worship, and of conversations with her spiritual guide. Here

by himself to his wife's son-in-law, William Jones. He
himself had not a near kinsman in the world. His
friends of the Wolf-clan, to which he belonged, determined that his remains should be carried to the church
in which they worshipped, and buried in the ground belonging to the Christian party. The funeral was numerously attended, not only by his own race, but by the
white people who gathered in from the adjacent country. Among the latter were some of the leaders of the
infidel white men who had acted in concert with the deceased in his opposition to Christianity. These latter
came with high expectations of beholding a splendid
pagan funeral, accompanied by the howlings of women,
and all the barbarous rites and ceremonies incident to
savage funerals in the days when "darkness brooded"
over the wilds of the continent. Great, therefore, was
their disappointment on finding themselves in the train
of a Christian funeral, attended only by its simple and
solemn observances.* Thus died the renowned Sà-go-

was the mission-school, in which her grand-children were receiving gratuitous instruction in the elementary principles of knowledge. Here was the chapel, to
which, since the change in her religious views, she had become very much attached; and here were the missionary and his family, whose instruction and
counsels she had for some time been accustomed to regard as those of friends to
her people.

   * My authority for the preceding account of the last days of Red-Jacket's
life, including the last council summoned by him, and his funeral, is the Rev. Mr.
Harris, with whom I have had repeated and full conversations upon the subject,
and whose report, written at the time, and published in the Missionary Herald,
vol. xxvi., I have consulted. Very grievous misrepresentations in regard to the
conduct of this gentleman at the death and funeral of the chief were sent abroad
by the disappointed white pagans, referred to in the text, some of which unfortunately found their way into the sketch published in the Indian Biography of
Colonel M'Kenney. I quote a few passages:—"There had long been a mis-

ye-wat-ha, whose great talents, and matchless gifts of
oratory, had so long exerted such a powerful influence
over the councils of his nation.

Some of the speeches of Red-Jacket, as noted down
in the closing conversations of his life, were prophetic,
and have already been fulfilled. " The craft and avarice of the white man will prevail," said he.   And they
have prevailed.   Less than nine years had elapsed
after his decease, when every remaining foot of the ancient inheritance of the Senecas was ceded to the white
man, in exchange for a tract of country west of the Mis-

sionary among the Senecas, who was sustained by the party among the natives
who had procured the deposition and disgrace of Red-Jacket. This gentleman
of ' the dark dress' was of course looked upon with high disfavor by Red-Jacket,
who considered him one of the agents by whom his nation had been distracted."
Now it has been seen by the statements in the text, that the chief was desirous of
dying in peace with the missionary. Again it is recorded in the same work, and
has thus gone upon the records of history, that,—" The neighboring missionary,
with a disregard for the feelings of the bereaved, and the injunctions of the dead,
for which it is difficult to account, assembled his party, took possession of the
body, and conveyed it to their meeting-house. The immediate friends of Red-
Jacket, amazed at the transaction, abandoned the preparations they were making
for the funeral rites, and followed the body in silence to the place of worship,
where a service was performed, which, considering the opinions of the deceased,
was as idle as it was indecorous. They were then told from the sacred desk
that if they had any thing to say they had now an opportunity. Incredulity and
scorn were pictured on the faces of the Indians, and no reply was made, except
by a chief called General Blanket, who briefly remarked—" This house was
built for the white man ; the friends of Red-Jacket cannot be heard in it." Notwithstanding this touching appeal, and the dying injunctions of the Seneca chief,
his remains were taken to the grave prepared by the whites, and interred.
Some of the Indians followed the corpse, but the more immediate friends of the
deceased took a last view of their lifeless chief, in the sanctuary of that religion
which he had always opposed, and hastened from a scene which overwhelmed
them with humiliation and sorrow." Now all this is very well told, and with
good dramatic effect. But, like most other dramatic compositions, it is an entire
fiction.

souri, to which the remnant of their people and the Tuscaroras are to remove.   When this removal takes place,
it may be considered the final dispersion, if not the extinguishment, of the once mighty confederacy of the
Five Nations.

This confederacy was never, perhaps,—certainly not
within the knowledge of the white man,—so great in its
numerical strength as has been supposed, or as might
be inferred from their deeds, and the extent of their do-
minion.   And yet, within that period, from their superior
organization, their discipline, and their prowess, their
name was terrible over a large section of the American continent.   It is within the knowledge of the white
man that the cry of " Mohawk !" would cause the Indian to fly in terror.*   The Delawares were conquered
and made tributaries by them.   They drove the Algonquins and the French before them, sacking Montreal,
and raising their war-whoop almost before the gates of
Quebec, while at the west and south their arms were
extended to the mouth of the Ohio, and the confines of
Florida.   For upward of a century they formed a living barrier between the English colonies and the French;
and for more than two centuries have they been strug-
gling against the gradual encroachments of the white
men, striving but in vain to bear up against a hundred
successive storms of adversity, and maintain an independent existence.   During this period, nation after nation of their hapless race has melted away and disappeared from the face of the earth.   Fate in her stern

* Colden's Six Nations.

behests has at length decreed that the Five Nations are likewise to be numbered among nations lost on earth.

The fate of this people is a subject for deep and anxious reflection. What is the destiny of those who yet remain? Are they,—any considerable portion of them, at least,—eventually to yield to the influences and usages of civilization, and thus to be rescued from extinction? Or is it among the inscrutable designs of Providence that the whole race shall disappear before the all-conquering Anglo-Saxons? Their destiny has been the subject of the gravest and most interesting contemplation, almost from the day of the discovery to the present. Philanthropists, for more than two hundred years, have been endeavoring to guide them into the paths of civilization, and Christians to win them from the gloom of paganism to the brighter hopes and promises of the gospel. But the efforts of both have been exerted to very little purpose. Small numbers, at various periods, have been prevailed upon to yield a faint assent to Christianity, but sound conversions, illustrated by subsequent lives of virtue and temperance, pureness of living, and truth, have been rare, while even among supposed converts the opinion has often been expressed by themselves, that Christianity was a better religion for the white people than for them; and their reformation, in but too many instances, has only been attended by the loss of many of their savage virtues, in exchange for which they have contracted the vices peculiar to civilized society.* Upon civilization the unsophisticated Indians have looked

* President Kirkland—Mass. Hist. Coll., vol. iv.

with contempt. But as they have been brought into close contact with civilized life, many of them have been constrained to acknowledge the superior dignity and happiness of such a state, and to wish that their children might participate in its benefits, as the only means of saving them from extinction. "If they sometimes reflect on us for being cowardly, effeminate, and tame spirited, they do it not so much from a real contempt of us, as to relieve that uneasy sense of inferiority which mortifies and oppresses them. Still, when they have acknowledged the importance of industry and the arts to their happiness, respectability, and even existence, they will add,—'Indians can't work.' They feel fast bound by the power of their savage habits, and do not summon resolution to practice according to their conviction."*

But Red-Jacket, as the reader has observed in the progress of the present work, during the latter thirty years of his life, would make no concessions in favor, either of Christianity or civilization ; and for the same reasons that operated upon his mind, the larger number of his race have entertained the same opinions. These reasons have already been adverted to more than once or twice. They were slow to comprehend the principles of Christianity, and could not well discriminate between the real and nominal Christian. Among the border-men, with whom they were first and most frequently brought into communication and contact, they were sure to find more of the latter class than of the former. Nor did

---

* President Kirkland—Massachusetts Historical Collections.

it commend the new religion to their untutored minds, that they constantly saw these professors of that religion practising every little art, and watching every opportunity to overreach them, and deprive them of their property, especially of their lands. They were early alarmed at the rapacity of the whites to obtain their lands, to which, always when sober, they clung with great tenacity. "I have heard a naked savage," says the eloquent Lord Erskine, "in the indignant character of a prince surrounded by his subjects, addressing the governor of a British colony, holding a bundle of sticks in his hand, as the notes of his unlettered eloquence, demand, being encroached upon by the restless foot of English adventurers:—'Who is it that causes 'this river to rise in the high mountains, and to empty 'itself into the ocean? Who is it that causes to blow the 'loud winds of winter, and that calms them again in 'summer? Who is it that rears up the shade of those 'lofty forests, and blasts them with the quick lightning 'at his pleasure? The same Being who gave to you 'a country on the other side of the waters, gave ours 'to us: and by this title we will defend it,' said the warrior, throwing his tomahawk upon the ground, and raising the war-sound of his nation. These are the feelings of subjugated man all over the globe."* Especially have they ever been the feelings of the American Indians; and having for two centuries seen the "knavery and

* Speech of Lord Erskine, in the great libel case of Stockdale. Lord E. had served in America, in early life, in the British army, and was present at an Indian council.

strength of civilization" exerted " by alternate stratagem
and force," to dispossess them of their proud inheritance,
thus derived, is it a subject of wonder that they alike
spurned the religion and civilization from whose advances they had so much to apprehend?

It was the opinion of Dr. Ramsay, the historian, expressed in a letter to the Massachusetts Historical Society,
so long ago as the year 1795, that the American Indians
are a people who cannot be civilized.   The doctor had
once regarded the belief as unphilosophical ; but reflection and experience had brought him to the opinion that
to tame wolves would be no more impracticable than to
civilize the Indians.   Hence he had almost adopted the
melancholy belief that they would ere long cease to be
a people.   He gave nevertheless but few reasons in support of his gloomy anticipations of their destiny; and
the subject was followed by a more extended discussion,
in the autumn of the same year, by General Benjamin
Lincoln, who had enjoyed large opportunities of studying
the Indian character.   General Lincoln concurred fully
in the opinion of the doctor, that they would never be
civilized ; but he did not anticipate their entire extinction.
Among the causes of their decrease of numbers, he
enumerated the change in their habits of dressing, by
substituting linens and calicos in the place of their natural and ancient covering, the furs, retaining, in other
respects, their partiality for the savage life, and exposed
to all the sufferings from the inclement seasons, and
rigorous winters of the high northern latitudes under
which they live.   A knowledge of fire-arms has led them

to measures producing the worst effects, and serving to diminish their numbers. The game upon which they previously subsisted, and the skins of which served them for clothes, was afterward wantonly destroyed; while the possession of fire-arms, and other implements of war composed of metal, fired their ambition, and enkindled a hope in their breasts, that with these weapons they would be enabled to avenge all their wrongs and recover their country. Stimulated by these delusive hopes, they have rushed heedlessly into wars which have greatly reduced their numbers. Another cause of this diminution of their numbers is found in the reluctance of their women to bear children, prompting them to employ means to prevent an increase of maternal responsibilities. Indian mothers have been greatly affected by the loss of their sons in their frequent wars, until, to quote their own expressive words, " *they have become tired of bearing children to be slain in war.*" Other causes of the decrease of this people are adduced by General Lincoln, and he accounts for their reluctance to become either civilized or christianized, upon the principles already explained.*

On the question of the ultimate destiny of the race, the communication referred to concludes as follows:—
" Should the Indian nations in general never become civilized, we may, I think, point to the consequences. Nature forbids civilized and uncivilized people possessing the same territory; for the means pursued by the civilized to obtain a support counteract the wishes and

*Letter to Dr. Ramsay—Mass. Historical Collections.

designs of the savage. While the former are busily
employed in removing from the earth its natural growth,
as necessary to the establishing themselves as husband-
men, the latter are wishing to increase that natural shelter
and hiding place for the beasts of the forest; for without
a covering they cannot be retained, but will seek new
feeding-grounds. Consequently the savage must retire
to those lands where he can with more ease obtain a
supply. Yet their new position cannot long avail them;
for civilization and cultivation will make rapid strides,
and advance fast toward them; and they must necessarily make way for such approaches, by following the
game, which takes the first alarm, or leave their present
pursuits and modes of living, and oppose the cultivator
by cultivation. The savage arm is too feeble, in any
other way, to counteract the progress of their civilized
neighbors; but it is hardly to be expected, considering
their attachments and prejudices, that they will see the
importance of this measure in time for self-preservation;
but will continue retiring before the enlightened husbandman, until they shall meet those regions of the north
into which he cannot pursue them. There, probably,
they will be set down and left, in the undisturbed possession of a country unenvied by any; as the last resort
of a people, who, having sacrificed every thing to their
love of ease, were at length compelled, by the effects of
their obstinacy and disobedience, to give up all hope of
ever regaining those hospitable tracts of country from
which they had retired, and which they had surrendered
to others; while nature had furnished them with the

power of having forever participated in the enjoyment of them. Being thus shut up in a country where subsistence can only be obtained by the chase, they will probably continue as a people until time shall be no more."

Such, with but a trifling change of phraseology, were the conclusions to which a gentleman of intelligence, sound judgment, and deep study of the Indian character, arrived more than forty-five years ago. Experience has in a great measure tested the correctness of his views, although as yet there have been no indications of a tendency on the part of the Indians to escape contact with the white man by seeking a refuge in the hyperborean regions. They could, doubtless, live there, as do the Esquimaux; but their attachment to the places of their birth, and their desire to linger around the graves of their ancestors, induce them to cling to their native soil with death-like tenacity. And although a close proximity to the whites has almost invariably caused a rapid diminution of their numbers, yet nation after nation of this extraordinary and in many respects noble people has melted away, and disappeared, or been reduced to a few degenerate relics, who at last relinquish their distinctive character by mingling with the fragments of other nations also in a rapid decline, but perhaps not quite so near positive extinction as themselves. This is a melancholy subject of contemplation, but it seems thus to have been decreed by an inscrutable Providence; and the flight of the feeble and broken remnant of the once proud and haughty AQUANUSCHIONI before the march of civilization, is but another and yet stronger illustration of the sad conclusion, that their destiny is to be,—EXTINCTION!

The orator, whose life has been traced in the preceding pages, and who, with all his faults, was a man of great talents and sagacity, foresaw the event almost with a prophet's vision, and labored for many years with all the energies of his soul to avert, or at least to put off the evil day. It was kindly ordered that he should not, with his natural vision, behold the extirpation of his people from the beautiful country so long their own, and he was gathered to his fathers in peace. For nine years after his decease, neither a stone nor other memorial marked his resting-place. But during the summer of 1839, while on a visit to Buffalo, HENRY PLACIDE, Esq., a gentleman of the histrionic profession, determined that the place of his sepulture should no longer remain undistinguished. A subscription was set on foot under his auspices, and the result was the erection over his grave of a handsome marble slab, bearing the following inscription :—

SA-GO-YE-WAT-HA,

(HE-KEEPS-THEM-AWAKE,)

R E D - J A C K E T ,

CHIEF OF THE

WOLF TRIBE OF THE SENECAS,

THE FRIEND AND PROTECTOR OF HIS PEOPLE,

Died Jan'y 20, 1830,

Aged 78 years.

The grave is surrounded by a neat picket fence ; and it was noted as an interesting coincidence, that during the visit of the gentlemen to superintend the erection of the tablet, a funeral feast, as is the custom of the Indians, was in progress, at an adjoining wigwam, in commemoration of the death of Red-Jacket's daughter, which occurred five months before, and during the ceremony his aged widow was distributing the moccasins, clothes, trinkets, etc., of the deceased.

Charlevoix and Colden, among the earlier Indian historians, and De Witt Clinton among the modern, have instituted comparisons between the ancient league of the Five Nations and the Romans. The coincidence was in some respects remarkable, especially in their foreign policy. The counsellors of the Five Nations had never heard of the Romans; and yet their ambition of foreign conquests, and their policy of planting military colonies in the countries they had subjugated, were the same. Other resemblances might be indicated were it necessary to the present purpose. With as much justice as Rienzi has been styled the last of the Romans, may Red-Jacket be denominated "the last of the Senecas." Though in the main the characters were widely dissimilar, and the one acted in great matters and the other in comparatively small, yet there is in one respect a striking coincidence : " Rienzi was more energetic in speech and council than in action, and failed in courage and presence of mind in great emergencies."

HO-NA-YE-WUS,

OR

FARMER'S-BROTHER.

FARMER'S-BROTHER.

AMONG the Indian contemporaries of Red-Jacket, the reader of the foregoing pages will have frequently observed the name of FARMER'S-BROTHER. It was an arbitrary name,—his real one, in his own language, being HO-NA-YE-WUS. Beyond all doubt he was one of the noblest of his race,—in both intellect and eloquence fully equal to Red-Jacket, and infinitely above him in courage and all the moral qualities of the man. But it seems not to have been his ambition to shine in council, as he might have done,—taking the few specimens of his eloquence that have been preserved, and the opinions of his contemporaries, as the criterion of judgment. On the contrary he was a warrior, in principle and practice,—spurning agriculture, and every other civilized art, with the contempt of Red-Jacket himself.

The time of his birth is uncertain; but as he was believed to have been between eighty and ninety years old at the time of his death, in the autumn of 1814, he was probably born about the year 1730. It has been stated that he was in the bloody battle in which General Braddock, with fool-hardiness, lost his life, and nearly the whole of his army, in July, 1755. On the score of age he may very well have been there; but the fact is not certain.

The first authentic mention of his name, as a warrior, is found in connexion with the horrible massacre of the "Devil's Hole," in the neighborhood of Niagara Falls,—an event that occurred in the year 1762, or 1763. Like their brethren, the other nations of the Iroquois confederacy, the Senecas had in general been the faithful allies of the English against the French, down to the war which ended in the conquest of Canada by the former. The Senecas were formerly engaged for a series of years in a war with the French and Adirondacks, during which the forces of the latter had invaded their country several times, and laid waste some of their towns and villages. At length a peace was concluded, and the French succeeded in detaching the Senecas from the English, and converting them into allies. Hence, in the war of 1755—1763, they tooks ides with the former, although it is said they regretted this connexion, and renewed their alliance with the English before the close of that contest.

The French fort at Niagara fell before the arms of Sir William Johnson, in the summer of 1759, as also did the smaller fortress at Schlosser, situated about two miles above the great cataract. These two posts were of great importance to the English, for the protection of the means of communication with the posts above, on the upper lakes. In 1760 a contract was made between Sir William Johnson and a Mr. Stedman, to construct a portage road from what is now the Lewiston Landing to Fort Schlosser, a distance of eight miles, in order to facilitate the transportation from one place to the other. In conformity with this agreement, on the 20th of June, 1763, Stedman had completed his road, and appeared at Lewiston Landing with twenty-five portage wagons, and one hundred horses and oxen, for the transportation to Schlosser of the king's stores destined to Detroit, &c.

Sir William was even at this time suspicious as to the designs of the Senecas, although the French power in that neighborhood had been extinguished four years before; for there were various indications of an uneasy and hostile disposition among them. In order, therefore, to protect the teams, goods and drivers from harm, a strong detachment of troops* was ordered to guard them across the portage. The caravan, under this escort, started from the landing,—the troops in advance, and Stedman, mounted upon a fine horse, riding between them and the teams. A small redoubt had been thrown up on an inconsiderable eminence, near the Devil's Hole, garrisoned by twelve men, as a competent guard for ordinary occasions against the depredations of the savages. The place, even at this day wild and dismal, must have been frightfully so then. It is about three miles below the cataract, on the American side of the strait, and is often visited by the inquisitive traveller in search of the picturesque. Indeed, as it has been justly said, "the mind can scarcely conceive of a more frightful looking den. A large ravine, made by the falling in of the perpendicular bank, darkened by the foliage of the birch and cedar, which had taken root below, and the low murmuring of the rapids of the chasm, added to the distant and solemn thunder of the cataract itself, contribute to render the scene grand and awful."†

The escort approached this gloomy place without apprehension, and the teamsters were whistling cheerily along, unconscious of danger. Fatal security! A large body of Seneca warriors had been sagaciously disposed in ambuscade under the conduct of Farmer's-Brother, who only awaited their arrival at a designated point, to

---

* In the life of Mary Jemison the number is stated at three hundred, but that must be altogether too great.
† Thatcher.

leap upon them like so many tigers. They did so, and
their descent was like a storm-cloud in its fury. Falling
upon the troops, teams and drivers, and the guard of
twelve already mentioned, every man in the company,
but three, was either killed outright, or by being precipi-
tated, together with the teams, headlong down the precipice, was dashed in pieces! One of the Indians seized
Stedman's horse by the bridle, and was attempting to
make a prisoner of him; but some extraordinary act of
the bloody scene diverted his attention for a moment,
and was the means of Stedman's escape. Quick as a
flash the latter cut the reins yet in the Indian's hands, and
putting spurs to his horse, the animal bounded over
the dead and dying, and speedily placed his master beyond the reach of their bullets, although sent after him
in a shower. Two others also escaped, one of whom
was a drummer,—a fortuitous circumstance, since his
rescue from death was owing to the strap of his drum,
which caught the limb of a tree in his descent into the
chasm, and broke his fall. The third had his thigh
broken by the fall, but he nevertheless succeeded in
crawling out of the den and finding his way back to the
garrison, below the cataract. The Indians themselves
were so much pleased by the brave conduct of Stedman, that they gave him a handsome tract of land as a
reward for his dauntlessness.*

During the whole contest of the American revolution,
Farmer's-Brother was upon the war path, as an active
and bold yet sagacious leader of his people in the cause
of the British crown. But after the conclusion of peace
with the United States, he maintained his pacific relations with the most unwavering fidelity to the end. He
was one of the party of chiefs who visited Philadelphia

* Old manuscript cited by L. S. Everett, formerly of Buffalo, in a letter to
the author of Mary Jemison's Life.

on a friendly mission in the spring of 1792, and was among the attendants upon the funeral and burial of Peter Jaquette, whose life and death have been noted in the history of Red-Jacket. He was also one of the chiefs who replied to the speech of the governor of Pennsylvania, welcoming them to Philadelphia.

In the spring of the following year he was present at a grand Indian council held at Niagara, the deliberations of which were connected with the war then raging between the United States and the north-western Indians. Those hostile Indians were represented in the council, and the debates were long and ardent. Farmer's-Brother signalized himself on this occasion by a speech of three hours long, of great eloquence and power, as it was reported, in favor of peace. Unfortunately the speeches of the council were never written.

The speech, or composition, of Farmer's-Brother, which has been most admired, was delivered at a council held by the Six Nations, at Genesee River, on the 21st of November, 1798, and has already been referred to in the preceding life of Red-Jacket. It was intended as a communication to the legislature of the state of New-York, and was transmitted to that body as such, though first delivered in the form of a speech. The occasion was this: Messrs. Jones and Parish, whose names have repeatedly occurred in the foregoing pages, as Indian interpreters, had been taken captive by the Indians, in the war of the revolution, and adopted by them. Their confidence in and affection for both was strong, and it was now their desire to give them a substantial mark of their favor by a donation of land. But by the laws of the state, no transfers of Indian lands could be made to private individuals, unless by permission of the government. Hence the following communication in the form of a speech, from Ho-na-ye-wus, to the white sachems around the council fire at Albany:—

The Sachems, Chiefs and Warriors of the Seneca Nation, to
  the Sachems and Chiefs assembled about the great Council
  Fire of the State of New-York :—

" BROTHERS : As you are once more assembled in council
for the purpose of doing honor to yourselves and justice to
your country ; we, your brothers, the Sachems, Chiefs, and
Warriors of the Seneca Nation, request you to open your ears
and give attention to our voice and wishes.

" BROTHERS : You will recollect the late contest between
you and your father, the great king of England. This contest
threw the inhabitants of this whole island into a great tumult
and commotion, like a raging whirlwind, which tears up the
trees, and tosses to and fro the leaves, so that no one knows
from whence they come, or where they will fall.

" BROTHER : This whirlwind was so directed by the Great
Spirit above, as to throw into our arms two of your infant
children, Jasper Parish, and Horatio Jones. We adopted
them into our families and made them our children. We loved
them and nourished them. They lived with us many years.
At length the Great Spirit spoke to the whirlwind, and it was
still. A clear and uninterrupted sky appeared. The path of
peace was opened, and the chain of friendship was once more
made bright. Then these our adopted children left us, to seek
their relations. We wished them to return among us, and
promised, if they would return and live in our country, to
give each of them a seat of land for them and their children
to sit down upon.

" BROTHERS : They have returned and have for several years
past been serviceable to us as interpreters. We still feel our
hearts beat with affection for them, and now wish to fulfil the
promise we made them, and to reward them for their services.
We have therefore made up our minds to give them a seat of
two square miles of land lying on the outlet of Lake Erie,
about three miles below Black Rock, beginning at the mouth of
a creek known by the name of Scoy-gu-quoy-des Creek, running one mile from the river Niagara, up said creek, thence
northerly as the river runs two miles, thence westerly one mile
to the river, thence up the river as the river runs two miles
to the place of beginning, so as to contain two square miles.

" BROTHERS : We have now made known to you our minds.
we expect and earnestly request that you will permit our friends
to receive this our gift, and will make the same good to them,
according to the laws and customs of your nation.

" BROTHERS : Why should you hesitate to make our minds
easy with regard to this our request ? To you it is but a little
thing, and have you not complied with the request, and confirmed the gift of our brothers the Oneidas, the Onondagas

and Cayugas to their interpreters? And shall we ask and not be heard?

"BROTHERS: We send you this our speech, to which we expect your answer before the breaking up of your great council fire." *

This brief speech has been uniformly regarded as one of the most interesting specimens of Indian eloquence, from its boldness of figure. The gentleman who wrote down the translation, at the time, in furnishing it for publication, remarked in a note to the editor, that for one expression Longinus would have given him credit for the true sublime : " The Great Spirit spoke to the whirlwind, and it was still."

* The copy of this speech was furnished to the author by James D. Bemis, Esq., of Canandaigua, from the original publication. Messrs. Jones and Parish, in whose behalf the application was made, both died in the summer of 1836,—the former aged seventy-two, and the latter sixty-nine years. The lives of both were eventful, and were marked with incidents of a remarkable character. Captain Horatio Jones was born in Chester county, Pennsylvania, in November, 1763, and while quite young emigrated with his parents to Bedford county, in the same state. In 1799, and at the age of sixteen, he enlisted as a volunteer under Captain Boyd, in an excursion against the New-York and Canada Indians, who, led on by the notorious Butler, Brant, and Bob Nellis, had committed many atrocious massacres in that peaceful neighborhood, sparing neither age nor sex from the tomahawk and scalping knife. Boyd's company, consisting of thirty-two, in their pursuit of Nellis, were surprised by a large ambuscade of Seneca Indians, on a branch of the Juniata, about half the party killed, and eight made prisoners; among the latter was the subject of this notice. He was conveyed to the Genesee Valley, went through the horrid and savage ceremony of "running the gauntlet," was adopted into an Indian family, and for five years remained a captive, suffering all the privations and hardships incident to Indian life. After the treaty of 1784, he was appointed an interpreter for the Six Nations by General Washington, the duties of which office he discharged with great ability until a year or two previous to his death. Possessed of uncommon mental vigor and quick perception, he was enabled to form a just estimate of character, and determine with readiness the springs of human action.

His bravery, physical power, energy and decision of character, gave him great command over the Indians with whom he was associated and he obtained their entire confidence, which afforded him an opportunity of rendering valuable service to the government in our subsequent treaties with the northern and western tribes. He was the favorite interpreter of Red-Jacket, and his style on all occasions was chaste, graphic and energetic. Sincere and ardent in his attachment, —frank and hospitable in his intercourse with the world, he commanded the respect and esteem of all who knew him. He retained the full possession of his mental faculties until the last moment, and has gone down to the grave full of years and with a character above reproach. In the various relations of husband, father, and citizen, his loss is sincerely and deeply deplored.—*Livingston Register.*

The early life of Captain Jasper Parish was likewise marked by inci-

In the month of December, 1811, Farmer's-Brother addressed a letter to the Hon. William Eustis, then Secretary of War, of which the following is a copy:—

" BROTHER : The sachems and chief warriors of the Seneca nation of Indians, understanding that you are the person appointed by the great council of your nation to manage and conduct the affairs of the several nations of Indians with whom you are at peace and on terms of friendship, come at this time as children to a father, to lay before you the trouble which we have on our minds.

" BROTHER : We do not think best to multiply words. We will therefore tell you what our complaint is.

" BROTHER : Listen to what we say. Some years since we held a treaty at Big-tree, near the Genesee River. This treaty was called by our great father, the President of the United States. He sent an agent, Colonel Wadsworth, to attend this treaty, for the purpose of advising us in this business, and seeing that we had justice done us. At this treaty we sold to Robert Morris the greatest part of our country. The sum he gave us was one hundred thousand dollars.

" BROTHER : The Commissioner who was appointed on your part, advised us to place this money in the hands of our great father, the President of the United States. He told us our father loved his red children, and would take care of our money, and plant it in a field where it would bear seed forever, as long as trees grow or waters run. Our money has heretofore been of great service to us. It has helped us to support our old people, and our women and children. But we are told the field where our money was planted has become barren.

" BROTHER : We do not understand your way of doing business. This thing is heavy on our minds. We mean to hold

dents which gave interest to his character. He was born at Windham, Connecticut, in March, 1766, and while a child emigrated with his parents to the Lackawaxen, Luzerne county, Penn. In 1778, at the age of eleven years, when the British and Indians, led on by those ruthless chiefs Butler and Gi-en-gwah-toh were waging an unrelenting warfare upon the inhabitants of Wyoming Valley, he was made a prisoner by the party of Delawares who had a few days previous committed the atrocious " Massacre of Wyoming." He remained a captive among the Indians seven years, during which time he was transferred from one tribe to another of the Six Nations, suffering privations incident to Indian life. He was released from captivity at Fort Stanwix, (now Rome,) under the treaty of 1784. He had acquired, and could speak fluently, five different languages of these tribes, which enabled him to be useful in our subsequent intercourse with them, and he possessed, moreover, much of their confidence. Under Washington's administration he was appointed interpreter to the Six Nations, and afterwards sub-agent; both of which offices he held more than thirty years, and until Jackson's administration. He was an early settler in Canandaigua, having resided there since 1792 ; and he well sustained the relations of a husband, father and citizen. *Canandaigua Repository, of July* 19, 1836.

our white brethren of the United States by the hand. But this weight lies heavy. We hope you will remove it.

" BROTHER : We have heard of the bad conduct of our brothers toward the setting sun.* We are sorry for what they have done. But you must not blame us. We have had no hand in this bad business. They have had bad people among them. It is your enemies have done this.

" BROTHER : We have persuaded our agent to take this talk to your great council. He knows our situations, and will speak our minds."†

On the declaration of war by the United States against Great Britain, in 1812, Farmer's-Brother, although upwards of eighty snows in years, was among the earliest to proffer his services to the United States, and was among the foremost upon the war-path when the services of the Indians were at last accepted. The part he bore, and an interesting incident in his career, have already been noted in the life of Red-Jacket, and need not here be repeated.

Unlike the greater portion of his race, he had the fortitude to abstain from ardent spirits, and lived and died a sober man. He was remarkably well-formed, and erect in his carriage, and trod the earth with a firm step to the last—ever grave in his demeanor, and conversing, but only through an interpreter in English, with great precision. " He was as firm a friend where he promised fidelity, as a bitter enemy to those against

---

* Referring to the rising of the north-western Indians, under Tecumseh and the Shawanese Prophet.

† Mr. Erastus Granger, the Indian agent of the United States, certified that this communication was delivered by Farmer's-Brother, in the form of a speech, and being reduced to writing, was signed by the Seneca chiefs as follows :—

Farmer's-Brother, his mark		X	Wheel-Barrow, his mark			X
Little Billy,	do	X	Jack Berry,	do		X
Young King,	do	X	Twenty Canoes	do		X
Pollard,	do	X	Big Kettle,	do		X
Chief Warrior,	do	X	Half-Town,	do		X
Two Guns,	do	X	Keyandeande,	do		X
John Sky,	do	X	Captain Cold,	do		X
Parrot-Nose,	do	X	Esquire Blinkey,	do		X
John Pierce,	do	X	Captain Johnson,	do		X
Strong,	do	X				

whom he contended; and would lose the last drop in his veins sooner than betray the cause he had espoused. He was fond of recounting his exploits, and dwelt with much satisfaction upon the number of scalps he had taken in his battles and skirmishes with the whites."* At the time of his visit to Philadelphia, as already mentioned, General Washington presented him with a silver medal, bearing his own likeness, which the chief prized highly, and ever afterward wore suspended from his neck,—always declaring that he would lose it only with his life.

He was bold and uncompromising, and nobly fearless in his resentments;—and although on many occasions implacable and unrelenting, he not unfrequently manifested instances of feeling and sensibility of compassion which few savages discover. Not like Tecumseh, not like Pontiac, he at times listened to the appeals of suffering humanity even when strict policy demanded the sacrifice,—and at all times when strict policy did not demand it. He was indeed a noble instance of a great and magnanimous mind, covered by a rough and savage, but commanding and princely exterior. No man who looked upon Farmer's-Brother could imbibe feelings of contempt, disgust or hatred; on the contrary, all who saw him were impressed with respect, if not veneration and esteem. There was no meanness, no littleness, no low enterprise, intrigue or management in his deportment or conduct. All was open, great, dignified and fearless. The impress of integrity and honor chastened and softened the sterner outlines of his character.†

Soon after the close of the Niagara campaign of 1814, the veteran paid the debt of nature, at the Seneca village, where, as a mark of respect for his character and distinguished bravery, the fifth regiment of United States

* B. B. Thatcher.   † MS. Collections of Joseph W. Moulton.

infantry interred him with military honors.* A friend
of the author residing at Buffalo,† who knew him well,
thus describes his character and bearing :—" He was
every way a great man,—truly one of nature's nobles,

——The front of Jove himself,
An eye like Mars to threaten and command
A station like the herald Mercury.

None who ever saw him will fail to recollect his majestic mien and princely bearing, much less will they
who have heard him in council forget the power and
deep toned melody of his voice,—his natural and impressive gestures, and the unaffected but commanding dignity
of his manner. Unrivalled as a warrior, and only
equalled by Red-Jacket in eloquence, speaking in the
verity of sober prose, it may be said that his was

A combination and a form indeed,
To give the world assurance of a man.

With such attributes, it is not surprising that his influence with his nation, though its form of government is
essentially democratic, was controlling—nor is it less to
his true glory, that his open-heartedness, his fidelity to
truth and his 'generous magnanimity, secured for him
the admiration and esteem of every white person who
had the honor of his acquaintance."

* B. B. Thatcher. † Hon. Albert H. Tracy.

GA-NIO-DI-EUH,

OR

THE CORNPLANTER.

CORNPLANTER.

FEW names are of more frequent occurrence, in the modern history of the Six Nations, during a period of more than three-quarters of a century, than that of THE CORNPLANTER. His Indian name was *Ga-nio-di-euh*,[*] or *Handsome-Lake*, and supposing him to have been twenty years old at the defeat of General Braddock, in which bloody affair he was engaged, he must have been born at least as early as the year 1735. It has already been stated, both in the life of Red-Jacket and in the pre- ceding sketch of Farmer's-Brother, that the Senecas fought in alliance with the French during the war of 1755, —1763, and the defeat of Braddock was entirely owing to them, since the French were exclusively indebted to Indian tactics for that signal victory. What part was sustained by Cornplanter in that memorable action,— whether he was a chief, or whether he had not yet ar- rived at that dignity,—cannot be told; but in either case he doubtless acquitted himself bravely, for he was a brave man. He was a native of Conewaugus, in the valley of the Genesee River; being a half-breed, the son

---

[*] Great difficulties are continually encountered in settling the orthography of Indian names. Every original writer fixes upon the orthography from the sound, and scarcely any two of them agree. The Indian name of Cornplanter has usually been written *Gyantwaia*. The orthography adopted by the author was received from Pierce, a Seneca chief, educated at Dartmouth college.

of an Indian trader from the Mohawk Valley, a white man, named John O'Bail.* His father, during his frequent journeys from Albany to Niagara and back, became enamoured of a squaw, and Cornplanter was the fruit of their attachment. Of his early life but very little is known, beyond the fact already stated, that he was in the engagement against the British and provincial troops under General Braddock, near Fort du Quesne, in July, 1755. His boyhood was in nowise distinguished from that of his juvenile contemporaries, according to his very *naive* letter, written long afterward to the Governor of Pennsylvania :—

" When I was a child," he said in that letter, " I played with the butterfly, the grasshopper, and the frogs; and as I grew up, I began to pay some attention, and play with the Indian boys in the neighborhood; and they took notice of my skin being a different color from their's, and spoke about it. I inquired of my mother the cause, and she told me that my father was a resident in Albany. I still ate my victuals out of a bark dish. I grew up to be a young man, and married me a wife, and I had no kettle or gun. I then knew where my father lived, and went to see him, and found he was a white man, and spoke the English language. He gave me victuals while I was at his house, but when I started to return home, he gave me no provision to eat on the way. He gave me neither kettle nor gun." *   *   *   *

The conflict of the American revolution found Cornplanter a war chief of his tribe, in the full vigor of manhood, and of high rank. He was active, sagacious, eloquent, and brave. But from that period to the close of his life, his history was from necessity so closely interwoven with the lives of Brant and Red-Jacket, that with the exception of the few of his letters and speeches that have been preserved, a mere rapid outline is all

* This name, too, has been variously written, O'Bail, O'Beal, and Abeel. I have preferred the former, in the absence of positive information, because it is the orthography observed in the life of the Seneca white woman, Mary Jemison.

that can be necessary to the present purpose. He is
believed to have participated in most of the principal
engagements in which the Indians bore a part, during
that war. The cruelties of Wyoming and Cherry Valley were chiefly enacted by the Senecas, and Cornplanter was doubtless present in both affairs, although his
name does not appear in the accounts. He was on the
war-path with Brant, during the campaign of General
Sullivan against the Indian towns of the Cayugas and
Senecas, in 1779, in the course of which it may be remembered he had occasion to reproach Red-Jacket for
his cowardice. And when, in a subsequent year, the
Indians fearfully avenged the invasion of Sullivan, by
sweeping with fire and sword through the valleys of the
Schoharie-Kill and the Mohawk, under the command of
Brant and Sir John Johnson, Cornplanter was the leader
of the Senecas. It was during this expedition that he
paid another visit to his father, who was then residing in
the vicinity of Fort Plain. Having ascertained the residence of his sire, he made him a prisoner, but with
such caution as to avoid an immediate recognition. After marching the old man some ten or twelve miles up
the river, he stepped before him, faced about, and addressed him in the following terms :—

" My name is John O'Bail, commonly called Cornplanter.
I am your son ! You are my father ! You are now my prisoner, and subject to the customs of Indian warfare. But you
shall not be harmed : you need not fear. I am a warrior !
Many are the scalps which I have taken ! Many prisoners I
have tortured to death ! I am your son ! I was anxious to
see you, and greet you in friendship. I went to your cabin
and took you by force. But your life shall be spared. Indians
love their friends and their kindred, and treat them with kindness. If now you choose to follow the fortune of your yellow
son, and to live with our people, I will cherish your old age
with plenty of venison, and you shall live easy. But if it is
your choice to return to your fields and live with your white

54

children, I will send a party of my trusty young men to conduct you back in safety. I respect you, my father : you have been friendly to Indians, and they are your friends."

But the elder O'Bail preferred his white children and green fields to his yellow offspring and the wild woods, and chose to return. He was therefore discharged by the chief, and escorted in safety back to his own habitation.*

In addition to these greater movements, Cornplanter was ever active in smaller war parties and partizan forays; nor did his white blood modify his Indian propensities, or cool the temperature of his vengeance ; for his tenderest mercies were cruel. He was probably engaged in the battle of Oriskany, and was certainly lurking about the precincts of Fort Stanwix at subsequent stages of the war, ready to fall upon every light detachment or straggler from the garrison; and by his own confession, he was the murderer of a little girl who was shot under the guns of the fort, while engaged in picking blackberries.†

But notwithstanding the cruelty of his hostile practices while the war continued, he became the fast friend of the United States when once the hatchet was buried; nor did he afterward falter in his pacific course. It has already been seen, both in the lives of Brant and Red-Jacket, that he was the efficient agent in effecting the treaty of peace concluded at Fort Stanwix, in 1784, in opposition to the eloquent persuasions of the greatest orator of his nation. He very well knew that by assenting to the large cessions of territory exacted by the treaty, he was jeoparding his popularity with his own people. But if others had not, he had the sagacity to perceive

* Mary Jemison.   † Vide Life of Brant.

that, although he and his people had served the crown
of Great Britain with all fidelity, they had nevertheless
been abandoned to their fate by their more powerful
ally, and were now by consequence reduced to the miserable alternative either of giving up as much of their
country as the United States required, or of yielding
the *whole* of it.   His course, and it was also the course
of wisdom, was prescribed by the necessity of the case ;
and by the energy and ability with which he conducted
the negotiation he yet retained for his people an ample
and beautiful territory.   In a subsequent negotiation,
five years afterward, at Fort Harmer, in a mixed council of his own and several of the northwestern nations,
he assented to the cession to the United States of an im-
mense tract of territory, situated beyond the Seneca
country proper.   This country was claimed by the Six
Nations by right of conquest from the Eries and Delawares, the former of whom they had exterminated.   There
were conflicting Indian claims to the same territory ;
and disputes ensued which were the cause of numerous
and protracted difficulties.   Very soon afterward, in the
same year it is believed, viz., 1789, another treaty was
held with the Indians at Marietta, which, according to
contemporary accounts, " terminated entirely to the satisfaction of all concerned.   On this occasion an elegant
entertainment was provided.   The Indian chiefs behaved with the greatest decorum throughout the day.
Good wine was served after dinner, and Cornplanter took up his glass and said :—' I thank the Great
Spirit for this opportunity of smoking the pipe of
friendship and love.   May we plant our own vines,
be the fathers of our own children, and maintain
them.' "*

---

* Quotation from Carey's Museum, by Drake.

But the satisfaction which prevailed at the conclusion of the treaty, and on this festive occasion, was not diffused among the Senecas and others of the Six Nations at home. Far from it; the course of Cornplanter at Fort Stanwix, Fort Harmar, and Marietta, was severely censured by his people, and in the bitterness of their reproaches his life was threatened.

Red-Jacket, as has been stated in the preceding life of the orator,—more eloquent and artful than his elder rival, but less frank and honest,—adroitly availed himself of the unpalatableness of those treaties for his own aggrandizement, and the consequence was that Cornplanter found himself beset with difficulties at home on every side. In this emergency he resolved to appeal to " the Great Father of the Fifteen Fires," General Washington, for counsel, and perhaps for relief. Repairing to Philadelphia, the then seat of the federal government, accompanied by *Half-Town** and *Big-Tree*,† chiefs or

---

* The Indian name of *Half-Town* was *Achiout*. After the war of the revolution was terminated, and peace with the Six Nations concluded at Fort Stanwix, Half-Town became the white man's friend, and during the subsequent wars with the more western Indians, he communicated to the garrisons of the United States every suspicious movement of the tribes of whom doubts were entertained. Hostile bands for a long time hovered about the post of Venango, which, but for the vigilance of Half-Town, and other friendly Indians, would have been cut off. In April, 1791, Cornplanter and Half-Town had more than one hundred warriors in and about that garrison, and kept runners out continually, " being determined to protect it at all events. Their spies made frequent discoveries of war parties. On the 12th of August Half-Town and New Arrow gave information at Fort Franklin, that a sloop full of Indians had been seen on Lake Erie, sailing for Presque Isle, and their object was supposed to be that fort; but the suspicion proved to be groundless. He was also one of the chiefs at the council of Fort Harman, in 1789, and with Cornplanter signed the unpopular treaty. The legislature of Pennsylvania rewarded his fidelity by granting a quantity of land.

† The Indian name of *Big-Tree* was *Ke-on-do-wa-nea*, [Drake's orthography is Ki-an-do-ge-wa, but the author's authority is an ancient manuscript received from Thomas Morris, derived from Timothy Pickering.] Big-Tree was with General Washington during the summer of 1778, as may be seen in Campbell's Annals, and my Life of Brant. He returned to the Seneca country in the autumn of that year, passing through the country of the Oneidas, who were at all times friendly to the United States, and by whom he was received and entertained with hospitality. Arrived among the Senecas, he used his eloquence to dissuade them from longer fighting under Brant against the United States, but to no good purpose. He had promised the Oneidas to return to them, and having staid longer amon the Senecas than was expected, a messenger was despatched to him to

sachems of consideration, the following pathetic appeal
for a reconsideration of the several treaties beforemen-
tioned, and for a modification of some of the stipulations, was presented to the President. It forms a touching chapter of grievances, and its composition was the
work of Cornplanter, his associates in the mission approving thereof by their signatures. The document is
long; but the talents of the author would not be justly
appreciated, nor the history of the Six Nations rendered
complete, without it :—

*The Speech of Cornplanter, Half-Town, and Big-Tree, Chiefs
and Councillors of the Seneca nation, to the great Councillor
of the Thirteen Fires.*

"FATHER : The voice of the Seneca nation speaks to you,
the great councillor, in whose heart the wise men of all the
Thirteen Fires have placed their wisdom. It may be very
small in your ears, and we therefore entreat you to hearken
with attention ; for we are about to speak of things which are
to us very great. When your army entered the country of
the Six Nations, we called you the *Town Destroyer;* and to this
day, when that name is heard, our women look behind them and
turn pale, and our children cling to the necks of their mothers.
Our councillors and warriors are men, and cannot be afraid ;
but their hearts are grieved with the fears of our women
and children, and desire it may be buried so deep as to be
heard no more. When you gave us peace, we called you
father, because you promised to secure us in the possession of
our lands. Do this, and so long as the lands shall remain,
that beloved name shall live in the heart of every Seneca.

"FATHER : We mean to open our hearts before you, and

know the reason. He returned answer that when he arrived among his nation
he found them all in arms, and their villages, Kanadaseago and Genishaw,
crowded with warriors from remote tribes, who at first seemed inclined to hearken
to his wishes ; but soon learning from a spy that the Americans were about to
invade their country, all flew to arms, and that he had put himself at their head,
" determined to chastise" he said, " the enemy that dared to think to presume
to invade his country." After the peace he became an abiding friend to the
United States. He lamented the disaster of St. Clair's army, and was heard to
say that he would have two scalps for General Butler's, who fell in that bloody
battle, and was scalped. The legislature of Pennsylvania made him a grant of
land, comprising an island in the Alleghany river. Being on a mission to Philadelphia, in 1792, he died, after a short illness, on Sunday the 22d of April, and
was buried with suitable attention. His descendants are yet persons of some
consideration among his people.

we earnestly desire that you will let us clearly understand what you resolve to do. When our chiefs returned from the treaty at Fort Stanwix, and laid before our council what had been done there, our nation was surprised to hear how great a country you had compelled them to give up to you, without your paying to us any thing for it. Every one said that your hearts were yet swelled with resentment against us for what had happened during the war, but that one day you would reconsider it with more kindness. We asked each other, 'What have we done to deserve such severe chastisement?'

" FATHER : When you kindled your thirteen fires separately, the wise men that assembled at them told us, that you were all brothers, the children of one great father, who regarded, also, the red people as his children. They called us brothers, and invited us to his protection; they told us that he resided beyond the great water, where the sun first rises; that he was a king whose power no people could resist, and that his goodness was as bright as that sun. What they said went to our hearts; we accepted the invitation, and promised to obey him. What the Seneca nation promise, they faithfully perform; and when you refused obedience to that king, he commanded us to assist his beloved men in making you sober. In obeying him we did no more than yourselves had led us to promise. The men that claimed this promise told us you were children, and had no guns; that when they had shaken you you would submit. We hearkened to them, and were deceived, until your army approached our towns. We were deceived; but your people, in teaching us to confide in that king, had helped to deceive, and we now appeal to your heart,—is the blame all ours?

" FATHER : When we saw that we were deceived, and heard the invitation which you gave us to draw near to the fire which you had kindled, and talk with you concerning peace, we made haste towards it. You then told us that we were in your hand, and that by closing it you could crush us to nothing, and you demanded from us a great country, as the price of that peace which you had offered us;—as if our want of strength had destroyed our rights. Our chiefs had felt your power, and were unable to contend against you, and they therefore gave up that country. What they agreed to has bound our nation; but your anger against us, must, by this time, be cooled; and although our strength has not increased, nor your power become less, we ask you to consider calmly,— were the terms dictated to us by your commissioners, reasonable and just?

" FATHER : Your commissioners, when they drew the line which separated the land then given up to you, from that which you agreed should remain to be ours, did most solemnly promise that we should be secured in the peaceable possession of the lands which we inhabited east and north of that line. Does this promise bind you?

"Hear now, we beseech you, what has happened concerning that land. On the day in which we finished the treaty at Fort Stanwix, commissioners from Pennsylvania told our chiefs that they had come there to purchase all the lands belonging to us within the lines of their state, and they told us that their line would strike the river Susquehannah below Tioga branch. They then left us to consider of the bargain till the next day. On the next day we let them know that we were unwilling to sell all the lands within their state, and proposed to let them have part of it,—which we pointed out to them in their map. They told us that they must have the whole; that it was already ceded to them by the great king, at the time of making peace with you, and was *their own;* but they said that they would not take advantage of that, and were willing to pay us for it,—after the manner of their ancestors. Our chiefs were unable to contend at that time, and therefore they sold the lands up to the line which was then shown to them as the line of that state. What the commissioners had said about the land having been ceded to them at the peace, our chiefs considered as intended only to lessen the price, and they passed it by with very little notice; but, since that time, we have heard so much from others about the right to our lands, which the king gave when you made peace with him, that it is our earnest desire that you will tell us what it means.

"FATHER: Our nation empowered John Livingston to let out part of our lands on rent, to be paid to us. He told us that he was sent by congress, to do this for us, and we fear he has deceived us in the writing he has obtained from us. For since the time of our giving that power, a man of the name of Phelps has come among us, and claimed our whole country northward of the line of Pennsylvania, under purchase from that Livingston, to whom, he said he had paid twenty thousand dollars for it. He said, also, that he had bought likewise from the council of the thirteen fires and paid them twenty thousand dollars more for the same.

"And he said, also, that it did not belong to us, for the great king had ceded the whole of it, when you made peace with him. Thus he claimed the whole country north of Pennsylvania, and west of the lands belonging to the Cayugas. He demanded it; he insisted on his demand, and declared that he would have it *all.* It was impossible for us to grant him this, and we immediately refused it. After some days he proposed to run a line, at a small distance eastward of our western boundary, which we also refused to agree to. He then threatened us with immediate war, if we did not comply.

"Upon this threat, our chiefs held a council, and they agreed that no event of war could be worse than to be driven, with our wives and children, from the only country which we had any right to ; and, therefore, weak as our nation was, they determined to take the chance of war, rather than submit to such unjust demands, which seemed to have no bounds. Street, the great trader to Niagara, was then with us, having come at the request of Phelps, and as he always professed to be our great friend, we consulted him upon this subject. He also told us that our lands had been ceded by the king, and that we *must* give them up.

"Astonished at what we heard from every quarter, with hearts aching with compassion for our women and children, we were thus compelled to give up all our country north of the line of Pennsylvania, and east of the Genesee River, up to the fork, and east of a south line drawn from that fork to the Pennsylvania line.

"For this land, Phelps agreed to pay us ten thousand dollars in hand and one thousand a year for ever.

"He paid us two thousand and five hundred dollars in hand,— part of the ten thousand,—and he sent for us to come last spring and receive our money ; but instead of paying us the remainder of the ten thousand dollars, and the one thousand dollars due for the first year, he offered us no more than five hundred dollars, and insisted that he agreed with us for that sum, to be paid yearly. We debated with him for six days, during all which time he persisted in refusing to pay us our just demand, and he insisted that we should receive the five hundred dollars ; and Street, from Niagara, also insisted on our receiving the money, as it was offered to us. The last reason he assigned for continuing to refuse paying was, *that the king had ceded all the lands to the Thirteen Fires,* and that he had bought them from you, and *paid you for them.*

"We could bear this confusion no longer ; and determined to press through every difficulty, and lift up our voice that you might hear us, and to claim that security in the possession of our lands which your commissioners so solemnly promised us. And we now entreat you to inquire into our complaints, and redress our wrongs.

"FATHER : Our writings were lodged in the hands of Street, of Niagara, as we supposed him to be our friend ; but when we saw Phelps consulting with Street on every occasion, we doubted of his honesty towards us, and we have since heard that he was to receive for his endeavors to deceive us, a piece of land ten miles in width west of the Genesee River, and near forty miles in length, extending to Lake Ontario; and the lines of this tract have been run accordingly, although no part of it is within the bounds which limit his purchase. No doubt he meant to deceive us.

" FATHER : You have said that we are in your hand, and that by closing it you could crush us to nothing. Are you determined to crush us ? If you are, tell us so; that those of our nation who have become your children, and have determined to die so, may know what to do.

" In this case, one chief has said he would ask you to put him out of pain. Another, who will not think of dying by the hand of his father or his brother, has said he will retire to the Chateaugay, eat of the fatal root, and sleep with his fathers in peace.

" Before you determine on a measure so unjust, look up to God, who has made *us* as well as *you*. We hope he will not permit you to destroy the whole of our nations.

" FATHER : Hear our case : many nations inhabited this country; but they had no wisdom, and therefore, they warred together. The Six Nations were powerful, and compelled them to peace; the lands for a great extent were given up to them; but the nations which were not destroyed all continued on those lands, and claimed the protection of the Six Nations, as the brothers of their fathers. They were men, and when at peace had a right to live on the earth. The French came among us and built Niagara; they became our fathers, and took care of us. Sir William Johnson came and took that fort from the French; he became our father, and promised to take care of us and did so until you were too strong for his king. To him we gave four miles around Niagara, as a place of trade. We have already said how we came to join against you; we saw that we were wrong; we wished for peace; you demanded a great country to be given up to you; it was surrendered to you, as the price of peace, and we ought to have peace and possession of the little land which you then left us.

" FATHER : When that great country was given up, there were but few chiefs present, and they were compelled to give it up, and it is not the Six Nations only that reproach these chiefs with having given up that country. The Chippewas, and all the nations who lived on those lands westward, call to us, and ask us,—' Brothers of our fathers, where is the place you have reserved for us to lie down upon ?'

" FATHER : You have compelled us to do that which has made us ashamed. We have nothing to answer to the children of the brothers of our fathers. When, last spring, they called upon us to go to war, to secure them a bed to lie upon,

55

the Senecas entreated them to be quiet, till we had spoken to you. But on our way down, we heard that your army had gone toward the country which those nations inhabit, and if they meet together the best blood on both sides will stain the ground.

"FATHER: We will not conceal from you that the Great God, and not man, has preserved the Cornplanter from the hands of his own nation. For they ask continually, 'Where is the land which our children, and their children after them, are to lie down upon?' 'You told us,' say they, 'that the line drawn from Pennsylvania to Lake Ontario, would mark it for ever on the east, and the line running from Beaver Creek to Pennsylvania would mark it on the west, and we see that it is not so. For first one and then another comes and takes it away by order of that people which you tell us promised to secure it to us.' He is silent; for he has nothing to answer. When the sun goes down, he opens his heart before God, and earlier than that sun appears upon the hills, he gives thanks for his protection during the night; for he feels that among men, become desperate by their danger, it is God only that can preserve him. He loves peace, and all that he had in store he has given to those who have been robbed by your people, lest they should plunder the innocent to repay themselves. The whole season, which others have employed in providing for their families, he has spent in his endeavors to preserve peace; and at this moment, his wife and children are lying on the ground, and in want of food; his heart is in pain for them, but he perceives that the Great God will try his firmness, in doing what is right.

" FATHER: The game which the Great Spirit sent into our country for us to eat, is going from among us. We thought that he intended we should till the ground with the plough, as the white people do, and we talked to one another about it. But before we speak to you concerning this, we must know from you whether you mean to leave us and our children any land to till. Speak plainly to us concerning this great business.

" All the lands we have been speaking of belonged to the Six Nations; no part of it ever belonged to the King of England, and he could not give it to you.

" The land we live on, our fathers received from God, and they transmitted it to us for our children, and we cannot part with it.

" FATHER: We told you that we would open our hearts to you. Hear us once more.

" At Fort Stanwix we agreed to deliver up those of our people who should do you any wrong, that you might try them, and punish them according to your law. We delivered up two men accordingly, but instead of trying them according to your laws, the lowest of your people took them from your magistrate, and put them immediately to death. It is just to punish murder with death; but the Senecas will not deliver up their people to men who disregard the treaties of their own nation.

"FATHER : Innocent men of our nation are killed one after another, and our best families; but none of your people who have committed the murders have been punished.

"We recollect that you did not promise to punish those who killed our people, and we now ask, was it intended that your people should kill the Senecas, and not only remain unpunished by you, but be protected by you against the revenge of the next of kin ?

"FATHER : These are to us very great things. We know that you are very strong, and we have heard that you are wise, and we wait to hear your answer to what we have said, that we may know that you are just.

It may be remembered that a brief reference to the preceding speech was made in the Life of Red Jacket; and it will not have escaped the reader's attention, that other grievances than those connected with the treaties of Fort Stanwix and St. Clair, are in this document presented. In his reply, President Washington was evidently embarrassed by a struggle between his feelings and the sterner behests of duty. Commiserating the situation of the chiefs and their people, it may well be conceived that his humane inclinations were in favor of the supplicants. On the other hand, the terms of the treaties, particularly in regard to the difficulties with Oliver Phelps, did not justify the complaints of the Indians. He doubtless said all he could for their encouragement, under the circumstances of the case, evading some of their complaints, and passing entirely over others. He assured them that no fraudulent means of obtaining their lands would be sustained by the government, and that in one particular act complained of, (the purchase of their lands by Livingston and others,) the whole transaction had been declared null and void. The

persons who had murdered several of their people, he
assured them should be dealt with in the same manner
as though they had murdered white men, and that
all possible means should be used for their arrest
and proper rewards offered to stimulate exertions for
that purpose. In regard to the lands conveyed to the
United States by treaty, the President could only assure
them that he had no authority to interpose in the premises.   On the whole, his reply to them was such as to
soothe their feelings, and to afford them a little encouragement, but not all they hoped for. In the course of
this answer, General Washington bore the following testimony to the character of the head of the deputation:
" The merits of Cornplanter, and his friendship for the
United States, are well known to me, and shall not be
forgotten; and, as a mark of esteem of the United
States, I have directed the Secretary of War to make
him a present of two hundred and fifty dollars, either
in money or goods, as the Cornplanter shall like best."

Cornplanter and his associates rejoined to the speech
of the President, referring again to some of their real or
fancied grievances, and pleading for the restoration of a
small portion of their lands which had been ceded by
the treaty of Fort Stanwix, comprising the village of
Half-Town and his clan. As one reason for making
this application, they urged that the treaty at Fort Stanwix was made while the United States were too angry
with them, and that the exactions then insisted upon,
were unwarrantable and unjust. This rejoinder was
made by Cornplanter, and is here inserted at large:—

*The Speech of Cornplanter, Half-Town, and Great-Tree,
Chiefs of the Seneca Nation, to the President of the United
States of America.*

" FATHER : Your speech, written on the great paper, is to
us like the first light of the morning to a sick man, whose

pulse beats too strongly in his temples, and prevents him from sleep. He sees it and rejoices, but is not cured.

"You say that you have spoken plainly on the great point. That you will protect us in the lands secured to us at Fort Stanwix, and that we have the right to *sell* or to *refuse* to sell it. This is very good. But our nation complain that you compelled us at that treaty to give up too much of our lands. We confess that our nation is bound by what was there done; and, acknowledging your power, we have now appealed to yourselves against that treaty, as made while you were too angry at us, and therefore unreasonable and unjust. To this you have given us no answer.

"FATHER: That treaty was not made with a single state,— it was with the Thirteen States. We never would have given all that land to one state. We know it was before you had the great authority, and as you have more wisdom than the commissioners who forced us into that treaty, we expect that you have also more regard to justice, and will now at our request, reconsider that treaty, and restore to us a part of that land.

"FATHER: The land which lies between the line running south from Lake Erie to the boundary of Pennsylvania, as mentioned at the treaty at Fort Stanwix, and the eastern boundary of the land which you sold, and the Senecas confirmed to Pennsylvania, is the land in which Half-Town and all his people live, with other chiefs who always have been and still are dissatisfied with the treaty at Fort Stanwix. They grew out of this land, and their fathers grew out of it, and they cannot be persuaded to part with it. We, therefore, entreat you to restore to us this little piece.

"FATHER: Look at the land which we gave to you at that treaty, and then turn your eyes upon what we now ask you to restore to us, and you will see that what we ask you to return *is a very little piece.* By giving it back again you will satisfy the whole of our nation. The chiefs who signed that treaty will be in safety, and peace between your children and our children will continue so long as your land shall join to ours. Every man of our nation will then turn his eyes away from all the other lands which we then gave up to you, and forget that our fathers ever said that they belonged to them.

"FATHER: We see that you ought to have the path at the carrying-place from Lake Erie to Niagara, as it was marked down at Fort Stanwix, and we are all willing that it should remain to be yours. And if you desire to reserve a passage through the Conewago, and through the Chataugue Lake and land, for a path from that lake to Lake Erie, take it where you best like. Our nation will rejoice to see it an open path for you and your children while the land and water remain. But let us also pass along the same way, and continue to take the fish of those waters in common with you.

"FATHER: You say that you will appoint an agent to take care of us. Let him come and take care of our trade; but we desire he may not have any thing to do with our lands;— for the agents which have come among us and pretended to take care of us, have always deceived us whenever we sold lands; both when the King of England and the States have bargained with us. They have by this means occasioned many wars, and we are therefore unwilling to trust them again.

"FATHER: When we return home, we will call a great council, and consider well how lands may be hereafter sold by our nation. And when we have agreed upon it, we will send you notice of it. But we desire that you will not depend on your agent for information concerning land; for after the abuses which we have suffered by such men, we will not trust them with any thing which relates to land.

"FATHER: There are men that go from town to town and beget children, and leave them to perish, or except better men take care of them, to grow up without instruction. Our nation has looked round for a father, but they found none that would own them for children, until you now tell us that your courts are open to us, as to your own people. The joy which we feel at this great news, so mixes with the sorrows that are past, that we cannot express our gladness, nor conceal the remembrance of our afflictions. We will speak of them at another time.

"FATHER: We are ashamed that we have listened to the lies of Livingston, or been influenced by threats of war by Phelps, and would hide that whole transaction from the world and from ourselves, by quietly receiving what Phelps promised to give us for the lands they cheated us of. But as Phelps will not pay us even according to that fraudulent bargain, we will lay the whole proceedings before your court. When the evidence which we can produce is heard, we think it will appear that the whole bargain was founded on lies, which he placed one upon another; that the goods that he charges to us as part payment were plundered from us; that if Phelps was not directly concerned in the theft, he knew of it at the time and concealed it from us; and that the persons we confided in were bribed by him to deceive us in the bargain; and if these facts appear, that your court will not say that such bargains are just, but will set the whole aside.

"FATHER: We apprehended that our evidence might be called for, as Phelps was here, and knew what we have said concerning him; and as Ebenezer Allen knew something of the matter, we desired him to continue here. Nicholson, the interpreter, is very sick, and we request that Allen may remain a few days longer, as he speaks our language.

" FATHER : The blood which was spilled near Pine Creek is covered, and we shall never look where it lies. We know that Pennsylvania will satisfy us for that which we spoke of to them before we spoke to you. The chain of friendship will now, we hope, be made strong as you desire it to be. We will hold it fast, and our end of it shall never rust in our hands.

" FATHER : We told you what advice we gave the people you are now at war with, and we now tell you that they have promised to come again to our towns next spring. We shall not wait for their coming, but will set out very early, and show to them what you have done *for us*, which must convince them that you will do for them every thing which they ought to ask. We think they will hear and follow our advice.

" FATHER : You give us leave to speak our minds concerning the tilling of the ground. We ask you to teach us to plough and to grind corn ; to assist us in building saw-mills, and to supply us with broad-axes, saws, augers, and other tools, so as that we make our houses more comfortable and more durable ; that you will send smiths among us, and, above all, that you will teach our children to read and write, and our women to spin and to weave. The manner of your doing these things for us we leave to you, who understand them ; but we assure you we will follow your advice as far as we are able."

The President replied to this appeal in a spirit of kindness, reminding the chiefs that the treaty of Fort Stanwix had been fully confirmed at Fort Harman in 1789,—again stating to them that it was not within his power to annul the provisions of a treaty,—more especially of one that had been concluded before his administration commenced,—but assuring them that Half-Town and his people should not be disturbed in the peaceful occupancy of the territory which they desired to reclaim. The President also suggested that he had in contemplation the adoption of some measures for teaching the Indians the use of letters, of domestic animals, and the arts of husbandry. The stay of the chiefs in Philadelphia was protracted until the 7th of February,

when they took leave by the following letter to the
President :—

The Speech of Cornplanter, Half-Town, and Big-Tree, Seneca
Chiefs, to the great Councillor of the Thirteen Fires.

" FATHER : No Seneca ever goes from the fire of his friend,
until he has said to him, ' I am going.' We therefore tell you,
that we are now setting out for our own country.

" FATHER : We thank you, from our hearts, that we now
know there is a country we may call our own, and on which
we may lie down in peace. We see that there will be peace
between your children and our children; and our hearts are
very glad. We will persuade the Wyandots and other western nations, to open their eyes, and look towards the bed which
you have made for us, and to ask of you a bed for themselves,
and their children, that will not slide from under them.

" We thank you for your presents to us, and rely on your
promise to instruct us in raising corn, as the white people do;
the sooner you do this the better for us. And we thank you
for the care you have taken to prevent bad men from coming
to trade among us; if any come without your license we will
turn them back; and we hope our nation will determine to
spill all the rum which shall hereafter be brought to our towns.

" FATHER : We are glad to hear that you determine to appoint an agent that will do us justice, in taking care that bad
men do not come to trade among us; but we earnestly entreat
you that you will let us have an interpreter, in whom we can
confide, to reside at Pittsburgh; to that place our people, and
other nations, will long continue to resort; there we must send
what news we hear, when we go among the western nations,
which we are determined shall be early in the Spring. We
know Joseph Nicholson, and he speaks our language so that
we clearly understand what you say to us, and we rely on what
he says. If we were able to pay him for his services we would
do it; but, when we meant to pay him, by giving him land, it
has not been confirmed to him; and he will not serve us any
longer unless you will pay him. Let him stand between, to
entreat you.

FATHER : You have not asked any security for peace on our
part, but we have agreed to send nine Seneca boys to be under
your care for education. Tell us at what time you will receive
them, and they shall be sent at the time you shall appoint. This
will assure you that we are, indeed, at peace with you, and determined to continue so. If you can teach them to become
wise and good men, we will take care that our nation shall be
willing to receive instruction from them.

This letter was answered in behalf of the President by General Knox, Secretary at War. He cautiously informed them that instead of taking a portion of their youth away from their country, to be educated abroad, it was proposed by the President to send a schoolmaster to reside among them. Two or three farmers were also to be planted in their country, to teach them the arts of husbandry. With these and other favorable assurances, Cornplanter and his associates departed for their homes. Arriving at Pittsburgh, they ascertained that some fresh outrages and additional murders had been committed by the whites against and upon their people, whereupon Cornplanter immediately addressed the following letter of just complaint to the President:—

Message from the Cornplanter, New-Arrow, Half-Town, and Big-Tree, Chiefs of the Seneca nation of Indians, to the President of the United States.

"PITTSBURGH, *March* 17, 1791.

" SIR : When we rose from the Great Council of the Thirteen Fires, we mentioned that we meant to have a council with the chiefs of the bad, angry Indians. Through the whole Quaker State, as we came up the road, we were treated well, and they took good care of us until we came here. One misfortune happened only, that one of our wagons is not yet arrived here ; the one we first engaged, with the goods you presented to us.

" FATHER : Your promise to us was, that you would keep all your people quiet ; but since we came here, we find that some of our people have been killed,—the good honest people who were here trading.

" FATHER : We hope you will not suffer all the good people to be killed ; but your people are killing them as fast as they can. Three men and one woman have been killed at Big Beaver Creek, and they were good people, and some of the white people will testify the truth of this. When we heard the news we found one boy had made his escape, and got to the trader's house, who saved his life ; we now wait to see him.

" FATHER : We have been informed that twenty-seven men came from another state, and murdered these men in the Quaker State, and took away nine horses, and all the goods

56

they had purchased from the trader. Our father, and ruler over all mankind, now speak and tell us, did you order those men to be killed?

" FATHER : Our word is pledged to you that we would endeavor to make peace with all warrior nations. If we cannot do it, do not blame us; you struck the innocent men first. We hope you will not blame us, as your people have first broke good rules; but, as for our people, they are as firm and friendly as ever.

" FATHER : We must now acquaint you with the men's names who did this murder at Beaver Creek; Samuel Brady, formerly a captain in your army, and under your command; also a Balden, were persons concerned in this murder.

" FATHER : We can inform you little more; therefore will conclude with asking you how we should have come to the knowledge of this, or how we could have informed you, had it not been for our good friend Joseph Nicholson? Therefore we beg you may grant him an appointment as interpreter; for we cannot see how we can do without him. We know of no other man who speaks your language and ours so well as he.

" CORNPLANTER, × his mark.
" NEW-ARROW, × his mark.
" HALF-TOWN, × his mark.
" BIG-TREE, × his mark.

" P. S. The boy who made his escape at Beaver Creek has arrived at this place, and I have taken him under my protection. Father, your despatches from Detroit have been unavoidably detained, heretofore; but to-morrow Big-Tree and one other shall set off with them, and will also take the boy mentioned here, and deliver him to his relations. We part, to-day, at this place; Big-Tree is going among the Cross Indians to see if they will make peace, and I go to my own people to call them to council.

" CORNPLANTER."

The Secretary at War replied to this message on the 28th of March, disclaiming and denouncing the outrages committed by Brady, and assuring the Indians that General St. Clair, then commanding in Ohio, should make full inquiry into the circumstances of the case, reimburse the Indians for the property destroyed, and discover and arrest the offenders if possible.

It will have been observed from the last two communications of Cornplanter and his associates, that Big-

Tree and Half-Town were about to proceed into the country of the Indians then at war with the United States, upon an embassy of peace. An arrangement to this effect, which was to include Cornplanter also, had been made during the visit of the chiefs at Philadelphia. Still it had been judged advisable for Cornplanter himself to proceed home in the first instance, for the purpose of convening a general council of the Six Nations, to meet Colonel Proctor, in whose company, and for whose protection, it was proposed that he should make his journey among the hostile tribes. The proceedings under this part of the arrangement have been detailed in the life of Red-Jacket. The mission of Colonel Proctor was a failure,—he being unable to proceed among the hostile Indians. Yet at a subsequent period Cornplanter performed the mission, at great personal hazard, but without any favorable results. There were many at that time, as in all Indian wars, who entertained doubts of the fidelity of such Indians as professed friendship for the whites, and Cornplanter did not escape suspicion. But his subsequent conduct showed that those suspicions were unjust. Among other evidences of his integrity, a letter from Fort Franklin bore the following testimony to his fidelity : "I have only to observe that Cornplanter has been here, and in my opinion he is as friendly as one of our own people. He has advised me to take care ; ' for,' said he, ' you will soon have a chance to let the world know whether you are a soldier or not.' When he went off, he ordered two chiefs and ten warriors to remain here and scout about the garrison, and let me know if the bad Indians should either advance against me, or any of the frontiers of the United States. He thinks the people at Pittsburgh should keep out spies toward the salt licks, for he says, by and by, he thinks the bad Indians will come from that way.' Another evidence of his good faith may be found in the following advertisement, signed by him and published in the same year,—1792 :—" My people having been charged with committing depredations on the frontier inhabitants near Pittsburgh, I hereby contradict the assertion, as it is certainly without foundation. I pledge myself to those inhabitants, that they may rest perfectly secure from any danger from the Senecas residing on the Alleghany waters, and that my people have been, and still are, friendly to the United States."* Another instance, and a painful one, goes to establish the same truth. At or near the time of his departure on his message of peace to the west, " as three of his people were travelling through a settlement upon the Genesee, they stopped at a house to light their pipes. There happened to be several white men within, one of whom, as the foremost Indian stooped down to light his pipe, killed him with an axe. Another of the party was badly wounded with the same weapon, while escaping from the house. They were not pursued, and a boy of the number escaped unhurt."† When Cornplanter became acquainted with the foul transaction, instead of seizing his tomahawk, and rushing at the head of his clan upon the nearest American settlement for revenge, he charged his warriors to remain quiet, and was heard only to say :—" It is hard, when I and my people are trying to make peace for the whites, that we should be thus rewarded. I can govern my young men and warriors better than the Thirteen Fires can their's!" This rebuke would have done honor to a Christian philosopher.

During all the troubles of those days between the United States and the Indians, until after the decisive victory of Wayne, and the treaty of Greenville, Cornplan-

* Drake.
† Idem. This poor wounded Indian, when almost recovered from the injury, was bitten by a serpent, which caused his immediate death.

ter was ever neutral, and always the friend of peace. His exertions to this end are referred to in the life of Brant, and more fully set forth in the preceding life of Red-Jacket. He was present at the several treaties held with his people by Colonel Pickering, ending with that of Canandaigua, in 1794. Nothing farther is heard of the veteran chief until the treaty with Thomas Morris, held at Big Tree, in 1797, when he again appeared upon the stage of action, as stated in the former part of the present volume.

He had ever entertained a profound regard for the character of Washington, and on the eve of the retirement of that great man from the public service, as President of the United States, Cornplanter made a special visit to the seat of the federal government, to take an official leave of the great benefactor both of the white man and the red. The following manly speech from the forest chief was delivered on the occasion at the interview :—

Speech of The Cornplanter to General Washington,—Philadelphia, 28th February, 1797.

"FATHER : I thank the Great Spirit for protecting us through the various paths which we have trod since I was last at this place. As I am told you are about to retire from public business, I have come to pay my last address to you as the great Chief of the Fifteen Fires, and am happy to find that I have arrived here in time to address you once more as father, and to advise with you on the business of our nation. You have always told us that the land which we live upon is our own, and that we may make such use of it as we think most conducive to our own comfort and the happiness of posterity.

" FATHER : I wish whilst I am able to do business to provide for the rising generation. Our forefathers thought that their posterity would pursue their tracks, and support themselves by their hunts, as they did in the extensive forests given them by the Great Spirit, and by them transmitted to us. But the great revolution among the white people in this country has extended its influence to the people of my color,—turn our faces which way we will, we find the white people culti-

vating the ground which our forefathers hunted over, and the
forests which furnished them with plenty now afford but a
scanty subsistence for us, and our young men are not safe in
pursuing it. If a few years have made such a change, what
will be the situation of our children when those calamities increase?

"FATHER: To those points I wish to draw your attention,
and once more to have your candid and friendly advice on
what will be best for the present race, and how we can best
provide for posterity. Your people have a different mode of
living from ours;—they have trades and they have education,
which enables them to take different pursuits; by which means
they maintain themselves, provide for their children, and help
each other.

"FATHER: I am also told that your people have a strong
place for their money, where it is not only safe, but that it produces them each and every year an increase without lessening
the stock. If we should dispose of part of our country and
put our money with your's in that strong place, will it be safe?
Will it yield to our children the same advantages after our
heads are laid down as it will at present produce to us? Will
it be out of the reach of our foolish young men, so that they
cannot drink it up, to the prejudice of our children?

"FATHER: You know that some of our people are too fond
of strong drink, and I am sorry to observe that your people
are too apt to lay that temptation before them.

"FATHER: The last time I was here I mentioned to you
that my mind was uneasy in regard to Mr. Oliver Phelps's
purchase, to which you desired me to make my mind easy,
and said that you would inquire into the business. On my return I met Mr. Phelps at Canandaigua, where he promised to
give me a piece of land and to build me a house, and give me
some cattle. With this I was satisfied, till I saw him again
some time after, when he, to my surprise, had almost forgotten
it,—but when I put him in mind of it he gave me a horse and
two cattle, but refused the house and land because land had
raised so much in value.

"FATHER: To one thing more I wish your attention :—
When I was returning home the last time I was here, I was
plundered by some of your unruly people, of several things,
amongst which was a paper given me by General Parsons, en-
titling me to one mile square of land at Muskingum, which I
have never been able to recover, and without your friendly
assistance must lose the land.

"FATHER: I congratulate you on your intended repose
from the fatigues and anxiety of mind which are constant attendants on high public stations,—and hope that the same

good Spirit which has so long guided your steps as a father to a great nation will still continue to protect you, and make your private reflections as pleasant to yourself, as your public measures have been useful to your people."

The manuscript of the preceding speech has been preserved among the papers of Thomas Morris. The circumstances of this visit being unofficial, or rather not being connected with the public service, it is not mentioned in the Indian state papers, and the reply of Washington seems not to have been preserved. No doubt it was characteristic of that illustrious man,—considerate as well as kind.

The relations between the United States and the Indians having now been settled upon a permanently pacific basis, the life of Cornplanter was no longer connected with the general history of the country. His labors were consequently thenceforward devoted to his own people. Like his great Mohawk contemporary, Thayendanegea, he was anxious for the civilization and moral and social improvement of his race, and his efforts were directed to that object. He saw all around him the evils of intemperance, and exerted himself with zeal, in conjunction with his brother, Gos-kuk-ke-wa-na-kow-ne-di-yu, the prophet, to effect a reformation upon this subject. In the course of his exertions in this cause he made a visit to President Jefferson, in the early part of his administration, for counsel and encouragement. Shortly afterward he received a beautiful and characteristic letter from Mr. Jefferson, which, not having been elsewhere published, is here inserted :*

" *Washington, November* 3, 1802.
" BROTHER HANDSOME LAKE : I have received the message in writing which you sent through Capt. Irvine, our confiden-

---

* The author has been favored with the original of this letter, by Mr. Pierce, a young Seneca chief of the Alleghany clan, to whom reference has before been made.

tial agent, placed near you for the purpose of communicating and transacting between us whatever may be useful for both nations. I am happy to learn you have been so far favored by the Divine Spirit, as to be made sensible of those things which are for your good and that of your people, and of those which are hurtful to you; and particularly that you and they see the ruinous effects which the abuse of spirituous liquors have produced upon them. It has weakened their bodies, enervated their minds, exposed them to hunger, cold, nakedness, and poverty; kept them in perpetual broils, and reduced their population. I do not wonder, then, brother, at your censures, not only on your own people, who have voluntarily gone into these fatal habits, but on all the nations of white people who have supplied their calls for this article. But these nations have done to you only what they do among themselves. They have sold what individuals wish to buy, leaving to every one to be the guardian of his own health and happiness. Spirituous liquors are not in themselves bad. They are often found to be an excellent medicine for the sick. It is the improper and intemperate use of them, by those in health, which makes them injurious; but as you find that your people cannot refrain from an ill use of them, I greatly applaud your resolution not to use them at all. We have too affectionate a concern for your happiness to place the paltry gain on the sale of these articles in competition with the injury they do you; and as it is the desire of your nation that no spirits should be sent among them, and I am authorized by the great council of the United States to prohibit them, I will sincerely co-operate with your wise men in any proper measures for this purpose which shall be agreeable to them.

" You remind me, brother, of what I have said to you when you visited me the last winter, that the land you then held would remain yours, and should never go from you but when you should be disposed to sell. This I now repeat, and will ever abide by. We, indeed, are always ready to buy land; but we will never ask but when you wish to sell; and our laws, in order to protect you against imposition, have forbidden individuals to purchase lands from you; and have rendered it necessary, when you desire to sell, even to a state, that an agent from the United States should attend the sale, see that your consent is freely given, a satisfactory price paid, and report to us what has been done, for our approbation. This was done in the late case of which you complain. The deputies of your nation came forward in all the forms which we have been used to consider as evidence of the will of your nation. They proposed to sell the state of New-York certain parcels of land, of small extent, and detached from the body of your other lands. The state of New-York was desirous to buy. I sent an agent in whom we trust, to see that your consent was free, and the sale fair. All was reported to be free and fair. The lands were your property. The right to sell is one of the rights of property. To forbid you the exercise of that right would be a wrong to your nation. Nor do I think, brother, that the sale of lands is, under all circumstances, injurious to your people; while they depended on hunting, the more extensive the forests around them, the more game they would yield. But, going into a state of agriculture, it may be as advantageous to a society as it is to an individual who has more land than he can improve, to sell a part and lay out the money in stocks and implements of agriculture, for the better improvement of the residue. A little land, well stocked and improved, will yield a great deal more without stock or improvement. I hope, therefore, that, on further reflection, you will see this transaction in a more favorable light, both as it concerns the interest of your nation, and the exercise of that superintending care which I am sincerely anxious to employ for their subsistence and happiness. Go on, then, brother, in the great reformation you have undertaken. Persuade our red men to be sober and to cultivate their lands; and their women to spin and weave for their families. You will soon see your women and children well fed and clothed: your men living happily in peace and plenty, and your numbers increasing from year to year. It will be a great glory to you to have been the instrument of so happy a change, and your children's children, from generation to generation, will repeat your name with love and gratitude for ever. In all your enterprises for the good of your people you may count with confidence on the aid and protection of the United States, and on the sincerity and zeal with which I am animated in the furthering of this humane work. You are our brethren of the same land; we wish your prosperity as brethren should do. Farewell!

(Signed,)   " TH. JEFFERSON."

It was in the course of these labors for the moral elevation of his people, that Cornplanter became involved in the contest for the ascendancy with Red-Jacket, as related at large in the life of the orator. There had never been any good will between them since the treaty of Fort Stanwix; and the effort now made by Cornplanter to regain the influence he had lost through the intrigues and subtlety of his rival, by means of the pretended visions and revelations of his brother, the prophet, having signally failed, as heretofore stated, the old war-chief remained, during the residue of his extended life, in retirement and comparative obscurity. The residence of his clan was upon the banks of the Alleghany, and its tributaries, the Oil and Connewango creeks, partly within the bounds of New-York, and partly in Pennsylvania. The legislature of the latter state having made him a special grant of land on the Alleghany, about seven miles below its junction with the Connewango, Cornplanter removed thither and continued there to reside, cultivating a large farm, until the day of his death.

In the year 1816, the late Rev. Timothy Alden, then President of Alleghany College, made a visit to the old chief, whom he says he found on the banks of the Alleghany on a piece of first-rate bottom land, a little within the limits of Pennsylvania. He was the owner of thirteen hundred acres of land, upon six hundred of which stood his village, exhibiting the signs of industrious inhabitants. "It was grateful," remarked Dr. Alden in his journal, " to notice the present agricultural habits of the place, from the numerous enclosures of buckwheat, corn and oats. We also saw a number of oxen, cows, and horses ; and many logs, designed for the saw-mill, and the Pittsburgh market." The chief was a professing Christian, and hailed with joy the visits of his fellow Christians. He was delighted with the arrival of Dr. Alden, and lost not a moment in welcoming him to his village, and insisted on waiting upon him in person. He had many of his people under his command, but he preferred serving his visitor, and even cutting and bringing from the field the forage for his horse, himself. The Western Missionary Society at that time were sustaining a school in Cornplanter's village, which Dr. Alden described as being in a condition promising good success. One of his sons, Henry O'Bail, had been educated in

Philadelphia ; but on returning to his people he became a drunkard and was discarded by his father. He afterward attached himself to the Pagan party under Red-Jacket. Cornplanter had other sons, but he resolved that no more of them should be educated among the whites, since, as he said, "it entirely spoils Indian !"* Notwithstanding his profession of Christianity, Cornplanter was very superstitious. "Not long since he said the Good Spirit had told him not to have any thing to do with the whites, or even to preserve any mementos or relics that had from time to time been given to him by the pale-faces ;—whereupon, among other things, he burnt up his belt and broke his elegant sword."

From the time of Dr. Alden's visit until the month of February, 1822, the name of this extraordinary man is found in connexion with no public event. It appears that in 1821–'22, the State of Pennsylvania attempted to exact a tax from Cornplanter and his people. The blood of the chief, though chilled by the cold of almost a hundred winters, became warm again. Such a demand never having been made of him before, he conceived it to be not only unlawful, but a personal indignity. He therefore resisted payment, and only submitted when the civil officers appeared and were about to enforce their demand with fire-arms. The tax was then paid, whereupon Cornplanter applied to the governor of the state for a redress of the grievance, in the following letter not actually written, but entirely dictated by himself. It is worth preserving, not only as it relates to the subject in dispute, but as a curious piece of Indian autobiography :—

" *Alleghany River*, 2d *Mo.* 2d, 1822.
" I feel it my duty to send a speech to the Governor of Pennsylvania at this time, and inform him the place where I was from,—which was Conewaugus, on the Genesee River.

* Judge E. T. Foote, of Chautauque, as cited by Drake.

" When I was a child, I played with the butterfly, the grass-hopper and the frogs. As I grew up, I began to pay some attention, and play with the Indian boys in the neighborhood, and they took notice of my skin being a different color from theirs, and spoke about it. I inquired of my mother the cause, and she told me that my father was a residenter in Albany. I ate still my victuals out of a bark dish—I grew up to be a young man, and married me a wife, but I had no kettle or gun. I then knew where my father lived, and went to see him, and found he was a white man, and spoke the English language. He gave me victuals while I was at his house, but when I started to return home, he gave me no provision to eat on the way. He gave me neither kettle nor gun, neither did he tell me that the United States were about to rebel against the government of England. *

" I will now tell you, brothers, who are in session of the legislature of Pennsylvania, that the Great Spirit has made known to me that I have been wicked; and the cause thereof was the revolutionary war in America. The cause of Indians having been led into sin, at that time, was that many of them were in the practice of drinking and getting intoxicated. Great Britain requested us to join with them in the conflict against the Americans, and promised the Indians land and liquor. I, myself, was opposed to joining in the conflict, as I had nothing to do with the difficulty that existed between the two parties. I have now informed you how it happened that the Indians took a part in the revolution, and will relate to you some circumstances that occurred after the close of the war. General Putnam, who was then at Philadelphia, told me there was to be a council at Fort Stanwix, and the Indians requested me to attend on behalf of the Six Nations, which I did, and there met with three commissioners, who had been appointed to hold the council. They told me they would inform me of the cause of the revolution, which I requested them to do minutely. They then said that it had originated on account of the heavy taxes that had been imposed upon them by the British government, which had been for fifty years increasing upon them; that the Americans had grown weary thereof, and refused to pay, which affronted the king. There had likewise a difficulty taken place about some tea, which they wished me not to use, as it had been one of the causes that many people had lost their lives. And the British government now being affronted, the war commenced, and the cannons began to roar in our country. General Putnam then told me at the council at Fort Stanwix, that by the late war the Americans had gained two objects;

---

* This paragraph has been already quoted, as chronologically belonging to the opening of the present sketch.

they had established themselves an independent nation, and had obtained some land from Great Britain to live upon, the division line of which ran through the lakes. I then spoke, and said that I wanted some land for the Indians to live on, and General Putnam said that it should be granted, and that I should have land in the state of New-York for the Indians. General Putnam then encouraged me to use my endeavors to pacify the Indians generally; and as he considered it an arduous task to perform, wished to know what I wanted as pay therefor? I replied to him, that I would use my endeavors to do as he had requested with the Indians, and for pay thereof, I would take the land. I told him not to pay me money or dry goods, but land. And for having attended thereto, I received the tract of land on which I now live, which was presented to me by Governor Mifflin. I told General Putnam that I wished the Indians to have the exclusive privilege of the deer and wild game, which he assented to.

" The treaty that was made at the aforementioned council has been broken by some of the white people, which I now intend acquainting the governor with. Some white people are not willing that Indians should hunt any more, whilst others are satisfied therewith; and those white people who reside near our reservation, tell us that the woods are theirs, and they have obtained them from the governor. The treaty has been also broken by the white people using their endeavors to destroy all the wolves, which was not spoken about in the council at Fort Stanwix, by General Putnam, but has originated lately.

" It has been broken again, which is of recent origin. White people wish to get credit from Indians, and do not pay them honestly, according to their agreement.

" In another respect it has also been broken by white people, who reside near my dwelling; for when I plant melons and vines in my field, they take them as their own. It has been broken again by white people using their endeavors to obtain our pine trees from us. We have very few pine trees on our land, in the state of New-York; and white people and Indians often get into dispute respecting them. There is also a great quantity of whiskey brought near our reservation by white people, and the Indians obtain it and become drunken.

" Another circumstance has taken place which is very trying to me, and I wish the interference of the governor. The white people who live at Warren, called upon me sometime ago, to pay taxes for my land, which I objected to, as I had never been called upon for that purpose before; and having refused to pay the white people became irritated, called upon me frequently, and at length brought four guns with them and seized our cattle. I still refused to pay, and was not willing to let the cattle go.   After a long dispute they returned home, and I understood the militia was ordered out to enforce the collection of the tax.   I went to Warren, and, to avert the impending difficulty, was obliged to give my note for the tax, the amount of which was forty-three dollars and seventy-nine cents.   It is my desire that the governor will exempt me from paying taxes for my land to white people ; and also cause that the money I am now obliged to pay, may be refunded to me, as I am very poor.   The governor is the person who attends to the situation of the people, and I wish him to send a person to Alleghany, that I may inform him of the particulars of our situation, and he be authorized to instruct the white people in what manner to conduct themselves toward the Indians.

" The governor has told us that when any difficulties arose between the Indians and white people, he would attend to having them removed.   We are now in a trying situation, and I wish the governor to send a person, authorized to attend thereto, the forepart of the next summer, about the time that grass has grown big enough for pasture.

" The governor formerly requested me to pay attention to the Indians, and take care of them.   We are now arrived at a situation that I believe Indians cannot exist, unless the governor should comply with my request, and send a person authorized to treat between us and the white people, the approaching summer.   I have now no more to speak."

The appeal was not in vain.   An act was passed by the legislature of Pennsylvania, exonerating the chief from the tax, and two commissioners repaired to his village to explain the matter to him.   He met them at the court-house in Warren, a town of Pennsylvania situated at the junction of the Connewango Creek and the Alleghany, on which occasion he delivered the following speech,— excellent of its kind, and eminently characteristic of his race :—

BROTHERS : Yesterday was appointed for us all to meet here. The talk which the governor sent us pleased us very much.   I think that the Great Spirit is very much pleased that the white people have been induced so to assist the Indians as they have done, and that he is pleased also to see the great men of this state and of the United States so friendly to us.   We are much pleased with what has been done.

" The Great Spirit first made the world, and next the flying animals, and found all things good and prosperous.   He is immortal and everlasting. After finishing the flying animals, he came down on earth and there stood. Then he made different kinds of trees, and weeds of all sorts, and people of every kind. He made the spring and other seasons, and the weather suitable for planting. These he did make. But stills, to make whiskey to be given to Indians, he did not make. The Great Spirit bids me tell the white people not to give Indians this kind of liquor. When the Great Spirit had made the earth and its animals, he went into the great lakes, where he breathed as easily as any where else, and then made all the different kinds of fish. The Great Spirit looked back on all that he had made. The different kinds he made to be separate, and not to mix with and disturb each other. But the white people have broken his command by mixing their color with the Indians. The Indians have done better by not doing so. The Great Spirit wishes that all wars and fightings should cease.

" He next told us that there were three things for people to attend to. First, we ought to take care of our wives and children. Secondly, the white people ought to attend to their farms and cattle. Thirdly, the Great Spirit has given the bears and deers to the Indians. He is the cause of all things that exist, and it is very wicked to go against his will. The Great Spirit wishes me to inform the people that they should quit drinking intoxicating drink, as being the cause of diseases and death. He told us not to sell any more of our lands, for he never sold lands to any one. Some of us now keep the seventh day; but I wish to quit it, for the Great Spirit made it for others, but not for the Indians, who ought every day to attend to their business. He has ordered me to quit drinking any intoxicating drink, and not to lust after women but my own, and informs me that by doing so I should live the longer. He made known to me that it is very wicked to tell lies. Let no one suppose this I have said now is not true.

" I have now to thank the governor for what he has done. I have informed him what the Great Spirit has ordered me to cease from, and I wish the governor to inform others of what I have communicated. This is all I have at present to say."

If there are any farther memorials of the life of Cornplanter, they have escaped the researches of the author. The old chief appears to have again fallen back into entire seclusion, taking no part even in the politics of his people, which, owing to the conduct of Red-Jacket, and the dissensions concerning him, were not of the most quiet description, until the close of his earthly career. He died at his residence, on the 7th of March, 1836, at the age of one hundred years and upward. His last speech, at Warren court-house, discloses a curious combination in his mind of the history of the creation, and of the rudiments both of Indian and Christian theology. Whether, at the time of his death, he expected to go to the fair hunting grounds of his own people, or to the heaven of the Christian, is not known.

HENRY O'BAIL.

THE name of this chief, the son of Cornplanter, has been mentioned a few pages back, and also several times in the life of Red-Jacket. He was a boy of fine spirit and promise, and his father sent him to Philadelphia for the benefit of an English education, under the charge of the Quakers, who placed him in a suitable school, and directed his studies. A few anecdotes and traditions are related by way of illustrating his character.

He was not only received in good society in Philadelphia, but was caressed. On one occasion, being at a ball, while dancing with a beautiful girl, the jealousy of one of the young gentlemen present was excited, and he gave vent to his vexation by muttering the dislike he felt at seeing the young lady " dance with a d——d Indian." The quick ears of young Harry caught the sound, and after the figure was ended, having invited the angry swain to the head of the stairs, he thrust him out, and opposing his foot to his seat of honor, gave an impulse that sent him headlong down. " There !" said he ; " you may now boast that you have been kicked down stairs by a d——d Indian !"

Another story is told respecting him, of a more senti-

mental character ;—rather too sentimental, in fact, to be
in keeping with the usual stoicism of his race. "Harry," says the narrator, "had been too long the wild boy
of the mountains to be pleased with confinement, or
bear patiently his monotonous exercises. He wasted
and pined till he became pale and emaciated. Possessing not that spirit of reserve and laconic manner of
speech, so characteristic of the Indian, he was courte-
ous and kind,—exercising a suavity of manner peculiar
in the forest chieftain. ' My sister,' he would say emphatically, ' my sister is not here, and there is another
who is not with me.' He thirsted for the bright waters
of his native valley, and longed to breathe once more the
pure air of the Alleghanies. The crowded streets of
the city had no charms for him. He stayed but a few
months, and bursting from his confinement, bounded
back, with the alacrity of a wounded deer, to the green
mountain haunts of his boyhood, the sweet tones of his
sister, and the gentle cooings of his forest dove. The
following year, Mr. N——, a gentleman from Philadelphia, who had known the young chief there, came on
an errand of agency to our country, where he has since
resided. Having no acquaintance here, and feeling a
deep interest in the welfare of his young friend, he
penetrated through the dark wilds of Potter and
M'Kean, and soon found himself at the village of the
Cornplanter. Harry welcomed him cordially, presenting him to his father, his sister, and his friends,—
but there was a sadness visible in his countenance, a
quick restlessness in his movements, which betrayed
how deep were the workings within. Mr. N—— then
asked him for the gentle dove he had described to him,
in days gone by. 'She is gone;' said he,—and he led
him to her grave. Here Harry, after the custom of the
whites, had planted flowers; not the forget-me-not, nor

58

the rose, nor the myrtle, but pale spring violets, refreshing them with his tears, and breathing from this hallowed spot his invocations to the Great Spirit."*

The subsequent career of Henry O'Bail but ill accorded with such a gentle and pensive beginning. He
opposed his father's efforts for the moral and social improvement of his race, and even attached himself to the
adherents of his father's bitterest enemy and successful
rival, Red-Jacket,—becoming ultimately very dissolute
and intemperate. He was, nevertheless, a brave man,
and did good service in the Niagara campaign, during
the last war with England, under General Porter. He
was at one period a man of handsome property. Having squandered this, he removed from the Seneca reservation to Tonnewanta. Shortly afterward a tradesman to
whom he had contracted a debt, for which he had given
his note, meeting with him at a public house, took the
note from his pocket, and asked for his pay. Henry
taking the note into his hand and looking at it for a moment, inquired of the holder,—"This is a good note, is
it not?" "Why, certainly it is," replied the creditor.
"Then you had better keep it," coolly answered the
Indian, handing it back with all possible gravity. The
note was never collected, and Henry died not long afterward,—a miserable drunkard. Alas, for the poor Indian! His arrow is broken!

BLACK-CHIEF'S DAUGHTER.

THE proverbial stoicism of the Indians has been referred to in the preceding brief sketch of the young
Cornplanter, as casting a shade of doubt over the ro-
mantic incident furnished by the lady of Wellsborough,
connected with an affair of the heart, and the untimely

* MS. letter from Miss Jackson, of Wellsborough, (Pa.)

death of the object of his attachment. And yet these apparently moody sons of the forest are not always so insensible to the finer feelings of the common race of Adam, when acting by and for themselves, as most of the pale-faces suppose them to be. Mr. Washington Irving, in his prairie-rambles, has said, as other writers before and since have done, that the Indians, in their own circles, have their wits and their humorists, and indulge in their pleasantries, their jokes, brisk repartees and merrymakings, as well as the whites. Why, then, should they be thought insensible to the thrill of the tender passion, and incapable of feeling acutely the pangs of sorrow? The anecdote of Henry O'Bail and his betrothed woodland nymph, if true, illustrates one division of the interrogatory. A marked illustration of the other is afforded by the touching story of Black-Chief's Daughter.

Forty years ago, Black-Chief was Sachem of the clan of Senecas residing at Squawky-Hill, in the valley of the Genesee River. He was famous for his skill and bravery in war, and the pursuits of the chase, and withal endeared to his people by his amiable temper and generous qualities. After his death his clan honored with their esteem an only daughter of the chief, remarkable for her beauty and intelligence, and resembling her deceased father in native goodness of heart. Indeed, so highly was she regarded that by a formal decree in council, notwithstanding her extreme youth, she was clothed with the authority of a princess. The brightest fish from the waters, the sweetest flowers, and the richest and rarest fruits of the forest, and the proudest trophies of the hunt, were left, in reverence, at the door of her wigwam. Old men prayed daily to the Great Spirit that her years might be long in the land; for their hoary seer had assured them that during her lifetime the ancient glories of the Senecas would be in part restored.

But as with the white man, so with the Indian, it is
well that the future is a sealed book. A malignant fever which had nearly depopulated the flourishing village
of Connewaugus, extended its ravages to Squawky-Hill.
The strong man was laid low,—woman grew pale, and,
with the infant at her bosom, perished. The dog howled
over the festering carcass, and hunger, in alliance with
the fell distemper, filled the cup of misery to overflow-
ing. In vain every precaution was taken to avert the
blow from the head of their beloved princess. After the
panic had in a great measure abated, and signs of returning health became visible, the destroyer entered her
lodge, and amid wails of grief, and groans of despair,
proceeding from a hundred lips, her young heart was
stilled for ever.

When a distinguished individual expired, it was the
custom of the Senecas to deposite the remains in a simple
structure of unhewn logs, called " The Cabin of Death."
But such was their enthusiastic affection for the chief-
tainess, that they departed from this ancient rite by
erecting a high scaffold in a neighboring grove. After
adorning the body with beads, shells, feathers, and other
barbaric ornaments, they placed it in an upright posture
on the rude throne they had thus upreared. A drum,
formed of the untanned hide of a deer, drawn tensely
over a section of the hollowed trunk of a tree, cut to a
proper length, and beaten upon by a war-club, gave out
its dull and dismal note, while men, women and children, moved in a slow and solemn dance around the
dead.

To the Seneca towns of Tonnewanta, Connewaugus
and Caneadea fleet runners hastened with the melancholy tidings, and the principal men of those places accompanied them back to take part in the sorrowful ceremonies. Garlands of flowers, ears of corn and valu-

able furs were thrown in profusion at the feet of the lifeless object of their idolatry. By night, fires were lighted,
and watchmen were stationed to guard the hallowed
spot, and keep the gaunt wolf at a distance. And every
morning the solemn rites of the preceding day were
renewed. After a partial decomposition of the body
had taken place, it was removed and committed to the
earth with tears and loud lamentations.*

But these rites were not peculiar to the Senecas, or
to the Five Nations. The Chippewas, who pitch their
tents on the shores of Lake Superior, proudly called the
"Father of Waters," and other nations of the great
northwest, honor their dead with obsequies somewhat
similar. It has indeed been conjectured that the Chippewas derived their picturesque funeral observances
from the Iroquois, with whom they often met in conflict,
for they were enemies of old, notwithstanding the vast
wilderness that separated their hunting-grounds. Nade-
wa-we-gu-nung, in Michigan, nine hundred miles from
the great council fire at Onondaga, was the scene of a
terrific battle between them "long time ago." On the
death of a sachem, or other person of note, the Chippewas, after dressing the body in the vestments of the living, and by the aid of colors extracted from plants and
clay having given a life-like appearance to the countenance, deposite the relics on two cross-pieces nailed or
tied with thongs to four posts set firmly in the ground.
With pious veneration they plant near the poles or posts
the gadding wild-hop, or the flaunting woodbine, in order that the revolting process of decay may be rendered
less offensive by the refreshing verdure of vegetable
beauty, and in a short time the corse is thickly em-

---

* This little narrative was written down from the lips of Mrs. Hosmer, of
Avon, who, reared as it were amidst the Senecas, was acquainted with the facts,
and, I believe, with parties.

bowered with leaves and flowers. There is something
strikingly poetical in these simple rites of the untutored
savage. While the enlightened pale-face yields to the
sunless custody of the tomb the beautiful and brave,
his wild brother of the woods mourns over the loved
and the lost with a lasting sorrow, and deems it hard to
cast into the cold embrace of the earth

> " Countenances benign,—and forms that walked
> But yesterday so stately o'er the earth."*

Glowing are the histories of departed monarchs lying
in gilded pomp, while in the crowns that rounded their
cold temples

> ———" Kept Death his court,
> Scoffing their state, and grinning at their pomp,"—

—of Inez de Castro, disinterred and arrayed in the glittering trappings of royalty ;—but where is the heart that
would not be less touched by those descriptions of the
learned narrators than by the unstudied recital of the
simple funereal honors paid by the Senecas to the beloved
daughter of Black-Chief?

* See Heckewelder's description of Indian funerals, Transactions of Philadelphia Philosophical Society, for much interesting matter upon this subject. Also,
Lewis and Clarke's Expedition. The Indians suppose that when the soul is
separated from the body, it preserves the same inclinations which it had when
both were united. Hence they bury the implements of war and the chase with
their bodies, and bring provisions to the grave. Some of the Indian nations believe in the transmigration of souls,—especially of the souls of those who die
young, and who therefore have the privilege of commencing a second life, because they enjoyed so little of the first. Hence children are buried along the
highways, that the women, as they pass, may receive their souls. From this
idea of their remaining with the body arises the duty of placing food upon their
graves; and mothers have been seen to draw from their bosoms that nourishment
which those little creatures loved when alive, and shed it upon the earth which
covered their remains.—*Charlevoix.*—*Dr. Jarvis's Historical Discourse.*

APPENDIX.

APPENDIX.

[A.]

THE deputation sent from the Six Nations as messengers of peace, to the hostile Indians at the Miami of the lakes, in the autumn of 1792, returned in November. General Chapin, the agent of the Six Nations, was absent at the seat of government when they returned, and the council to receive their report was called by his son, Israel Chapin, Jun. It was held at Buffalo Creek, on the 16th of November, and was attended by Major Littlehales in behalf of Governor Simcoe, then commanding in Upper Canada. The following is the report of the deputation, as rendered into English by Mr. Parish, the interpreter.

BUFFALO CREEK, *November* 16, 1792.

BROTHERS,—PEOPLE OF THE UNITED STATES, AND KING'S PEOPLE, *take notice !*—Last winter the President took us by the hand, and led us to the council fire, at Philadelphia ; there they made known to us their friendship, and requested us to proceed to the westward, and to use our influence to make peace with the hostile Indians. We went accordingly, and made known to them our agreement.

When we returned from Philadelphia to Buffalo Creek, the chiefs that remained at home on their seats, were well pleased with what we had done at Philadelphia ; and after we had determined to proceed on our journey, some of our chiefs were detained on account of sickness.

BROTHERS,—PEOPLE OF THE UNITED STATES AND KING'S PEOPLE :—After we arrived at the westward, we met with an agreeable reception ; they informed us we were their oldest brothers, and appeared as the sun risen on them, as they always looked to them for advice.

It is now four years since we have heard your voices, and should be happy now to hear what you have to relate to us.

The Six Nations then requested of the western Indians what they had to relate to them, as they kindled the council fire.

The WESTERN INDIANS replied : About four years since, your voices came to us, desiring us to combine ourselves together, as we were the oldest people of this island, and all of one color, that our minds may be one.

59

This, they informed us, they had attended to, and exhibited a large bunch of wampum, to prove the same, from each nation.

To confirm it still further, they informed us we sent them a pipe, which passed through all the nations at the west and southward ; all smoked out of it, both women and children ; and as this pipe has been through the nations, and all smoked out of it, they returned it to us, and bid us to smoke out of it ourselves.

BROTHERS : Listen once to your eldest brothers. Our forefathers have handed down to us, that we are one people, of one color, on this island, and ought to be of one mind, and had made our minds strong, and had become as one people in peace and friendship.

This being done, our chiefs agreed to hand it down to future posterity, and the same combination to continue down to them.

The nation called the Unions, took a brand from our fire and kindled it, and became a people with us ; then we considered ourselves as one people, combined together.

And now there is a white people on this island, who are watching our conduct ; but let us attend to our own concerns, and brighten the chain of friendship with our nations ; and as our minds are one, let us consider future posterity and not consider those young warriors who are in the prime of life, and so much engaged in the pursuit of land, &c., which is the cause of so much difficulty at present.

BROTHERS : Consider your country, which is good, and conduct yourselves in such a manner as to keep it to yourselves and posterity.

Now, BROTHERS : You present us the pipe,—you say your eldest brothers sent you ; you say your head chiefs all smoked out of it, and returning it to us again, all took it and smoked out of it ourselves, in friendship. Now, as we are thus combined together, we are able to lift a heavy burden.

THE SHAWANEE NATION said :--OUR ELDEST BROTHERS : We have heard what you have related,—we have heard it with attention ; we consider it as if you delivered it from the outside of your lips ; although you consider us your younger brothers, your seats are not at such a distance but what we can see your conduct plainly ; these are the reasons why we consider you to speak from the outside of your lips ; for whenever you hear the voice of the United States, you immediately take your packs and attend our councils.

We see plainly folded under your arm the voice of the United States,—wish you to unfold it to us, that we may see it freely and consult on it.—[Speaking on a string of wampum of three strings, throwing it across the fire to us, instead of handing it in a friendly manner.]

[Then we proceeded to relate the instructions of congress, which is too tedious to relate, and which they already know ; but when we first related it we failed for interpreters, so that they had not a proper idea of it ; they appeared to be very much ruffled in their minds, and adjourned the counsel to the next day ; then it was interpreted properly to them, and they appeared easy in their minds.]

ELDEST BROTHERS : You desire us to consider our country and property ; we will accept of your advice, and proceed accordingly.

THE SIX NATIONS said :—Let us look back to the time of white people coming into this country ; they very soon began to traffic for land.

Soon after, Sir William Johnson was sent as an agent from the king, and he began to purchase at the treaty at Fort Stanwix, and purchased all east of the river Ohio.

A few years after this purchase, the people of the States and the king's people broke apart, and we being persuaded to take the king's part, became very bad for us. After a few years, the king was beat ; then the States took possession of all the land the English formerly took from the French.

You tell us, we come with the voice of the United States ; we do, together with the advice of the king. He tells us not to throw our minds on either side, but to listen to reason, &c., and remain a people confederated.

THE SHAWANEE NATION,—Now ELDEST BROTHERS : You come to us with your opinion, and the voice of the United States. It is your mind to put an end to all hostilities. Brothers : now, we will relate what took place last fall in our country. General Washington sent an army into our country, which fell into our hands; their orders were thus,—to proceed into our country as far as the Miami towns, to the Glaize ; thence to Detroit, but not to molest the king's people, and if the army should meet any people that appeared friendly, to leave them behind their backs, without harm.

The President of the United States must well know why the blood is so deep in our paths. We have been informed he has sent messengers of peace on these bloody roads, who fell on the way. And now, as he knows that road to be bloody, no communication can take place through that bloody way, as there is a path through the Six Nations' country, which is smooth and easy. If he wants to send the voice of peace, it must pass through this road.

ELDEST BROTHERS : We have been informed the President of the United States thinks himself the greatest man on this island. We had this country long in peace before we saw any person of a white skin ; we consider the people of a white skin the younger.

BROTHERS : You inform us it is the wish of the white people to hold council with us, General Washington being the head man ; we will consent to treat with them ; we desire you, our older brothers, to inform General Washington we will treat with him, at the Rapids of Miami, next spring, or at the time when the leaves are fully out.

We consider ourselves still the proper owners of some land on the east side of the Ohio.

But we will deliver up that, for money that has been paid to some individuals, for land on the west side of the River Ohio.

BROTHERS : You have have given us a dish, and one spoon, desiring the whole combination to eat with them ; we accept of them, and shall do accordingly.

We are now about to complete the business you came on. When you return you will make known to the President what we have done ; it may be he will not consent to what we have proposed ; and if he will not, we must call on you to assist in the heavy burden that will lie on us. We have opened a path, and pointed out a way, and, if he will not walk in it, we must have your assistance.

Now, OUR ELDEST BROTHERS : When the President came to you, he took you aside to hear what he had to say. He desired you to come to us and deliver the messages ; you have delivered them, and we desire you to deliver the messages we have given you to deliver to him, and desire him to send a message back what he will do concerning what we have done and concluded on ; to forward it to you, and you to us. We will lay the bloody tomahawk aside until we hear from the President of the United States, and when this message comes to us, we will send it to all the different nations. (Speaking on three strings of wampum.)

Speech from the Six Nations to the President.

You sent us on the westward with a message of peace to the hostile Indians.

We proceeded accordingly to your directions, and was protected, going and coming, by the Great Spirit. We give thanks to the Great Spirit that we have all returned safe to our seats.

While we were at the westward we exerted ourselves to bring about peace. The fatigues we underwent are not small. Now, it is our desire for your people on the Ohio to lay down their arms, or otherwise it is all in vain what we have done.

Now, if you wish for peace, you must make every exertion, and proceed through this path we have directed for you. If peace does not take place the fault must arise from your people.

We now desire you, Brothers, to send forward agents, who are men of honesty, not proud land-jobbers, but men who love and desire peace. Also, desire they may be accompanied by some Friend or Quaker to attend the council.

We wish you to exert yourselves to forward the message to the western Indians as soon as possible ; and we are taken by the hand, and have agreed, next spring, to attend the council at the Rapids of Miami, when we shall hear all that takes place there.

Hostile Indians to Governor Simcoe.

Brother : We have been informed the late governor is a good man ; we desire that you will take the governor by the hand and lead him to the council next spring. Exert yourselves to get him up, that he may not be backward ; that he may sit side and side with the Americans at the time of the council. And when you take him by the hand, desire him to furnish us with provisions necessary for the treaty.

Six Nations to the Governor.

Brother : Now, we have laid all our proceedings before you, which took place at the westward. You have heard the request of your western brothers, therefore wish you to exert yourself to grant their requests.

You informed us to listen to the voice of peace, wherever we might hear it. Now we hear the voice of peace ; we call on you for assistance, that we may obtain peace through this island.

Brother : We now sit here together ; you are the man who represents the United States ; we have discerned that too great a degree of pride has subsisted between the two governments ; we desire that it may be laid aside.

When the agents from the United States come forward to the council, we desire they may bring forward all the records, plans, maps, and documents, that any way respect the lands purchased from the Indians.

Fish-Carrier's Speech.

Desiring this degree of pride, which has heretofore existed, may be done away, and that each government may mutually consent and agree on terms of peace.

Cornplanter's Speech.

He informs, that he has always attended treaties that have been held, and has always wished for peace, and has done all in his power for peace ; that he has not advised any hostilities to commence on either side, and now wishes each government to lay aside all pride and preju- dice and to use their endeavors for peace.

After the council was over, Major Littlehales, who represented Governor Simcoe on that occasion, answered the Indians as follows :—

BROTHERS : I shall lay before the governor your requests ; and respecting his furnishing you with provisions, &c., I doubt not but he will do it agreeable to your wishes. And also to procure all records, plans, and documents, which shall be thought necessary, and to do every thing in his power to bring about a peace, so interesting to the United States, as well as to the British government.

[B.]

THE PRESQUE ISLE QUESTION.

At a council of the Six Nations, held at Buffalo Creek, on the 18th of June, 1794, Captain O'Bail (Cornplanter) spoke as follows in behalf of the Indians :—

BROTHER : We are thankful that you have attended to the call of the Six Nations, and that you have been preserved by the Great Spirit, &c.

BROTHER : (Addressed to the President) I have for a long time aimed at the good of both parties,—I have paid you different compli- ments, as that of brother and father, and now I call you friend. We were pleased when we heard that you were appointed to have the chief command of the United States.

BROTHER : The Great Spirit has so ordered, that every nation shall have some one to be at their head—you are to look over your people, and settle all difficulties—and we, the Six Nations, expect that you will not be unmindful of us, but see that we have justice done us, as well as your own people.

BROTHER : We, the Six Nations, now call upon you ; we pay no attention to what has heretofore been done by congress ; their pro- ceedings we consider as unjust. We wish for nothing but justice, and hope that will take place.

BROTHER : You know our demands—we ask but for a small piece of land, and we trust as you are a great man, you can easily grant our request.

BROTHER : You wish to be a free people in this country, who have come from the other side of the water, and why should not we, whose forefathers have lived and died here, and always had possession of the country.

BROTHER : We, the Six Nations, have determined on the boundary we want established, and it is the warriors who now speak.

BROTHER : You have the map on which the boundaries are marked out which we want established.

BROTHER : We want room for our children. It will be hard for them not to have a country to live in after that we are gone.

BROTHER : It is not because that we are afraid of dying that we have been so long trying to bring about a peace. We now call upon you for an answer, as congress and their commissioners have oftentimes deceived us, and if these difficulties are not removed, the consequences will be bad.

This speech was delivered with eight strings of black and white wampum.

BROTHER : We have opened this fire upon two different kinds of business—we wish you to listen to them with attention.

BROTHER : We are in distress—a number of our warriors are missing, and we know not what has become of them, but suppose that they have been killed by the Americans.

BROTHER : Last fall an Indian chief by the name of Big-Tree, left this country and went to the American army in a friendly manner, and we have since been informed that he was killed by them.

BROTHER : The other day a very unfortunate circumstance happened. One of our nephews (of the Delaware nation,) was killed at Venango, by a party of warriors who were going to Presque Isle, without giving us any notice whatever.

BROTHER : You are sensible this must be very hard, to have a man killed in time of peace—one who was sitting easy and peaceable on his seat—you certainly would complain if we were to treat your people in the same manner.

BROTHER : It has been customary, when one person has killed another, that those who have done the injury go to the injured party and make satisfaction.

BROTHER : We told you that we had two pieces of business to attend to,—we hope that you will pay attention to them both.

BROTHER : The establishing a garrison at Presque Isle may occasion many accidents, as the southern Indians may do injury, and we may be blamed without a cause.

This speech was delivered with ten strings of black wampum.

Captain O'Bail then addressed himself to Captain Chapin :—

BROTHER : When we sent for you, it was because we placed great dependence upon you,—we hoped that you would not fail of doing every thing in your power to assist us.

BROTHER : We now expect that you will exert yourself in removing those people off of our lands. We know very well what they have come on for, and we wish them pushed back.

BROTHER : We now wish that you and Mr. Johnson would go together and remove those people back over the line which we have marked out upon the map.

BROTHER: If these people remove off immediately we shall consider them as our friends,—if not, we shall consider them as no friends.

BROTHER :—We expect that you and Mr. Johnson will go together on this business, and we shall send ten warriors to attend you ; and we shall expect that you will bring us word when you return.

This speech was delivered with six strings of black and white wampum.

General Chapin's answer to the speech delivered by Captain O'Bail :—

BROTHERS : I have heard the speeches which you have delivered with great attention, and have thought seriously on what you have communicated to me. You have requested me to go to Presque Isle, —as I wish to do every thing in my power, both for the United States and the Indians, I shall comply with your request.

BROTHERS : I can do no more to those people than to give them my advice. It is not in my power to drive them off.

BROTHERS : You must be sensible that I am obliged to look to the interests both of the United States and the Indians, and consider myself accountable to both for whatever I do ; and you may depend that when I return, I will give you a just account of whatever takes place.

BROTHERS :—This business is of a serious nature, and is really a matter of importance to both parties. You may rest assured that the President is your friend, and that he will pay attention to the business which you have laid before him.

BROTHERS : You observed that you would send ten warriors to attend me. I must also request that you would send two of your chiefs.

BROTHERS: The business which you desire me to do, is what I had little thought of. I am unprepared for the journey ; however, as I have informed you that I would go, I shall set out immediately.

BROTHERS : The speeches which you have delivered for the President, shall be sent on as soon as is convenient, and you may shortly expect to receive an answer.

General Chapin to the Secretary of War :—

Canandaigua, July 10, 1794.

DEAR SIR,—The evening before I returned my son arrived in this place. He brought letters from the Secretary of War, which mention nothing to counteract any of our proceedings while I was at the westward ; but rather in favor than otherwise.

I sent Parish immediately to Philadelphia with despatches, after my return, including the whole of our proceedings while at Buffalo Creek, and Presque Isle, &c. ; and from every information by my son I am in hopes and believe the dispositions of the President and of General Knox are such as will render satisfaction to the Six Nations.

It is a fact that the President was not concerned in the business of ordering this party to Presque Isle, but so far from it, (that after the Governor of Pennsylvania had ordered the party to march to Presque Isle,) for fear of ill consequences, the President sent them counter orders to stop and remain at Le Bœuf. Matters appear more favorable with regard to war between Great Britain and America. They have ceased in some measure to take our vessels in the West

Indies, and it is to be hoped that the present negotiation with Mr. Jay, will be the means of settling the difficulties subsisting between both parties.

As soon as Parish returns I shall communicate the answer,—as soon as possible. Yours, &c.,

ISRAEL CHAPIN.

[C.]

THE CANANDAIGUA TREATY.

COLONEL PICKERING TO CAPTAIN BRANT.

Canandaigua, November 20th, 1794.

SIR : When I wrote you on the 17th, I had not time to express any opinion relative to the Mohawk nation, as implicated in the present treaty. As one of the Six Nations, I did not think it proper to name it as not included in the treaty ; nor to omit it by enumerating the other five. For general concerns, I consider the whole six as forming one confederate nation.

The great object of this treaty (like almost all other Indian treaties) was to remove complaints respecting lands. The particular tract in question I supposed especially concerned the Senecas ; but it was natural that an object so important to one, should interest the whole. By the terms of the present treaty, the complaints which were the immediate occasion of it have been removed ; and, as I observed in my former letter, all appeared to be satisfied; and many individual chiefs, in strong terms, expressed their satisfaction. So, I trust, no heart burnings for past transactions will be felt, nor reproaches used, in future.

It is the nature of the present settlement which has led me to contemplate the case of the Mohawk nation.

"This settlement," said one of the chiefs to me, " appears like a great light to us." And to me it seems like a new era. With much pleasure, therefore, I should see presented to that nation, a token for participating in the general satisfaction which this treaty has produced. The goods in my power to dispose of have been distributed ; and to convey a share of them to your people would have been impracticable ; and therefore I abandoned the idea of it ; but if it should not meet your approbation, I persuade myself that an equivalent in money would cheerfully be presented. On this subject I shall be happy to see your mind expressed in a letter to General Chapin, (whom I have consulted on this occasion,) or to me. In the meantime a copy of this letter will be given to the Secretary of War, for the President's information.

The Onondagas and Cayugas, residing at Grand River, who were not present to receive a part of the goods given at this treaty, may doubtless be also comprehended in providing a gratuity on the present general settlement with the Six Nations. Before I closed my letter of the 7th, I intended to give you a sketch of the terms of the treaty ; but a throng being about me, and your nephew waiting, it was omitted. By former treaties the Six Nations relinquished all their lands west of a line running due south from the mouth of Buffalo Creek. Now I have given up the claim of the United States to a large tract of land lying between this due south line and the meridian which makes the eastern boundary of the triangular piece of land which the United States sold to Pennsylvania. The tract now relinquished probably contains four times as much land as that triangle, and was peculiarly important to the Seneca nation, as several hundred of their nation were dwelling on it.

I have also relinquished the United States' claim to the strip of land four miles wide, including the carrying path from Lake Ontario to Lake Erie, along the Niagara strait, except that part of it which, in a treaty held thirty years ago with Sir William Johnson, the Seneca nation ceded to the King of Great Britain, to whose right therein I considered the United States as succeeding. Or, as the chiefs expressed it, "that piece became ours (the United States) by the right of war." Its eastern boundary is a line from Johnson's Landing to Stedman's Creek, and thence to Niagara Straits, and the strait itself bounds it on the west and southwest. Besides these relinquishments, I have stipulated a perpetual annuity of four thousand five hundred dollars, to be applied to the benefit of those of the Six Nations, and their Indian friends and associates, residing among and united with them, who do or shall reside within the boundaries of the United States; for the United States do not mean to interfere, by any permanent arrangements, with nations elsewhere resident. The terms I have stipulated, will, I trust, be approved by the President and Senate, and then the treaty will be obligatory on both sides.

I am, Sir, &c.,
(Signed) TIMO. PICKERING.

P. S. My letter of the 7th was delivered to the care of Henry Young Brant, who I understood was your nephew. In that I enclosed a copy of my speech relative to the appearance of a British agent at a council fire kindled by the United States.

Capt. Jos. BRANT.

CAPTAIN BRANT TO COLONEL PICKERING.

Niagara, 30th December, 1794.

SIR: Your letters of the 17th and 20th November, '94, from Kanandaigua, I have now before me, and I have to say, that at all our meetings during the whole of last summer, our thoughts were solely bent on fixing a boundary line between the confederate Indians and the United States, so as that peace might be established on a solid basis, for which reason we pointed out the line we did, well knowing the justness of it, and that it would be ratified by the whole Indian confederacy.

As an individual I much regret to find that the boundary so pointed out has now been abandoned, the establishment of which, I am well convinced, would have been the means of bringing about a lasting and permanent peace. This object, so earnestly to be desired, has ever made me exert every nerve, wishing for nothing more than mutual justice. This line, you will recollect, was offered to Governor St. Clair at Muskingum, and notwithstanding the two successful campaigns of the Indians, after this I still adhered to the same, and still do. This, I hope, will satisfy you that my wish ever was for peace. The offer was rejected by Mr. St. Clair, and what the consequences have been you well know. I should be sorry if your endeavors would be crowned with no better success, as your exertions I hope are not influenced by similar motives with his. You must also recollect that I differed even with my friends respecting this boundary, and to the last two messages you then received, my name was to neither of them, because I thought them too unreasonable. This made me take more pains and trouble to bring the Indians and you to an understanding, than I was under any obligations to do, otherwise than humanity dictated to me, having nothing but our mutual interests in view, and as to politics I study them not. My principle is founded on justice, and justice is all I wish for, and never shall I exert myself in behalf of any nation or nations, let their opinion of me be what it will, unless I plainly see they are just and sincere in their pursuits, doing what in every respect to justice may belong. When I perceive such are the sentiments of a people, no endeavors shall be wanting on my part to bring neighbors to a good understanding.

I must again repeat that I am extremely sorry this boundary, so long since pointed out, should have been abandoned,—it being an object of such magnitude, and which much depends on the whole Indian confederacy being interested. I should therefore have supposed it would have been more for mutual interests and would have had a better effect, to have dealt upon a larger scale than within the small compass of the Five Nations, the meeting being intended solely to talk over the business of the boundary, and then to have acquainted the whole confederacy with what had passed, so that something final could have been determined on, as all that part of the country is a common to the whole of us.

You say on your part every thing has been openly and fairly explained, and that you shall be disappointed if the chiefs do not acknowledge your candor. I can, for my own part, form no opinion, whether it is so or not, being perfectly ignorant of what has passed, but ever look upon it that business fairly transacted should be adhered to as sacred.

And that you are still ready to make peace with the western nations,—this has made me say much about the boundary line, in order that peace and friendship might be established between you. This obliges me to say they ought to have been included in this treaty, and to have been consulted with, as well as those who were there, they being equally interested with the Six Nations in this line. *As to the British,* they are an *independent nation,* as well as the United States and the Indian nations, and of course they act for *themselves,* as well as other white nations do.

My mentioning in my letter to you, that I was sorry Mr. Johnson was looked upon as a spy, was because I knew the Five Nations so often erred in their transactions with the white people,—it being myself in person, from the wish of the Indians, that requested Mr. Johnson should go to the treaty ;—in consequence of which request he was permitted. I was well aware at the same time of the reception he would meet with, as we are an independent people. I ever thought our councils should be private ; but must at the same time say, we have an undoubted right to admit at our councils whom we please.

Of course the United States have it optional whether they will treat or not with any nation or nations, where foreign agents are present.

You seem to think, in your letter of the 20th, that the Senecas are the nation most concerned in the tracts in question, agreeable to the lines you point out. At the different treaties held since the year '83, I allow, the Senecas from their proceedings seemed to be the only nation concerned in that country, although the whole Five Nations have an equal right one with the other, the country having been obtained by their joint exertions in war with a powerful nation, formerly living southward of Buffalo Creek, called Eries, and another nation then living at Tioga Point, so that by our successes all the country between that and the Mississippi, became the joint property of the Five Nations,—all other nations now inhabiting this great tract of country were allowed to settle by the Five Nations.

This I hope will convince you that the Mohawks have an equal claim, and right to receive in proportion, with the others of the Five Nations. But as I am ignorant of the transaction,—knowing nothing of what has passed, and what was the result of the treaty,—must, therefore, defer saying any thing farther on the subject until I know the particulars, which I hope will be ere long. As to the others of the Five Nations residing on the Grand River, they must answer for themselves. I am not so particular in that as I might be, seeing no great necessity for it,—as I hope to see General Chapin ere long.

In reading the speech you have sent me, I perceive that you say we requested you might be sent to kindle the council fire, &c. This I knew to be a mistake. In our speech to General Chapin, we wished the President of the United States to send a commissioner to our fireplace at Buffalo Creek, (your name being mentioned,) not that you was to come and kindle a council fire elsewhere—and that you requested our assistance to bring about a peace, &c. You did, and every thing has been done by us faithfully and sincerely, by pointing out the medicine that would accomplish it, your relinquishing part of your claims in the Indian country.

You also say that I told General Chapin at Winny's that it was the British prevented the treaty taking place. I said so then, and still do. What enabled me to say so, was the gentleman belonging to the Indian department in that quarter, interfering in the business. Had the line, as pointed out by us been accepted of by the United States, their interference could not have prevented peace then taking place, as the five nations had pledged themselves to see it ratified.

As to the business of the white nations, I perceive it at present to be a lottery—which will be uppermost cannot be known until drawn— the most powerful no doubt will succeed; but let who will be successful, our situation is the same, as we still have whites to deal with whose aims are generally similar.

You mention the people of *France* took the Indian method, all their warriors turning out. The Indian warriors are always ready to turn out in defence of their just rights,—but Indian warriors would not be ready to *butcher* in an *inhuman, shocking* manner, their *king, queen, nobles and others.* This is acting worse than what is called savage. The Indians are not entirely destitute of humanity—but from every appearance it has fled from *France.* I must therefore say the *French* have not acted as Indians do.

You likewise mention that you told the deputies from the westward who met you at this place, that though you were willing to run a new line, yet it was impossible to make the Ohio the boundary. This, I believe is a mistake, as the word Ohio was never mentioned at that time.

You may now perceive that I do not swerve from any expressions I have made use of. I know the necessity for being candid, especially at this critical juncture, and still earnestly hope that peace may be established without further bloodshed, and that friendship may reign between the people of the United States and the Indian nations. This, be assured, is the sincere wish of, Sir,

Your most obedient humble servant,

TIMOTHY PICKERING, ESQ.			JOS. BRANT.

[D.]

CAPTAIN BRANT TO CAPTAIN CHAPIN.

" Niagara, 21st of May, 1803.

" DEAR SIR,—

" Your friendly letter by Aaron, I have the felicity of acknowledging, and ought to have answered it long ere this. But I trust you'll excuse me for this neglect,—particularly so, when I assure you of my high esteem for you. I trust you'll continue your friendly correspondence, as the love I bear you is sincere, and as there was a degree of confidence and friendship that subsisted between your worthy and much to be lamented father and myself. This I look upon, (exclusive of our personal friendship and acquaintance,) to be a sufficient reason for continuing our mutual friendship toward each other. Be assured nothing on my part shall be wanting to keep this flame of friendship alive.

" I certainly regretted to hear of your removal from office, but trust it will not be long before you again fill it,—an office in which you have certainly done credit to yourself, and justice to those Indians over whom you presided. To you did they look up as their friend and patron. Your removal is one of the natural changes incidental to republican governments. When a person is elevated to a high office, it is expected from him, and it is but natural to suppose that he will provide for his friends, at the expense of others,—perhaps more honorable than the favorite to be provided for. I am happy that you bear your dismissal with manly, virtuous, and patriotic fortitude. This surely must redound to your honor, and raise you even in the estimation of the person who dismissed you.

" I hope before long to have the pleasure of seeing you personally, and condoling with you for your loss, if you look upon it as such. In all revolutions, some changes for political reasons will take place,— perhaps through whim, caprice, or prejudice.

" I will thank you to pay attention to your friend Oghgwage-Joseph, who is the bearer of this, and am, dear sir,

" Your friend and well-wisher,
" JOSEPH BRANT."

" CAPTAIN ISRAEL CHAPIN."

[E.]

GENERAL PORTER TO THE AUTHOR.

Niagara Falls, Oct. 25, 1840.

DEAR SIR :—I have received your favor of the 9th ultimo, enclosing a number of the manuscript sheets of your intended biography of Red-Jacket, containing a notice of the repulse of a detachment of British troops under the command of Colonel Bishop, at Black Rock, in July, 1813,—being the first occasion on which our Indians were engaged in battle as auxiliaries of the Americans ; and embracing also an account of the march and operations of the American army under General Brown, from the time of their entering Canada, on the 3d of July, 1814, until shortly after the battle of Chippewa, when the Indians took leave of us for their respective homes ; and asking for such additions, corrections and remarks as the subject may suggest.

While I will cheerfully comply with your request as regards the affair at Black Rock, I will not disguise the satisfaction which the receipt of your communication has given me, in so far as it affords me an opportunity of doing an act of justice, too long withheld from the Indians and volunteers engaged in the battle of Chippewa ; by presenting, with your permission, and in a shape and connexion where it will be sure to meet extensively the public eye, a minute account, (so far at least as the Indians and volunteers were concerned,) of the various movements and incidents of that day ; and thus rescuing their characters from the charge of cowardice, preferred against them for their conduct on that occasion.

It is to be regretted that we have no fair, intelligent and connected history of the interesting campaign of 1814, on the Niagara frontier, prepared by some one whose knowledge of the views and plans of those who conducted it, as well as of its incidents, gives him a right to be heard. But of those best qualified to perform the task, many have doubtless been deterred by considerations of delicacy in the narration of events in which they had a deep personal interest or agency ; and thus involving the necessity either of becoming their own panegyrists, or of suppressing important facts,—the preservation of which is due to the integrity and truth of history.

Many, if not most of these, have already left the stage of life, and the only hope of preserving the recollection of many interesting events of that period, rests upon the occasional and voluntary contributions of those who remain. I observe, with much satisfaction, that our friend, Major Douglass, has been employed in delivering, in your city, a course of lectures on the subject of the "Niagara Campaign." He was, if I mistake not, personally engaged in several of the principal battles of that year ; and, although then young, and fresh from West Point, he was an intelligent and active officer, and will doubtless gratify the public expectations with many interesting reminiscences.

Will it, then, my dear sir, be presuming too much to offer for your acceptance the accompanying narrative of the operations of the army during the few days to which it extends, and embracing the battle of Chippewa, as a substitute for the sheets you sent me ? In exchange for the loss of style and spirit in its composition, I can only promise a more minute detail, and probably somewhat greater accuracy in the relation of facts. If the story should appear to be a long one, I hope that this defect will not be ascribed wholly to the proverbial garrulity of an old soldier, but to the impossibility of doing justice to the several parties engaged in that severe conflict, without a full knowledge of its complicated incidents. The whole history of this battle, as it has appeared in most of our publications on the subject, may be comprehended in two simple propositions :—the one, that our volunteers and Indians, when met and attacked on that day, by the regular columns of the British army, retreated and were pursued with great precipitation. The other, that these same British columns were, immediately thereafter, met and beaten by our regular troops, and obliged in their turn, to retreat with equal precipitation.

Now, both these propositions are literally true : but whether the inferences that have been drawn from them are just, can only be decided by reference to the whole operations of the day, and these it has been my purpose to detail. I have however introduced some circumstances that were not strictly necessary to an exposition of the merits of the battle, merely because I thought they would be interesting to readers of the present day.

I remain, dear Sir, very truly and respectfully, yours,

WILLIAM L. STONE, ESQ. P. B. PORTER.

[F.]

THE INDIAN TREATIES.

The following are the leading provisions of these treaties as agreed upon in council on the Indian reservation, January, 1838. We presume they have been ratified essentially as they were originally made. The government gives the New-York Indians 1,824,000 acres of land, west of Missouri, being 320 acres for each person, to be held in fee simple by patent from the President, which is never to be included in any state. The Indians are to have the right of holding in severalty, under such regulations as they may prescribe, and are to enjoy their own form of government, subject only to the laws of Congress.—They are to be secured in their new possessions, and if aggressions are committed upon them, and redress cannot be obtained of the aggressor, then the government is to make good the loss. It is to remove them and subsist them for one year. It is also to erect for them council-houses, churches, school-houses, a saw and grist-mill, gunsmiths' and blacksmiths' shops ; find coal, iron and steel ; and pay teachers, millers, blacksmiths and a gunsmith for ten years, and as much longer as the President may deem proper.

Fifty thousand dollars are set apart to be invested to support a high school, or college, the teachers of which are to be Indians, if those of suitable qualifications can be found. Twenty thousand dollars are set apart to make erections and enclosures for poor people, after their arrival west.

Ten thousand dollars a year, for five years, are to be paid them in domestic animals, farming utensils, spinning wheels and looms, and to support persons to teach them the use of the same.

It is farther provided, that those who wish to remove in their own conveyances, can do so, and be paid what it costs the government to remove others, and a physician is to accompany each party of emigrants, if they desire it.

The only cession of land to the government, is of the Green Bay tract, from which is expected a reservation now occupied by the Oneidas. Those who do not remove to the new country in five years, or such time as the President may appoint, forfeit their right to the country set apart for them. The Senecas, Cayugas, Tuscaroras, and the Onondagas, residing on the Seneca reservations, agree to remove in five years, and a portion of the Oneidas are to do so, as soon as the Governor of New-York will purchase their lands.

Several sums of money are to be paid to several nations and individuals, to remunerate them for losses and services, which it is supposed the United States ought to pay. There are also several separate provisions for each tribe, and distinct branches of a tribe.

A separate treaty was also made in January, 1838, with the Senecas and Tuscaroras, for the purchase of their lands, (except one reservation conveyed by the latter to the United States in trust,) by the representatives of the state of Massachusetts with the assent of a superintendent from that state. The consideration money for the sale of the Seneca reservation is to be paid to the United States, and be held in trust for the nation. One hundred thousand dollars of which is to be invested for the use of the nation ; and the balance ($102,000) is to be distributed among the owners of the improvements on the reservation.

The government agrees to have one of its agents reside among the Indians at their new homes, and to pay them their annuities there.

These are the leading provisions.

By this treaty the Tuscaroras cede to the Ogden Company, who have purchased the pre-emptive right 1920 acres ; to the United States about 5000 acres, of which the Indians owned the fee, and which is to be sold by the United States, and the nett proceeds paid to the Indians.

The Senecas cede to the pre-emptive owners about 115,000 acres, all lying in the western part of this state,—upwards of 50,000 of which is the reservation near this city.

The other reservations are, one at Tonnawanda, one at Cattaraugus, and one at Alleghany.

The tract which the Indians obtain, lies directly west of, and adjoining the State of Missouri, being 27 miles wide and about 106 deep. It is watered by the little Osage, Marmaton, Neosho, and branches of the two Verdigris and Turkey-foot rivers.—These are all clear rapid streams, abounding in fish. The country is healthy and fertile, with sufficient timber along the borders of the rivers for all practical uses. Besides this, on the tract are found coal, fine stone quarries, and, in the immediate vicinity, salt in abundance.

Such was an outline of the treaty as at first concluded in 1838. While under discussion in the Senate of the United States, it was amended as follows :—The special provisions for the erection of houses, churches, mills, shops, providing various utensils, coal, iron, steel, &c. &c., it was thought might open the door to fraud and speculation, and in lieu thereof, after a careful estimate of the fair probable cost of all these things, the Senate struck them all out, and inserted instead the specific sum of $400,000, which is to be expended under the direction

480 APPENDIX.

of a superintendent in providing every thing promised by the treaty, which it was believed would cover the whole expense.

[The following article, copied from the New-York Journal of Commerce of December 30, 1840, affords a history of the negotiations with the Senecas which resulted in the treaty-so-called, that has been concluded. The article is a review of two important publications, which the nefarious transactions here unveiled, have called forth.]

REPORT on the memorials of the SENECA INDIANS and others. Accepted, November 21, 1840, in the Council of Massachusetts. Boston : Dutton & Wentworth, State printers, 1840. pp. 28.

THE CASE of the SENECA INDIANS in the State of New-York, illustrated by facts. Printed for the information of the Society of Friends, by direction of the Joint Committee on Indian Affairs, of the Four Yearly Meetings of Friends, of Genesee, New-York, Philadelphia, and Baltimore. Philadelphia : Merihew & Thompson, 1840. pp. 254.

To all who can sympathize with the Indians in the afflictions which are consuming them from the face of the earth, these are deeply interesting publications ; and the character of the sources from which they emanate, must command respectful attention to their contents. Nor can the truth of their statements be questioned ; for all the important facts are sustained by authentic documents, given at full length. A brief abstract of their contents seems the more desirable, as the Senecas aver that a powerful influence, exerted over the press in their vicinity, has hitherto prevented them from laying the story of their wrongs fully before the public.

The present number of the Senecas is said to be 2,449. They claim four "Reservations" in the State of New-York, viz : the Tonnawanda, 13,000 acres ; the Buffalo, 53,000 acres ; the Cattaraugus, 22,000 ; and the Alleghany, 31,000 ; in all, about 119,000 acres. Much of this land is among the most fertile and valuable in the state, and the whole is supposed to be worth at least two millions of dollars. At the close of the war of the revolution, Massachusetts claimed an interest in this and other land belonging to the Six Nations. By articles of agreement, dated at Hartford, December 16, 1786, Massachusetts ceded to New-York the sovereignty and jurisdiction over those lands, and New-York ceded to Massachusetts, its grantees, their heirs and assigns, the right of pre-emption to the lands themselves. It was "provided, however, that no purchase from the native Indians by any such grantee or grantees should be valid, unless the same should be made in the presence of, and approved by, a superintendent, to be appointed for such purpose by the commonwealth of Massachusetts, and having no interest in such purchase ; and unless such purchase shall be confirmed by the commonwealth of Massachusetts." This agreement was sanctioned by Congress in 1787.

By an agreement, dated March 12, 1791, the commonwealth contracted to sell its pre-emptive right to Samuel Ogden, his heirs and assigns ; and by several transfers, that title has come into the hands of a company, now known as the "Ogden Land Company." Under this title, several purchases have been made of the Indians, and confirmed by the commonwealth.

The United States had made three treaties with the Six Nations,

previous to the negotiations which have given occasion to these publications. The first was a treaty of peace and boundaries, in 1784.
The second, in 1789, was little more than a confirmation of the first.
The third, which continued to be the rule of intercourse between the
parties for more than forty years, was made in 1794. It contained
two important provisions, bearing on the questions which have lately
arisen. First, it acknowledged and guaranteed the right of each of
the Six Nations, to its own reservations ; so that the Six Nations
could not, thenceforth, dispose of any of the land of any one tribe
of the confederacy against its will. Secondly, while other Indians
are restrained from selling their land except to the United States, this
treaty conferred on each of the Six Nations, separately, the right to
sell any or all of its lands to citizens of the United States, whenever
and however they might choose. The Indians agreed never to set
up any claim to any other land within the United States. Under
these arrangements with the United States and Massachusetts, the
Indians frequently sold land to companies and individuals, and conveyed it, not by treaties, but by ordinary deeds of conveyance.

It would seem that the United States had now no further connexion
with this business. It was, however, for the interest of the Ogden Land
Company, that the United States government should be involved in
some train of measures for removing the New-York Indians. For
this purpose,—as it was stated by Mr. Sevier, Chairman of the Committee on Indian Affairs, in his speech in the United States Senate,
March 17, 1840,—the Company induced two small bands to apply to
President Monroe, in 1818, for permission to purchase, with their
own means and on their own account, the title of the Menomonies, to
certain lands near Green Bay. Mr. Sevier asserts, that evidence of
the Company's influence in this movement is on file in the War Department. Mr. Monroe gave his assent. The agents of the "two
small bands," as they assert, purchased the land and paid $12,000 for
it, and the bands began to remove. The Menomonies denied the
purchase. A controversy arose, and the United States Government
was called upon to make peace. The government made peace
in 1832, by purchasing the land of the Menomonies, paying back
to the "two small bands" the $12,000 which they professed to have
paid for it, and paying $35,000 to the Oneidas and $5,000 to the
St. Regis Indians, as a remuneration to them for purchasing and
removing to the Green Bay lands, under Mr. Monroe's permission.

This treaty of 1832 was made with the Menomonies ; and neither
the Senecas, nor any other Indians residing in New-York, were present, or had any thing to do in making it. Yet by this treaty the
United States purchased, for $20,000, of the Menomonies, 500,000
acres of land, as a home for all the New-York Indians ; and it was
stipulated that the New-York Indians should remove to it within
three years, or their right to it should be forfeited, and revert to the
United States. This, it was hoped, would induce them to sell their
reservations in New-York to the Ogden Company on easy terms. The
Senecas, however, paid no attention to the treaty. They were satisfied with their old homes, and cared nothing for the forfeiture of lands
which they had not purchased and did not want. In the hope that
they might be brought to change their minds, a supplementary arti-

cle was procured, by which the time for their removal was left to the discretion of the President.

So matters remained till 1837. About this time, certain new agents appeared, acting for the Land Company. It does not appear from the documents before us, but has been currently reported at and around Buffalo, and is understood to be acknowledged by the gentlemen themselves, that five men agreed to obtain a treaty for the removal of the Senecas within a specified time ; for which some of them were to receive $25,000 each, and some of them $20,000 and certain profitable agencies. These agents took hold of their work in good earnest. Mr. Sevier, in his speech already quoted, read a contract between one of these agents, on behalf of the Ogden Land Company, and a Seneca chief, in which the said chief agreed to " use the best of his exertions and endeavors" to procure such a treaty as the Company desired, by " the active application of his whole influence at councils, and in confidential interviews," and in such other ways as he should be advised; for which, and for his " improvements," he was to receive two thousand dollars within three months after the ratification of the treaty, and a lease, at a nominal rent, during occupancy, of the farm on which he lived. By the treaty, if made, he would of course be paid for his " improvements" a second time. Mr. Sevier read another contract, by which the same agent agreed to pay another chief, for similar services, five thousand dollars. How many such contracts were made, is not known. Mr. Sevier mentioned six others. By these eight, the Company were bound to pay $21,600 to eight chiefs for such services as have been described, besides leases for years, or for life, or grants in fee simple, of the lands they then occupied. By this arrangement, he remarked, " the emigrating party were to stay at home upon their leases, and the non-emigrating party were to be transported beyond the Mississippi."

To accomplish the object, the intervention of the United States was necessary, and was obtained. A commissioner was appointed, to purchase of the Senecas their right in the Green Bay lands, which they always had refused to accept as a gift. A council was called. Two instruments were laid before the council. One was a treaty, by which the United States were to give 1,800,000 acres of land, west of the State of Missouri, and $400,000 in cash, for the Green Bay lands. The other was a deed, conveying the Seneca reservations in New-York to the Ogden Land Company, for $202,000, the receipt of which was acknowledged,—though the treaty provides that it "*shall* be paid" to the United States, to be used as stipulated for the benefit of the Senecas,—and though the Senecas have never yet received any part, either of the principal or income. To this treaty forty-five signatures, purporting to be those of chiefs or head men, were obtained. The effect of these bargains would be, that the United States would remove the Senecas at an expense of 1,800,000 acres of land, and $400,000 in cash ; and the Ogden Land Company would purchase $2,000,000 worth of land for $202,000.

The party among the Senecas who were opposed to emigration, asserted that this treaty had been obtained by fraud and corruption ; but they do not seem to have had, at that time, the means of proving their assertion. The contracts referred to by Mr. Sevier, had not then come to light. The sale was approved by the government of

Massachusetts ; but the United States Senate found its provisions so enormously liberal that they refused to ratify it. They amended it, so as to make it almost a new treaty ; either wholly annulling, or commuting for others which the Senecas might think less valuable, six important inducements to sell their lands and remove. They sent the amended treaty back to the Senecas, with a resolution, that it "shall have no force or effect whatever, nor shall it be understood that the Senate have assented to any of the contracts connected with it," till it should have been explained by the United States commissioners in open council, and received the assent of a majority of the chiefs. This provision was added, to prevent such frauds in obtaining signatures as the Senecas had complained of.

The Commissioner returned, called a council, explained the amended treaty, and urged the Senecas to assent to it. Among other things, he told them that the head of the Indian Bureau at Washington thought the sale to the Land Company valid, whether the treaty was ratified or not ; so that they must assent to it, or be left without a home. Gen. Dearborn, who attended as superintendent on the part of Massachusetts, told them that the Governor of Massachusetts thought otherwise,—that if the treaty was not ratified, the contract was void. The Commissioner called for signatures. One of the chiefs proposed that those opposed to the treaty should sign a remonstrance ; but the Commissioner refused to authenticate it. One was drawn up, and authenticated by Gen. Dearborn. The treaty was signed by 16 chiefs, and the remonstrance by 63. The Commissioner then invited the chiefs to sign the treaty singly and secretly, at his private lodgings, in a tavern at Buffalo. Runners were sent out, chiefs were brought in, paid various sums of money for their signatures, made drunk and induced to sign, or their assent was procured at their own houses. In various ways, 15 more signatures were procured, making 31 in all. The treaty was sent to Washington, and five more signatures were sent after it ; but they were rejected by the Department of War. The Commissioner continued his labors, and obtained ten more signatures, including three who had been made chiefs illegally, for the purpose of signing the treaty, and making 41 in all. The whole number of undisputed chiefs is 75. Of these 29 appear to have signed the amended treaty. The whole number who are claimed to be chiefs by both parties, is 97, of whom 41 appear as signers. Six of those whose names are attached to it, solemnly swear that they never signed it, knowing what they did, nor in any way authorized others to sign it on their behalf. The "Friends" in one of the works mentioned at the head of this article, give at full length the "bribery contracts," as they call them, and one affidavit, testifying that twenty-five dollars was offered to a certain Seneca, if he would forge the name of a chief to the power of attorney for signing the treaty, and then swear that the signature was genuine.

The treaty went again to the Senate, who advised the President to make proclamation of it and carry it into effect, whenever he should be satisfied that it had received the assent of the Senecas, according to the true intent and meaning of the Senate's former resolution. In August, 1839, the Secretary of War and Gen. Dearborn met the Senecas in council. Of the result, the President says : "No advance toward obtaining the assent of the Senecas to the amended treaty, in council, was made ; nor can a majority of them in council now be obtained ;" and again : " That improper means have been employed to obtain the assent of the Seneca chiefs, there is every reason to believe." It was referred, in the Senate, to the Committee on Indian affairs, who reported a resolution for rejecting it. The Senate, however, March 25, 1840, passed a contrary resolution, it is said, by the casting vote of its presiding officer ; and the President, April 4, proclaimed it, as a part of the law of the land. The ratification of a treaty requires the assent of two-thirds of the senators present. Whether this vote was a ratification, and therefore void for want of the constitutional majority, is a disputed question.

The Senecas then applied to the government of Massachusetts, as their ancient protector ; and the "Friends" of the four "Yearly Meetings" sent on their memorial. These papers were referred by the Governor and Council, to a Committee, of which John R. Adan, Esq., was Chairman. The Report was accepted by the Council and approved by the Governor, November 21, 1840. It is brief, but able. It concludes that the assent of the Commonwealth to the sale of Reservations, though made in ignorance of important facts, which, if known, would have prevented it, cannot be retracted. It sets forth several strong arguments against the validity of that sale ; but these only raise a " legal question,—a question of title to the lands, which must be determined by a judicial tribunal, and cannot be determined by the Executive Department of Massachusetts." " Considering the nature of the objections to the Ogden Company's title, we think the character of that Company, and of those who conduct its affairs, as well as the interest of both parties, require that those objections should be fairly met and judicially settled without delay. Until that shall be done, the Senecas will probably remain at their *old homes ;*—and the Ogden Company may not find it easy to sell them, or any part of them, to any prudent purchaser."

Such is the present situation of this affair. Those who wish to examine in detail the long and sickening series of astounding frauds by which it has been brought into this situation, may consult the publications from which this abstract has been made.

Thus far the Journal of Commerce. It should be stated, in order that his name may be held in everlasting remembrance,—for good if he has done good, and for evil if evil,—that the name of the United States Commissioner, under whose conduct such proceedings have been had, is Gillett, recently a member of Congress from the county of St. Lawrence, N. Y. His duty, in theory, was to watch over the interests of the Indians, and shield them from the rapacity and fraud of the white man. How far, and with what degree of fidelity he has performed that duty, is a question which the public must decide.